THE
ZEROES

THE
ZEROES

MY MISADVENTURES IN THE DECADE
WALL STREET WENT INSANE

RANDALL LANE

PORTFOLIO

PORTFOLIO
Published by the Penguin Group
Penguin Group (USA) Inc., 375 Hudson Street, New York, New York 10014, U.S.A.
Penguin Group (Canada), 90 Eglinton Avenue East, Suite 700, Toronto, Ontario,
Canada M4P 2Y3 (a division of Pearson Penguin Canada Inc.)
Penguin Books Ltd, 80 Strand, London WC2R 0RL, England
Penguin Ireland, 25 St. Stephen's Green, Dublin 2, Ireland (a division of Penguin Books Ltd)
Penguin Books Australia Ltd, 250 Camberwell Road, Camberwell, Victoria 3124, Australia
(a division of Pearson Australia Group Pty Ltd)
Penguin Books India Pvt Ltd, 11 Community Centre, Panchsheel Park, New Delhi–110 017, India
Penguin Group (NZ), 67 Apollo Drive, Rosedale, North Shore 0632,
New Zealand (a division of Pearson New Zealand Ltd)
Penguin Books (South Africa) (Pty) Ltd, 24 Sturdee Avenue,
Rosebank, Johannesburg 2196, South Africa

Penguin Books Ltd, Registered Offices: 80 Strand, London WC2R 0RL, England

First published in 2010 by Portfolio, a member of Penguin Group (USA) Inc.

1 3 5 7 9 10 8 6 4 2

LIBRARY OF CONGRESS CATALOGING-IN-PUBLICATION DATA
Lane, Randall.
The zeroes : my misadventures in the decade Wall Street went insane / Randall Lane.
p. cm.
Includes index.
ISBN 978-1-59184-329-0
1. United States—Economic conditions—2001–2009. 2. Financial crises—United States—History—21st
century. 3. Wall Street (New York, N.Y.)—History—21st century. I. Title.
HC106.83.L36 2010
330.973'0931—dc22   2010001959
Printed in the United States of America
Set in Garamond 3
Designed by Elyse Strongin, Neuwirth & Associates

To Mom, for the unconditional trust and love, and the idea to write this

CONTENTS

Part 2 MANIA: 2006-2008

6
We Want Your Money (Late 2006–Mid-2007)   137

7
The Blank Check (2007)   161

8
Fight Night (Mid-2007–Late 2007)   186

9
Nails (Late 2007–Early 2008)   211

10
Maxed Out (Early 2008)   239

Part 3 RECKONING: 2008-2009

11
Leverage (Mid-2008)   265

12
The Party's Over (Late 2008–Early 2009)   296

13
See It, Spend It, End It (2009)   329

PROLOGUE

Anyone who has ever been on an active trading floor can testify to the din that can emanate from full-bodied, full-throated men locked in daily combat over large sums of money. On November 1, 2007, my company, Doubledown Media, publisher of *Trader Monthly*, *Dealmaker*, and *Private Air*, the magazines that had set the tone for the decade's wanton earning and spending on Wall Street, stacked almost one thousand of the financial elite three layers high in New York's century-old Hammerstein Ballroom, a grand hall designed to challenge the Metropolitan Opera House acoustically, for our first-ever Wall Street Boxing Charity Championships.

We fattened them up, proffering beef tenderloin seared medium rare. We liquored them up, placing at each table a five-liter bottle of Imperia vodka, a just-launched "premium spirit" owned by a newly minted Russian oil billionaire who claimed to have rediscovered a nineteenth-century formula that Czar Alexander III had once decreed the standard for all vodka: winter wheat taken from the black soil of the Russian steppes, distilled with glacial water from Lake

Ladoga, and twice-filtered through quartz crystals hacked from the Ural Mountains.

If our guests wanted a little privacy, they could sit in a $400,000 Mercedes Maybach, a three-ton rolling first-class cabin for those who had graduated from the burden of driving to lounging in a backseat outfitted with eighteen-direction adjustable leather seats, foot and head massagers, and a Champagne fridge in the middle armrest. If those venturing into our custom cigar tent wanted a nicotine fix, we foisted upon them unlimited $30 Zino Platinum Crowns, a blend of one Peruvian and three Dominican tobaccos, aged four to five years and wrapped in a leaf developed at a boutique plantation in Connecticut. We were providing the kind of full-sensory experience required to distract any attendee from noticing that we had lightened their wallets by as much as a thousand bucks each.

I was surely in the poorest one percent of those assembled, a guy who drove a dented '97 Subaru Outback. But as the CEO and editor-in-chief of Doubledown Media I had the best seat in the room to view my creation in all its craven glory. My ringside tablemates included Gerry Cooney, the gregarious former heavyweight contender whom we'd paid $2,000, cash up front, plus cab fare, to mingle with the guests, and Emile Griffith, the former middleweight champ best known for tragically beating Benny "the Kid" Paret to death during a nationally televised bout in 1962. (Griffith, I discovered, suffers from dementia owing to a few thousand hits to his head, which made him extremely hard to understand. That helped explain his meager appearance fee—$200, no cab fare.)

Halfway through the second fight, I pulled myself away from my famous rent-a-friends and gazed around. The collective wealth and conspicuous consumption was breathtaking, especially when compared to the scrappy style of our perpetually underfunded company. This was a world as innately foreign to me as a gorilla troop in the African plains. But over the past five years, I had gradually learned the language and the customs, and become, at first, a tolerated observer, a Jane Goodall with some cool magazines. As our products gained influence, the financial community slowly accepted me as a trusted insider. And now, as the markets ascended to unprecedented heights,

I found myself, as Wall Street's scorekeeper, fueling the make-and-spend machine. I hadn't created the wealth in front of me. In order for my company to flourish, however, we needed to embrace it.

Eating, drinking, and consuming, the Wall Streeters arrayed before me were doing a fantastic job celebrating their status at the precise apex of our country's financial pyramid. But judging from the almost primal noise now shaking the Hammerstein's century-old foundations, our guests, in their Armani tuxedos and Brioni suits, had actually come for something even more innate than the steaks and vodka. They had come for blood. Preferably, it seemed, blood from the one group that almost everyone on Wall Street could agree embodied all that was evil and wrong with the world: the tiny substratum of their peers who made even more than they did.

"Goldman . . . Sucks!" the crowd thundered in unison. "Goldman . . . SUCKS!"

Poor Shane Kinahan, I thought, watching him march toward the boxing ring as the bagpipers he'd personally hired for his entrance futilely tried to drown out the profanity now raining on him. A vice president at Goldman Sachs, an institution whose name was now being collectively mocked, Kinahan was guilty of a mortal Wall Street sin: inspiring jealousy. Once bonuses were doled out a few months hence, Goldman would pay its thirty thousand employees an average of $661,000 for 2007, more than any bank on the Street or similarly sized company in the world. It was a figure that took into account every secretary, janitor, cafeteria worker, and Town Car driver. Our crowd, of course, did far better: Kinahan was surely well into seven figures, and some of his colleagues would nudge past $100 million for the year. Rooting for Goldman Sachs was thus about as much fun as rooting for Kim Jong-il on Election Day in North Korea.

To make matters worse for Kinahan, he was fighting Josh Weintraub, who had the double advantage of a college boxing background and the underdog's chip on his shoulder. No matter that Weintraub was one of the biggest hitters on the Street, the guy who made millions running Bear Stearns's "private label" mortgage trading desk— selling mortgages so junky that neither Fannie Mae nor Freddie Mac would guarantee them—packaged under a euphemism that made them sound as benign as Sam's Club cola (*"It's just as good as Coke, but one-third the price!"*). The math in the room was just as simple: Bear versus Goldman. David versus Goliath.

Rather than tap gloves at the beginning of the round, as is traditional in amateur fights, Weintraub taunted Kinahan, sticking his face out the way a mongoose might bait a snake. Trinity Gym, a boxing specialist in New York's financial district, had spent four months training each of our fighters, and part of the mantra had been to put on a good show for the paying customers. If you were outclassing an opponent early, carry him a little bit, then take him out in the third round. Not Weintraub. He tore at Kinahan mercilessly—*a left cross for Kinahan's secretary, who made three times more than Weintraub's secretary, a right jab for the three top earners Goldman had stolen from Bear the year before*—finally stunning him with a right hook that dropped the Goldman trader after ninety seconds.

The crowd cheered like it was V-E Day, led by a boisterous Weintraub entourage. He had personally forked out $65,000 for premium tickets for friends, family, and crew, followed by an after-party at a nearby club. As eight sets of boxers slugged through the night, traders and bankers streamed toward Hammerstein, unfurling rolls of hundreds in hopes of charming the check-in girls and buying their way into the capacity event. Via text messages and cell phone calls, The Word had gone out: Wall Street was celebrating tonight.

The past month had seen the Dow Jones Industrial Average surge past 14,000 points for the first time. Guys like Josh Weintraub were making fortunes by creating securities more complicated than the Rosetta stone and also far more valuable. And Bear had just beaten Goldman. For these guys—*my* guys, for better or worse—all was right and just with the world.

No one had yet developed a name for this era, this decade with the once-a-millennium calendar quirk of two zeroes perched in the middle. As I gazed across the room in front of me, "the Zeroes" seemed fairly spot-on. Wall Street's breathless pursuit of zeroes, that easy-money mentality, had permeated every aspect of our culture. In my role as Wall Street's scorekeeper, I too had fallen prey to the mind warp.

But I had no inkling that, when the figures were tallied at the end of 2009, there would be zero increase in household net worth for the decade. Zero net job creation. Zero median income growth. Zero stock market appreciation. Or that the global economy, imperiled by a group of collective zeroes, faced an imminent meltdown that would wipe out millions of people financially—myself included. Given my unique perch, perhaps I should have. But wealth and excess have a blinding effect, especially amid the kind of greedfest that comes along only once every thousand years.

That was exactly the problem. It calls for an explanation.

PART 1

FEVER

(2001–2006)

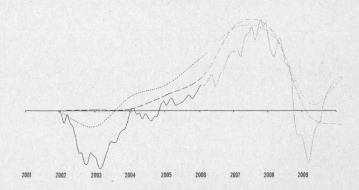

—— S&P GLOBAL 100   ------ WORLDWIDE BONUSES   — — — GLOBAL CDO ISSUANCE

2001   2002   2003   2004   2005   2006   2007   2008   2009

1

See It, Make It, Spend It

(2001–2004)

London's labyrinthine financial district is known as the City. It would be quite in character for the local traders and bankers to dub their part of town so arrogantly, as if the rest of the metropolis were merely a densely packed suburb, but this mile-square zone was actually London's entirety back in the Middle Ages. Though only 8,000 people now live in the City—down from a more properly Dickensian quarter-million in 1700—some 350,000 still pile in each weekday morning trying to conquer the globe, as thoroughly as the tall ships that sailed from here on behalf of the British Empire.

Andy Priston was one of those 350,000 on Tuesday, September 11, 2001. Twenty-four and recently out of Loughborough University, Priston had been the first college graduate ever trained by a City trading outfit named MacFutures. Until he came along, the scruffy firm trended less educated and more colorful, including one trader named Roberto, who had the unique habit of stripping off his clothes in the middle of the day, and then playing the markets buck naked.

A thin triathlete with a soft face, Priston followed his usual routine that day. As a "scalper," he perused the global exchanges, looking for market swings in complicated interest rate and bond derivatives. When he saw action, whether up or down, he'd jump in and out in the appropriate direction, "scalping" himself a small profit within a few seconds, perhaps minutes, versus holding a position days or weeks. But the markets were slow this Tuesday. Rather than force a trade, Priston decided to call it a day and go play soccer. That's when he *felt* an impact on his computer. "The market jolted weirdly," he remembers. Turning the communal televisions above the MacFutures trading floor to SkyNews, Priston saw smoke billowing from one of the World Trade Center's towers, and then a streaking plane disappear into the second.

The entire world saw tragedy unfurling in front of its eyes. Priston saw something entirely different: *opportunity*.

Without pausing, he returned to his desk, sold stocks and oil futures, and, borrowing heavily, bought any and every European government bond that came on the market, tens of millions of dollars of them. His hunch: the panicked investing hordes, once they overcame their shock, would retreat massively into the comfort foods of capitalism—notably the government bonds he was snatching up.

This move wasn't precalculated. Priston had no time to ponder it. It was pure, cold-blooded instinct, orchestrated electronically with trading partners across the planet. Within twenty minutes, he made several hundred thousand dollars. Grasping that this was an *attack*, not an accident, he then repeated the trick, more aggressively, before the markets shuttered trading.

In that window, less than an hour from the time the first plane hit, Priston made himself $1.5 million.

A few years later, when Priston recounted this story for me, I got queasy. He felt guilty enough about it afterward that he tithed 20 percent of his 9/11 take to the New York City Fire Department. But to his awed City colleagues, he was a hero, a legend. They even bequeathed him a nickname, befitting one sure of his righteousness and fearful of nothing: Braveheart.

$ $ $

My path, the one that would cross with Braveheart's, began on the same day, September 11, 2001, at almost exactly the same time he felt the markets jolt. The second airplane was flying south directly above the Hudson River while I was riding south directly below it. I lived less than two miles from the World Trade Center, and had arisen early that morning, kissed my longtime girlfriend, Jennifer Reingold, and quietly caught a train to Philadelphia, to repeat what I'd been doing almost every day for the past year: rattling my cup for yet another magazine idea.

The decade so far had been a dud for me. In the very first week of this optimistic new millennium, Freedom Communications, the company funding the men's business magazine I had cofounded, *P.O.V.*, pulled the plug after four years. It felt like losing a limb. My partner, Drew Massey, and I had maxed out credit cards and drained bank accounts to launch it. Freedom had been impressed enough to throw in $18 million, and *Adweek* named us 1996's "Startup of the Year." But as other business magazines fattened up on the ephemeral dot-com Kool-Aid, and other men's magazines got far bigger, far faster emphasizing "beer and babes," we were stuck in the middle. While the rest of the world welcomed a new era, as artificially defined by the calendar, we had to lay off fifty people, including ourselves.

After moping around for six months, a pre-midlife crisis, at age thirty-two, that mostly involved drinking copious amounts of wine under the guise of getting my professional sommelier degree, I dusted myself off and began raising money for a new magazine concept, *Justice*. Think *People* meets *Law & Order*, tapping into America's growing obsession with real-life drama. Condé Nast and Hearst had agreed to distribute it, and by late summer 2001, one of Europe's biggest publishers, Burda, stood poised to fund it as their American flagship. Those prospects collapsed with the twin towers I could no longer see, amid a giant cloud of gray smoke, as I lurched toward Manhattan on the first train allowed back in that afternoon, while thousands streamed out.

A saying took root across America: "9/11 changed everything." As I flashed my driver's license so I could get home past the police barricades (downtown Manhattan, enveloped in an acrid smell that would last months, had been quarantined for nonresidents), that sure seemed right. But amid the insanity, the world felt strangely purposeful; and all the projects I'd been working on suddenly felt stupid and trite.

Over the next few weeks, I fed rescue workers, attended funerals, and chronicled the heroes and scenes of Ground Zero for various magazines, and subjects and strangers alike later called me, in tears, thanking me for what I'd written. I tried harder to do right by those who loved me. I decamped to Florida to help my mother and stepfather, as they dealt with a brain tumor that hit in lockstep with 9/11 and took him almost as swiftly. And on a reporting assignment in tension-filled India, sandwiched artlessly between a terrorist trying to explode a shoe-bomb on a plane over the Atlantic and Pakistani and Indian troops massing angrily at the border, ratting nuclear sabers, I proposed to Jennifer at the Taj Mahal.

This new, empathetic America revealed itself to me in full thirteen days after the attacks, when I found myself at the New York Hilton with a dozen top African American leaders, led by the Reverend Jesse Jackson. Though I was invited by one of the guests, my presence caused much distraction—this was supposed to be a private affair, a post-9/11 "unity dinner," and its candor was compromised by a scribbling writer. I took the point and prepared to leave.

As I did, the group, from CEOs to Wall Street heavies to politicians, including the soon-to-be Democratic nominee for governor of New York, Carl McCall, clasped hands and lowered heads, launching their meal with a standing prayer circle. For what seemed like forever, I listened for the invocation, before Jackson opened his eyes and stared archly across the room at me. *"Are you going to join us?"* Wedging between the reverend and McCall, a dozen black powerbrokers and one broke white guy were united for a moment by shock and grief.

"Burdens to share," Jackson intoned, in his famous rhyming cadence, "make them easier to bear."

That *was* the national sentiment, so I put forward the sharpest skill set I had: starting magazines. As part of a public diplomacy program similar to Radio Free Europe or Voice of America, the State Department had allocated more than $4 million a year to launch a magazine about American culture, which would be translated into Arabic and sold across the Arab world. Other than a corny name, *Hi!*, the one English word everyone on the planet knows, it was an empty vessel. To fill it, the State Department hired a well-regarded Washington-based custom media company, TMG, which in turn hired me and a squad of naturalized Arab Americans, including a smart, opinionated Libyan, Fadeel al-Ameen. For the part of the world that hated us most, I would craft America's public face, as translated via the cover and substance of a glossy magazine.

It was fun distilling America every month, explaining baseball, or the culture of Silicon Valley, or the new battle between smokers' rights groups and public health advocates. I had taken the gig on the promise that it would be politics-free. Culture is the first building block to understanding. There was nothing to be gained by being either a propagandist or an apologist.

But as the memory of 9/11 began to fade, so did the magazine's utopian mission. Congressmen began complaining that rather than *show* young Arabs how Western society works, *Hi!* should *tell* them why American policies are right. A State Department panel of ham-fisted political appointees now began actively reviewing our content before we printed it as the new war in Iraq turned increasingly unpopular. One of my favorite sections loosely translated to "Window on America." It was a simple conceit: a photo essay showing what America actually looks like, unfiltered. A bass fishing tournament, a breast cancer walk, the Puerto Rican Day parade—these were exotic images to most Arabs, too often poisoned about the United States by their inflammatory local press. But during one review meeting, held before a star chamber of ten high-level State Department officials, the co-leader specifically took offense to a photograph from a classic western scene: campers and pack mules heading out on a rugged weekend expedition.

Our team always remained vigilant about cultural sensibilities, avoiding the bottoms of shoes, or bare arms or other innocuous images for Americans that could backfire with the Arab audience. This official's concerns, however, were more parochial. She held up the offending photo, as wholesome as a Norman Rockwell painting, and pointed to a pack mule that, by other names, might be known as a donkey. *This has to go*, she said. *Too pro-Democrat*. And out it went.

It was time to do something else. Six months prior, I had received an old-fashioned letter from a London trader—Braveheart's boss—named Magnus Greaves, with a simple request: *Can I pick your brain about a financial magazine idea?* For an hour, I relayed to him, in great detail, the problems with the business in general, ending with a checklist of things he needed to answer if was he serious. Shockingly, to me, Magnus had now returned, asking to hire me as a consultant.

In considering this new project, I thought about an incident in Morocco. Part of developing *Hi!* included a two-week trip across the Arab world, interviewing hundreds of young adults from Abu Dhabi to Beirut about their views of the United States. The most memorable session had been a near-riot in Casablanca, where two hundred college journalism students, enthralled by the opportunity to rail against actual Americans, packed into a classroom built for fifty and blasted invective for two hours, as our small group, including one embassy official, tried to parry. ("Half of these kids have never seen an American in person," the school's dean told us beforehand. "They wanted to be sure you all didn't have guns.")

Afterward, the crowd rushed us and the meager security scrambled—unnecessarily, it turned out. Politics time was over. *How do I get a job in America?* we were asked, with urgency. *How can I get a visa? How can I make my fortune?*

One student, wearing a red leather jacket, wanted detailed advice on how he could start a Web site exposing Moroccans to the wonders of heavy metal. "Ozzy rules," he said as his salutation, his pinky, pointer, and thumb outstretched in perfect formation. For the next few months, I mentored him in his quest to introduce Arabs to a less-obvious piece of American culture.

Another student, in a blue sweater-vest, shyly waited his turn. He pulled me aside as we were about to leave, with an equally pressing query about what he heard was really going on in America: *How can I become a stock trader?*

The global mood had changed. The War on Terror would be conducted with bullets, not magazines, while the rest of the world tried to forget about it. And domestically, President Bush's post-9/11 message to Americans about their patriotic duty—go shopping—had taken root. The Zeroes really started on 9/11. Everything before had just been nineties flotsam. What I didn't realize then, but would slowly over the ensuing months and years, was that Braveheart's experience on that miserable day, rather than mine, was the more definitive one.

$ $ $

You can always tell a trader by his watch. They're the wedding rings of the financial world, an accessory that informs knowing observers of the bearer's status. A typical trader's watch generally contains enough metal to construct an Eastern European automobile, and lots of internal "complications" designed, as the term implies, to make the science of time-telling, properly mastered five centuries ago, difficult yet again. They demonstrate to all who notice, *Yes, I can afford to spend $32,000 for something that performs no better than the giveaway at the bottom of a cereal box.*

The chunkiest I'd ever seen, a Franck Mueller with Roman numeral hands that melted like a Salvador Dalí painting, adorned the wrist of the twenty-nine-year-old who greeted me with a bear hug in late 2003, my reward for successfully navigating the ancient City alleys to find our lunch spot.

On Magnus Greaves, with a name fit for Greek mythology, it seemed proportional. Six-foot-four, three hundred pounds, Magnus projected still larger, owing to his normal-sized head, which bobbed above his thick torso like a cherry atop a giant ice cream sundae. Yet there was nothing intimidating about him: the gap-toothed grin, the squashed nose, the nearly shaved head, all combined into a handsome version of the friendly giant Shrek.

"Buddy," he said. "Welcome to my little corner of the world."

That Magnus's corner and mine had ever come in contact had all the probability of two specific meteors striking each other somewhere in suborbital sky. He was a black Canadian college dropout turned successful trading tycoon who lived in a luxury apartment in London. I was a white American college-graduate-turned-failed-media-entrepreneur who lived in a fourth-floor walk-up in New York. Together we severely tested the theory that any two people on earth are within six degrees of one another. The unlikely connection that prompted his letter to me came via Roger Karshan, the boyfriend of the sister of the girlfriend of the colleague of my wife.

For the past few months, I had been teaching Magnus how the magazine business worked. Now he was reciprocating with a grand tour of trading culture, starting with his watch, the first accessory a successful trader buys. "There's such a high at work," he explained, in a pleasant accent that melded proper London and the *ehs* and *oos* of his native Vancouver. "Traders need to keep that going in their spare time. They like buying things that perform. And our guys are young, so being flashy comes naturally. They like showing everyone how successful they are."

The next purchase is generally a car, as demonstrated by MacFutures' garage, a pit of concrete pillars and oddly shaped nooks filled incongruously with wealth and power: Mercedes, Bentleys, and Ferraris, including Magnus's silver Ferrari 360 convertible, which he was now dropping my bag into, before we headed upstairs to check out his office. As best I could tell, driving anything less than a Porsche to MacFutures was as socially unacceptable as wearing a tank top to a wedding.

When you boil it down, Magnus's traders didn't actually *earn* money—they *made* it. For most of us, money equals time. Work a fixed amount of hours, get paid a fixed amount, whether $8 an hour for a teenager at McDonald's or $20 million for Harrison Ford to spend eight weeks on a movie shoot. At MacFutures, there was no correlation: a Breitling watch or a Lotus Esprit Turbo wasn't six months' work—it was an impulsive reward for one smart, or lucky, push of a button.

"We never thought in terms of percentages," Magnus remembers, referring to the return his traders averaged. "We thought about it in terms of how many dollars you needed to make that month. If you had $50,000 in your account, that was just the deposit you used to make another $50,000." Blow through it in January, make it again in February. Then repeat. At MacFutures, every day was Christmas, every night was shore leave.

The idea he had originally reached out to me with was called "InBusiness"—a hipper, stylish business magazine for men. It sounded a lot like my last magazine, *P.O.V.,* giving me 18 million reasons to caution him. But he was undaunted. His parents met in a bookstore, and his dad burned into him a literary life lesson: *never be caught without something to read.* To Magnus, starting a magazine was the ultimate fulfillment of that advice, and my role as his consultant centered on helping him develop the idea fully enough to take it to a big publisher like Condé Nast or Time Inc. So I dutifully noodled with editorial templates, design treatments—one clever logo merged the two words of the title, "busINess"—and daunting financials, until Magnus, almost offhandedly, mentioned the idea of a supplement for professional traders.

Trader Monthly. Now *that* was a good idea. Advertisers have all the benevolence of Aryan eugenics theorists: they hate diversity and crave purity. They use an elegant five-letter word for any men looking at female-based advertising, or women perusing a campaign for males: "waste." Ninety-seven percent of traders were men. Still better for the advertising Nazis: income purity, since almost all of these men made six figures; some, I would soon learn, far more. In other words, no journalists like me (aka "waste") eyeballing ads for $200 bottles of Scotch.

The more I talked about *Trader Monthly*, the less Magnus talked about "InBusiness." Not long after my visit to the City, we stopped mentioning it altogether.

$ $ $

A few floors above the garage lies the MacFutures trading floor, the manifestation of the most ascendant—and, ultimately, the most destructive—economic force of the decade, and one I would soon play a part in enabling.

The first thing I noticed were the women. Or, specifically, the lack of them. All 120 traders in MacFutures' London headquarters were male. (A bad day for equality; a happy one for advertisers.) The only female in the office was the receptionist.

The second thing I noticed was their age: almost entirely in their twenties, complete with fraternity nicknames for each other. There was Razors, a fast talker perpetually touting his "deal of the week." There was Pub Dart, an information repository for the world's most dubious sport. Unsurprisingly, the dress code was pretty much up to the lofty standards of a gym. Except for the discus-sized watches, they looked almost destitute. The standard uniform seemed to be jeans or shorts, T-shirts, and flip-flops, though Roberto, the naked trader, had graciously opted for clothing that day. "All that matters is that they're comfortable," said Magnus, shrugging. "There's enough stress as is." It was a full-sensory experience, complete with the funky smell that comes from a roomful of men, dressed for sport, sweating profusely.

These ten dozen young men were divided between two rooms of equal size, and then stacked like crated calves at a veal farm, but far more wired. "Physically, it was like a sweatshop," remembers Braveheart. Each trader stared at up to six screens, teetering haphazardly within their three-by-five-foot workstations. A few had tried to personalize their areas—a soccer picture here, a Post-it reminder of good trading habits there—the way a prisoner might doll up his jail cell. One screen carried a news wire. Another, a Bloomberg terminal, digitally housed every piece of financial data known to man. Two were for charting; with a couple of keystrokes, trends and comparisons could spring to life visually. And most important, the final two were trading screens, the gateways to "electronic trading."

While the term seemed anachronistic by 2003, conjuring images of copper wire and vacuum tubes, the modern reality was that Magnus's 120 traders could buy and sell, directly, in real time, from Chicago to Hong Kong to Budapest to Johannesburg.

Until recent years, trading had been a parochial business. Coffee traders in Chicago stuck to coffee, municipal bond traders in New York stuck to municipal bonds, and so on. You took care of your specific contract, traded physically in front of you, and it took care of you. Some made great fortunes, but most traders had merely served as middlemen, facilitating trades between institutions, mutual funds, or perhaps your broker, as he fiddled with your retirement account. For decades, all this middlemanning kept the typical Wall Street executive solidly positioned in his suburban house, with a new car every two years, next to his neighbors, the doctor, the lawyer, and the corporate manager.

That was beginning to change when Magnus, a nimble math student who viewed college as nothing more than a four-year delay to getting rich, arrived in the City in 1996. The giant Swiss bank UBS accepted him as a trainee for an entry-level spot on the floor of the London International Financial Futures and Options Exchange (LIFFE). Everyone in the trading world called it "The Life." And it was. Created in 1982 to trade currencies after the UK deregulated its controls, The Life was surging into other areas by the time Magnus arrived.

Nonetheless, trading was still done the way it had been done on exchanges for centuries. Men jostled in pits, like an enormous rugby scrum, placing orders by either barking them out or using elaborate hand signals: palms-in meant buy, palms-out meant sell, one hand's vertical fingers represented one through five while the same fingers horizontally signaled six through ten. For six-and-a-half hours a day, the guys who could get the closest, shout the loudest, and signal above the fray got the trade. It's why trading had long been a haven for male ex-jocks like former high school basketball star Magnus Greaves.

Electronic trading doomed these physical trading pits, an evolution Magnus was quicker to grasp than most. So with three partners, including one, Jamie MacLeod, fronting most of the money, the new MacFutures rented a glorified closet in the City, bought a bunch of computers, began playing video games for money, and facilitated that move for others.

MacFutures' position in London at the beginning of the Zeroes wasn't much different from having a monopoly renting pans and blue jeans during the California Gold Rush. As the physical floor wound down, a trickle of Life refugees became a stream and then a torrent. MacFutures became a place where you learned about electronic trading. Magnus would provide those magic boxes—the information and access to the global markets—in exchange for a piece of their action. And that model scaled. Magnus began opening offices globally, nabbing pit refugees in every trading hub: New York, Sydney, Paris, Miami, Gibraltar. By 2003, MacFutures was operating in ten cities, overseeing 550 traders.

None of these guys were middlemen. Computers now largely handled that task. The official term was "proprietary" or "prop" trader, as in an independent guy trading for himself. In reality, they were rank speculators. MacFutures, meanwhile, was technically known as an "arcade," which seemed appropriate for a roomful of guys playing high-stakes video games, yet also glossed over what it really was: a global casino.

In the early part of the Zeroes, the tables were smoking. MacFutures' first trainee recruited straight out of college, Braveheart, now twenty-seven, was making almost $1 million *a month*. He had proven so consistently successful in the two years since 9/11 that Magnus slowly reinvented his company around reverse-engineering him. Rather than take the Life's detritus and turn them into electronic traders, he began taking smart kids with instincts and math skills and training them to scalp.

During the trading day, this group was quiet. Unlike the movie scenes of noisy trading floors, the only boisterousness came during market lulls, when horseplay ruled. When there was money to be made, there was no shouting, no phones ringing, no one taking orders (a middleman's job). Instead, these men stared intently at their screens, looking for trends, new flashes, openings, anything that gave them an edge. While most generally specialized in two or three types of contracts, whether New Zealand's currency, the kiwi, or the Bobl, a type of German bond, Magnus's machines offered literally hundreds of thousands of trading options.

Occasionally, the relative silence was broken by the guy Magnus called "the analyst," in reality more like a news anchorman, conveying a headline over a loudspeaker.

Unemployment numbers out in France.

Or maybe he said Australia. Or the United States. I don't remember, and it doesn't really matter. Electronic traders didn't even need to know, at any given time, *what* they were trading, owing to the second half of the MacFutures name. Futures were originally invented as a way for farmers to lock in a price for their products each spring, thus assuring they'd have enough money to harvest in the fall. Food companies (and traders) could then buy and sell the right to take delivery of that product at a set point in the future, but the farmer now had protection: he wouldn't get rich, but he wouldn't bet the farm every year, either. In the 1970s, futures began gaining favor as a tool for companies to lock in interest rates, or, as "options," to incentivize management.

But what started out nobly—markets ensuring our food supply—was now just fodder for the global casino. Increasingly powerful, fast, and interwoven computers were creating endless synthetic ways to wager, with the numbers of capitalism used as the game's points. The idea of people buying and selling a piece of something tangible had given way to betting whether a contract—any contract—would trade at a certain price at a certain time. The only thing a scalper cared about was *volatility*. Whether a market was up or down was wholly irrelevant—what killed them was a *flat* market. So they scanned the world's exchanges for waves to surf, and once the analyst found a crest, the herd could stampede anywhere, traveling instantaneously via electronic trading to plunder or be plundered. It was little different from wagering on which of two birds would fly off a wire first.

For anyone with the direct market access of Magnus's machines, the global casino was a twenty-four-hour operation. The MacFutures crew tended to stick with European hours, and then go out to enjoy the fruits of their pillaging. One rival, TransMarket Group, based in Sydney, Australia, had traders come in three shifts, like a factory trying to maximize production, trading around the clock as the gambling hall that was planet Earth rotated through opens and closes.

The house made sure the gamblers had access to money. Futures exchanges let traders borrow up to two hundred times the value of a contract. So a $20,000 cash position on some synthetic contract like the Australian dollar's movement against the Canadian dollar became a $4 million bet. With that much on the line, movements down to the fourth decimal place, an increment called a "pip," could produce a fortune. Or wipe you out.

$ $ $

Part of MacFutures' testing process for its trainees involved their comfort level with risk. Anybody unnerved by the idea of having a fortune splayed across the electronic ether wasn't going to make it as a trader. Early in our relationship, I asked Magnus what his risk tolerance was, and his response, told in a breathless, giddy tone that rolled on for emphasis, was one word: *unliiimmmiiitttted*.

As the *Trader Monthly* concept evolved, so did Magnus's thinking in terms of pushing it forward. Magazines are risky ventures. How could it be harnessed, without going over the edge?

Magnus dealt with this balance on an everyday basis. During my visit to his London offices, I noticed, in the middle of all that testosterone, a glass-enclosed cube—a cage, really, except the animals being watched were on the outside. "Those are the two most important guys on the floor," Magnus had said, pointing. Their official titles were "risk managers." While they wanted Magnus's crew to take the chances necessary to make money, it was their job to make sure nobody blew up anything.

That was no small concern during the Zeroes. The decade's post-9/11 turning point, geopolitically, had occurred a few months earlier, when a United States–led coalition invaded Iraq, looking for "weapons of mass destruction" that didn't exist—a blunder that eroded our moral high ground in the War on Terror and made the doomed *Hi!* project exponentially more difficult. It was while working with Magnus, though, that I found the Zeroes' biggest, most dangerous cache of WMDs. They were sitting not in the bowels of Saddam Hussein's palaces, but on trading desks worldwide.

In both theaters, technology had amplified the dangers. Rather than bully neighbors, a rogue state with biological or nuclear weapons could threaten the world. In the financial arena, the floor trader of yore, visible to all and limited to one market, posed only so much mischief capability. But now any of those trading screens, anonymously tied into almost every exchange on the planet and armed with near-infinite debt, could wreak havoc on a massive international scale.

The City, an early adapter of electronic trading, was an especially active hive of financial shenanigans around the time I visited. Memories were still fresh of Nick Leeson, the twenty-eight-year-old "rogue trader" whose parting gifts to Britain's oldest bank, Barings, were a two-word note on his desk ("I'm Sorry") and $1.3 billion in furtive losses he'd buried in a dormant error account, number 88888, within the firm's computers. Barings, financiers of the Louisiana Purchase, collapsed three days later. ("I had a good moment in a pub the other day," Leeson later told one of our reporters, after serving four years in prison and having Ewan McGregor play him in the movie. "This old Irish bloke slapped me on the back. He said, 'Aw, you know, Nick, if they can't take a joke, feck 'em.'")

By 2003, the schemes had become far more sophisticated, with names straight out of the spy movies. Most weren't even illegal. The year before, a City trader named Anthony Ward had used the anonymity of the computer screen to quietly corner the world's cocoa supply via futures contracts on the Life, garnering himself a James Bond–worthy nickname—"Chocolate Finger"—and $15 million in profit.

Meanwhile, a few blocks from Magnus's offices, five Citigroup traders were plotting a trade they dubbed "Operation Dr. Evil," after the satirical villain from the Austin Powers films. Their plan, carried out the following August, involved selling $16 *billion* worth of government bond futures they didn't actually own—an aggressive technique known as short-selling—within a period of a few seconds. Hidden behind their screens, they were able to mask the fact that just one group of traders was selling, causing panic in Europe's capitals, and a price collapse. The traders then immediately *bought* the bonds, at far cheaper prices, to cover their sales, pocketing a cool $20 million, and prompting a massive investigation into how five guys at a bank could roil the ability of Europe's governments to pay their bills.

Magnus hadn't been immune to the nonsense. During MacFutures' nascent days, it had shared its space with a twenty-seven-year-old Eton graduate and Credit Suisse alum named John Ho Park. Over a forty-eight-hour period around Christmas 1998, Park had followed the Leeson two-act script perfectly: trader makes dumb bet, trader uses computers to hide bigger and bigger secret bets in a vain attempt to dig out of the hole. He lost $10 million he didn't have on German bond futures, and because his trades were mixed in with MacFutures, Magnus's firm lost several hundred thousand, too, almost collapsing. ("I once saw John walking down the street," recalls Magnus. "That prick was wearing the same Rolex he used to wear when he was trading in our office. It took every fiber of my being not to go up to him, rip it off his wrist, and call us even.")

As Magnus evaluated what to do next with *Trader Monthly*, his gut said *unliiimmmiiitttted*. And increasingly, he saw me as a kindred spirit. In my twenties, I had always felt the need to challenge myself, to put myself in uncomfortable situations to test my own mettle. Generally, it had been stereotypical stupid guy stuff—running with the bulls in Pamplona, competing in no-limits open highway races, and all manner of ill-conceived macho writing assignments, such as a month spent hanging with a Northern California offshoot of the Bloods street gang, which ended when a PCP-loaded member of an affiliated Samoan group punctured my eardrum. Life was an endless adrenaline rush.

But I eventually channeled that into entrepreneurship. There was still risk—I threw in thousands of dollars during the credit card launch of my first magazine, *P.O.V.*, eventually leaving a safe, plum job, as Washington bureau chief of *Forbes*, to pursue that dream. But it was constructive, rather than gratuitous, thrill-seeking.

Now *Trader Monthly* beckoned, a chance to avenge the lessons of *P.O.V.*, with a far more focused, far more desirable audience and a wiser business model (rather than vainly spend millions soliciting subscriptions, we'd send a magazine to every professional trader in the country for free). Life had presented a do-over.

Plus the risk-reward tilted toward the latter. Whether journalist or entrepeneur, I was never motivated by money. My car, dinged up from years of street parking, had ninety thousand miles but it ran fine. My apartment didn't have air-conditioning in the living room but was plenty comfortable. For the expensive things I did like— good food, good wine—I wove them into my professional life. As a fattening hobby, I was the chief restaurant critic for a popular weekly magazine, *Time Out New York*, and ran a small wine-buying service, snapping up cases at auction for others and taking my fee in bottles rather than in cash. But now financial security was an issue. Jennifer was pregnant with our first child; Sabrina would arrive bearing coal eyes and strawberry blond hair in March 2004. "When I started trading, I made a lot of money," Magnus once explained to me. "But it's when I had other traders working for me that I really became successful." So how much would it be worth to connect every trader in the world? Certainly a house with a yard, and a college fund for Sabrina.

But perhaps the biggest attraction was the *energy*, the clear world-changing phenomenon that Magnus had tapped into. Utopian visions of an interlinked planet where we'd all speak Esperanto—something way past even the *Hi!* ideal—had already come true. Only the connectivity came through computers, and the language was money.

Soon after my visit to Magnus's offices, I phoned him, with some urgency.

"Hey, Magnus, I want you to stop paying me."

"Excuse me?"

"I don't want you to pay me anymore. I want to be partners. And partners shouldn't be paying each other. I want you to put that money into the company."

"Buddy," he said, "I've been waiting for you to say that for months."

So rather than me cooking up a business plan for Magnus to shop around to various media companies, we would *become* a media company. Our skill sets were yin and yang, but in terms of risk profile,

Magnus saw that we were conjoined for better or worse, with no one inclined to ever step on the brakes. We came out with an appropriately *unliimmmiiitted* company name—Doubledown Media. And we intended to launch as many good media concepts as we could off of this platform.

As Magnus also had a new baby—his wife, Elise, had just given birth to a son, Felix—we implemented some risk management. We wouldn't launch until we could get some advertisers to commit, a sign of proof-of-concept. And Magnus wouldn't put in all the money himself. Most likely, he'd put in $500,000, and pass the hat for the rest of the $2 million or so we figured it would cost to launch. I would run it. My salary until we received more funding would be zero, and after that, I would simply take enough to live on. In terms of ownership we agreed to a fifty-fifty split, with Magnus, or his coinvestors, getting additional stock based on money put in. That incentivized him to keep us well funded, and encouraged me to run a lean ship.

We sealed our deal the way partners do in Jimmy Stewart movies: with a handshake.

For the next two years, it was the only contract he and I needed.

$ $ $

With his perfect, creaseless hair, bespoke suits, and Cambridge-trained diction, complete sentences rolling off his tongue like a movie screenplay, Phillip Bennett, CEO of Refco, looked every bit the cold-hearted poster boy of corporate villainy he would soon become. But in early 2004, as I sat waiting in his offices in New York's World Financial Center to meet Refco's marketing chief, amid a contemporary photography collection so valuable that it spawned a coffee table book, he would assume another role: *Trader Monthly*'s godfather.

Bennett did this unknowingly, and with complete self-interest, spurred by his desire to create a Wall Street giant out of a checkered futures broker. In the unique semaphore of the trading pits, a Refco transaction had been signaled via holding a thumb and one finger to the lips, as if smoking a joint. It was a wordplay on Refco and reefer, but it could just as well have implied the misdemeanor that came along with the toke. Refco's steady rise had come with more than one hundred citations from federal regulators, including fines for multiple attempts to corner markets in frozen pork bellies and other farm commodities. Either despite or because of such antics, Refco had quietly grown with the futures market to 200,000 customers in fourteen countries generating $1.9 billion in revenue, of which $187 million was profit.

But Bennett, the firm's head since 1998, wanted more. He was preparing to take the company public, with a valuation expected in the $3 billion range, providing the kind of war chest and profile needed to fulfill his grand aspirations. That also required that a company previously invisible to the outside world—save some notoriety in 1994, when it was discovered that First Lady Hillary Clinton, during the Whitewater scandal, had turned $1,000 into $100,000 trading cattle futures under the tutelage of a Refco broker named Robert "Red" Bone—engage in a completely foreign art: marketing and advertising.

That's how I ended up, amid the photos of praying nuns and graffiti-covered chairs, shaking hands with Robert Mercorella, a pleasant-looking man in his forties with a full head of dark hair. His business card had a fancy title—Senior Vice President—which hid the fact that at a company valued on a par with General Mills and Chrysler, he was the entire marketing department. Magnus had made the introduction: Mercorella needed a shotgun blast to everyone in the trading world, which made advertising in *Trader Monthly* a snug fit.

So Mercorella went to Bennett, and Bennett signed off on my first proposal: a $360,000 advertising campaign over our first year of publication. A huge sale even for major magazines like *Fortune* or *Forbes*, albeit a rounding error to Refco, and an ample proof of concept for us.

It got even cozier. In tandem with the marketing, Bennett was also on a major acquisition binge, gobbling up smaller companies with a futures bent. Right around the time Magnus and I were throwing in together, he authorized a $50 million offer for MacFutures. Even after partners and taxes, Magnus now had enough money to fund Doubledown Media himself. It was financially reckless—the company's finances would rest solely on his personal shoulders—but that's what someone with *unllliiimmmittted* risk tolerance does when he believes in something.

When we shook hands, I had made him a solemn promise: *"I'll treat your money like my money."* Magnus had spent the past eighteen months visiting my apartment, filled with used furniture left over from my last business. He watched me sleep on friends' couches whenever I visited him in London. I treated him to the best restaurants in New York through the meals I got as a restaurant reviewer—paid through my fingertips and keyboard late at night. His trust in me was complete, and mine in his. As profligate as our audience was, I instituted a strict operating philosophy, encompassing two steps: first, spend as little as possible, on every single budget item, to get the job done well; second, be as creative as possible in accomplishing the first step. We began calling it the Doubledown Way.

I had found a seven-thousand-square-foot office on one of the snootiest blocks in New York—Forty-fourth Street, between Fifth and Sixth avenues, home to the Harvard and Penn and New York yacht clubs, the Royalton and Mansfield and Algonquin hotels, and a Daniel Boulud restaurant best known for its head-turning $28 foie gras–stuffed hamburger. It cost us just $7,000 a month, a fifth the per-foot rate most of the rest of the neighborhood was commanding. The catch: it was a near-windowless bunker, and we had a thirty-month sublet, the kind of short-term lease most loathed. To fill this dungeon, I asked the real estate law firm that was vacating to leave the old furniture rather than throw it out—boxy wooden lawyer desks, bric-a-brac desk chairs, and rows of mismatched legal filing cabinets.

We scoured Craigslist for used computers, which invariably came with a treasure hunt of random software already installed, plucked at 10 cents on the dollar from a slew of dot-com start-ups that had finally burned through their venture money, the last fumes of the Internet bust that had taken hold four years before. To take care of those constantly malfunctioning computers, a two-person tech start-up, Helix Systems, would serve as our de facto IT department in exchange for a small office. Rather than hire a fleet of editorial assistants to report and fact-check—or, still worse, run articles without fact-checking them—we brought in interns looking for a career break, and spent the year training them as they did all the little things that make media products work.

Most critically, I scrambled to reunite the *P.O.V.* band by cherry-picking the best of that group, giving us an inordinate amount of talent for a raw, cash-conscious start-up, with the advantage that these all-stars had all played together before. Florian Bachleda, a designer with an elegant touch, would oversee the magazine's upscale look, which would roll out atop glossy paper thick enough to sleep in. Ty Wenger, a verbal perfectionist, would edit the lifestyle coverage and produce in-depth features. Rich Blake, a gruff, barrel-chested, and plugged-in market expert who carried himself like a trader, would handle financial coverage.

On the business side, Rachel Pine, *P.O.V.*'s frizzy-haired, frenetic publicist, came on to handle communications, and most critically, Marc Feifer, impeccably organized and immaculately honest, would return to run the finance department. He was Doubledown's risk manager.

This group was loyal. Loyal to each other, and loyal to me. I had given Brian Dawson, a brilliant word machine now charged with overseeing the copy and enforcing deadlines, his first job out of college. He had been the "employee of the year" at a music magazine called *Blender*, which entitled him to a week at flamboyant owner Felix Dennis's mansion on the Caribbean island of Mustique. He forfeited the trip to join me at *Trader Monthly*. Wenger, an avid duffer, would give up his job testing the best courses in the world for *Travel and Leisure Golf*. Feifer, whose profession dictated that he not take risk, left a higher-paying job at stable Viacom.

Pine was more complicated. Besides *P.O.V.*, her other long-term job had been working for Harvey and Bob Weinstein at Miramax Films; years later, resentment for perceived slights stewed deep enough that she wrote a roman à clef, filled with thinly veiled venom against two brothers who made movies. As a courtesy, I read a draft, and she in turn dedicated the entire book to my "exquisite" newborn daughter. My wife found that gesture—in combination with frequent, manic early-morning phone calls that too often coincided with our vacations—creepy. I just saw it as fervent loyalty. This time, I hoped we could all win together.

$ $ $

During one of Magnus's increasingly frequent New York visits, he and I became determined to develop a slogan, a few words that could concisely describe *Trader Monthly*. For inspiration, I brought him to a popular traders' hangout in midtown called Tao.

Actually, *hangout* is the wrong word: it was a meat market, one of the preeminent spots where that classic Wall Street trade—looks for money—takes root. Pale, swollen guys in $4,000 Kiton suits buy rounds for lithe women dressed to impress. The loud music thankfully drowned out the insipid banter, but it also made for difficult brainstorming. So we retired to the upstairs bar, which looked down upon a giant, smiling golden Buddha that lorded over the ground-floor carnage.

Magnus was in a good mood. He fished into his wallet for a photograph and, with all the pride of a father showing his son in a resplendent Little League uniform, revealed a picture of a black Lamborghini Murcielago—wedged into the belly of a Virgin Atlantic 747, a foot or two on each side to spare. Besides Doubledown, Magnus was bankrolling a cross-country race—*Cannonball Run* meets the *Robb Report*—with an appropriate market-friendly name: the Bull Run. Since the whole point of such rallies is to show off the wheels you've overpaid for, Magnus was planning to ship his new $300,000 baby to the starting line in Los Angeles. Rather than subject it to a drawn-out boat trip through the Panama Canal, it would travel the way he did, first-class.

I pondered the absurdity, and his joy in it. Then, over a few Bass ales, I pushed Magnus to encapsulate what drives a trader.

Magnus's mind worked sequentially. He was partial to lists and bullet points, and after mulling a few moments, he spat out a crisp three-step process.

"First, you need to see the money, see the opportunities in front of you.

"Second, you need to know how to capture them.

"Third, you want to enjoy the fruits of your labor, the best life has to offer."

As I listened to Magnus, reflecting on his many tales, it clicked. I grabbed a cocktail napkin, and regurgitated six words that tried to encapsulate everything Magnus had just explained.

His winning grin stretched ear-to-ear, looking at the chicken scratch that seemed to embody the zeitgeist of the era: *"See It, Make It, Spend It."*

Those six words resonated across the summer of 2004. Since neither our lease nor payroll commenced until July, my reunited editorial crew held regular meetings at a bar called the White Horse Tavern in New York's Greenwich Village, whose previous literary claim to fame was that poet Dylan Thomas put down eighteen shots of whiskey a half-century earlier, then went into a coma and died. A plaque near the bar commemorates his patronage.

The exercise at the White Horse was simple. I would spit out a character trait or interest area that I'd noticed from my talks with Magnus or my visit to his trading floor, and then we'd collectively brainstorm a fun or interesting way to convey it within the context of "See It, Make It, Spend It." It was a similar exercise to when I had distilled America for the Arab world with *Hi!* magazine, an audience that seemed just as foreign.

The bread-and-butter content—the "See It" and "Make It" parts—revolved around trading strategies practical across any market. Johnny Chan, the ten-time World Series of Poker champion, signed up for a surprisingly perceptive column about the parallels between the tables and the markets. We created a tongue-in-cheek section, "Cojones," which allowed everyone from Air Force test pilots to poisonous snake hunters to explain how they manage risk. ("I have no fear of heights," said a skyscraper antenna repairman, "but I respect them.") We enlisted a hedge fund manager, Jonathan Hoenig, to profile palladium and natural gas and other trading contracts as if they were Hollywood starlets: where they were born, how they evolved, how they got popular, what makes them angry, what makes them tick. Most of all, we would feed the anxiety, by publishing, and celebrating, what the top dogs made—the *Trader Monthly* 100.

In channeling "Spend It," we celebrated gluttony. The magazine would showcase soup-to-nuts restaurant feasts, under a column we called "The 5,000 Calorie Meal," that would give Caligula indigestion. Readers sent in their most egregious expense reports—the $7,600 dinner for four traders at London's Nobu, including nine bottles of first-growth Bordeaux, which we'd wryly annotate. ("Gosh, free soup. And after only $1,600 so far!") Besides the de rigueur reviews of new cars and watches and Scotch, we offered impulse items, such as "Buy This Island," for those interested in, say, a twenty-two-acre speck off the coast of Rio de Janeiro; rather than a guesthouse, the $9 million property had a guest island, connected by a 450-foot tram.

All of these ideas were either spawned by or fed into Magnus, who would tweak or correct them, a one-man focus group, in lieu of the millions a big media company might spend on market research. Rather than a bunch of journalists swilling beers, imagining what traders might like, Magnus gave us the inside knowledge and industry credibility for us to brag that the magazine was "for traders, by traders."

To front this strange brew of success and decadence, we tapped Braveheart. A magazine cover, like a cereal box or a movie poster, is a visual introduction to the world, a chance to project what's inside. The magazine's core mission—uniting the global community of traders—necessitated one of their own. Specifically, one of their own who fit their glorified collective self-image, complete with the toys. Hence, Braveheart, whose moneymaking abilities now split time between his home (London), his girlfriend (Montreal), and warm-weather working holidays (Miami, Gibraltar), the very embodiment of the electronic trading revolution.

To save money on the cover shoot, we used my apartment as the staging area. Braveheart huffed four floors up, his shiny face reinforcing that he was still just a few years out of college—this was, in fact, his first-ever visit to New York. The photography team pressed Braveheart into a $300 burgundy Prada shirt, covered by a $2,000 black Prada suit, and paired him with a female model who looked like a young Sophia Loren, with an imperfectly crooked nose that made her more beautiful. We then took him out on the cobblestone streets of New York's Meatpacking District and leaned him against the frame of a sky blue 1964 Austin Healey, borrowed from my poker buddy for the afternoon.

Nathaniel Welch, a photographer who had worked with stars from Tom Petty to Snoop Dogg, rotated the insta-couple, testing the lighting and the composition with Polaroids until stumbling upon the pose that would become an immediate hallmark. The background was the city—the urban jungle, where the fit survive and the fittest thrive. The foreground, the classic car, was the manifestation of the rewards that await the victor. At left center, the model, her hair flowing in the wind, her hand on her gentleman's chest, her eyes cast straight at him as if straight out of a male fantasy. And smack in the middle, Braveheart, his eyes locked straight at the camera, daring our egocentric readers to connect the dots: *either this is you, or it should be.*

$ $ $

The Time Warner Center was the first major skyscraper to be completed in New York after 9/11, and its two identical towers, each soaring 750 feet, served as both as a sober coincident and a triumphant statement that in 2004 the city was back.

It was also the physical embodiment of what Doubledown Media was trying to do. While the World Trade Center had been filled with the *Trader Monthly* audience during the day, the Time Warner Center was focused on housing them at night. The top floors were filled with luxury apartments overlooking Central Park that commanded the highest square-foot price in North America. David Martinez, the founder of Fintech, which bought and sold international debt, had just plunked down $54.7 million for a penthouse. On the bottom four floors was New York's first luxury mall (although "mall" itself was a four-letter word; the developers instead dubbed it "The Shops at Columbus Circle"): Armani, Coach, Davidoff, and the like, with nary a Linens 'n Things to be found. Sandwiched in the middle was a media company, Time Warner, along with the glamorous Mandarin Oriental Hotel, from whose thirty-sixth-floor ballroom, staring across Central Park and the Manhattan skyline, *Trader Monthly* officially launched on November 15, 2004.

See it, make it, spend it. For invitations to prospective advertisers and other outsiders, we stoked the stereotype, silk-screening a big green dollar sign onto burlap bags—ones you might see in a silent movie bank robbery—and then filling them to the rim with gold-foiled chocolate coins, necked with a tag announcing "Come Meet the New Moneybags." We hired models, dressed as Brink's guards, to hand-deliver the loot sacks all over town.

Over eight hundred crammed into the giant ballroom. From the ceiling we hung a trapeze and giant swaths so that lithe dancers could perform Cirque du Soleil–style. The bar poured Moët Champagne, Chivas Regal—the good stuff, aged eighteen years, not much younger than many of the multimillionaire guests. Level Vodka offered a special martini bar where imbibers could choose from six kinds of olives. Davidoff cigars were puffed in violation of New York's new antismoking ban. Foie gras canapés were passed and buffet tables offered heartier fare. Hummer-branded body wash, mini bottles of the Chivas, and vouchers for $500 off a Tourneau watch and $5,000 off a private jet flight filled the extreme-goodie bags. And onstage, in gold lamé, the Godfather of Soul, James Brown himself, warbled and danced, breaking the kind of sweat necessary to become the hardest-working man in show business, backed by a seven-piece band. *Hit me!*

"You can't cut corners," I declared to an attending reporter. "That means the Mandarin. That means foie gras floating around."

Of course, this also meant doing things the scrappy Doubledown Way. The booze and goodie bags had been solicited by our new publisher, Wilkie Bushby, from advertisers eager to foist their concoctions down the throats of the ultimate target market. The aerialists were recruited by Doubledown's new marketing director, Marla Nitke, from a gymnastics school in exchange for $500. A literal ton of chocolate—two thousand pounds of coins—had been purchased for a similar amount, wholesale, from a factory in Pennsylvania, and rather than pay for UPS, we rented a cargo van and hired some guy on the Internet to drive all night and fetch it. And "James Brown" was actually Black Velvet and the Green River Blues Band, an unknown but enthusiastic act that I caught randomly, at a small local bar in the Bronx after a Yankees game. I didn't think anyone would take them seriously—the invites specifically said that Black Velvet was playing—but years later, people still asked how I got James Brown to play our launch party. This was my element, a guerrilla start-up, and the smoke and mirrors necessitated by our limited resources only made it more fun for me.

The only real cost was for the Mandarin Oriental Hotel itself—the room, staffing, the food—but they too were eager to meet the New Moneybags, and passed on those services at cost. The entire event, from invitations to cleanup, ran $35,000. And that was pricey by our standards. Earlier, like a Broadway show, we'd opened in Chicago. A Hard Rock Hotel had just launched there and, keen to spread the word to traders, management gave us their hotel ballroom absolutely free, complete with rooms for Magnus and me. Other than incidentals, that party didn't cost us a dime.

This was our coming-out party to three audiences simultaneously: the New York trader community, still the world's most influential, who had come to ogle themselves and then pursue women; advertisers and potential advertisers, who had come for free drinks and to observe the first group to see if they were as affluent as we had promised, the way a father might observe his daughter's new potential boyfriend; and the media, who would judge both groups.

The traders and the advertisers were impressed. The former for finally being recognized as the superstars they always thought they were; the latter because these New Moneybags actually showed by the hundred, as promised, and indeed appeared to have cash. But perhaps the most interesting reaction came from the media, which showed up by the dozen.

Between the magazine and live parties, a foreign world had been unveiled, and the media treated us as if we had brought them inside a royal castle. The story had everything. Impossibly young guys were making and spending impossible sums of money, and the anonymous idea of a "trader" now had a face. "I went to the *Trader Monthly* launch party," admitted Susan Lisovicz, a redheaded business anchor, when I appeared on CNN. "Live band, great food, free drinks, fancy cigars. I really enjoyed the vicarious experience!" Jim Cramer, the manic former fund manager and TheStreet.com cofounder now emerging as the Oprah of stocks, also took a shine. "It has the buzz of the CNBC floor and of all my trading friends," he said while introducing me on his nationally syndicated radio show, "and I want everyone to check it out."

But I was just a journalist-entrepreneur; the media really wanted to meet actual traders. With Magnus uncomfortable embodying the stereotype, the coming-out tour increasingly became the Braveheart show. He had jetted in for both the Chicago and New York parties, where he was fawned over like a glistening celebrity. "They were treating me like a rock star," remembers Braveheart. "Chicks were chasing me around the room. It was *mental*." And then he started making appearances for us, including a breakthrough performance on CNBC's *Power Lunch* shortly after the issue hit.

"You have been incredibly successful in this market," gushed the CNBC anchor, Sue Herera. "You make an eight-figure income, as we mention. How did you do it?"

"As a trader you have to be quite emotionally balanced, quite strong, mentally tough," responded Braveheart, via satellite from Montreal. "You have to have a good appreciation for what moves the markets. And you have to have good risk awareness as well."

As Braveheart droned into trader talk, specifically the choppy direction of the equities market, Herera peeked at her screen. "Every single single woman at CNBC," she blushed, "has now requested that you come into the studio to do an interview."

When he responded that he had a girlfriend, Herera spoke for a smitten media worldwide: "She's a lucky lady."

The coming-out party was a worldwide success. The New Moneybags were rock stars. The media was watching closely. The advertisers were clamoring for space. Experiencing our business unfold, we really did feel like the future was *unliiimmmiiittted*. Whatever a risk manager would have whispered to us would have fallen on deaf ears.

2

Starmakers

(2005)

"Are you Randall Lane?" the woman on the phone asked urgently, the heavy New Jersey accent inflecting an almost menacing tone. "*Are . . . you . . . Randall . . . Lane?*" When I assured her that I was indeed, the other end paused, which seemed both a sigh of relief and a necessary breath for the torrential run-on sentence about to emerge. It went something close to this:

"You know, I had to ask five different people before someone would give me your number . . . so you're the guy who chooses who goes on the cover . . . why haven't you put my husband on the cover yet . . . he's one of the best traders in the world . . . and he's very good-looking . . . you need to put us both on the cover . . . I used to be a model, you know . . . you should do the photo shoot at our house . . . we have a gorgeous house in New Jersey . . . you should take pictures of the house . . . you should do a big story on us . . . we should write for you . . . we love to travel . . . we should write a column about travel . . . we go to the first-class places . . . we just got back from the Dominican Republic . . . it was unbelievable . . . we could do the cover shoot down there. . . ."

After what felt like ten minutes, but was probably closer to two, I finally managed to get in a question of my own.

"Um, who are you?"

Adrienne Bolling was, as she promised, a former model, thin and blond with curves in the right places. Devoted to her two kids, knowledgeable about what her husband did for a living, and appreciative of what that living did for her, she was, according to many other traders who would later offer me their unsolicited opinion when they found out I knew her, the paragon of what a trader's wife should be. The Alpha Female.

Eric Bolling, who met her at a party for *Sports Illustrated* swimsuit issue cover model Elle Macpherson, was, as she promised, one of the most successful traders in the country. Baseball was his intended career, until a ground ball changed his life. A third baseman for the Pittsburgh Pirates' minor league club in Bradenton, Florida, Bolling picked up the grounder, turned to throw, and *pop!* went his shoulder. So Bolling did what six-foot-one ex-jocks from Chicago were supposed to do in the 1980s bull stock market. He wedged himself into the trading world, securing a spot on a Prudential-Bache desk, albeit a sleepy one: energy.

Fortuitously, the same forces that made Refco into a juggernaut and enriched the young gamblers of MacFutures had turned energy trading, and its hub, the New York Mercantile Exchange (NYMEX), into a millionaire machine.

Energy as a trading chit had its pitfalls—when California partially deregulated electricity prices in 2000, a Houston-based trading giant named Enron figured out a way to game the system, causing disruptions that led to "rolling blackouts" in the state and an eventual voter recall of the governor, Gray Davis. Enron itself went out of business, spectacularly, in 2001, in an accounting scandal so profound—its executives capitalized on the byzantine intricacies of futures trading to mask how, or even if, it made money—that it also took down its auditor, the august Arthur Andersen. Nevertheless, the energy markets marched on and thrived. Between 2001 and 2004, the amount of energy trading at the NYMEX surged 50 percent, as price volatility made traders fortunes: between early 2002 and the middle of 2008, the price of a barrel of crude oil exploded from $20 to almost $140.

Eric Bolling was in the thick of it, controlling as much as 5 percent of the NYMEX's action. By the time I met him, at the *Trader Monthly* cover shoot Adrienne had so forcefully pursued, the forty-three-year-old had expanded from mere trader to mini-empire. He controlled numerous exchange "seats"—de facto licenses that prevent a free-for-all and allow each seat holder a profitable oligopoly—on the NYMEX, as well as related exchanges that handled a huge percentage of the world's coffee, sugar, cotton, cocoa, and orange juice, as well as most metals. Bolling was personally making $10 million to $15 million a year.

Bolling still liked spending all morning in the open-outcry pits (badge name: RBI), because most of the volume for energy, in 2005, was still on the physical floor. But in the afternoon he'd repair to a nearby office, where he'd watch and trade contracts electronically. Energy is the most global of commodities and what happens in Russia or the Middle East or South America can cause huge and immediate ripples. He had started trading crude oil futures, which he likened to playing blackjack at a $100 minimum table, and then moved his operation aggressively to the real high-roller area: natural gas futures—known as "nattie gas" or, more ominously, "the widowmaker," owing to its harrowing price hiccups.

Adrienne's call, and Eric's eager cooperation, was indicative of a turning point. When *Trader Monthly* was launched the previous fall it had emerged as a media phenomenon, covered slavishly by the global press as these mysterious creatures—hedge fund managers and traders—were unveiled for public viewing. And in tabulating who made what, as well as displaying the bling, we reached near-immediate global penetration on trading floors. ("It's a bit like the *People* magazine phenomenon," *The New York Times* declared right after it launched. "People chide it, but everyone seems to read it.") What was missing, as indicated by the *Times* quote, was credibility.

About six months after that first issue, once it became clear that we had staying power, attitudes about *Trader Monthly* began changing. The first few issues had been filled with traders who knew us well enough to take a chance on an untested product, whether Braveheart, who worked for Magnus, or Joe Butler, a bond trader for a top French bank, BNP Paribas, who was the brother-in-law of a buddy. By the middle of 2005, Wall Street started to call *us*. "From the first issue, it felt like you guys had always been around," Refco's Mercorella told me on one of my periodic visits to the World Financial Center. (Translation: I'm not asking for my $360,000 advertising contract back.)

If we hadn't yet achieved universal respect, there was certainly more than acceptance. When the first issue hit, a lot of traders looked through the pages of the issue, the way you look at photographs of yourself, and said, "Do I really look like this?" Six months in, the collective attitude seemed to be, "Hey, I really look like this." For his *Trader Monthly* cover, Bolling was shot in the same composition that Braveheart had branded: an iconic backdrop, the Empire State Building shooting up infinitely; Eric, thick and muscular in a $400 Gianfranco Ferré shirt accented by a Rolex Submariner watch, and a $3,000 blue Armani Collezioni suit, staring intently off the page, the bottom half of a goatee sitting on his square jaw; and Adrienne at his side, starting straight at him, a ring with a row of four diamonds dangling off her finger. The day after the cover came out, Bolling's pit buddies made fifteen seven-foot blowups, which they postered across the NYMEX floor, supplemented by a few hundred eight-by-elevens. "I'm coming up the escalators, crude is trading up two dollars, so the markets are going crazy," remembers Bolling, "and everyone is staring at me." They all had a huge laugh, but what might have been tainted with derision a few months earlier was now tinged with jealousy. Bolling's cover pose displayed, as the *South China Morning Post* noted, "an expression that indicated the kind of confidence and cockiness that only money can buy."

$ $ $

By the middle of 2005, the most famous face in trading may have been someone who didn't actually trade anymore: Magnus Greaves.

As the magazine "For Traders, By Traders," we thrust Magnus out in front every chance we could. He was our six-foot-four emblem of legitimacy, the Richard Branson of liquid markets. His name soared across the top of the masthead, his mug inserted into every party photo, his founder's letter fronting each issue, accompanied by a frequently updated headshot.

It helped that he was universally recognizable, with his hulking three-hundred-pound frame, caramel complexion, and shaved, undersized head. Walking down the street with him in Chicago, the ultimate traders' city, was no different from strolling with any local pro sports figure not named Jordan or Ditka. "Mag-nus! MAG-nus! MAG-NUS!" you'd hear from across the street, young men in trading jackets and $5,000 watches, pumping their fists. Whenever I visited him in London, his adopted town, it was even worse. In New York, we'd head down for beers at Figaro, a generic Italian joint wedged into the ground floor of our office building, and a second round would arrive subtly, with a tip of the forehead from random Wall Streeters at the end of the bar.

I remained relatively anonymous, but for those, like Adrienne Bolling, who knew who chose the story and cover subjects, I was also more powerful. A trader could create gold, Midas-like, with his fingers, but as proven by what *Trader Monthly* had done for Magnus, I had something more rare in the financial subculture: the ability to confer fame.

For the twenty or so decades since twenty-four stockbrokers sat under a buttonwood tree at 68 Wall Street, which now faces a BMW dealer, and created what became the New York Stock Exchange, such power would have been viewed as a threat rather than an asset. "Loose lips sink ships" wasn't a war slogan, it was a business credo. Tactically, traders go through elaborate rituals to mask their strategy, rather than promote it. From a regulation standpoint, attention is even worse. The rule of thumb is that the only thing attention will get you is an SEC investigation, in the same manner that public bragging among Mafiosi leads to attention from the feds.

But in this new Gilded Age, hedge fund managers were the new robber barons—and their relative youth, wealth, and swashbuckling aura made them A-list figures in their cities. Discretion went out the window—rather than worry about investigations, too many traders wanted to be rock stars, especially if becoming a mini-celebrity could translate into still more cash. The cover of *Trader Monthly* quickly emerged as a hugely desirable piece of real estate.

John Devaney saw the allure. Raised a Miami child of privilege, complete with boats and boarding school, he was appropriately tanned and blond when I met him. He looked even younger than his thirty-five years, and he was very eager to show me, and anyone else, how he backed up that golden boy image. Like Magnus, after a few years of trading, he had grasped an emerging opportunity (creating something tradable out of a bunch of IOUs) and founded his own firm, United Capital Markets, in 1999. Devaney focused on taking bundles of junky asset-backed securities—whether overdue credit card debts, dicey airplane leases, or mobile home loans—and repackaging them into trader-friendly units.

For example, in 2005, right before we met, he had bought up, at a huge discount, $150 million worth of loans that had been used to buy airplanes and might not be paid back. Devaney then sliced up the loans into pieces, taking out insurance on the best stuff so that he could resell them as a guaranteed, blue-chip investment to someone who wanted a safe return, and dividing the rest into three different buckets, each riskier than the next, for hedge funds on the hunt for aggressive returns.

Asset-backed securities were soaring—in 1999, when Devaney started his firm, they totaled less than $300 billion; by 2005, they approached $1.3 trillion—and Devaney's cash stack had followed suit. As these kinds of securities generally had whatever imaginary value he could convince someone to buy them for, he imagined himself a profit of a couple million on the airplane loan deal, a drop in the bucket toward the $50 million we estimated he would make personally just for 2005. That haul was poised to grow considerably: rather than just run a financial butcher shop, buying the sick cows cheap, and strategically carving them up, why not keep the best cuts for himself? He started a series of hedge funds under a suitably sunny name, Horizon, and was in the process of raising $500 million.

Devaney wasn't shy about showing off his precocious fortune. He basically annexed Key Biscayne, a posh island sitting between Miami and South Beach, starting with a rented house that served as headquarters for his eighty-person firm. Devaney then snapped up separate mansions for his mother, mother-in-law, father-in-law, and sister-in-law. For himself, his wife, Selene, and their three tanned, blond children, this capitalist gunslinger bought the 12,000-foot palace revered by a generation of gangsters: Al Pacino's movie home from *Scarface*, the place where a coked-up Tony Montana asked some well-armed trespassers to "say hello to my little friend." Except that Devaney's little friend was his 142-foot-long yacht, the *Positive Carry*, docked right in his backyard, paid for by all the lousy loans homeowners and plane buyers and others were taking out.

Like Bolling, Devaney was keen to do the *Trader Monthly* cover. We, in turn, were excited by the location. By the mid-Zeroes, Miami's role as the gateway to South America, and the city's weather, made it an emerging trading capital. Dozens of companies, including Magnus's Refco division, were setting up Miami offices so that their traders, like white-haired snowbirds, could trade and recreate in the warm clime for a few months, the ultimate testament to the transient lifestyle afforded by electronic trading. In scouting for a location, unlike the Braveheart cover which was designed, *Rashomon*-style, to be whatever trader city the reader imagined, we wanted something unmistakably South Florida. We focused on Miami Beach's Ocean Drive, securing photo permits and renting a vintage convertible, which Devaney could lean against with the famous neon and Art Deco behind him. We sent down a photographer and fashion editor, who in turn picked up an assistant, a stylist, lighting equipment, and other necessities to make these guys look as good as they thought they were. And so the stage was set.

Then my crew waited. Throughout the day, our chief photographer, Ian Spanier, high-strung on shoot day, texted me in New York urgently. *Where is he? Where is he?*

Four hours late, Devaney finally showed. The sun was setting and Spanier was frantic to get started before the remaining light departed.

"This isn't me," Devaney replied, surveying the scene. He didn't do South Beach, didn't drive a vintage car. Spanier texted me again: *Trouble!*

And then communication from him went dark. I figured the cover was lost, the money wasted. Not so. Devaney decided that if he was going to be shot for the cover of *Trader Monthly*, it would be with *his* toys, not someone's rentals. So the entire crew was dragged to a nearby airplane hangar. Opening the giant doors, Devaney walked his visitors in. Parked in front was his brand-new, jet-black Rolls-Royce Phantom (price: $328,750). Next to the Phantom, for longer hauls, he pointed to his white Sikorsky S-76 helicopter, complete with vast leather seats in the passenger cabin, satellite phones, and mini-fridge ($11 million), and to the left was the king of the runway, the best private jet a man could buy in 2005, a Gulfstream IV with seating for ten, a six-foot-high cabin, leather chairs, and a flight crew ready to take off to almost anyplace with an airport ($35 million).

Insistent that Spanier fit all three toys into the frame, Devaney, in a navy blue three-button suit and no tie (this is Miami, after all), posed for the cover. This didn't sit well with everyone. Somebody with inside knowledge (we didn't announce our cover subjects in advance) created a Yahoo account, your_next_cover, and sent a staccato e-mail, written in the manner of an old-time telegram when people were charged by the word:

"John Devaney / United Capital / under elevated investigation by SEC and NASD / fact"

His marketing deputy laughed it off. "We're under perpetual investigation." The cover was sending a message to the world, not unlike what Bonnie and Clyde did when they playfully posed in front of their fancy getaway car, guns at their side: *Come and get me.*

$ $ $

The bridge we had created between Wall Street and popular culture, which drove the ruckus when we launched, was now cast firmly in concrete, and glory-seeking traders were striding across it. The resonance came from our newfound influence on television. Producers deduced that the *Trader Monthly* mix—see it, make it, spend it—was good television even before there was *Trader Monthly*. A documentary outfit named Blue Chip Films had approached Magnus and me while we were still in our planning stages about doing a reality TV show about our planned magazine, something we ultimately declined because the necessary currency of the genre—filmed conflict—didn't mesh with our goal of building a respected media company for the long term. Ultimately, no one used the bridge better than CNBC.

The network, one of the most profitable in the world during 1990s day-trading mania, had suffered commensurately during the dot-com bust. In the mid-Zeroes, it began clawing back—ratings doubled, and the network's estimated profits jumped to $300 million—by following the same formula we had stumbled onto: deifying these financial wizards to the Main Street audience who hoped to jump on the gravy train. If traders were the new rock stars, CNBC intended to be MTV.

So to that extent we were quite useful. As everyone in media well knows, television sits atop the information food chain, letting those who deal in words ferret out priorities, and then swooping in for the glory. In the Zeroes, network news parroted *The New York Times*. Cable news parroted the political blogs. For hour-to-hour coverage, CNBC aped Reuters and Bloomberg; for starmaker suggestions, it followed *Trader Monthly*. We'd bring forward the world's top trading talent from behind their anonymous computer terminals, deliver them on-air, usually on the morning *Squawk Box* or midday *Power Lunch* shows, and they'd then cherry-pick the most articulate and best looking for further roles with the network. While lower-level CNBC friends would privately apologize for our emerging role as their uncompensated talent scouts, we shrugged. Serving as CNBC's farm team, the gatekeeper to mainstream fame, carried huge advantages besides credibility for our brand, and thousands of visitors to our

Web site: it strengthened our influence and my unexpected role as the broke kingmaker among the financial titans.

In April 2005, CNBC summoned us to meet with their three top producers about a "secret" project that was in the "embryonic stage." The month before, they had launched a show called *Mad Money*. It starred my old friend Jim Cramer, who basically riffed for an hour about stocks, yelling at the camera—it was *The Wall Street Journal* meets sports talk radio. And from what we were being told, it was a big hit.

The new idea was something akin to a traders' version of *The View*, Barbara Walters's successful daytime kaffeeklatsch. A group of professional traders, fresh from battle, would head to the studio after the closing bell to swap war stories, analyze the day just past, and provide picks for the day to come. Since *Mad Money* had worked so well (what was money in the Zeroes if not stark *craaaazy*?) they would call this new show something even more basic, *Fast Money* (in the Zeroes, clearly, no one need actually *wait* for cash).

Historically, the idea that regular people would want to hear traders talk to each other about their day was as absurd as the idea that legitimate traders would actually want to spend their weeknights sharing their trading secrets. But the former proved out—*Fast Money* was an immediate smash when it launched in June 2006—as did the latter. Over the first year, a healthy chunk of the *Fast Money* panel came ripped from the pages of *Trader Monthly*, including linebacker-turned-trader Pete Najarian and a hedge fund trader named Karen Finerman.

Finerman represented a turning point for *Trader Monthly*. Since a magazine has a personality—complete with habits and affectation and attitude—there's a perpetual internal battle about whether it should lead the readers, like a respected elder sibling, or reflect them, like a buddy. For the first four or five issues, I had leaned toward the latter, and thus, astride the strategies and the glitz, came chauvinistic flourishes: the superfluous cover models, "Kobe's Korner" (gifts to buy your way out of the doghouse, named for wayward basketball star Kobe Bryant), and, most notably, a column with a name too catchy not to use: "Trader Dater." In concept, it was simply establishing a market—a clearinghouse of gold diggers to match the huge pool of young, rich, single men—and it was an immediate sensation, the traders gawking at their options the way they did at the antique car listings in two-inch-thick *Hemmings Motor News*.

But women on Wall Street immediately complained that rather than push trading culture into the future, we just reinforced its past. They were right. And our quick success gave us the luxury of setting up a soapbox on this issue. So while 90 percent of the magazine remained structurally intact, we did a 180-degree switch. Adrienne Bolling would be the last woman to appear on our cover as arm candy. Instead, we proactively addressed the iniquities of a field so predominantly male despite the shift from brawn in the pit to brains on the computer. "They're Tougher, Smarter and Better Than You" touted one cover story on female traders. We began having giant "Women of Wall Street" parties, attended by everyone from out-of-college stereotype-breakers to industry legend Muriel Siebert, the first woman to own a seat on the New York Stock Exchange (she famously had to cross the street to go to the bathroom).

CNBC, which faced just as big a gender imbalance as we did, eagerly integrated any female trading talent we highlighted. They booked Kristen Dove, a blond trader at ABN Amro, who graced our cover. They tried to develop an entire show around Shahnaz Hussain, a young Brit who controlled enough of the market for the Schatz, a slow-trading German government note, that she was known widely as "Bond Girl." Finerman, meanwhile, was a hedge fund hitter whom we plucked from obscurity, performing well enough in an on-air interview we coordinated for CNBC producers to place her right at the center of the five-person *Fast Money* panel, albeit with her hair softened and lightened. This was, after all, still television.

The breakout star of *Fast Money*, however, was surely Eric Bolling. He and I had slowly become friends since his cover appearance. In the awful aftermath of Hurricane Katrina, while many of his NYMEX peers pounced on the uncertainty surrounding the rigs in the Gulf of Mexico (one named Steve Berkson, we reported, made $20 million), Bolling reached out to me about how we could raise money for victims in New Orleans. We, in turn, used the biggest megaphone we had, our relationship with CNBC, to get word out about how traders could pitch in. Bolling discovered he loved the camera, and it pretty much reciprocated. "When they called me in to talk about *Fast Money*, they had the *Trader Monthly* cover on their desk," says Bolling. "It was a huge factor." Stripped of the "RBI" nickname by which I had first known him, CNBC rebranded him "The Admiral," for his chart-reading skills.

Once, over dinner at his favorite restaurant, the Palm Too, which he frequented so often that the managers painted a mural of Eric and Adrienne smooching on the cover of a cartoonish *Trader Monthly*, I asked him about his typical day. "Crazy, man, I get up at six a.m. Trade like crazy in the morning, do research for the show, trade the close, then start heading into the studio about two thirty."

I didn't ask how much CNBC was paying him, because it really wasn't a factor. They might as well not have paid him, given how much he was leaving on the table due to the hours and distraction required to appear on the show. I sketched it out. If Jay Leno was maybe the best-paid television personality of the Zeroes, pulling in over $30 million a year to tell corny jokes at 11:35 p.m., Eric Bolling was certainly the worst-paid: his TV passion had be *costing* him a couple million a year, easily. But it didn't matter. He was famous.

$ $ $

Sitting at our midpoint between Wall Street and media, watching traders pine to become rock stars, we noticed that something even stranger was happening: the rock stars were pining to be traders.

What else could explain why early on February 7, 2005, a few hours after the New England Patriots had defeated the Philadelphia Eagles for their second straight Super Bowl win, Refco's midtown Manhattan trading floor was suddenly graced by one Richard Melville Hall, better known to the world as Moby? The great-great-great-grandnephew of Herman Melville, Moby had sold ten million copies of *Play*, the most popular electronica album of all time, and was five weeks away from releasing *Hotel*, which would go double platinum. Into this hectic period, he had slotted a day for some high stakes trading.

Playing off the fame-finance nexus we had created, I concocted a column for the magazine called "Celebrity Trader." The gimmick was simple: we (okay, Magnus) would give each celebrity $50,000 to trade with for a week, and turn them loose on the professional markets, no-holds-barred: derivatives, options, futures, the works. Whatever they made off our nest egg, we (Magnus) would then donate to the charity of their choice, with a $5,000 minimum donation guaranteed, no matter what.

Just as staid Wall Street had become taken with fame, the celebrity set found that playing Andy "Braveheart" Priston or Eric Bolling for a week was now a perfectly A-list exercise. They just asked us not to make them look stupid, which is why we always provided access to a professional trader "buddy."

"Honestly, I don't even know what I invest in," shrugged actor Billy Bob Thornton. "I told my manager I don't want to know." We generally coordinated the trades by phone, and while we encouraged the celebrities to move in and out of the markets as much as they wanted across the week, many seemed content to just make their picks Monday morning and then hear how they fared late Friday afternoon.

The best-selling artist in the history of electronic dance music, however, wanted some hands-on electronic trading. So as Christian Faber, the head of Refco's New York prop trading operation, peered out over his floor, in came his newest trader, his trademark shaved head bobbing over the terminals, jeans and a blue hoodie over a strange white T-shirt with a picture of a Moby-looking bald alien, with two antennas protruding.

Moby stared intently through his oversized horn-rimmed glasses at the screens, questioning what each one did. He had dabbled in buying up tech stocks during the late nineties and, like the rest of us, thought himself a market genius, until that bubble crushed him. "Now I trade like a seventy-year-old man," he said. Overall, he didn't seem overly impressed with Refco's advanced weaponry; in the end, they were powerful computers that just happened to be directly connected to every market in the world.

Those computers gave him infinite options. But just as having one thousand cable channels, in the days before DVR, drove you to the four networks you really liked, the musician's trades leaned Moby-specific. A noted vegetarian, he snapped up stock in the rapidly expanding Whole Foods chain. A Bush-hater who endured watching the president get reinaugurated two weeks prior, he decided to buy euros on the currency market. And appropriate for a guy who helped establish a music subgenre called "chill out," he expressed empathy when buying shares of Martha Stewart Living Omnimedia. "Now that she's been humbled, that makes her a lot more appealing."

NBA superstar Dwyane Wade, faced with a similarly infinite menu and the luxury of Magnus money to play with, also reverted to what made him comfortable. He bought stock in Carnival Cruise lines, because his team, the Miami Heat, was owned by Carnival CEO Micky Arison. He bought Bank of America because that was where he had his money stashed ("they do everything right"), and Abbott Laboratories, because they made the baby formulas, Similac and Isomil, that his toddler son Zaire had gobbled up.

To the scalpers and speculators of the Zeroes, such a "buy what you know" credo, which had been popularized by Peter Lynch and had dominated individual stock-picking for the past two decades, seemed as quaint as an Amish horse-and-buggy driver on the Pennsylvania Turnpike. But the celebrity point of view reflected that of the general public: while fascinated by this new Wall Street culture, they still had no fundamental concept of what traders actually did. Moby and Dwyane Wade and your aunt Carol all still believed that Wall Street was in the business of investing (i.e., building value over time) versus trading (casinos with securities). And even when given the full slate of options, as Moby had been, modern trading was impossible for laymen to decipher, a foreign language spoken only by those with mastery over a Bloomberg terminal.

Our trader coaches tried to translate. Wade's new buddy, Scott Jacobson, took the point guard's boss-pleasing Carnival play and suggested that he buy options, which would move exponentially if the stock popped. It did, and Wade's otherwise flat performance blossomed to 1.1 percent, an outstanding 59 percent on an annual basis.

Faber, meanwhile, spent a good half-hour tutoring Moby on a complicated "pairs" trade, where he simultaneously bought cash futures for the Dow, while shorting them on the Nasdaq. While Moby's emotionally based picks didn't do much, Faber's trade scored—the bet against the Nasdaq returned 10 percent for the week, while the Dow component paid, too. Overall, Moby was up 4 percent—an annualized return that would make Braveheart blush.

But they were exceptions. As the goal was to coach the celebrities, not trade for them, our professional buddies generally guided them toward the exotic new markets where the real money was being made and let them fend for themselves. Encouraged to buy metal, Billy Bob Thornton insisted on silver because "I always thought gold looked gaudy—silver is more rock and roll." Pushed to dabble in currencies, Thornton decided to refight World War II, shorting the yen and the euro ("I'm very patriotic"). And when the idea of commodities was introduced, he brushed off the analytics and insisted on soybeans— because he's allergic to dairy. "If I have milk," he explained, "I have migraines and break out." Such a stellar set of rationale led to a 0.4 percent loss for the week.

Many did worse. The Peter Lynch model worked so well for so long because it was rooted in business fundamentals, and anyone could understand it. The speculators' game was too complex to give the little guy a fair shake, even if he theoretically knew the rules. Those swaggering few who correctly surmised that they were simply entering a global casino, and knew better than to bet money based on food allergies, still generally met the fate that keeps the lights so bright in Vegas. "I don't know shit about trading, but it's just legalized gambling, right?" comedian Denis Leary announced on our first phone call. "It's Vegas-style, baby, and we've got five grand in our pocket guaranteed! Let's roll the dice!" (He crapped out, down 1 percent, our third-worst performance ever.) "Let's pick some high-risk stuff with some big upside because *Trader Monthly* is covering the losses," tennis star Andy Roddick declared at the beginning of his week. (He did, and we did, following a negative 2.7 percent disaster, the second-worst ever.) "In a way it's gambling," Jamie-Lynn Sigler, a trader favorite for her role as the attractive Mafia princess in *The Sopranos*, told me, when I recruited her for the contest. "You have to be willing to lose it." After listening to her husband, an ex-broker named A. J. DiScala, who put her into a student loan company "a friend of ours told us about," she lost it, logging negative 3.2 percent, the worst ever. (She asked for a divorce within the year.)

The professional athletes, unsurprisingly, were the most competitive. There's a reason so many ex-jocks become traders. They wanted to win—and when they did, they wanted everyone to know about it. Over four years of "Celebrity Trader," baseball superstar Alex Rodriguez was the only one who insisted on trading without a buddy. He shorted the euro and gobbled up gold futures. After he popped a 0.68 return, which annualizes to a stellar 35.4 percent, someone in his camp then leaked his prowess to the *New York Post*. The August 3, 2005, headline read "Wall Street's Got Nothing on A-Rod."

A Yankee legend of an earlier era, Reggie Jackson, did even better, nailing a spectacular 5.4 percent one-week return with a basket of Silicon Valley stocks like Apple, Cisco, and Oracle, and then walking across our fame bridge for his date with CNBC, a live interview on *Power Lunch* with host Bill Griffeth. "I mostly have focused on the tech sector, Bill. . . . It's always been extremely interesting to me, 'cause they stay on the cutting edge," posited Mr. October, before he launched into an analysis of how layoffs at Ford would affect the auto industry's performance.

The Magnus Greaves of the A-list, however, was unquestionably hip-hop producer Damon Dash. Jay-Z's business partner combined the bravado of rap ("I've got nerves of steel; I never sweat"), the instincts of Braveheart ("I know what's going on," he said, outlining an aggressive purchase of oil futures; "gas prices are going up . . . oil is black gold"), and, well, the ignorance of Billy Bob Thornton. "The pound is worth more than the dollar," he declared, justifying why he was betting on "the cable," a popular trade comparing the British pound to the U.S. greenback. *"It weighs more."*

Two out of three turned out fine. Dash's performance, even by the highest professional standards, backed up the big-money name he had chosen for his label, Roc-A-Fella. Fed chairman Alan Greenspan kept interest rates flat, making his knuckleheaded cable play a winner, while Russian leader Vladimir Putin rattled sabers against Russia's oil monopoly and Hurricane Ivan raked the oil rigs of the Gulf of Mexico. It was a literal perfect storm that helped Damon crank out the kind of return any hedge fund manager would kill for over a year—23.9 percent—in *one week*. "I figured going in I wanted to hit at least 15 percent, so I did pretty well," he said with a shrug afterward. "It's fun—trading is like playing Monopoly." If ever there was a sign that we were in a bubble, that was it.

$ $ $

As our little bridge to fame matured, our role in the conversation between Wall Street and Main Street began to morph. At first, we had been dragging the world's most important traders over it, kicking and screaming. Then, we started marching arm-in-arm with large-talent and large-ego types like Eric Bolling and John Devaney, burnishing each other's reputations. As we achieved some cultural resonance, we encountered a curious new dynamic: traders with more moxie than talent determined to get us to carry them to fame by any means necessary.

The most headaches, by far, came from a group of honorees we dubbed the 30 Under 30, our annual attempt to ferret out the up-and-comers of the trading world. Only the *Trader Monthly* 100 rivaled it in terms of the buzz it generated. These were punk kids, barely out of college, controlling vast swaths of the global economy, with all the entitled ignorance of the ten-year-old child-soldiers then terrorizing vast swaths of west Africa. The very idea fascinated the outside world. CNBC would feature members of the list every day for an entire week whenever it came out, and their hometown papers would write paeans to them.

Unlike their more press-reticent elders, this younger group of traders craved attention. Andy Warhol's concept of everyone getting their fifteen minutes had emerged as the Zeroes' dominant culture thread. A television show named *Survivor* that stranded regular people in a deserted island environment, *Lord of the Flies*–style, and filmed the results, debuted in 2000 and quickly became American television's best-rated show. It was followed by *Big Brother* (regular people stranded in a house together), *The Amazing Race* (regular people dash across the globe), *Fear Factor* (regular people compete to see who can eat the grossest things or stay locked in a coffin the longest), *The Apprentice* (regular people compete for a job working for Donald Trump), and of course, *American Idol* (regular people compete for a record contract), which was the biggest show on television by 2004 and remained that way for the rest of the decade.

Cable networks began turning over their lineups to the "reality genre," and in 2005, Rupert Murdoch dispensed with any pretensions, launching an entire cable network, Fox Reality. The whole "reality" phenomenon was, of course, little more than a reaction to the Internet; those coming out of college in the Zeroes were the first to have grown up in a culture where even a kid in high school could broadcast his musings to the world; by 2005, social media tools like YouTube and Twitter and Facebook were on the cusp of becoming cultural forces.

Thus to the younger traders, the 30 Under 30 was viewed as something of a reality contest, complete with commensurate prizes. The banks hated when we highlighted individuals—their fees were based on the notion that the brands Goldman Sachs or Merrill Lynch superseded any one person's contributions—as recruiters would make calls up and down the list, waving job offers that would result in the trader either engineering a salary match, or a profitable exit. A lucky few even tried to raise money for a hedge fund armed with the validation we (and our CNBC pipeline) offered. The party that we threw after each edition, generally in August, drew upwards of a thousand people. The beverage giant Diageo sponsored it each year, and we'd present each of the young guns the ultimate trophy for those too young and too rich— a bottle of Johnnie Walker Blue Label, a handmade Scotch that blends more than a dozen whiskies, some more than a century old, retailing for $200 a bottle, with their name engraved. When *The New York Times* covered the 2006 soiree (headline: "Traders' Night

Out"), the story proved one of the most popular in the history of their "Dealbook" blog.

For the most part, we got the 30 Under 30 list right. As trading got more technological, it mirrored the phenomenon Silicon Valley had absorbed over the past decade. Age and experience were no longer automatic virtues; comfort with cutting-edge technology and no preconceived notions about how to implement it were. For the first time in human history, naïveté was a strength as, combined with some killer smarts, it allowed kids to conceive entirely new ways to make money.

But starting with that first edition, in the fall of 2005, some self-promoters, recognizing the prizes available, would invariably con us into putting them on the list. For example, a short, smarmy trader named Zach Michaelson drew our attention because he ran a hedge fund as a college student, and now managed a large pile of money at Fortress Investments, a surging firm. The problem was, he had lost his job sometime between getting on our radar and the list going into production, an inconvenient fact he neglected to tell us, even during the fact-checking process. Fortress, as typical on Wall Street, had left Michaelson a phone and an e-mail address while they paid him his severance. Our fact-checkers also called Fortress, who, clearly leery of any possible lawsuit, confirmed that he "worked" there. When his face popped up on CNBC as part of the package, the Fortress traders deluged our office with howling e-mails.

Our worst pick, however, involved a manic twenty-three-year-old, Tim Sykes. So as not to feature thirty Goldman Sachs traders, our team of editors would generally showcase a couple who'd achieved success nontraditionally. Sykes fell neatly into that category. He had a cute story—he claimed to have parlayed $12,000 in bar mitzvah money into over $1 million—that he would happily share with anyone who would listen, including several of our reporters and, at a party that we hosted for traders at Trump Tower in 2005, me.

That event, held in the massive four-story boutique for Asprey, a British purveyor of precious things no one really needs, like $500 umbrellas, leather-bound first-edition books, and "Christmas crackers" (a sort of time-capsule-looking thing filled with silver trinkets), was a watershed moment for our company. It proved that our mailing list, which had surged into the tens of thousands, could be applied to turn out the actual trading world in force. With the drop of an e-mail, seven hundred traders filled the store, as one of our sponsors, Rolls-Royce, idled cars outside, ready to give them rides home. It was the first real chance since launch to interact with our readers en masse, and as Magnus wasn't able to attend, I was swamped by proxy, with traders either singing *Trader Monthly*'s praises, or their own.

Among the fifty or so traders I must have met that night, Sykes stood out for his sheer braggadocio. "How do I get on your 30 Under 30 list?" he asked, not even bothering with small talk.

"You trade well, and in a manner that we can verify."

"I have the number one long-short microstock hedge fund in the country, according to Barclays," he responded, using a euphemism for penny stocks, the runt of trading contracts, and thrusting me his card, from the Cilantro Fund, which in reality was $1 million mostly from friends and family.

His over-the-top sales pitch was a turnoff. But when one of our reporters included him on our list, I didn't think enough of his overbearing manner to remove him, especially since he had scored so well with Barclays. (Only later did I learn that it wasn't the august Barclays, the three-hundred-year-old British bank, the UK's second-largest, that had rated him so well, but rather the Barclay Group, a small research company based in Fairfield, Iowa, run by a Transcendental Meditation disciple, one of dozens of that religion's adherents who had decamped to the cornfields to practice their rituals and make a living from the markets.)

Once he was on the list, he ran with it. He touted his bar mitzvah story on Reuters and CNBC, as part of the wall of traders we put forward the week the 30 Under 30 was released, and from there he began putting himself everywhere: CNN, Fox, the Internet.

Then came a larger invitation. Right along with every profession from cooks (*Top Chef*) to fashion designers (*Project Runway*) to hair stylists (*Blow Out*), reality television was coming to the trading world. A network named Mojo TV, available only by satellite, approached our staff about leveraging our fame bridge to help them produce a show called *Wall Street Warriors*, which would chronicle different financial types. Two of our editors, Rich Blake and a savvy trader named Andrew Barber, would serve as on-air experts, providing overarching explanations of the financial world, and we presented them with a menu of some of the talent we had profiled.

So Sykes, the made-for-television trader, invited the crew into his living room "office" to watch him trade on a regular basis in his bathrobe. We saw Sykes, the gentleman, reflexively and angrily terming his losing position as a "bitch." We saw Sykes, the dutiful son, letting in cameras to film his mother, on her knees, scrubbing his toilet. "She's kind of my personal slave," he scoffs. When she asks him what the handcuffs in his kitchen drawer are for, he ultimately responds, "Leave me alone, I'm down five fucking grand." ("I don't really care what my friends think," she shrugs to the camera, defensively.) And Sykes the sportsman, inviting the camera crew for a round of "drunken golf," in which he stumbles around, trying to run down deer with his electric cart and taking off his clothes to retrieve an errant ball in the lake. ("My goal is to build my hedge fund and be taken seriously by the industry," he had said earlier.)

Perhaps most disturbingly, though, we see Sykes the trader. Managing other people's money, as Sykes was now doing, carries far more fiduciary responsibilities than stewarding your own like, say, Eric Bolling, whose new TV habit affected only him. Sykes's "strategy" varied all over the map, but the one consistency on *Wall Street Warriors* seemed to involve hemorrhaging cash. On one episode, he conducted an awkward, seemingly contrived meeting with a "potential investor" in his apartment, walking away from his computer while several short-term trades remained open. While he was acting for the cameras on TV, the real money he was managing for his family and friends was suffering. "This is fucking perfect, and I fucking missed it!" he screamed upon his return to his computer.

Those unfortunate enough to have entrusted their money to him began noticing. "Things are going well, it's just going to take us a while to turn around," we hear him telling one investor, after his fund has lost $300,000 in one month, a huge percentage of the money he was managing. When the investor wasn't persuaded by that reasoning, insisting on a refund, Sykes reacts by violently kicking a standing fan across the room.

"Greed is ugly," he said at each episode's beginning, flipping his collar up. "Make as much money as you can so you can get out of there before it turns you to the Dark Side." Fame, it seemed, could prove ugly, too.

3

The Jealousy Machine

(2005)

My middle-class nose had been pressed up firmly to the glass of American wealth and power from birth. The odd-shaped stone house of my childhood directly abutted the 3,600-acre Rockefeller family estate in Westchester County, an hour north of New York City. Every morning, as I waited for my school bus at the foot of the driveway, my feet shuffled over a century-old metal plaque denoting the property line and inscribed "J.D.R."—John D. Rockefeller, founder of Standard Oil and America's first billionaire.

Gazing right from the driveway, I saw endless suburbia: pleasant houses filled with regular professional folk, including my parents, a public university professor and a stay-at-home mom/writer. Gazing left, I saw the endless trees of Pocantico Hills, the Rockefellers' compound with ten mansions dotted over *six square miles* of estate. My grade-school friends were the children of Rockefeller servants; my Boy Scout troop convened in the tiny Rockefeller family church filled with stained glass windows from Chagall and Matisse. In high school, after my parents divorced, weekends were spent drinking beer at all-night bonfire campouts deep into the estate, known casually by my crew as "Rocky's," oblivious to the irony that the safest place from unwanted police attention was the vast private backyard of America's greatest financial dynasty.

Perhaps as penance, I wound up working for the bible for these financial elite, *Forbes* magazine, right out of college. As the rookie reporter, I was relegated to their equivalent of water boy duty: a full-year as capitalism's scorekeeper, tracking down, appraising, and profiling America's richest people for their annual *Forbes* 400. While the editors viewed it as an appropriate hazing, it proved transformative. Tycoon by tycoon, I deconstructed and tabulated the American economic engine, deducing everything from how much Bill Cosby made syndicating *The Cosby Show* ($300 million) to the value of a secretive industrial valve company in Cleveland ($700 million), whose paranoid owner left the old signs in place when he bought a new office or factory building.

Armed with that skill set, I was then deployed by *Forbes* as its designated wealth hunter, throwing me into assignments head-dizzying for a twenty-five-year-old who went to public school. Nike founder Phil Knight toted me around the Olympics; George Lucas hosted me for three days on the Skywalker Ranch; the Coors family dragged me across Colorado. Personally, it was heady and fun. Professionally, it was better than a Harvard MBA. Rather than academically dissect companies, as that business school's vaunted case study methodology encourages, I got under the hood, spending hours one-on-one with the founders and CEOs, always inevitably answering a single question: what's this thing really worth?

If you spend your youth pretty much broke, surrounded by the richest people on the planet, one thing pops out at you: the titans of any field are less focused on how they're doing than on how they're doing *relative to their peers*. When I spent a week alternating between the offices of Arnold Palmer and Jack Nicklaus, decades after their on-course rivalry ended, all they could both talk about was how much better they were doing, in business, than the other guy. Steven Spielberg detailed, with minutiae, how he got "gross points" (a cut of the sales) while those other saps got "net" (a cut of the profits). A sports-based comic strip named "Tank McNamara" once depicted a fight between baseball players and race car drivers, citing the *Forbes* list of highest-paid athletes, which I oversaw. "To Randall Lane," read the autographed inscription on the original artwork, which the cartoonists sent to me, "who fuels the jealousy machine."

Trader Monthly offered the most high-powered jealousy machine fuel I'd ever encountered. There is nothing subjective about what traders do, and they don't create anything that can be debated, like art or writing or even corporate performance. Success and failure are perfectly quantified and the points are consistent and universal: dollars. So for all the expensive toy reviews and personality profiles, the only question anyone ultimately wanted answered from a magazine "for traders, by traders" during this dizzying run-up was: who's making what? Someone needed to keep score. As much as anything, it was our willingness to do so—for the first time, the secret pay packages of the entire financial elite would be shared with the world— that put *Trader Monthly* on the map.

Serving as Wall Street's scorekeeper, however, quickly required me to check reality at my weathered office door each morning. Over the past year, I had slowly come to grips with the idea of Magnus flying around his Murcielago, as I drove my beat-up Subaru, or Braveheart making $10 million a year playing high-stakes video games, as I logged seventy-hour unpaid weeks trying to get a start-up rolling. But as our team started making calls and crunching the numbers for the *Trader Monthly* 100, the number of zeroes coming back looked like decimal errors. When I was assured that they weren't, I felt the way the small group watching the first atomic bomb test in the New Mexico desert must have; I was witnessing something blinding, staggering, nauseating, with the world at large still oblivious it to it all.

No longer were the best financial industry players content with a payday to make a Yankees shortstop blush. Instead, sometime around 2002 or 2003, compensation hit a new stratosphere mimicking the GNP of small countries. Rich Blake and his reporters calculated the 2003 figures for our launch issue and then followed up, in early 2005, with a tally for 2004. The results revealed dozens upon dozens of obscure hedge fund traders personally making $50 million a year, with many making far, far more.

But more than just the totals, what was most telling were the people hauling them in. In 2004, the group in ascendance, as measured by the only score they counted, were the *quants*. With electronic trading maturing worldwide, the emerging superstars could amalgamate this suddenly limitless, accessible data—literally billions of data points across tens of thousands of potential contracts within hundreds of markets around the globe—sift through it, and find quantitative, predictable, actionable *patterns*. So for all the little-known but stereotypical jock types our Trader 100 sleuths were digging up, like Michael Novogratz, a forty-year-old former U.S. Army helicopter pilot who was pulling in $50 million a year (half the GDP of the Falkland Islands) at Fortress Investment Group, or Mark Kingdon, a third-degree tae kwon do black belt who in 2004, we estimated, surged past $75 million (half the GDP of the Republic of Kiribati), the serious brainiacs—the kind of people who in a better world would be proving the Riemann hypothesis, or curing cancer, or breaking terrorist code—were concocting algorithms that could make 1 + 1 = 3.

Rather than drink beer or read Shakespeare, thirty-five-year-old Ken Griffin had spent his time at Harvard developing a mathematical model for convertible bond arbitrage (in English: take advantage of price differences, even a penny per share, in contracts involving a bond that has the right to become a share of stock). His Chicago-based hedge fund Citadel had gone so far as to mostly do away with traders entirely; instead, special computer programs, known as "black boxes," would surf electronic markets on their own, and trade when conditions met preset parameters. Black boxes like Griffin's were systematically making prices so efficient that the human scalpers, including Magnus's old crew, who profited off of market hiccups, were being wiped out like Civil War musket troops marching into Gatling gun fire. We calculated that Griffin's black boxes earned him $250 million in 2003, and then another $100 million in 2004.

One generation of nerds older, James Simons, a Berkeley PhD and a math professor who, true to his alma mater, lost his job with the Defense Department for opposing the Vietnam War, had also developed a black box to skim pennies. He made no secret about his edge—he named his Long Island–based hedge fund Renaissance *Technologies*—and in 2003, we figured that he personally took home about $400 million; by 2004, his annual income swelled to a *half-billion dollars*, or about $2 million each and every workday.

But standing atop both the 2003 and 2004 scorecards was a man whose name made him sound like he was eight years old, but who was, by numbers and acclamation, among the small circle who knew him, the greatest trader in the world: Stevie Cohen. For 2003, *Trader Monthly* estimated that Cohen took home almost $550 million, and followed that in 2004 with a $650 million personal payday: *$1.2 billion for two years' work*. And unlike the Bill Gates and Warren Buffett types whose net worth can fluctuate that much in a single day depending on how their company's stock is trading, this was cash, ready to come off the table or, in most cases, roll into another year's worth of bets.

Stevie Cohen was a mystery, the Greta Garbo of the markets. He never talked to the press, eschewed industry events, and made his employees sign thick nondisclosure agreements. Public photos of him didn't exist, but as described by our sources for his *Trader Monthly* 100 profile, "he looks a little like George from *Seinfeld* and dresses like a suburban accountant." But anonymous in stature, infantilized in name, Stevie Cohen was also a freak of nature, the son of a dressmaker and a piano teacher who began devouring sports statistics and then stock prices as a kid, before taking down hundreds of dollars at all-night high-stakes poker games in high school. He was, in brains and constitution, the perfect trader: a mathematical genius who thought like a quant, able to detect patterns and foresee price movements, with the raw instincts for anticipating how the crowds would react that had typified pit traders for centuries.

His trading operation was mercurial. He holed up in Stamford, Connecticut, a minor city an hour northeast of New York that, owing to its proximity and lower taxes, had emerged as a trading mecca. Magnus's old firm, UBS, opened the world's largest trading floor there, which stands at 103,000 square feet, or roughly two football fields; to cars cruising I-95, which bisected the city, it appeared like an elevated sports arena floating above the sidewalks. A few blocks away, Stevie Cohen's shop, SAC Capital, at a mere one-third of a football field, didn't compete on size, but its volume was head-dizzying. On a typical day, Stevie Cohen's team of two hundred traders and analysts divided into forty separate trading units did 2 percent of the trading on the world's two biggest stock markets, the Nasdaq and the New York Stock Exchange. That's 20 million shares of stock bought and sold each day.

Amid this trading hive, kept at a brisk temperature to keep everyone alert, Cohen sat in the center, the fleece-clad queen bee, staring at eight screens of information, while a small camera stared back at him. All the worker bees at SAC Capital got a live feed of Cohen on one of their screens—Stevie TV—so that they could see at all times what the queen was doing and react accordingly. Cohen would absorb fantastic amounts of data, fed both from his traders and also a huge number of brokers around Wall Street. His was one of the last shops that, just as in Wall Street's easy days, actually paid brokers a full commission to execute trades. In 2004, he likely shelled out about a quarter-billion dollars in these fees, most of which was unnecessary, since electronic trading increasingly meant cutting out, or cutting down, the middleman. What Cohen was really buying was information, a legal version of the challenge the fictional Gordon Gekko gave the cold-calling young broker Bud Fox in the movie *Wall Street*. ("Money itself isn't lost or made," Gekko tells Fox, "it's simply transferred from one perception to another.") The biggest tipper gets the best service, and Wall Street's waiters fell over each other to feed him tidbits ahead of their other clients in exchange for the odd million or two he might leave for them on the table.

Cohen would then process all the data fed to him, calmly filter it, and react rapid-fire. His philosophy, tailor made for the electronic trading age, was to get in and out of stocks fast. He was especially vigilant about walking away from losers, a skill learned from poker. When he didn't see opportunity, he could create it. So great was Cohen's clout, in terms of trade size and reputation, that he could personally move the market, with the parasitic copycats jumping in behind him as soon as the word spread that Stevie was making a play. So in one tactic, according to a 2003 *BusinessWeek* story on Cohen (the only article of significance on his shop I had ever seen), Cohen would have his traders sell a small amount of stock they liked, watch the rest of the market jump in and drive the price down further, then gobble the shares up at a lower price. Another one would have them flood a market, buying every available share of a stock, forcing banks that always needed an inventory to buy some back at higher prices.

Everything about him—the obscene hauls, the force he created in the world's biggest stock markets, the low profile—made Stevie Cohen the closest thing our readers had to Elvis. We in turn tried to cement his celebrity. He became *Trader Monthly*'s leitmotif, as we snuck references to him into almost every issue the way Al Hirschfeld buried his daughter Nina's name into all his illustrations. Among our audience, Stevie Cohen represented everything to aspire to.

$ $ $

Stevie Cohen's payday was a half-century in the making. In fact, it was entirely appropriate that our magazine was born of hedge funds, as hedge funds had been born of a magazine. A writer for *Fortune* named Alfred Winslow Jones, in the course of preparing a story on stock market forecasting, developed a strategy that held that selling some stocks short (betting that prices will go down) while simultaneously buying others, and borrowing against both types of trade for added oomph, would provide a "hedge" against market risk, at least matching the overall market in good times while greatly outperforming it in bad. "Speculative techniques used for conservative ends," as he put his leveraged "long-short" philosophy. In 1949, he raised $100,000—$40,000 of which was his own—and thus the first "hedge fund" was born.

By the mid-1960s, Jones had proven phenomenally successful, and copycats abounded, notably Michael Steinhardt and George Soros, the latter of whom became far better known by the Zeroes for plowing his trading riches into democracy-building in Eastern Europe and left-leaning causes domestically. Most, however, did not adhere to Jones's long-short model, and the roiling 1970s markets efficiently punished that oversight; by 1984, a researcher could locate only sixty-eight hedge funds globally.

But Jones's influence was far from finished. In 1952, three years into his fund, Jones institutionalized an innovative compensation system for himself. He didn't follow the structure of a mutual fund—perhaps the most important investment innovation of the twentieth century, the idea that regular folks can buy into a diversified, professionally managed basket of stocks—which generally charges 2 percent of all money managed to cover costs and its fee. Rather, Jones arranged to get 20 percent of the profits. In other words, while a mutual fund manager was mostly incentivized to *not lose* money, Jones was incentivizing himself to *make* money, and taking an outsized cut if he did.

What Jones was homing in on was the concept of *alpha*. Boiled down, alpha represents how much better you can perform than the overall market itself. Delivering alpha gives a trader value-added—it's the trait that guarantees he can't and won't be replaced by a computer. Alpha conveys upon a trader the ability to create gold with his fingertips, translated through a keyboard. If a typical market rises 4 percent in a year and you're able to get 10 percent, your alpha skills have created an extra $60,000 out of thin air for every $1 million you control. Thus, pensions and endowments and the run-of-the-mill superrich with plenty of these millions to put to work, each eager for all those extra $60,000 checks, lined up to get behind highly touted hedge fund managers, some of whom achieved cult status among the moneyed set. Parking your money with Stevie Cohen or Ken Griffin or James Simons had become de rigueur, akin to having a summer house on Gin Lane, a child at Dalton, or a golf membership at the Round Hill Club.

Part of the exclusivity was legally fueled. Unlike mutual funds and many other investment vehicles, hedge funds aren't allowed to advertise or promote themselves and they can take money only from "accredited investors." That means investors with $1 million in net worth, or earnings above $200,000 a year, as well as institutions— because rich people, evidently, ought to know better than your Grandma Beatrice about what crazy place they're putting their money in, and the crazy price they're paying to do so.

In exchange for only dealing with so-called sophisticated investors, hedge funds had none of those pesky rules designed to protect the little guy. In fact, they had no rules at all. They were completely unregulated, free to short sell, gobble risky derivatives, or buy up goat farms in Appalachia. And by the Zeroes, the vast majority of hedge funds were doing all of the above, elegantly ignoring the lessons of the 1970s. Once again, there was no "hedge" in most hedge funds. A hedge fund was nothing more than an unregulated compensation system. The gold rush was on. In 2000 there were about 2,500 hedge funds, managing $350 billion; by 2005, those ranks quintupled: 12,250 hedge funds controlling $1.4 *trillion*.

In the pay department, modern hedge fund managers had done Jones one better. Rather than take just 20 percent of profits, they would take the pay system those poor slobs running mutual funds had concocted and layer that atop their pile, too. So a hedge fund manager in the Zeroes would get 2 percent of everything managed *and* 20 percent of the profits, or "2-and-20" in hedge fund shorthand.

The most ridiculous pay scale ever devised came into widespread acceptance at the exact time that electronic trading turned the entire world into a free-for-all global casino. Two-and-20 was sacrosanct. No self-respecting manager would take less. They couldn't even if they wanted to. Nobody would put their money with a cut-rate hedge fund manager any more than they would buy a discount crib or smoke alarm. You don't cheap out on your kids, your health, or your stash.

In reality, 2-and-20 didn't even reward alpha: 20 percent of the *profits* means your fund can be "up" 5 percent when the market as a whole is up 8 percent (in other words, you delivered *negative alpha*) and you still kept one-fifth of whatever the fund "made," in addition to the 2 percent fee, of course, skimmed off the top.

What 2-and-20 *did* was encourage risk. You got to keep 20 percent of everything your fund made, while someone else had to pay 100 percent of everything your fund lost. *Heads I win, tails you lose.* Except that the first 2 percent serves as a safety net, generating your run-of-the-mill $1 billion fund a nice $20 million to spread around even if it keeps all the money in cash in a file cabinet. In other words, a hedgie was set for life the second he raised the money. So it was actually *heads I win, tails you lose . . . but I still win.*

As any quant could tell you, with that math, the riskiest move for a hedge fund—particularly since they were completely unregulated—was *not* taking risk. Magnus's prop traders, at least, had been kept honest because any money lost was largely their own. Not so the hedgies, who were quick to embrace the three most glorious letters on Wall Street: OPM (Other People's Money). Alfred Winslow Jones had calibrated this danger a half-century before; he was the largest shareholder in his own fund, disincentivizing him from making irrational bets. But like hedging itself, that inconvenient concept had been forgotten by most.

The only hedgies who didn't practice OPM, naturally, were the small handful that could actually be counted on to profitably manage it. Which brings us back to Stevie Cohen and how someone can earn $650 million, cash, in one year. Cohen had consistently proven that he really did have the ability to generate alpha. He was a legitimate human ATM, and endowments, foundations, and the superrich tried to get their money managed by Stevie Cohen with all the vigor that they tried to place their spawn in $40,000 private schools. Cohen's quant mind, of course, recognized the imbalance between supply and demand, and adjusted his own price accordingly. He would take *3-and-50.* You don't like it? Tough. Not only was Cohen turning people away, he was actually giving money back to investors. By 2004, he had been making enough money for enough years that he increasingly began managing his own money. (His new model: 0-and-100.) It was alpha compounding alpha, the kind of cash snowball, fueled by his army of frigid, fleece-clad traders, that yields two-thirds of a billion dollars in one year.

$ $ $

As important as cars were to Magnus, Braveheart, and their seven-figure crowd, the nine-figure hedgies put that same passion into their houses: they earned one hundred times more, so their toys needed to scale similarly. They went after the $30 million mansion rather than the $300,000 Murcielago.

While Manhattan, London, and the Hamptons all boasted a large degree of housing absurdity, Greenwich, Connecticut, was becoming the world's first city where a $1 million salary made you officially middle-class. Little Greenwich, a town of 63,000 between New York City and Stamford, nudged right up against the border of Westchester County, had freakishly emerged as perhaps the fifth most important trading hub in the world, with only New York, London, Chicago, and Hong Kong ahead of it. In 2004, there was more than $1.2 trillion managed by hedge funds, and 10 percent of it—a full $120 billion—was controlled out of Greenwich.

Greenwich emerged a century earlier as a summer retreat for New York's robber barons, who didn't feel like decamping the family all the way out in Newport, instead sprinkling dozens of gorgeous mansions across its 47.8 square miles. The interstate transformed the cottage town into your typically Waspy Connecticut suburb. Then Paul Tudor Jones, a legend from the 1987 crash, moved up there in 1994, and the city of hedge funds sprouted, like some neighborhood in Queens that becomes an Armenian enclave because an influential Armenian happened to settle there. Except Greenwich was no melting pot. The place was being leveled. In a town of 23,000 households, 176 were approved for demolition in 2005, up from around 50 in 2000.

In the place of these stately old mansions, modern castles emerged. Tudor Jones set the tone. He had paid some $11 million for a grand century-old house with a view of Long Island Sound built by the man who bankrolled the Dixie cup. It wasn't long until he and his new wife, an Australian model, tore it down, erecting a Monticello-influenced colossus that Nina Munk in *Vanity Fair* described as "a cross between Tara and a national monument," complete with a twenty-five-car garage.

Then Cohen made his move. Tudor Jones had nudged up his fee structure to 4-and-23, before Cohen leapfrogged to his mammoth 3-and-50. Cohen's house reflected the new math. In 1998, Cohen plunked down $14.8 million—cash—for a thirty-room mansion, built from fieldstone during the Roaring Twenties. Cohen then set about, with another $10 million or so, transforming the fourteen-acre estate into a hedgie paradise.

Trader Monthly had begun dabbling in events in Greenwich—showing off $400 black onyx cuff links and $240 water carafes at the Georg Jensen boutique and the like—and on one visit to town, I drove to check out La Casa Cohen. I was greeted by a twelve-foot wall, more appropriate for someone looking to weather a medieval siege. Which was kind of the point. Security was paramount throughout Greenwich, especially since January 2003, when whiz kid fund manager Eddie Lampert was abducted from a downtown parking garage at gunpoint by four masked men and taken to a local Days Inn. Lampert was handcuffed and blindfolded for a day and a half before convincing his captors, who in a moment of negative kidnapping alpha had used his credit card to order pizza, that they would now surely be caught if they didn't let him go. (True to Greenwich form, Lampert, whose financial backers included music mogul David Geffen, computer entrepreneur Michael Dell, and the Tisch family of CBS fame, returned to work within days. While the plot's mastermind earned fifteen years in prison, Lampert earned an estimated $400 million for the rest of the year.)

Cohen's compound offered something for everyone, according to people who have been inside the walled city. Romantics could stroll a mini-Versailles, complete with tree-lined walkways, formal gardens, a reflecting pool, and a giant fountain. The recreation-inclined—Cohen and his second wife, Alexandra, had seven kids between them—could use the tennis court, the indoor swimming pool, the two-hole golf course, the regulation basketball court, or the 6,734-square-foot ice-skating rink about the size of Rockefeller Center. (One visitor, describing the 720-square-foot cottage where the ice-resurfacing machine was stored, told *Vanity Fair*, "You'd be happy to live in the Zamboni house.")

The inside of the house swelled to 32,000 square feet, or precisely the square footage of the Taj Mahal, where I had proposed to my wife. Cohen, for his part, had installed a twenty-seat movie theater with a ceiling painted with the starry sky as it looked on the Cohens' wedding night. Above all, there was the art. Cohen, who made more from numbers than anyone in human history, had become enamored with the complete randomness of art. So during the first half of the Zeroes, he and his wife went on a *$700 million* buying spree, the largest, fastest major collection ever assembled. Vincent van Gogh's *Peasant Woman Against a Background of Wheat* and Paul Gauguin's *Bathers* (bought together from casino impresario Steve Wynn for $100 million) sat in the living room. A Jackson Pollock drip painting ($52 million) hung in the library. Andy Warhol's *Superman* ($25 million) graced the foyer. There was a Picasso ($25 million) and a Bacon ($16.5 million), a Degas and de Kooning, a Manet and a Monet.

Probably most emblematic was *The Physical Impossibility of Death in the Mind of Someone Living*, a sculpture by British artist Damien Hirst, which Cohen paid $8 million for. It was considered the most iconic piece of UK art from the past two decades (*The Times* of London labeled the sale "a big loss for Britain"), and in many ways it epitomized everything—Darwinism, aggression, fear—that was making hedge fund managing the world's most lucrative job, and in lockstep, Greenwich, the world's richest city: it was a dead fourteen-foot tiger shark, floating in a formaldehyde-fueled suspended reality, its nose jutting out, its mouth wide open.

$ $ $

The nuts and bolts of putting together the *Trader Monthly* 100 was daunting—especially in our launch issues—and required months of digging by our reporters. In some ways, we made it harder on ourselves. By 2004, the supremacy of the 2-and-20 model was so complete that we felt compelled, in order to mirror the constituencies of our readers, to institute a strange form of affirmative action to avoid a list with only hedgies on it. (A hedge fund publication, *Alpha,* already did that.) We blocked out twenty spots for bank traders, and another twenty for independent traders like Braveheart and Eric Bolling, reflecting the fuller breadth of the trading world.

The last group was simple, given that both pit traders like Bolling and prop traders like Braveheart still traded in physical proximity to many others; we thus had a good fix on who was making waves, and how big their action was. We called every person on the list for comment before publication. Some didn't take our calls, but many did—almost always on the condition that they would publicly deny doing so—to listen and then, like a true trader, haggle, trying to spin us either higher, or lower. Especially livid complaints were sent to me.

One of the world's best crude oil traders, Tom Gordon ranked among the most vocal. He hit the list with an estimated $10 million to $15 million in 2004 working the NYMEX pits near Bolling. "There are twenty guys ahead of me here," he screamed. "I don't make anywhere near that much."

My background in billionaire hunting came in handy here. At *Forbes* I operated on the assumption that anyone talking to me about their money was lying in one direction or the other. Most who controlled vast fortunes argued about making their number lower, for personal reasons: modesty, security fears, or because they didn't want hundreds of hard-luck cases asking them for money, or people on the street staring at them like the otherworldly creatures they actually were.

But a surprising number went to great lengths to push themselves higher, for financial reasons. The owners of privately held companies could use a high estimate of their business's value as an advantageous starting point with a group looking to buy them or invest. Or even more likely, they could use a high valuation to bully better terms out of banks. The real estate moguls, whose success was directly tied to how much they could borrow at what price, were particularly insufferable. Drawing Donald Trump as a subject meant weeks of pompous bragging about giant numbers he'd flail about trying to defend (he even sued a *New York Times* reporter for having the temerity to suggest he wasn't as rich as he said he was). The biggest strip mall builder in Texas, Jerry J. Moore, was so obsessed with his *Forbes* 400 ranking—he wanted to be listed as a billionaire—that he called me weekly for six months when I was working on that project. After the twin discoveries that I made only $27,000 and I was putting him on the list at "only" $500 million his last-ditch plea included offering my twenty-four-year-old self a $100,000 public relations job "with lots of golf."

But unlike bickering about *Forbes* 400 valuations, which were based on net worth, as much art as science, what someone earns in a year can be proven in black-and-white with a tax return. So I offered Gordon the same deal I had offered for all *Trader Monthly* 100 gripers: prove us wrong by showing me your tax return, and we'll humbly apologize and publicly correct the record. It was at this point that most would mumble something and then get off the phone.

Gordon took me up on my offer. He took an afternoon from trading—about $25,000 of time lost, based on our estimate of his per-minute trading income. One of the dwindling number of people still making their fortunes on the physical pit, he looked more like a plumber than a millionaire, dressed in jeans and a well-worn T-shirt (although, tellingly, the shirt was from Paul Tudor Jones's Robin Hood Foundation). He slid his return across the table. Page after page showed short-term trading gains (lots) and losses (few)—and sure enough, it totaled $5 million, one-half of the low-end range we'd pinned on him.

Gordon was polite and gracious, a gentleman proving a point of honor. I gave him his profuse apology. He in turn declined an immediate correction ("It would just draw more attention"); we instead noted our error, and the accurate figure, in the following year's edition.

The hedgies, in general, proved far trickier. They were the MI5 of finance, with secrecy ingrained into their culture. Employing market-beating strategies meant, by definition, that the rest of the market couldn't copy your pattern. Government rules both banned them from promoting themselves and shielded them from having to tell anyone anything about what or how they were doing, with the small exception of their investors, and that group was certainly not about to publicly kill any golden goose laying alpha-sized eggs. Peers and underlings were given huge nondisclosure forms. And even in their warped world, these hedgies understood well enough that crowing about the obscene paydays they were quietly enjoying was the surest way to end them. For months, Rich Blake and his reporters chiseled at the edges. In the weeks leading up to our launch, we all lay awake worrying that our supposedly definitive list would fall flat.

Then our publisher, Wilkie Bushby, introduced me to the Candyman, whose nickname came from a job that in Greenwich, Connecticut, made him more popular than Santa Claus. Rich families, college endowments, union pension funds, and run-of-the-mill billionaires gave the Candyman anywhere from eight to ten digits to parcel out to hedge funds. Virtually every hedge fund of significance, in turn, lined up to provide all their intimate financial information, which they hoped would lead to their allocation of candy. He knew how much money each fund managed, how much they made off that money in the previous year, whether their compensation varied from the 2-and-20 standard, and how much of their haul the top dog kept for himself: the four variables needed to peg a hedge fund manager's annual earnings almost to the dollar.

For us, the Candyman was as good a source as Watergate's Deep Throat. Like Deep Throat, though, the Candyman was paranoid about making sure his identity was shielded. And like Deep Throat, he didn't just want to give us the information, which would have taken him a few hours to crunch rather than the months that Blake and his team would have spent interviewing hundreds of sources, culling databases and searching financials, looking for information crumbs. Rather than out-and-out leak, he preferred to act as the ultimate tour guide, confirming, correcting, and shaping, nudging us a little higher on some, lower on others, pushing some managers off, and suggesting names that we missed.

"Where's Leon Cooperman?"

"How can you not have Stephen Mandel?"

"That's only one fund. He has another that didn't do well."

Even the Candyman was staggered by the wealth he was confirming. "Can you believe these figures?" he marveled, giddy to find other people as amazed by this historic money stream as he was.

I looped back to him a couple times, and the list began to shine. Not perfect, but credible, and headed toward definitive.

He had a lot to lose—literally, millions—if his identity was revealed. Yes, he was doing his old friend, Wilkie, and now his new friend, me, a favor. But there was clearly something else motivating him, as his risk-reward in helping us was atrocious. I finally asked him as much.

"If you guys are going to do this anyway," he responded, "you might as well get it right."

$ $ $

The truth. In the trading world, the banks had the biggest problem with that seemingly quaint concept. Wall Street's big firms had a unified position on us from the outset: ignore us until we go away. Publishing their occasional foibles (through our gossipy "Insider Info" column), fomenting the cars-and-watches stereotype, and, most critically, publishing their traders' incomes for the world to see—all these things were about as welcome as a gout flare-up. But once it became clear that we had dug in—and in fact were read across every trading floor in America, including their own—one by one, they begrudgingly accepted us, or at least tolerated us. They took our calls, and spoke off the record, in an effort to "correct" numbers they thought were inaccurate. As we grew, they began to acknowledge that they talked to us. Then they began actually pitching ideas to put in the magazine. And finally, firms like Credit Suisse and Merrill Lynch began to advertise with us and hire us to produce entire custom-published magazines on their behalf.

The sole exception was Goldman Sachs, the Evil Empire of Wall Street, whose firm's CEOs seemingly had an automatic appointment to be secretary of the treasury. Goldman pretty much treated us like a nonentity, unless we were printing their employees' salaries. Then, they'd start fibbing.

Goldman's employees gossiped like fourth-grade girls—particularly if it involved how big their bonuses would be and how much other people made—except that they were far more petty. Those who felt slighted were oh-so-eager to rat out those they perceived as having unjustly made more than they did. We generally received multiple confirmations, as we tallied their traders making $30 million, $40 million, $50 million a year.

For Goldman Sachs, denying the reality was a necessity: 2-and-20 was completely disrupting the way they were doing business.

To Washington regulators, hedge funds were a world unto themselves, a pool of rich people allowed to deal with one another in almost unfettered ways, on the premise (false, in my experience) that if you're wealthy, you're smart enough to know what you're getting yourself into. Compensation was viewed similarly. Stevie Cohen made a $500 million payday? It's just money sloshing back and forth between rich people, with no broader effects.

Except that 2-and-20 mania began hitting the banks directly. Yes, hedge funds were little more than compensation schemes for the managers. But the top performers at banks didn't need to tax their math skills to calculate that they were making a puny $10 million turning out the same performance as a hedge fund making $250 million. Alpha was alpha. But hedge funds were unfettered, while banks were regulated, publicly traded entities loath to hear the wrath of shareholders or regulators after giving some no-name math nerd a quarter-billion-dollar bonus.

So increasingly, bank traders—specifically Goldman traders—began starting hedge funds. The turning point was right around 2005. First, Eric Mindich, whom Goldman had made the youngest partner in the firm's history at age twenty-seven, walked away from his $15-million-a-year position and started a $3 billion hedge fund, Eton Park, along with three other former Goldman traders. Within a year, 2-and-20 was delivering him $100 million. Dinakar Singh went from running Goldman's arbitrage desk to his own $3 billion fund, TPG Axon. Geoff Grant, Goldman's foreign exchange star, wound up managing $1 billion for Peloton Partners. Then Grant's former deskmate, Christian Siva-Jothy, followed suit. Goldman's brain drain was on.

That posed an especially big problem for Goldman and the other banks, because they had been slowly turning themselves into hedge funds. Just as their top traders figured out the income disparity, bank management saw the immense profits their clients made trading all these new risky derivatives. Rather than just play boring middleman and skim profits, they began actively trading via "prop," as in proprietary, desks. The similarity in moniker to Magnus's "prop" traders isn't coincidence. These new bank prop desks were just blown-up versions of that model, trading independently with the bank's money, often competing with their own clients.

Given the Zeroes' bubble economy, these prop desks became wildly profitable. So profitable, in fact, that they became the most important components of these banks. By 2006 Goldman's Trading and Principal Investment division—their euphemism for prop desk—was pulling in $25.6 billion in annual revenues. The traditional roles of investment banks—serving as middlemen, or advising on a deal, or underwriting an IPO—seemed so passé, so nickel-and-dime. Why share a good idea with a client when you can trade it yourself?

Now addicted to risky prop trading, the banks began quietly paying mind-numbing bonuses to their cash cows in an effort, largely futile, to keep traders from jumping to hedge funds.

Which brings us to a thirty-nine-year-old with a name made for Scrabble, Raanan Agus. Empowered to deploy $10 billion in firm money into any trade he saw fit, Agus in 2006 became, as best we could tell, the first employee they ever paid $100 million in one year.

Goldman was not happy about having this information published. First, they went after us with the charm offensive, sending out their head of public relations, Peter Rose. As any baseball fan knows, it's very hard to take someone saying "trust me" seriously when his name is Pete Rose. But he tried. Rose's take followed the kind of logic that would shortly get the banks into big trouble: I'll tell you what he made—off the record—if that means you won't print what he makes.

Heated conversations turned into heated e-mails. When Rose finally asked what "additional proof" was necessary to "finally satisfy you and cause you to remove him from your list," my two-word response was "a W-2." Instead, I got a letter from Goldman's outside counsel, at the white-shoed law firm Clifford Chance, informing me that *Trader Monthly* "acts at its peril" if it published Agus's salary.

We published it anyway (along with Goldman's denial). But it would soon be academic. The hedgies were making such eye-popping money that we eventually felt it necessary to abandon our *Trader Monthly* 100 affirmative action. The gold rush was such that these Goldman earners, for all their protests, were merely middle class by Wall Street standards.

$ $ $

One of the problems I encountered as the pauper among the princes was how to reciprocate for kind gestures. You could send Stevie Cohen a check for $1 million and it would engender no greater change in his life than if I gave you a stick of gum. Traders had this problem with one another, as well. So the currency at the top of Wall Street, player-to-player, was leveraging connections. Can you ask your friend Sting to play my daughter's bat mitzvah? Can you get my nephew an internship with Paul Tudor Jones? Citigroup head Sandy Weill, responding to a memo titled "AT&T and the 92nd Street Y," helped (via a $1 million donation) get the kid of one of his analysts into an elite private preschool, and that analyst, Jack Grubman, shortly thereafter improved his rating of AT&T's stock.

A few days before the *Trader Monthly* 100 list came out, Wilkie Bushby suggested that his friend the Candyman would appreciate a "proper" night out as a thank-you for his help. In Wall Street parlance, *proper* means a strip club. This stripper culture flummoxed me. I'm not being prudish—I've been to plenty. But my social visits were always tied to a bachelor party, including my own. (Giving their buddies a socially acceptable excuse to visit strip clubs, as well as I can tell, remains the largest reason grooms-to-be even have them.) The exclusionary idea of a business relationship forged over the ogling of surgically enhanced women was indefensibly backward.

For traders from Houston to Chicago to London to New York, however, socializing at strip clubs was part of the culture, as everyday as catching up over double lattes and blueberry scones at Starbucks. It remained an ingrained misogynistic by-product of a trade that for centuries was all male, and valued aggression, testosterone, and physical size above all else. Throughout the latter of half of the twentieth century, the idea of the strip club as an extended financial firm conference room was usually tolerated, and often encouraged. One Wall Street partner, a twenty-five-year veteran, recalled to me one client golf outing in the early nineties where the host, a regional bank, assigned each twosome a bikini-clad stripper. The women would dangle on the back of the cart from hole to hole, and then prostrate themselves, legs open, on the putting greens, providing the traders a target.

Then there was the Boom-Boom Room. Female employees at a Long Island branch of Smith Barney sued, revealing their male superiors as loutish pigs who ran, among other things, a "boom boom" party room about as welcoming for female employees as a Hooters franchise. The suit was settled in 1997, with $2 million in lawyers' fees going to the plaintiffs and Smith Barney investing $15 million to hire and train women employees; a subsequent lawsuit from other women at the firm was settled for $33 million.

For the most part, Wall Street firms, more fearful of penalties than enlightened about how wrong such exclusionary traditions were, clamped down hard on endorsing this type of activity. Expensing it, as had been the practice for decades, was no longer an option.

So by 2004, Wall Street's strip club love affair had been driven underground. Requests for a "proper" night out, generally to pay back a favor, were made with a wink, and it was up to the favor recipient—in this case, me—to figure out how he was going to pay for it. Given that the Candyman was now the key to the *Trader Monthly* 100, without which we had no magazine, no business, no jobs, there wasn't much choice. For financial reinforcement, Magnus joined Wilkie and me.

The evening started at a steak house called Maloney & Porcelli, a trader hangout that blares CNBC on the bar's big-screens, even at night, and ended near the Hudson River at the Penthouse Executive Club. The only thing that could link Bob Guccione's pornography empire with the word *executive* was the financial crowd it catered to almost exclusively. "We're looking for the upscale clientele," the club's "COO," Mark Yackow, told a reporter in 2004. "The business-men, the Wall Street professionals, the brokers."

As we walked in, I can only imagine what we looked like to the "entertainers"—three guys dressed like millionaires, and one journalist-entrepreneur in a tattered suit. Steak to a death-row in-mate? Beer to a broke college student? A corner table was procured, and we were attacked like locusts by strippers who, sizing up the room, accurately saw the biggest profit opportunity. A rotating pa-rade of girls made themselves comfortable at our table, as Magnus ordered drinks (Myers's rum, a vodka tonic, Captain Morgan, a Black Russian and a Bud for me, tipping $100 on the $70 round)—and $500 worth of lap-dance vouchers (at $20 a dance) from the Pent-house Executive Club's "currency" department, to whom he tipped yet another C-note on top of the $100 "surcharge."

After about an hour, Magnus upgraded us to a private room, and upstairs we went, four gents and five ladies (the Candyman wanted a spare). Magnus ordered more drinks, including a bottle of Grey Goose ($350). Rather than a per-dance charge, these private rooms apparently rent on a metered basis, with a burly maître d' barging in every fifteen minutes to monitor the situation, and every hour to ask if we wanted more time. There was no difference between what hap-pened in the private room and the public floor, except for the illusion that this was just a naughty group date—and a questionable decision by Wilkie, for forty-five uncomfortable seconds, to shed his pants.

By 3:30 a.m., the party was wrapping up. A car service was sum-moned to take the Candyman back to his suburban mansion, and Magnus summoned his final bill. When I glanced over his shoulder,

I nearly passed out: two hours in the private room cost $6,000, plus a usurious $1,200 "surcharge." During the age of the Boom-Boom Room, strip club managers had picked up an Enron-like ability to muddy the accounting waters. The receipts were specifically from "Robert's," a generically named steak restaurant housed within the club that very few—presumably including Wall Street's controllers and CFOs—had ever heard of. The lap-dance vouchers and private room fees were listed consistently as "food/bev."

Even Magnus gaped at the large number. He paused for a while. Then, he did something unexpected. He laughed.

"That's an insane amount of money for lap dances," he said, plunking down his American Express card, and adding an additional $800 tip, bringing the night's damage to just under $10,000. "But it's cheap for a good story to tell." A yarn for $10,000? In the Zeroes, that apparently was a good trade.

The turnaround in the morning was brutal. Back at my desk within a few hours, groggy and hungover, I immediately heard from Wilkie. I was sure he was looking to replay the good $10,000 story that Magnus had so kindly bought for us. But, sounding even worse than I felt, he got straight to business.

"The belt!"

"What?"

"The belt. [Candyman]'s belt. It's gone."

Apparently, over the course of the night, the Candyman had somehow forgotten, like his briefly bottomless friend, that at strip clubs, dancers are the ones who are supposed to shed clothing. Most people, of course, would shrug it off as the kind of acceptable collateral damage incurred when blowing $10,000 at a strip joint. But, like the watch that Bruce Willis risked death to retrieve in *Pulp Fiction*, this belt apparently had a crucial provenance.

Was it a family heirloom from Dad? An anniversary gift from the wife? Father's Day gift from the kids? That information was apparently on a need-to-know basis. All I got was: "Dude, [Candyman]'s really freaked out. You've got to get that belt back."

It's not really a job you can delegate to an assistant. (*"Um, Alison, can you go to the Penthouse Club and pick up a belt?"*) So, less than eight hours after departing the Penthouse Club, I was back in our private room, looking under seats and kneeling on the shaggy carpet. As I mustered every fiber of willpower to avoid pondering what microbes might be lurking within, a manager, donning an impeccable brown suit with a cleanly shaven head, emerged, waving something like the Grail itself. *The belt.*

It was indeed a nice belt, soft and dark, a weave of a dozen-plus strands. I later would drop it into a messenger's envelope, fronted by an innocent note in case his secretary opened it: *Thanks for letting me borrow this. Perfect with my shoes!* And so I walked out onto the city streets, knowing that I had ably paid back the Candyman, in the currency money can't buy, thus assuring *Trader Monthly* a perpetually accurate pipeline into the absurd numbers being chalked up by America's new robber barons.

4

Doubling Down

(2005)

    Our company's name was specifically derived from a black-jack term. Doubling down helps explain why good players can get their odds close to fifty-fifty in a business that builds marble palaces by maintaining a significant numerical edge. For the uninitiated, blackjack rules allow you to double your bet after seeing your first two cards, as long as you hit at least one more time. There's risk, of course: you know neither what your next card will be, nor what the dealer is hiding, and a poor outcome inflicts double punishment. But if used judiciously, it doubles your profits in situations where you have a clear advantage: more risk in volume, less risk in outcome.

    Magnus and I had both previously absorbed this lesson. Magnus had gone from successful trader to trading tycoon by hiring 550 traders under him across ten offices worldwide—a far bigger bet than I had taken, with far better odds. My last venture, *P.O.V.*, ripped through $18 million putting one egg in one basket. While giants like Time Warner and News Corp. could spread out their overhead, and leverage their clout, *P.O.V.* withered and died alone. Magnus's positive experience, and my negative one, reinforced our shared goal:

layer on as many smart media products as possible across the infrastructure we were building. Just as much of America was borrowing money, using the equity in their houses to speculate, we wanted Doubledown to be very, very big.

We didn't like tying our fates strictly to the grotesque and grotesquely paid boys of the financial world. Which brought us back to *Justice*. Old ideas die hard—especially with me—and my pre-9/11 project had targeted a completely different demographic: middle-class women, a group I was admittedly not as familiar with as Wall Streeters. The magazine's working slogan, "Real People, True Stories," underscored that this was the polar opposite of the *Trader Monthly* fantasy world. That appealed to us.

So did the potential payoff. *Justice* was a big idea: turn the worldwide obsession with real-life crime stories and courtroom cliffhangers into little soap operas. The O. J. Simpson trial, which captivated tens of millions of Americans for almost two years during the 1990s, had created a demand that affected virtually every form of media. Prime-time television boasted no fewer than four versions of *Law & Order* and three of *CSI*. During daytime television, talk shows and actual soap operas were being replaced by judge shows, from *Divorce Court* to *Animal Court*, *Judge Joe Brown* to *Judge Judy*, a brash sixtysomething who had become a superstar, earning herself over $45 million a year to dispose of small claims cases, and challenging Oprah Winfrey's dominance of the housewife set. John Grisham and Scott Turow sold tens of millions of novels and spawned multiplexes of movies. But there was no magazine or Web site devoted to legal drama.

We'd tested the concept, but no one was inclined to plow in the tens of millions required for this big idea based on good results from sample subscription offers and glowing comments from potential advertisers. Only the German publishing company seeking an excuse to come to America had given it serious consideration, which 9/11 thoroughly dispatched.

Just as I had done with *P.O.V.*, our answer would be to put out a few test issues, turning our promises into quantifiable results, while leveraging Doubledown's infrastructure to keep costs down. Rather than a fun concept, we would have an actual media product, one targeting blue-haired Court TV watchers rather than slick-haired financial titans. We would have a diversified, balanced portfolio.

As this had been my baby for many years, I stubbornly insisted on editing it myself, leading to an odd mental dichotomy. Most of my time was spent pondering the foibles and whims of men who drove starter Porsches to their jobs betting up and down the lifeblood of the global economy. The rest of my time was spent hanging out with the crowd smoking cigarettes outside the courthouse, from celebrity defense lawyer Mark Geragos to former O. J. Simpson prosecutor Marcia Clark.

My best friend from the *Justice* world was a washed-up gangster named Henry Hill. If the name is familiar, it's because his life story was the basis of the movie *Goodfellas*, as depicted by Ray Liotta and brilliantly told by Martin Scorsese. I had recruited him to be the Mafia correspondent. The wiseguy who ratted out fifty members of the Lucchese family would now cover his old chums.

Henry had signed on in *Justice*'s primordial days, before we even had a fleshed-out business plan. He was desperate for money. In part due to cocaine addiction, he had been booted from the Witness Protection Program and now fended for himself while simultaneously trying to avoid getting whacked. Contacting him required the kind of elaborate smoke signaling lost to North America two centuries ago. I would pass word through an intermediary that I wanted to talk, and then at random times that generally coincided with waking me up, some mysterious third party would call from a blocked number, and then patch in Henry.

We bonded over our shared love of food. In a gravelly Brooklyn accent that came across like an agitated mumble, Henry began steering me to the restaurants where the wiseguys ate, including Vincent's in Little Italy, and Don Peppe near Kennedy Airport ("call it Don Pep's, or they'll know you don't belong"), where the dominantly male patrons really did wear tracksuits and the wine came home-brewed from the owner's garage.

But the more I talked with Henry—do-it-yourself witness protection can apparently be a lonely place—the more I realized that his background was more relevant, in many ways, to *Trader Monthly*.

Traders make their money skimming from legitimate businesses; so did Henry. "Anything that came through JFK, we could take a piece," he told me. "We wuz like a toll collector." It could just as easily have been Eric Bolling talking about nattie gas, albeit with a harsh accent. Like traders who made money from information, Stevie Cohen–style, Henry passed on the tip that led to the $5 million Lufthansa Airlines heist in 1978, the largest cash robbery ever on American soil. And like traders, he spent money as fast as it came in, knowing that he could always make more. "It was fucking ridiculous . . . we lived like kings."

Plus, he knew how to get money out of people. Since his $3,000-per-column salary would commence only once we began publishing, he had helped me pass the hat from day one. Well before I met Magnus, I cohosted dinners for prospective investors at Sparks, a Manhattan steak house infamous as the spot where John "The Dapper Don" Gotti rubbed out his predecessor, "Big Paul" Castellano. Henry would finish our PowerPoint presentations with an offer they couldn't refuse. "Hi, this is Henry Hill," his prerecorded message would announce menacingly, as a still from *Goodfellas* flashed on the screen. "I heard you're all eating at Sparks. A few years back, something bad happened to a friend of mine there. I don't want the same thing to happen to you, *so I suggest you fork over the money*."

With the money now forked over by Magnus, we added four new *Justice* employees to supplement Doubledown's squad of twenty or so. Our little crew did a nice job. Lots of celebrity mug shots and foibles. Meatier fare, such as women who fall in love with death-row serial killers. And above all, heroes. The Iowa mom who trapped the predator stalking her teen daughter. The students who freed an innocent man. The activist defending an oppressed Montana Indian tribe. Regular people doing exceptional things.

Unfortunately, it took exceptional effort just to find *Justice*. Like the rest of America, we were getting whisked into a real estate bubble. By 2005, eager-to-lend banks had changed a timeless equation: space on planet Earth was still finite, but money no longer was. Home prices across the nation were up 69 percent since 2000, the beginning of the largest real estate run-up in history.

Justice's real estate bubble came via supermarket checkout racks—the physical wire slots near where you bag your groceries at Safeway or A&P or Walmart. The majority of all magazine copies sell through these rented slots. The juicy subject matter made *Justice* a checkout natural. But just as in the housing market, prices were skyrocketing. Akin to reality television and legal drama, a national obsession had developed around the personal lives of celebrities, and every magazine company with access to dead trees was launching a title devoted to covering the same ten people—Brad and Jen and Angelina and Ben and J.Lo, in various permutations—snapping up any checkout rack they could. The checkout penthouses (eye-level) tripled in price in one year, the dreary basements (foot-level) went from unrentable to coveted. The supermarkets were now, like fancy apartment building landlords, demanding up-front money and multiyear commitments. We were the equivalent of a shaggy college student looking for a month-to-month lease, and were largely shut out.

More troubling, no marketer seemed interested in reaching the *Justice* audience. Crime was scary. Real people were frumpy. And there were lots of other ways to reach the female-skewing American middle. After six months of efforts, our sales staff, charged with bringing in $200,000 in advertising, had turned up all of twelve grand. Since we needed the magazine, going forward, to at least appear successful, I approved filling the ad slots with freebies to carefully selected friends. Yet it seemed we couldn't give the space away, eventually *calling in favors* to run ads, gratis, for the motley likes of Oreck vacuum cleaners and Gold Toe socks.

For all our goals of diversifying our markets, the marketers weren't having it. Another product catering to average folk held very little interest. They instead wanted our help reaching the financial elite. That was the game in the Zeroes.

$ $ $

Those financial elite could increasingly be found smack-dab atop Greenwich Mean Time, which cuts precisely through the heart of London. That quirk of cartography turned prescient during the Zeroes. The City, logistically situated so traders could catch the Asian close in the morning, the European markets through the day, and the American open in the afternoon, was now literally the center of the financial world.

Trader Monthly had thus proven an even bigger hit in the United Kingdom than in the United States, even though only a few thousand copies were shipped across the pond, passed around until dog-eared, like copies of *Playboy* smuggled into an all-boys sleepaway camp. "*Trader Monthly* is one of those ideas that is so obvious someone must have had it before," crowed the *London Daily Telegraph*, "and so inspired you're annoyed it wasn't you." A popular London comic strip, "Alex," spent a day poking fun at the jealousy provoked by who got the magazine and who didn't.

Much of the impact came from sheer concentration. Unlike the United States, where *Trader Monthly* found professional traders in all fifty states, with the banks providing large clusters in New York, the exchanges in Chicago, and the hedge funds in Connecticut, almost all the UK's traders—banks, exchanges, funds—were piled around London, mostly in the City, with many banks pushing farther east to Canary Wharf and many hedge funds moving to the posh Mayfair district, where increasingly higher-end art galleries and jewelers followed, hoping to scoop up some golden crumbs. The physical proximity created a little parallel society—modern-day freemasons, except more foulmouthed, with all sorts of customs and services completely invisible to regular people like me. On my semiannual visits to London, I would sometimes peek in.

As a whole, UK traders actually *surpassed* the stereotype we were portraying in the United States. In London, it was completely acceptable to park your Ferrari on the street. One City trader, we learned, forgot about one of his sports cars for a few months—until the police called him, informing him that it had been impounded after racking up over 10,000 pounds in congestion pricing tickets. They frequented their own bars and maintained their own clubs, including Fifty, a private casino that charged 650 pounds in annual dues for the privilege of losing your money with them.

The old adages didn't apply. Money, it seemed, *could* buy happiness, and health. Soon after we launched, I was invited to get a free exam by a curiously named outfit called Preventicum, located in London's Shepherd's Bush section, whose clientele was 70 percent financial types. No matter that every Brit had free insurance; UK traders had their own medical system. For roughly $5,000, Preventicum would check you out the trader way. It was an appealing offer, since it had been five years since my last checkup; until I got married in 2002 I spent the early Zeroes dealing with health insurance the American entrepreneur way—I went without it.

As with all Preventicum's patients—doctors see only four a day— they dispatched a Mercedes to fetch me. After changing into a robe in my private suite, complete with couches, high-speed Internet, and satellite television, I had seven staffers spend the next five hours pricking, poking, manhandling, and scanning every last inch of me. I submitted to a blood test, urine test, and treadmill stress test, and my inner organs were examined by ultrasound as urgently as if I had been carrying triplets. Then came the coup de grâce: a frighteningly thorough preemptive MRI that included twenty minutes for the heart, fifteen for the brain, and ten for the entire arterial system, plus twenty minutes for the colon, liver, kidneys, and spleen. I was warned that this latter examination might be "mildly unpleasant"; it was roughly as comfortable as being buried alive in a tiny coffin with a large water balloon wedged into a very tight, very personal space.

But I couldn't gripe. Preventicum used the MRI scans to immediately map me three-dimensionally, and the medical director, Dr. Garry Savin, then spent thirty minutes with me analyzing every last result, as if he were the surgeon general and I were the president. With a clean bill of health and my scanned images in hand, I was whisked back in the Mercedes to the real world.

These MRI'd traders traveled differently, too. With the City's increased prominence, the New York to London route became one of the world's busiest, a transatlantic shuttle with dozens of legs flown each weekday. Virtually every bank and trading outfit let its money warriors fly business or first-class, typically an $8,000 round-trip. As one trader explained about his personal policy, "I only go left," referring to the direction he turned upon entering the cabin door.

But flying in the front of the plane, shielded by a curtain from the riffraff in coach, was no longer good enough. Three start-up airlines popped up to offer the financial elite flights between New York and London composed *entirely* of luxury seats. A company named MAXjet bought up middle-aged Boeing 767s, ripped out the usual 200-plus seats, and plopped in 102, configured as endless rows of business class. Rival Silverjet also bought used 767s, retrofitting them down, like some leg-space arms race, to a mere 100 seats.

Both felt like Greyhound, though, compared to Eos, the Greek goddess of the dawn reborn as the trading world's transatlantic chauffeur. All three of these New York–London luxury shuttles advertised in *Trader Monthly*—Silverjet insisted on a special kind of silver ink for their ads, incurring thousands of dollars in extra production costs—and all threw in free tickets for us as part of the deal. But both Magnus, whose financial and physical girth meant he flew only first-class, and I, childlike at the prospect after a lifetime of middle seats in the back, would do whatever was necessary, schedule-wise, to use the Eos slots.

The sleek 757s, which normally held 220 seats, were outfitted with 48 pods, each like a studio apartment, except that beautiful flight attendants came over periodically to offer filet mignon and second-growth Bordeaux. Dozens of movies were available on demand, and the pods morphed into completely flat seven-foot beds, or two-person workstations, where you could take a meeting with someone else on the plane. The two dozen passengers—I never saw an Eos flight more than half-full—would eagerly eye each other to gauge who else might be sufficiently important. No one ever approached me. Maybe because, even after a year or two at the periphery of this world, I still didn't look the part. Or maybe because I was deep in reflection, praying for an in-flight delay that would result in a few more hours of peace and Taittinger Champagne before returning to my hovel.

This obscene City culture had piqued the interest of Jonathan Newhouse, who ran the European operations of the luxury publishing giant Condé Nast. Magnus had seen him in a restaurant shortly after I began consulting for him, and subsequently introduced himself through a letter.

Newhouse, nephew of Condé Nast CEO Si Newhouse, was intrigued. He suggested the idea of an investment to his colleagues in New York, but Condé Nast didn't do joint ventures, and we were clearly too small to buy. Using his autonomy in London, however, Newhouse offered to launch *Trader Monthly* as a separate UK publication, using a small division that produced magazines for others for a fee (known as custom publishing in the United States, and contract publishing in the United Kingdom). A savvy move on his part: he could keep tabs on our growth, and generate revenue rather than incur cost, since we would pay them for their services.

It seemed a savvy move for us, as well. One year earlier, the whole company had been nothing more than Magnus and I e-mailing each other across the Atlantic. Now we would own a magazine produced by the gold standard of golden media, complete with the legitimacy the Condé Nast association afforded us in both the United Kingdom and the United States.

The only issue was price. Condé Nast was the opposite of Refco, the Wall Street pirates who generously and patronizingly had left thousands on the table for us. Our dealings with Condé Nast, snooty publishers of *Vogue* and *GQ* and *Vanity Fair*, required us to fight for every nickel.

It was a classic good cop–bad cop routine. Newhouse's custom publishing chief, Sue Douglas, played the good cop. She was charming and smart and glamorous, a famous editor and a friend of the royals, who would host introductory lunches to unveil us to the likes of British media magnate Andrew Neil and editor-turned-reality-television-judge Piers Morgan.

Her deputy Tabitha played Dr. No. The contract publishing division's other clients included Ferrari and the Maybourne Hotels—companies that loved the glitzy Condé Nast association, but had no idea how much it cost to put out a magazine. We were the nightmare client: completely aware of the obscene markups and cash-strapped enough to point them out.

I flew into London for the final negotiations. Going through their proposal line by line, logic was irrelevant. Tabitha's first answer was always a variant of "I don't have authority to change that." Her second, usually after conferring with Sue Douglas, was "that's just how we do it at Condé Nast."

In fairness, it was. *Don't worry about costs*, I was told, *we'll just make it up in the advertising we're going to sell for you*. That formula had made Condé Nast the world's most successful magazine company. I just didn't see how it could work for us, especially given the cash flow. Condé Nast, of course, wanted their money up front before every issue. The revenue would trail over ninety days. It was a cash sinkhole.

We were at an impasse, which Sue gracefully tried to nudge forward: "Just a quick note in advance of our celebratory dinner tomorrow," she e-mailed. "Can we get the contract signed before then? Or else it'll be dry bread and water!!"

Magnus finally pulled me aside. "You just have to stop fighting them. They're not going to do it the Doubledown Way. We've come this far. We just have to jump in."

I was in no position to argue, especially given my *Justice* misadventure. This was Magnus's baby, and it was Magnus's money. He wanted to go forward. But I left him with a prediction: "It is going to cost us $1 million to make this work."

Once the contract was signed, the dynamics changed. Rather than base *Trader Monthly* out of posh Vogue House, their main headquarters, which looked like the residence of some duke or earl or other kind of secondary royal, we were shunted around the corner to a dumpy annex named, completely without irony despite centuries under the British heel, Ireland House. Visions of *GQ*'s crackerjack sales force packaging in ads for *Trader Monthly* gave way to an army of hired mercenaries who would cold-call clients like a boiler-room broker, trying to leverage the Condé Nast name. As a result, the magazine that was supposed to immediately break even was losing close to 50,000 pounds per issue—a double problem, since the pound during most of the Zeroes was worth two dollars—on top of the dire upfront cash requirements.

When we complained, we were given the Condé Nast solution: spend more money. Specifically, another launch party. And so we did. Magnus came up with $75,000, and we rented out Il Bottaccio, a two-hundred-year-old mansion near Buckingham Palace.

A party promoter helped organize a Monte Carlo–style casino, a Cuban cigar roller, and a burlesque show. The latter might have prompted lawsuits in the States, but in a country where the newspapers feature topless girls of the day next to updates on the Iraq war, it generated enthusiastic cheers from both the traders and the heavy dose of fashion models assembled.

To Magnus's credit, *Trader Monthly Europe* was a clear hit with the audience, with similar advertising potential to what we were seeing in the States. To mine, my unfortunate prediction of a $1 million requirement would come to pass. And that was quickly going to become a problem.

$ $ $

Monday, October 10, 2005, started out pretty auspiciously. *Trader Monthly*'s first anniversary issue, so denoted by a silver starburst right under the logo, hit trading desks across America. In the twelve months since that party at the Mandarin Oriental, our company had grown from an idea with potential to a multiproduct global enterprise, with twenty-five employees, a new partnership with Condé Nast, and more than $2.5 million in revenue. Not bad. The new issue was fronted by yet another young Braveheart-type emerging from a helicopter, dressed smartly in a Calvin Klein suit. It featured an exclusive interview with the original rogue trader, Nick Leeson, along with a listing of the thirty biggest trading blowups of all time, which we played up in giant letters on the cover.

Leeson's collapse of the Bank of Barings ranked third on our list, behind two other relatively recent meltdowns: that of a Japanese trader named Yasuo Hamanaka, dubbed "Mr. 5 Percent" because he supposedly controlled one-twentieth of the world's copper market, but who in reality electronically stashed billions in losses, Leeson-style; and the winner, Long-Term Capital Management's $1 trillion interest rate bet gone wrong that nearly collapsed the entire federal banking system in 1998, before Wall Street's banks bailed them out.

By that very afternoon, if we could have magically appended a new Number One to the list, we would have. A scam so damaging and insidious that it eventually earned the mastermind sixteen years in prison was about to burst into the public consciousness. And it had happened right under our noses.

Magnus's voice, exceptionally calm under almost any circumstance, was unnerved when he called with the news. "Buddy, are you sitting down?"

"What's going on?"

"Something's happening at Refco."

Just six weeks earlier, the IPO that had spurred Refco's marketing chief, Robert Mercorella, to throw us that $360,000 advertising contract had proven a smash success. What Magnus was now telling me, as news of it broke around the world, was that it had been a fraud. For all his immaculate tailoring and perfect British diction and Cambridge education, Refco CEO Phil Bennett had been perpetrating a scheme that was the stuff of financial thrillers. The plot: Have Refco regularly "loan" hundreds of millions of dollars to a hedge fund. That fund, in turn, returned the money to another company also named "Refco," except that, apparently unbeknownst to the hedge fund, this other Refco was nothing more than a secret bank account controlled by Bennett himself. Bennett then took the money in fake Refco and "bought" losses from the real Refco, effectively turning its junk into gold. All told, it amounted to $430 million in fictitious profits, allowing for the rosy IPO. Bennett had connived his way to $1.6 *billion* worth of personal stock.

For us, it was like finding out your father was a serial killer. Without Refco's buyout of Magnus and its advertising commitment to *Trader Monthly*, there never would have been a Doubledown Media. We were the spawn of dirty money. By Wednesday, police had handcuffed Bennett, the new Jeffrey Dahmer of accounting, and Refco's stock was in free fall, dropping from $28 to 8 cents. Within a week, it had filed for bankruptcy, the fourth largest in American history. "To this day, it doesn't make any sense," says a former Refco executive, shaking his head. "To do that and then do an IPO, which basically guaranteed you'd get caught." Thousands lost life savings, and thousands more were now out of work.

I worried desperately for the two dozen under my watch at Doubledown. The effect on our company was devastating. Three months earlier, I had been in a festive mood just a few hundred feet from Bennett, negotiating a contract renewal in Robert Mercorella's office. Refco's IPO was imminent, and Mercorella had been very pleased with the awareness we'd delivered as his de facto marketing division. It was a very good thing for us; when Wall Street is going well, no one's salary stays flat. You're up or out. So while we would have been content to maintain our $360,000 level, we were slated to get a raise, to a cool half-million.

That was now gone, of course, along with the $60,000 Refco still owed us for the ads appearing in the now hugely ironic blowups issue ("a salt-in-the-wounds coincidence," as *The New York Times* noted), including one page crowing "First Again," in reference to a new Singapore office—directly across from our kickoff of the Leeson interview.

Twenty percent of our revenue had just been nuked. Worse, that was all marginal profit. In other words, we still had to produce magazines, Web sites, and events—Refco didn't cause us any extra work, they just piggybacked on what we already did. That money would need to be made up from Magnus or other investors, as would the other revenue from trading companies who had bought into us based on Refco's credibility.

It could have been much worse. Most of Magnus's MacFutures earn-out wasn't due for two more years. But because his fast-growing company had hit its performance benchmarks early, Magnus had gone back to Refco to negotiate a longer-term deal. Rather than figure out a way to motivate them over time, Bennett did what greedy crooks do: he hoarded his falsely inflated stock, and paid Magnus and his partners immediately in cash. It was Magnus's greatest trade ever. Without it, he would have been crushed. He had funded Doubledown, and bought a house in London and a penthouse in Vancouver on the seemingly safe assumption that the Refco money was coming. And the company would have been shuttered that day.

But despite that masterstroke, Magnus was rapidly entering a vise. *Justice*, Condé Nast, and now the Refco implosion had more than doubled our burn rate; we were now mowing through $200,000 more a month than we were taking in. Payroll alone was $75,000 every two weeks. And while Magnus had plenty of assets, it was illiquid rich-guy stuff: real estate, private partnerships, and trusts. He was quickly running short on cash.

He also made the serial entrepreneur's classic mistake. He had fallen in love with our business.

"Buddy, I don't want us to stop doing any of the things that we're doing," he would say to me when I brought up our alarming burn. "I don't want to cheat what the company should become. I'll figure out the cash."

Every two weeks, as we faced payroll and other bills, money somehow showed up. Usually, from Magnus. And several times, it was from a guy named Henry.

I don't really know much about Henry. To this day, I still don't know his last name. The only thing I do know is that we should all have a Henry in our life. Henry was a mentor for Magnus, and thought well enough of him to front us up to $100,000, no questions asked. It was no different from spotting Magnus a five-spot for a burger. When some revenue came in, we would pay Henry back.

Meanwhile, our CFO, Marc Feifer, and I stretched the cash and sold whatever wasn't nailed down. Mostly, that meant our receivables. Each magazine issue was approaching $500,000 in advertising sales, but our blue-chip advertisers generally didn't pay for ninety days. So we contracted with a company from Fort Lee, New Jersey, called Prestige Capital that was anything but prestigious. It was a "factorer," or a pawnshop for IOUs. It would pay us 75 percent of the value of our advertising as soon as we printed, and keep 100 percent of the payments once they rolled in. It was a ruinous interest rate, but without it, we wouldn't have survived ninety more days to collect. We even sold the $60,000 Refco owed us for 20 cents on the dollar, to some lawyer willing to chase the company's remains in bankruptcy court for years to collect the rest.

Marc and I would sometimes postpone our salaries, occasionally enlisting one or two trusted employees like Wilkie Bushby, to take the hit with us. I also began to find my own mini-Henrys. The poetically named Robert Frost, who oversaw Doubledown's 401(k) plan, and even my mom—a widowed freelance writer who trusted me with her meager savings—would slip us $25,000 to cover shortfalls, as long as they were quickly paid back.

Nevertheless, we were still coming up short. On November 29, a few days after Thanksgiving, facing a 4 p.m. deadline to fund the payroll, Magnus called me, sounding desperate.

"Buddy," he said, "I have some bad news."

"Dude, we have one hour till payroll."

"My bank won't release any money," Magnus replied, sounding thoroughly defeated. "I can't find Henry."

This was a problem. Likely a fatal one. Small businesses get a lot of leeway; our vendors were working with Marc on payment conditions. But payroll is sacrosanct. Miss it, and you're dead. Even a late payment sends the entire company on a job hunt, and in the Internet age, public mention of a cash crisis becomes a self-fulfilling prophecy.

It wasn't a very long conversation. I had no doubt that he had tried everything he could, as he knew this meant our company, and the millions he'd sunk into it to date, would disappear.

I walked into Marc's office and told him the situation. He had a complexion befitting the hardest-working guy at the company, yet even he found a new shade of pale. We were ruined.

Looking at his face, and then around the office at the people who depended on us, I didn't think much about my next action. I was not a wealthy man. I did not own a house. I did not have the fancy clothes or cars of my readers. My Doubledown salary, $120,000, was respectable, but less than half of what I could make elsewhere, and my daughter Sabrina, now eighteen months, was requiring expenditures I never encountered before. But I did what I needed to do.

I took out my wallet, took a pen off Marc's desk, and wrote a check for $75,000, borrowed off the brokerage account which held my life savings, to cover payroll, knowing that unlike Henry, or Bob Frost, or my mom, this was a one-way deposit until a larger solution came around.

Marc, ever loyal, even with his own job at risk, tried to wave me off. "No, no, no . . . that's a lot of money. You can't afford to do this."

On the contrary, looking at the potential we had on the financial upside, and the human cost to the staff who had taken a chance on us, I couldn't afford not to.

It was perverse in so many ways. The following week we hosted a holiday party at the four-thousand-square-foot Tribeca penthouse of our first post-Refco cover subject, James R. Hedges IV. Movie-star looks, major art collector, and that name—yes, he was a hedge fund rainmaker—he was *Trader Monthly* central casting (and thus CNBC central casting, where he began guest anchoring).

His apartment was our apartment for the night. Framed by the king-sized bed in the master suite, an ironic James Pierson sculpture of asymmetrical wooden blocks read POOR BOY. Martinis made with "quadruple-distilled" Belvedere vodka were poured under a Dale Chihuly glass Macchia shell, which Hedges had purchased directly from the artist. Zino Platinum cigars were fired up on his 1,500-foot heated terrace. And the 175 guests, trading big shots, a few key advertisers, and a smattering of actresses and models, milled in the giant living room, dominated by a white marble fireplace above which sat a $600,000 painting Andy Warhol made by urinating on a canvas, then sprinkling gold dust on the results. In Jim Hedges's world, people really did piss gold.

Yet the party happened only because I had just written the biggest check of my life by a factor of ten. We were a chronically undercapitalized company—entirely reliant on an illiquid individual investor—that had cornered the market on the best-capitalized guys in the world.

When I called Magnus back to inform him of the Christmas miracle that had saved his investment and our company, I actually felt good about it. I had not yet internalized the Wall Street philosophy of Other People's Money. It just seemed fair to me. Magnus was in far deeper than he had planned, and as I was his partner, albeit the operator who was already taking a reduced salary, it felt right to have real skin in the game beyond sweat equity. We had both doubled down.

$ $ $

Mobster-turned-junkie Henry Hill haunted the first weeks of 2006. My phone friend had devolved back into addict mode before we launched *Justice*. He moved from Washington State to Nebraska, and began calling me wantonly, his number carelessly popping into my phone, his slurred voice bemoaning his fate and occasionally cursing me out, over what I never knew since half his words were undecipherable. There was no choice: I had to whack him. We replaced Henry as our mob columnist with another mafioso made famous by Hollywood, Joe Pistone, better known as "Donnie Brasco." Ray Liotta for Johnny Depp? Seemed like an upgrade. Pistone was sharp—when we had lunch, he would sit only at the corner seat of a corner table, so that no one could come at him from behind. And he was sober.

But Henry had clearly put some kind of Sicilian curse on us. By January, *Justice* was lurching severely. A few months earlier, I had tried to opportunistically solve our supermarket real estate problem. The legendary *TV Guide* had announced that it was ditching its purse-friendly digest size—the idea of printed TV listings was about as relevant as rabbit ear antennas—to compete as a full-sized, photo-heavy profile magazine, along with the dozen or so other *People* wannabes. Suddenly, tens of thousands of cheap, tiny checkout racks had freed up—they were foreclosed trailer home racks compared with the Hamptons beach house racks we had been fruitlessly chasing—so in a last-ditch attempt to survive, as *TV Guide* went big, the second and third issues of *Justice* went small.

But that wasn't enough. To showcase it properly, *Justice* still needed more time and hundreds of thousands more dollars than we had. I began talking to the likes of Court TV and American Media (publishers of the *National Enquirer*) about taking it off our hands. To make that easier, we frantically tried to create national buzz, investigating a neo-Nazi celebrity as he simultaneously tried to date our reporter and nailing a weepy jailhouse interview with Lindsay Lohan's felonious dad. Nothing.

With time ticking down, I launched a Hail Mary: A friend of mine in Miami had tipped me to the deli where O. J. Simpson ate his breakfast every morning. I, in turn, pressured Marcia Clark—she wrote a column, "The Advocate," that helped readers get personal justice when their landlord screwed them, or their ex-husband held back child support—to fly down there on the upcoming tenth anni-

versary of the verdict and engage in the cross-examination the world
had waited a decade to hear. We had numerous discussions about
this, with Marcia reverting into the skeptical prosecutor.

"So you want me to just go up to him out of nowhere?"

"Yes, counselor."

"And just sit down with him at his table?"

"Yes, counselor."

"In a bagel restaurant?"

"Yes, counselor."

"What if he's not there?"

"We'll have someone scout out the day before to make sure he's
in town."

"And if he goes somewhere the next day?"

"Then, you can hang in Miami until he gets back. Hey, where
could O.J. possibly need to go?"

"Randall?"

"Yes?"

"This sounds pretty crazy."

Desperate was actually a better word. We were grasping at straws.
A few days into the New Year, it was time to whack *Justice*. Even
though we were sending them into a good job market, looking into
the eyes of the four people I was laying off was dreadful. But within
a few days, that awful feeling gave way to relief. In theory, *Justice*
was a far sexier, bigger idea than *Trader Monthly*. Yet it had attracted
a microfraction of the buzz. The plow horse in our stable, in turned
out, was also the show horse.

Unfortunately, *Justice* was only one factor in our accelerating cash
crunch. And more critically, it didn't magically infuse money into
any of Magnus's bank accounts, particularly around the holidays,
when revenues slow down everywhere. Nights became endless. Sleep
was something that I had always taken for granted. I didn't need
much of it, and could generally take it whenever I wanted. But I was
now learning that your brain controls your body, not the other way
around, as every fortnight became an epic payroll struggle. After
Marc and I jerry-rigged some new solution, I would go home euphoric, full of swagger, like a bulletproof action hero. By the next

day, the stress would return, as I began trying to solve the next payroll problem two weeks hence.

We faced the wall several more times, and the personal financial nightmare became a recurring one. That first $75,000 infusion had simply bought time for a second one, it turned out. Another $50,000 was required after that. And finally, a $33,000 infusion, made on January 13, 2006, the day before I turned thirty-eight, a kind of reverse birthday present to myself. My total personal exposure was now $233,000. I obviously didn't have that kind of cash lying around, so I continued to borrow against the mutual funds that held my life savings. Fifteen years of scrimping for a security blanket, in exchange for covering four payrolls.

I wasn't mad at Magnus. He never asked me to put money in, and he was scrambling to risk more of his own. Yes, he had approved the expansion, and had committed to pay for it. But I had pushed him. We were both paying the price of *unliiiimmmiiittted* risk profiles. There had been no one to say no to us, and our eyes were bigger than our stomachs.

I was mad at myself, though. It was a lousy predicament. I never went into the office intending to write a check to the company. We were always crafting multiple solutions at work right up until payroll day, but on the weeks they fell through, it was left for me to either save the company or fold it. There was no choice, especially when half the staff had joined the company because of loyalty to me.

I couldn't even bear to tell my wife about it until months after the fact, which just made her more furious and scared when I finally fessed up. It was technically my money, accumulated before I knew her, still in the accounts I originally opened. But it was *our* future. Shortly after that last deposit, I learned that Jennifer was pregnant again. Chloe Lane would arrive that summer, in a hurry. She almost popped out in the taxi en route to the hospital, and emerged loudly as purple as a plum, her umbilical cord around her neck; it was as if Chloe knew she had to move quickly before trouble could happen. In that regard, she was already smarter than her dad. There would soon be two little mouths to feed, along with the leveraged pressure that came with that responsibility.

Waiting for one of Magnus's friends to emerge as a white knight was no longer feasible. I had avoided approaching other media companies about funding or buying *Trader Monthly* because it was too early; they wouldn't properly value what we accomplished, and the potential that lay ahead. But such subtleties go out the window when neither of your two principals has any access to cash.

Atlantic Media, publishers of *The Atlantic* magazine, *The Hotline* newsletter, and other properties targeting the influential, was in expansion mode. Their president signed off on a deal that would pay us $5 million—basically paying back all our investment, plus a chance for our whole team to make far more going forward. The only thing missing was the seal of approval from the company's sole owner, David Bradley, a billionaire consulting titan who had migrated to the world of ideas. A larger struggling company, Dow Jones, owners of *The Wall Street Journal*, was even more gung ho. They were keen to get into the events and glossy magazine business, and liked the idea of how Doubledown, a media rifle, fit with their broad shotgun. Bureaucratic, even by public company standards, Dow Jones had us meeting with two dozen of their top executives, as their acquisition team began scrubbing our financial records and personal backgrounds.

As those negotiations lurched forward, we frantically scrambled for backup plans. Magnus and I embraced a philosophy for desperate times: talk to anyone who even appears to have a serious bankroll, and then take those talks as far as they will lead.

That meant a lot of meetings, most of which were educational, and some were promising. Platinum-type investors like former Thomson CEO David Flaschen, advertising legend Charles Saatchi, and private equity pioneer Alan Patricof took a personal interest, kicking the tires and sending in underlings to look fully under the hood.

Then came the freaks. Compared with, say, an insurance company, sexy media deals tend to draw out the more colorful of the tire kickers. On paper, Jeffrey Epstein was perfect. A former Bear Stearns trader who made hundreds of millions managing money, largely for Victoria's Secret billionaire Les Wexner, he understood the audience. And his frequent companion, Ghislaine Maxwell, daughter of the late British press baron Robert Maxwell, made the introduction because he was now dabbling in start-up magazines. Unfortunately for Epstein, he was simultaneously dabbling in child prostitutes; a subsequent indictment, and guilty plea, explained why he had stopped returning our messages.

William Talcott "Billy" May's mischief was far more acceptable. The heir to a famous century-old real estate brokerage, William B. May, he took a shine to Doubledown over an afternoon coffee at a French bistro, and insisted that I meet him that night, a Monday, at midnight at a velvet rope club in Greenwich Village. The midnight meeting was appropriate because May had calibrated his body, like our UK traders, to Greenwich Mean Time. He would catch a few hours of sleep that evening, and begin his "day" at the club. "You don't know somebody until you hang out with them," he insisted, in a deep raspy voice similar to Harvey Fierstein's.

It seemed we could hang. Before I lurched out at 3 a.m. he emphatically jotted on a cocktail napkin—the music was too loud to talk—WE WILL BE PARTNERS. Unfortunately, like Epstein, he was a convicted felon. In 2001 he had planted fake bombs at the New Castle County Airport in Delaware, in something between a prank gone very wrong (his account) and bipolar disorder (his lawyer's). We wouldn't be partners, it turned out, after he asked yet another felon, a former white-collar crook just out of jail, to be his project manager on our prospective deal.

While perpetually under investigation, John Devaney, our former cover boy with his own jet, helicopter, Rolls-Royce, and Scarface house, was not an actual felon. I gave him the pitch in the back of his Town Car, as his mini-motorcade sped from Wall Street toward Teterboro Airport, where his private jet was idling. That pitch continued through the terminal, onto the tarmac, and then all the way up the stairs to his plane, ending with him voicing support for the idea, as the plane doors closed between us, ripping us apart at the crucial moment like the lovers at the end of *Casablanca*. But his angle was turning the magazine into a glossy marketing brochure for his company. It didn't go further.

Then there was Michael Fowler. With bad skin and greasy blond hair that looked like it had last been washed when Shaun Cassidy was still popular, he was no older than twenty-five and looked far younger, despite three-piece suits seemingly borrowed from his dad and a ubiquitous briefcase. His investment firm was called Fowler Thorn—the logo was a *T* with a little arm jutting off the right side to make an *F*—yet we had never met Thorn, and the Web site on his card didn't work.

But he had been introduced to Magnus by Rachel Pine, and went to great lengths to prove that he was in fact "money good," the deal-world term for someone who has the ready cash to meet the interest. He brought Magnus and me to the Four Seasons hotel, right around the corner from where we developed "See It, Make It, Spend It," to meet one of his alleged coinvestors, Ziad Abdelnour. One of Michael Milken's junk bond deputies at Drexel Burnham, Abdelnour was a legitimate power player in his own right, in New York and Washington, where he helped steer policy toward his native Lebanon, and spent most of our meeting on his cell phone buying an entire oil tanker on the cheap. Fowler began dropping us e-mails like "What about a magazine for real estate developers? Think Bruce Ratner, Nick Gouletas, Steve Ross, Mort Zuckerman . . . I know a majority of these guys personally as I've financed them." Or, referring to the Wyndham Hotel chain, "Lost the bid by $40M. I'll show you the model we did. Our price was $1.4B in cash. Feel free to contact me at your convenience." He once spent an hour showing me a "radical new" kind of security that he'd developed, which he said would tap tax-free government bonds as collateral to buy companies, risk-free. He called them High Yield Zero Coupon Secured Corporate Bonds. Zeroes, for short.

Fowler actually seemed to have a motivation to do this deal. He was promoting what had to be the stupidest magazine idea ever: a sex magazine for women called "Cake," edited by a nineteen-year-old from his New Jersey hometown who dropped out of NYU based on Fowler's promise that he'd help her launch it. Fowler committed to putting $5.5 million into the company if we helped them get "Cake" started, and backed that up with a nine-page term sheet outlining the proposal.

On the night we were supposed to discuss drafting a proper investment agreement, over pasta and wine, he instead desperately steered the conversation toward Stephen Glass, the notorious serial fabulist, memorialized in *Shattered Glass*, whom I had known when I lived in Washington. He asked me endless questions: *Did I know he was a faker? How did he get away with it for so long?* That night, rather than go home to the $7 million mansion he said was "under construction," he asked if he could crash on my couch. He slept in his three-piece suit, and then left quietly in the morning. And I never saw him again. There was never any mansion, of course, nor any lasting trace of Michael Fowler. Magnus and I remained alone.

There is a gambling corollary to doubling down, and it's not even specific to blackjack: the table maximum. If you ever wondered why every casino game has both a minimum bet and a maximum bet— shouldn't they want you to bet as much as possible?—here's the answer. A bettor who doubles his bet every time, until infinity, will always win. Whenever his luck turns, he'll get all the money he lost, plus a profit matching his initial wager. Do the math—it works. But table maximums prevent that. Rub up against one and you lose everything, a mighty fine disincentive to trying to infinitely double.

Magnus had several million invested. I was at $233,000, which relative to our respective net worths was actually the more dangerous amount. We were at our table maximum. If the next card or dice roll didn't go our way, we were busted.

5

Dealmaker

(2006)

There's a saying my grandfather, a professional greyhound bettor, used to tell me: you can tell everything you need to know about a man by standing at the track's rail with him. So what was I to make of the familiar, somewhat froggy bass voice bellowing from across the craps table at the El Conquistador Hotel in Puerto Rico, chanting rhythmically, manically?

Peee-ter! Peee-ter! Peee-ter!

The Peter in question was a magazine consultant whose claim to fame this night was an epic roll that was making the whole table a lot of money. The distinct voice belonged to one John McCain, a man determined to become leader of the free world in a few years. On this night, however, as he focused intently on the dice in front of him, he would unknowingly help me save Doubledown Media.

John McCain on a serious craps bender seemed perfectly normal as 2005 was turning into 2006. The entire planet was officially a big casino, with those populating the richest parts engrossed with the pursuit of easy money, whether flipping real estate using no-money-down loans pushed increasingly by companies like Countrywide Financial or borrowing against their houses to buy securities based on those kinds of loans.

McCain and I were both at this giant, musty hotel, ninety minutes east of San Juan, for the American Magazine Conference, an annual get-together of print media hoi polloi. The Arizona senator was giving the keynote speech the following morning, engaged in the classic rite of presidential aspirants trying to impress an audience with sway over tens of millions of voters. (At the following year's conference, I met another ambitious senator, Barack Obama, as he came off the golf course, his pants hiked up way too far above his waist.) My politicking was far more focused. I had to find one person who could pull Magnus and me out of our financial death spiral.

Twenty minutes earlier, I had heard the clarion call of a hot run—frenetic shouting—and wedged into the last slot at the lone craps table in the hotel's poky casino. The old Navy pilot was already throwing around a staggering pile of chips with the zeal of a Fleet Week sailor.

Give me the c-and-e. Horn-high yo! Press the six. Cover the hardways. McCain was a maestro of the felt, intently covering each roll with hundreds, perhaps thousands of dollars. I couldn't tell, exactly, how much the senator was plunking down—I was directly across the length of the table—other than that his chips were different colors from the stack I received for my $100.

The players around me were still buzzing about an altercation McCain just had. "Some woman was getting in his space," my table neighbor explained. A yelling match apparently ensued, with the woman either fleeing or getting led off. And McCain's turf battle paid dividends as the table stayed hot. McCain rolled, and made everyone money. Then came Peter, whose epic run lasted a good forty minutes.

Peee-ter, Peee-ter, Peee-ter!

When I got the dice, McCain was more formal: "Come on, big guy!"

Big guy! Big guy! Big guy!

When I hit my eight, he pumped his fist at me, in his herky-jerky style, as if I'd just delivered the early returns from New Hampshire.

I was up about $700 after about ninety minutes. McCain was surely up several thousand. I very much wanted to walk away. I really wanted McCain to walk away, too, both because he'd accumulated a tidy haul, and because I liked the idea of a president who knew when to leave a surplus alone. But this was the Zeroes. McCain didn't walk away, and I vowed to stay as long as he did. Who wants to tell their grandkids they bailed from a hot dice game with a president?

McCain tested me. After another hour my chip pile had been halved, as had McCain's. It was well past midnight. I had at least three hours of work to do before bed, and the program started at 7:30 the next morning. Yet McCain kept playing. I gave it another half-hour. McCain kept playing. It became clear that the former POW might well play until dawn. So I walked with my smallish profit, leaving the senator still rolling. For all I know, he's still there.

But the McCain-assisted bleariness the next morning paid dividends. While stumbling around for coffee outside the conference hall while some speaker droned I came across a slim blonde with a familiar name on her conference badge: Polly Perkins Johnson. I had met Polly once before. She had offered some free advice to *P.O.V.* It was a connection I remembered only after seeing her name, and which she barely recalled.

Polly was now an investment banker at AdMedia Partners, and briefly listened to the Doubledown proposition. We followed up in New York. Initially skeptical, she became smitten with our potential and took us on as a client, if only as something of a charity case. We couldn't afford a retainer. But Polly came from an old, almost extinct school of investment banking that centered on relationships. A half-century ago, when Goldman Sachs was an actual investment bank rather than a platinum-plated speculator, legendary CEO Sidney Weinberg promoted a culture that encouraged bankers to act as long-term counselors, charging only if and when a deal was consummated, even if it took decades.

During the early months of 2006, Polly and one of the firm's principals, Mark Edmiston, made introductions, advising us on our ongoing negotiations with Atlantic Media and *The Wall Street Journal*. Over that period, as our economic situation became increasingly dire, Polly would check on me periodically, the way you might a relative in a nursing home, just to make sure no one has been taken to the morgue.

While I was at a Passover seder in April 2006, Polly deluged me with an uncharacteristically urgent barrage of voice messages. When I finally got back to her, she was focused and intense.

"Do you know who Jim Dunning is?"

"Of course." While he was obscure to most of the world, everyone in magazines surely knew of Jim Dunning.

"Well, I've been holding back on this one. I'm still not sure I should do this. But I just had a conversation with him. He has money, he knows the game, and he wants to meet. Tomorrow. At two p.m."

$ $ $

For Jim Dunning, the third marriage was the charm. Eighteen months earlier, he had married Susan Magrino, the tall, stunning owner of the most influential luxury public relations firm in New York. The nuptials were at the exclusive Ocean Club on Paradise Island in the Bahamas, in a ceremony full of teak and orchids featured around the clock on a wedding program on the Fine Living cable network. Magrino's eponymous agency represented the likes of Dom Pérignon and Martha Stewart, and Jim scheduled our meeting at her offices, located on the twenty-eighth floor of an appropriately posh tower with views across midtown Manhattan.

I walked in accompanied by one of Polly's colleagues, a banker my age named Jay Kirsch, and got my first glimpse of Dunning. Jim appeared as small as Magnus was big—maybe five-foot-five, without an ounce of fat. A recent back injury had turned his usual ramrod bearing into a painful gait. He wore a cardigan sweater that retained the whiff of cigar smoke.

But even banged up, Jim exuded self-confidence, punctuating everything he said with the fervor stocked by three decades of success straddling the deal and media worlds. He had turned around *Rolling Stone* as its president, run a small investment bank, and then began buying and selling the Googles of the eighties: yellow page businesses. In 1996 he initiated the greatest deal in magazine history. As critics howled, he paid $450 million for a sleepy publishing company named Petersen (*Hot Rod, Motor Trend*). Rather than slash costs, he frantically invested, expanded, and acquired, taking the entire operation public in 1997 before selling the whole kit and caboodle in a leveraged buyout for $1.5 billion. Because so much of the initial purchase came from borrowed money, his backers made ten times their investment. Jim made a fortune.

Polly had been one of Jim's Petersen lieutenants. The reasons she'd hesitated to make the introduction were on immediate display at our meeting. She knew he'd sworn off media deals, and she knew he could be fearsome.

"Why did you bring your babysitter here?" he asked, looking at me archly, after Kirsch, doing what bankers tend to do to make themselves useful, tried to start the meeting with an overview. That was pretty much the last time Jay opened his mouth.

After six months on the professional begging circuit known as fund-raising, I had performed the Doubledown pitch at least a hundred times. I liked to start by bringing out a little DVD player I toted around, teed up to a four-minute video full of TV talking heads touting *Trader Monthly*, as well as scenes from our parties. Showing, rather than telling, the vibrancy and influence of our products. Thirty seconds in, Jim cut me off.

"That's the kind of crap you show advertisers," he barked. "I want to know what this business is about."

And so it went, in an infinite loop. I would open my mouth, and halfway through the sentence, Jim would cut me off, challenging the first clause before I could roll out the second. He'd then ask a question that would lead to a new sentence that he would then cut off again.

The plan I was haltingly throwing out was something Magnus and I had come to call the Rubik's Cube. Like the eighties toy, it was represented by a three-dimensional series of boxes, with different affluent careers shooting out in one direction, different global regions in a second, and different types of media in a third. The Doubledown Media we now envisioned would build a global database of the affluent, based on what people did for a living. If *Trader Monthly* works for traders, why not go after bankers, CEOs, and lawyers? If it resonated in the United States and the United Kingdom, why not reach these professions in China, Japan, Dubai? And not just separate magazines for each of these professions in each of these locations, but Web sites, events, conferences, newsletters. We wanted to double down again, but properly funded this time, and consistent with our strengths.

The meeting broke up after two hours of six-word bursts. Rumors had spread throughout Susan Magrino's office that the editor-in-chief of *Trader Monthly* was ensconced in the conference room. Once the door opened, a conga line of Susan's attractive reps bounded in to introduce themselves and explain which clients they represented and whatever initiatives they were being paid to push.

Out on the street, staring up at the ski slope top of the Citigroup building, Jay and I shrugged. "That didn't go too well," I said.

"Well," responded Jay, trying to buck me up, "he *did* ask a lot of questions."

Jay was right. I'd been through dozens of meetings throwing out so many silver sentences, and all the ensuing praise that gushed from legends and felons alike had yielded exactly zero dollars. Jim's interrogation stemmed from piqued interest. Tire kickers laud, serious investors grill.

Especially Jim. What I had experienced, Jim's friends would later knowingly tease me, was the "Dunning Treatment." It was a rite, and I'd just been broken in, with all the subtlety of a prosecutor attacking a hostile witness.

As the witness hadn't flinched, Jim began some due diligence.

First, his wife told him that her eager executives were interested in part because her luxury clients specifically listed *Trader Monthly* as a desired target; the reps' efficacy was measured in part on whether they could get their products placed in our magazine.

But did the people we sent the magazine to actually read it? Jim went home to his Sutton Place apartment, previously owned by New York's billionaire mayor Michael Bloomberg, and called his eldest son, James, who worked at Citi. Have you ever heard of *Trader Monthly*? "Absolutely, Dad," came the reply. "Every single trader picks it up."

Jim then dialed a friend of his son's, just out of college, ensconced at Goldman Sachs, and repeated the question. "Yes, Mr. Dunning," came the reply. "Whenever an issue comes out, I'm given a hundred dollars to go down and buy every copy off the newsstand so we have extras."

Jim made one final call, to a friend who also knew Gordon Crovitz, the publisher of *The Wall Street Journal*, one of the many top suits we were meeting with as Dow Jones continued its due diligence. Yes, the response came back, they were seriously considering purchasing us, confirming what I'd just told him. My credibility and Doubledown's attractiveness were both burnished. As with trading, information rules the deal world. Jim Dunning, master dealmaker, knew everything before I even got back to my office.

$ $ $

The following Monday, Jim called. "I'm going to be your coach," he announced. Jim had been a college hockey and baseball player. As a parent, he managed elite Connecticut teenage squads that included several future NHL players. As an entrepreneur, he bid aggressively in the 1980s to buy the New York Mets. Coaching was his natural inclination. "I was investing in *you*," he recalls. "There was genius in the presentation. You had a thoroughly forward-thinking business model."

We established a regular routine. He would call me every day at 9 a.m. sharp—"Hey, it's your coach calling"—and we'd go over my daily game plan. For the next few weeks, the game plan mostly involved having his full-time driver cart me around town in his BMW to meet more potential investors. Atlantic Media had turned us down, flummoxing our bankers who had been told it was a near-sure thing. Owner David Bradley was already investing in another magazine aimed at the elite, *02138*, which targeted Harvard graduates and was named for the zip code in Cambridge, Massachusetts. For Bradley, that was enough new risk for his portfolio. So Jim was introducing me to backups as we waited for the *Wall Street Journal* process to play out.

What coaching didn't involve was money. I never asked Jim to put in anything. The relationship seemed more intimate than a quick cash source, and I was careful to respect it as such. Magnus also met Jim, and we took to calling him our "tough love dad." He'd bark whenever he disagreed with a decision, but the Dunning Treatment always ended in a hug. The last thing a tough love dad wants to see is someone with his hand constantly jutting out. So every time payroll came due, he would watch while Marc Feifer and I pulled some rabbit out of a hat. Wilkie Bushby, our publisher, had heroically helped ease the crisis. Perceptive enough to foresee that a deal would get done with either Dow Jones or Jim, Wilkie also saw the surge of advertising about to break for us. Wilkie didn't have hedge fund money, but he came from that world, and one Connecticut friend loaned him $350,000, providing Doubledown a Band-Aid.

The less I asked Jim for money, the more he offered. The first $50,000 came with no strings attached, a gesture of goodwill when he could see we were struggling mightily to make payroll, but were too proud to ask for help. Other wires, in the same altruistic manner as Magnus's mysterious friend Henry, followed.

He began suggesting, unsolicited, investment scenarios for himself, albeit more tough than love. His first offer was the world's most expensive credit card: a half-million loan, with a 16 percent rate of interest, and 15 to 20 percent ownership of the company as a sweetener. Even in our desperate straits, we couldn't take that. In his gruff way, Jim respected us for that.

The more Jim hung around our company, in fact, the more he began to suggest that we shouldn't even sell to Dow Jones. Just as Magnus had envisioned a career past trading, and I hoped for a way to give my family financial security, Doubledown offered something for Jim: redemption. After Petersen, Jim had led a buyout of Ziff-Davis, the world's largest computer magazine publisher (*PC*, *Macworld*); that deal went south with the dot-com bust, and Jim was dumped by the board after arguing (correctly) for a more aggressive digital strategy. He lost $10 million, and face. Doubledown could erase that bad aftertaste. "This is the biggest opportunity I've seen since Petersen," he began to tell anyone who would listen.

The Dow Jones option proved moot. I had brought Jim to one meeting, where he had proceeded to give a roomful of twenty plodding executives the Dunning Treatment. *Why was some short tycoon drilling us*, I was later asked by their head of acquisitions, *when we are the ones, in theory, buying you?* More critically, Dow Jones's brand-new CEO, Rich Zannino, had a mandate for profitable, digital initiatives. Doubledown would have been his first transaction and, as constituted, we were the opposite: money-losing, print-dominated. As a consolation prize, since they wanted to start a relationship that could lead to a sale down the road, they agreed to take over as our European partner, freeing us from the financially draining Condé Nast partnership.

So Jim and I cut a deal. The rough details were straightforward enough: Jim would invest just under $2 million for 20 percent of the company. That was the cash part. The tougher negotiation was for a concept foreign to me, the "promote." In essence, Jim wanted extra stock in exchange for the benefits his platinum name would bring. In exchange, he was willing to jump in not just as investor, but as chairman of the company. I would carry the CEO title; Magnus would be named Founder. After a year of week-to-week living, frankly, it was a small price to pay for the peace of mind that came with flush pockets, contacts, and experience many times deeper than either Magnus or I had.

I e-mailed him with an offer of an 8 percent promote, bringing his total to 28 percent; he would have a shade more ownership than I would. Magnus, after all the money he had put in, would remain the largest shareholder. We had also carved out about 7 percent for the employees who had started with us, in the form of options that mimicked real ownership stakes. "So what say you?" my note read. "Will the coach become the partner-coach?!" Jim agreed, but with one additional condition. His money could not be used to repay any of the cash Magnus and I had plowed into the company. He wanted his money used for future growth, not past sins. Our money would come out only when his began to.

That was a big condition, as Magnus and I both would have a frightful amount locked in until some liquidity event could free us, the exact kind of motivation Jim wanted to give us. His point was nonnegotiable, and again we weren't in a position to quibble, as scary as the personal prospects were. Not only were our short-term cash flow needs taken care of, but now we had the resources to start filling in the Rubik's Cube.

A funny thing happens once a company no longer needs money: a dozen people suddenly line up, cash in hand. Having learned the lesson of the past twelve months, we took as much of it as we could— mostly from friends of Jim, who had seen the Dunning magic, and the more financially successful of my college buddies, who now saw it was safe to join the party. We raised over $1 million more, and expanded the number of people we could call on for help. While still cash-strapped personally, Magnus and I were no longer alone.

To celebrate our new partnership, Jim and I decided to have a date night and introduce our respective wives to each other. As many wonderful meals as I'd eaten as a restaurant reviewer, Jim was determined to show me the benefits of this new stratum I was now entering. He arranged through Susan to dine at the fabled Le Cirque, at the chef's table, located inside the kitchen itself. Through a tinted window that looked out over the dining room we could see the run-of-the-mill Wall Street slobs paying $200 a person merely to eat food served by waiters, compared to whatever the chefs chose to pamper us with, each dish described with gusto.

Joining us was one of our new investors, who doubled as Jim's best friend and the nation's top magazine circulation expert, Chip Block, along with his witty wife, Leanna Landsmann. Early in the dinner, however, Jim warned that the table for six might turn into a table for seven. One of Susan's best friends had no plans this Friday night, and thought she might jump in on the fun. Just before appetizers, Martha Stewart ducked into the kitchen and joined our table.

I had been inured to wealth since my youth adjacent to the Rockefellers, to fame in my twenties covering athletes and CEOs for *Forbes*. So the presence of one of the richest and most famous women in the world seemed somewhat normal. Time and again, I'd learned that the rich and famous are no different from anyone else, just more egocentric, and on principle I tried not to treat them any differently.

What was different, however, was how she treated *me*. My toe-to-toe dealings with the elite had previously been enforced by the power I wielded with my pen. Martha, however, immediately approached me as an equal, a friend. We both edited and published magazines. She worked with Susan, I worked with Jim, who introduced me to anyone who asked not as his star pupil, but as his new partner. Martha eagerly forked the half-eaten food off my plate, and made small, indirect jokes at her own expense about her recent jail time for insider trading, given that I ran a trading magazine.

That she went home by chauffeur to her estate in Bedford while Jen and I would take the subway back to our fourth-floor walk-up with no air-conditioning surely didn't occur to her. And no matter. Since I'd grown up abutting the Rockefeller estate, my nose had been pushed squarely against the glass of wealth and power. For the first time, I felt like I had been given a hall pass to visit the inside.

$ $ $

Just as Magnus had brought me into a secret trading culture, part of Jim's coaching mission was to educate me on the people who buy and sell *entire companies* rather than mere securities. If traders are the world's richest fraternity, then dealmakers, it was quickly apparent, formed the world's most powerful club.

Thus, not unlike Rotarians or Kiwanians, every deal mecca had a clubhouse. In Silicon Valley, it was the Sundeck, a bright grill situated at venture capital's capital, Sand Hill Road, which placed a cup of silver golf pencils between the salt and pepper so guests could scribble out valuations and terms on the butcher paper table coverings without fumbling in their pockets. In Washington, Charlie Palmer Steak got around lobbying restrictions, which forbade taking legislators to any meal involving silverware, by offering a special menu of deluxe vittles consumed by finger and toothpick. ("No knives, no forks, no problem," general manager Philip Gates told one of our reporters.)

New York had a couple of power headquarters, starting with San Pietro, where the heads of banks and trading exchanges jousted for one of the three tables near the window, dubbed Chairman's Row. "Most of the time, there's an unwritten law among these guys as to who gets to sit where," owner Gerardo Bruno explained. "They know who's 'in the moment' and who should get the best seats. But when they don't, I have to get to work—and it isn't easy." At Michael's, media honchos poked through $30 Cobb salads.

But those were niche spots, industry watercoolers dispensing Pellegrino. The real hitters, the small handful of people who could put together and break apart companies like LEGO blocks, regardless of type or size of business, lunched almost daily at the Four Seasons restaurant.

As part of my introductory tour inside the bubble, Jim invited me to join him at lunch for a history lesson and a chance to meet the gang. The Four Seasons, unaffiliated with the hotel of the same name, sits inside the foot of the landmark Seagram Building. New York's first tower to eschew gargoyles and needles and the other frills that traditionally constituted great skyscraper design, the Seagram Building instead highlighted the structure itself: steel, girders, I-beams. A postwar power statement. Appropriately, the same architects, Mies van der Rohe and Philip Johnson, designed a power commissary that was unchanged from its 1959 debut to almost a half-century later, when Jim and I ascended the grand staircase into the dining area.

There were actually two giant dining rooms, with ceilings so high that each space felt cubic. Soaring window columns, softened by a golden mesh, accentuated the effect. Each room had a name more appropriate for a country club than a public restaurant. To the left was the Pool Room, with a white marble fountain in the center. In front of me was the Grill Room, covered in grainy French walnut, an elegant dais rising across the back. Connecting the two spaces was a grand hallway displaying a rotation of Pablo Picasso tapestries, Frank Stella paintings, and other collection-worthy offerings. Mark Rothko had originally been commissioned to do all the restaurant's artwork, more than thirty pieces in all, but he found himself increasingly bitter, even back then, about the moneyed clientele and pledged to paint "something that will ruin the appetite of every son-of-a-bitch who ever eats in that room." He eventually returned his commission money, and the paintings are now housed in several museums, including London's Tate Modern.

The restaurant's silver-haired co-owner, Julian Niccolini, sprang up from the hostess stand to greet us like family. Jim and Susan had their New York wedding reception here for those who didn't make it to the Bahamas ceremony. At lunch, Niccolini was the master of ceremonies, his reservation sheet, penned by hand in elegant black ink, reading like a preview of the following week's *Wall Street Journal*, once you deciphered who had been sitting with whom.

As Jim and I were shown to our table in the Grill Room, the concentration of power before me was remarkable. There were more women than you would see on a trading floor, but it was still a predominantly male affair. On the elevated level sat bushy-browed Mel Karmazin, the former head of CBS, who now ran the Sirius XM satellite radio giant. On the main floor was Edgar Bronfman, Jr., who had inherited the Seagram liquor fortune responsible for the building overhead, and lost much of it chasing movie studios and record labels; Hank Greenberg, the billionaire who had turned AIG into an insurance giant; Vernon Jordan, the one-man Washington–Wall Street nexus, simultaneously wearing the hats of investment bank Lazard Frères, the *Fortune* 500 (he sat on American Express, Xerox, and a half-dozen other boards), and Democratic Party fixer (most famous for trying to help Bill Clinton assuage Monica Lewinsky with an internship). Sandy Weill, who had built Citigroup into the world's largest financial company, was at his regular table, number 33, eating his usual, grilled fish. And those were just the faces I recognized.

What I found interesting was how active this group was, bounding from table to table like it was a college cafeteria. Deals don't happen in a vacuum, and they don't happen by coincidence—they occur because the right people know the other right people, and know the businesses that are being bought and sold. That knowledge—*deal flow*, in this world's vernacular—was the ultimate currency. The game at lunch every day was acquiring it.

Ironically, this game was invented by the beefier version of Walter Cronkite who was waiting for Jim and me at our table. Few at the

Four Seasons knew the name Carl Hess, and still fewer recognized the man. Jim, who had invited him to join us, would have stared right through him, too, except that Hess was his neighbor on Sutton Place. Such are the inconveniences of living until you're ninety-four. But Hess was the last man alive who could take credit for creating the thing that was driving every conversation in the room: private equity.

Technically, robber barons like J. P. Morgan and Andrew Carnegie began buying and selling companies privately—versus taking them public—at the turn of the last century. But it wasn't until 1967, when Carl Hess founded AEA Investors, that a firm was actually formed for the purpose of buying and selling whole companies, rather than stock.

Hess's mind remained remarkably sharp. Although he no longer had a formal role, he still put on one of his bespoke suits, made by an Italian tailor named Carmine del Giudice, and went into the AEA offices five days a week. But his voice was largely shot—every word was diluted by a lot of air—and I had to strain mightily over the din of exuberant deal flow to hear a remarkable oral history that linked the twentieth century to the Zeroes.

As Hess and I both tucked into $53 Dover sole, he described what it was like, straight out of Dartmouth in 1934, trying to sell companies in the teeth of the Great Depression ("that's how I learned about business"). I would discover later that he had advised Western Union about selling its undersea *telegraph* cables. Mostly, he discussed how he had run the world's first private equity firm, after raising money from twentieth-century industrial royalty—the Rockefellers, the DuPonts, the Mellons, and S. G. Warburg himself.

As with hedge funds, AEA launched on the idea that borrowed money could lead to better results for investors. But he applied that rule carefully: he always bought companies with at least 40 percent cash down, taking no more than 60 percent as debt, often far less. "The banks always wanted to give us more," he whispered. "But I was never comfortable with that." Hess also pioneered the idea of a "commitment agreement," where investors would agree to put in money when called upon. Both practices still held during the Zeroes.

In the early 1970s, Hess gave Jerome Kohlberg a copy of AEA's investor contract, which he used as a template when starting Kohlberg Kravis Roberts, the KKR of *Barbarians at the Gate* fame.

Such swashbuckling hostile takeovers during the 1980s, powered by the levels of debt that Hess eschewed, gave "leveraged buyouts" a bad name. But by the Zeroes, the LBO game had roared back, redubbed with the friendly name that old-school guys like Carl Hess had given to the straightforward idea of buying and selling companies without going public: private equity. "Creating efficiencies" and "unlocking value" were the buzzwords, as huge numbers of private equity firms began pooling huge sums of money to buy mature, profitable companies (654 in the United States in 2006, for $375 billion, almost twenty times the level in 2003), which were then cut, merged, or expanded into something to be sold or taken public. These were the hedge funds of the deal world, complete with the same reckless pay structure for the managers: 2-and-20. Heads I win, tails you lose but I still win.

Among the more than 1,700 private equity firms at the time, the undisputed king was the Blackstone Group. Founded in 1985 by Richard Nixon's secretary of commerce, Pete Peterson (who was having grilled chicken paillard with a side of pasta and a potato a few tables over), and a former Lehman Brothers prodigy named Stephen Schwarzman, Blackstone now controlled more than one hundred companies, worth an aggregate of nearly $200 billion. They were the most respected/admired/loathed/feared private equity firm in the world, which, by math's transitive property, made Schwarzman, now Blackstone's CEO, the undisputed mayor of the Four Seasons.

As if on cue, Schwarzman came bounding around the Grill Room like he was running for office. He was fit, wearing a perfectly cut navy blue suit, with a slight tan and a salt-and-pepper comb-over appropriate for a man soon to turn sixty. Schwarzman was smack in the middle of a $39 billion bid for Equity Office Properties, the largest private buyout offer ever, surpassing KKR's legendary *Barbarians* quarry of RJR Nabisco by a healthy amount. But while making an offer equivalent to giving every man, woman, and child in the

United States $125, he still made time, as he did most days, to hit the Four Seasons.

Jim flagged him. "Hey, Steve, it's Jim Dunning.

"This is my partner, Randall Lane. He's the guy behind Double-down Media, *Trader Monthly*." Schwarzman shook my hand, acknowledging familiarity with the company, or at least pretending to.

Then he began introducing Hess. "Hey, Carl Hess!" Schwarzman exclaimed. "I met you in 1976. You haven't gotten any older." Pleasantries ensued, and off he moved to the next table.

Hess was having fun. The respect shown by Jim. The eager audience he had in me, as I scribbled notes of his more remarkable utterances, mindful that the world's oldest dealmaker would make a good story someday. The recognition from Schwarzman, the king of the field he had started and the mayor of the restaurant he had graced a thousand times.

Then came the real mayor. Michael Bloomberg, financial-information-billionaire-turned-unbribable-politician, wandered in. Again, Jim Dunning, ever the wallflower, intervened.

"Hey, Mayor," Jim bellowed, waving his hands. Bloomberg walked over and shook our hands as Jim again explained what we all did. Bloomberg didn't recognize his old neighbor Carl Hess, and didn't seem to recognize Jim. "I own your old place on Sutton Place," Jim reminded him.

"Oh, I had a *lot* of fun in that apartment," responded Bloomberg, wistfully. He meant that with all it implied, and seemed comfortable doing so in our company. That's why, after all, people like to be in a club.

$ $ $

Too many people think of Wall Street types generically, throwing around the terms "traders" and "bankers" interchangeably when they really just mean "some overpaid asshole in a suit." As Jim was demonstrating, there are in fact two sides of the financial world, as distinct as waiters are from cooks in a restaurant, with virtually nothing in common in terms of skills, temperament, or expertise.

Historically, Wall Street had been like one giant extended high school (a boys' high school). The jocks became traders—large, aggressive men who succeed in the pits based on heft and testosterone. The nerds went into banking, crunching numbers and pumping out spreadsheets to determine the efficacy of deals.

During the Zeroes that dynamic was neatly inversed. Electronic trading was ending the reign of the burly floor trader, with a PhD in math far more in demand than a four-year starter at right tackle. The mergers and acquisitions world, meanwhile, was becoming so exuberant that the most valuable person at a private equity firm, by far, was whoever could raise cash. A little deal flow and the magic of 2-and-20 would take care of the rest. So those with a dose of face-man charm and confidence were increasingly controlling the deal world.

Just as most traders were no longer content to serve as someone's glorified middleman, the deal world now held a similar view of the classic investment banker role, which had been like door-to-door sales work, shopping deals like encyclopedias. The best and the slickest poured into private equity, seeking to actually buy and sell companies. While a typical deal took five years from entrance to exit, versus the half-minute a typical trade lasted, the money could be just as good. Tens of thousands of M&A dealmakers were making well into six figures, a few thousand were pulling in $1 million plus, and the highest echelon were getting fantastically wealthy. My new lunch buddy Steve Schwarzman was planning to take Blackstone public, a move that in a few months would make him worth—for a time—$8 billion. One of the very richest men in the world.

This was, in other words, a group that fit naturally into the Rubik's Cube business model that Jim had bought into. The demand was there. Thousands of members of the deal community—bankers, venture capitalists, private equity, analysts, and the like—had been erroneously registering for *Trader Monthly*, or asking how they could get a magazine and Web site for their half of Wall Street. From a corporate standpoint, it was a no-brainer: twice as many rich guys to package to marketers, and a lot of synergy with our current staff.

So it was that in late 2006, we launched *Dealmaker*. Although most references at the time used "deal maker," I intentionally made it one word to underscore that rather than a cake baker or a telephone operator, this was a specific professional species, like a congressman. As we had with Magnus and *Trader Monthly*, the editorial team and I used Jim and some of our other new investors as an in-house focus group, buttressing the knowledge I'd soaked up in six months dabbling in Jim's world.

Culturally, we had to adjust our mind-set. While traders were the ultimate consumers, tearing through positions during a stress-filled, fixed-hour day, and then spending wantonly as they blew off steam with their easy money at night, dealmakers were *acquirers*. Ninety-hour workweeks minimized potential trouble, and their business required them to live with their decisions for years. They viewed purchases through the lens of appreciation. Rather than sports cars, *Dealmaker* evaluated classic cars. Rather than a chunky Panerai watch, we touted elegant Patek Philippe, a favorite at the auction houses. Dealmakers were more likely to collect rare Bordeaux than shoot back hundred-dollar shots of Johnnie Walker Blue. The magazine's slogan, "Acquiring Minds," was a far cry from "See It, Make It, Spend It."

That acquisition mind-set imbued the serious part of the magazine, too. With deal flow paramount, we came up with columns such as "The Courtship," which dissected deals in retrospect, finding out what both sides were really thinking as the negotiations had progressed, and "Inside the Deal Shop," a deep look at the portfolio interests of major private equity firms. In the page margins, we put a short bio of every person mentioned, so that readers could connect with subjects who had similar deal styles, industry expertise, or academic backgrounds. Boiled down, *Dealmaker* was a glossy networking event.

The audience immediately bought into it. Trading is inherently all about secrets: a zero-sum battle between you and the person buying or selling your security, where proprietary information is paramount and publicity has very little upside. The first word in "private equity" doesn't let on that the only way to find out about private deals is to let the world know what you're interested in. Because we billed the magazine, similar to the *Trader Monthly* pitch, as by dealmakers for dealmakers, we were invited in by firms that were secret to the point of paranoid in the outside world. That included the Carlyle Group, a Washington-based private equity firm that included the first President Bush, former secretary of state James Baker, and former UK prime minister John Major as key investors, and was often mentioned by government conspiracy theorists in the same breath as the Trilateral Commission. Rather than the furious pushback we received from the *Trader Monthly* 100, dozens lobbied and politicked to get into our "Rainmakers" package of top bankers and private equity influencers. "To these guys it was currency," one private equity managing director recalls, having seen several of our Rainmakers put reprints of their *Dealmaker* profile into their sales materials. "You were giving away currency."

I've launched nearly a dozen magazines. *Dealmaker* remains the one I'm most proud of. It completely understood its audience, made a desk job glamorous, and did so elegantly. During the Zeroes, a popular trade Web site called MediaPost ran a column, "Magazine Rack," that reviewed new magazines the way *Variety* reviewed movies or *Gourmet* did restaurants. Their take on *Dealmaker:* "One of the fastest-out-of-the-gate biz-pub launches in recent memory and one of the best . . . Presenting useful, timely information for an audience that traffics in it. Wow, what a novel concept. Really, this whole magazine thing ain't so hard; *Dealmaker* makes it look easy."

To celebrate our November 2006 launch, we returned to the Mandarin Oriental ballroom, the one place that allowed us proper glitz on a Doubledown budget. Since the hotel was foisting dim sum on us as part of our discounted package, we rolled with it, shifting the entire party's theme to China on the loose-but-accurate premise that the world's largest country was now a hotbed of M&A. We found a class of tai chi martial artists, willing to act, at nominal cost, as slow motion statues, and hired a Chinatown club to do a New Year's dragon dance, complete with firecrackers and drums. Fortune cookies, custom-ordered for a nickel each from Chinatown, offered up dealmaker quotes from the first issue ("I'm tenacious. I'm hard to knock down."—Sandy Weill).

The eight hundred guests threw back Chopin vodka in a concoction called "CEO martinis," Moët Champagne, and Stella Artois beer. Since Black Velvet, the James Brown impersonator, had gone AWOL, we hired my wedding band, which cut me a generous discount. I felt I deserved it after they, against my directions, played "Love Train," setting off a hundred-person conga line. (The *Dealmaker* party "seemed less like a stodgy Annual Shareholders Meeting," noted the *Huffington Post*'s reporter, "than your cousin's surprisingly fun wedding.")

People all over the world, the singer crooned, *join hands. Form a love train. Love train!* And as billions of dollars of deal talent did so over the twinkle of the Manhattan skyline, I felt hugely optimistic. The risk that I had taken with my life savings, and the related psychic beating of trying to hold everything together for myself and the team, now seemed like an intelligent one. Perhaps soon, my family and staff would see the financial security that the dancing revelers so enjoyed.

$ $ $

The bubble economy of the Zeroes, from real estate, to trading derivatives, to the buyout game, came down to one consistent problem: the world was swimming in cash, and there simply wasn't enough stuff of real value to buy.

Consider that, for each of the years 2002 and 2003, private equity funds collectively raised approximately $100 billion, and "put to work" roughly $100 billion. Between 2006 and 2008, funds raised roughly $500 billion each year, yet only invested about $200 billion. Pensions funds, university endowments, rich individuals, family trusts, charitable foundations, all were pouring money into private equity, desperately seeking the alpha needed for their swelling budgets or lifestyles. The funds, in turn, were increasingly at a loss to find worthy targets. Because their financial success derived from allocating whatever cash they had, they began looking harder. Even if that meant squinting.

Private equity firms frantically glommed on to "operators"—

executives with some expertise who could help them at least justify why they could "unlock value" from a target company that seemed just fine as it was. Sometimes, the operators came from the inside of a company; usually, the operator was an outsider.

This imbalance between buyout cash and viable targets caused prices to soar, and any company exhibiting even a weak pulse sought to take advantage. The average multiple of cash flow for acquisitions during the mid-Zeroes soared from seven to ten. (In English, that meant the price the company was acquired for, compared to the money generated by its ongoing businesses, not including taxes or any financial trickery foisted on it by creative dealmakers. Cash flow is the only figure that really matters when private equity kicks tires.) The same dynamic explained the exploding stock market. Between 2002 and 2007, the Dow Jones went from 7,850 to 14,165, the Standard & Poor's 500 from 777 to 1,565, and the Nasdaq from 1,114 to 2,859.

This all conspired to produce deals that, in retrospect, were completely preposterous, but that at the time seemed brilliant and logical. It was perfectly reasonable, say, for a tiny, money-losing company with $4 million in revenue—fueled by a private equity firm and a lot of debt—to spend $200 million to buy an overvalued-but-profitable company nearly twenty times its size.

I know this for a fact, because the $4 million company in question was Doubledown Media. Actually, we weren't quite a $4 million company. It was October 2006, and we were en route to $4 million in revenue for that year, almost double our 2005 performance but still not that far above what a typical McDonald's franchise takes in. So in fairness, we were *trending* toward $4 million, a $4 million *forward* revenue company, in dealmaker language. In the age of private equity, close enough.

The $200 million target meanwhile was described in the eighty-seven-page bound document labeled "Confidential Information Memorandum September 2006" and, in smaller type below a generic logo, "Phillips Investment Resources," that Jim had dropped on my desk. It was "the book," the de rigueur business overview and financial details that companies put together when they're looking to be purchased, an inch-thick résumé for companies looking for an inflated exit.

"You recognize that name?" Jim barked.

"Never heard of it." Once I started going through the book, it became clear why. Phillips Investment Resources had been founded by a small Baltimore-based publisher, Tom Phillips, who had achieved success with health newsletters that allowed people to keep up on the latest with their particular maladies. In 1974, he started something called *The Retirement Letter* for conservative penny-pinchers, and for the next thirty years followed his newsletter's own advice, growing safely and glacially.

But something happened to Tom Phillips's company in 2004. As I flipped through the numbers, what emerged was one of the secret success stories of the Internet age. In 2003, Phillips had achieved $5.2 million in cash flow. In 2004, that figure had exploded to almost $21 million. After ebbing a bit in 2005, to $15 million, it was again approaching $20 million as we ended 2006.

What happened? In 2004, Phillips fully embraced the Internet. All the economic factors that had done in my *P.O.V.* magazine and shackled Phillips—sending out millions of direct-mail pieces in the hope that a tiny percentage of people will actually request your product, followed by an endless battle to make them pay—had melted away. Phillips was now in the spam business: 156,008,834 e-mails in 2004, to be specific. And while their data showed a seemingly horrendous 99.96 percent failure rate, the measly .04 percent who took out their credit cards bought enough $250 newsletter subscriptions to translate into a huge business when multiplied by enough spam to reach just about every adult in America. Phillips's e-mail initiative brought in $18.8 million in orders that year, at $3.4 million in cost (mostly renting e-mail lists)—a $15.4 million advantage that explained most of the cash flow jump between 2003 and 2004.

Now with three years of Internet-pumped results under his belt, Tom Phillips was ready to take advantage of the ridiculous prices companies were fetching and cash out. He had already dumped his health newsletters the previous year for a nine-figure number, and was looking to repeat the trick.

"So what can we do with this company?" Jim asked.

"What do you mean?"

"If we bought them."

This, of course, was the kind of Dunning magic that justified his "promote." True to his Four Seasons lunch habits, he generated deal flow.

At first, besides marveling at their spam machine, it didn't seem like a fit. Phillips's customer base, as well as I could tell, was a lot of gray hair—82 percent of their customers were over fifty—keeping busy by actively managing their retirement accounts. What would tips on higher dividend yields from a newsletter called *The 25% Cash Machine* have to do with our six- and seven-figure professional gunslingers?

But digging deeper into the book, a couple things seemed to play to our strengths. Virtually none of Phillips's revenue came from advertising, our lifeblood and specialty. Phillips was also finding success selling big-ticket "Inner Circle" services, including special e-mail alerts about specific trades and access to proprietary reporting, for $5,000 a year. The market for this—professional-amateur straddlers like Tim Sykes who sat at home in their pajamas trading all day—nudged closer to our audience.

It became apparent in dissecting their numbers that the key to success was also what we did best: creating stars. Louis Navellier and Tobin Smith looked like corporate types, with their friendly grins, graying temples, and law firm partner names, but in Phillips's world, they were Lennon and McCartney. Both had been recommending stocks for a quarter-century, acquiring tens of thousands of fans along the way, fueled by plenty of TV appearances, who followed them, like groupies, from new product to new product. Navellier was the king of growth stocks, recommending them in four flavors (each with a separate fee, of course) from up-and-comers to blue-chip. Smith's ChangeWave brand, which espoused profiting from societal trends, also offered four different newsletter options, as well as the Inner Circle. Phillips was reaping so much from Navellier and Smith that it took large "key man" life insurance policies out on each, lest a scuba accident or falling piano force the company to instantly shut its doors.

So I was intrigued. More important, Jim had a private equity shop willing to back us as the operator. Chicago-based CIVC Partners had $1 billion to put to work. They had made a killing a decade earlier on Jim Dunning's massive Petersen deal, so when it came to our chairman, they were playing with house money.

Marcus Wedner, whose perpetual five o'clock shadow and designer eyeglasses made him one of the more stylish figures in dealdom, was the CIVC partner on the deal. Jim thought enough of Wedner's opinion that, right after he enlisted as my coach, Marcus was the first person he had me meet. "Really smart, but I'm skeptical of the magazine business," he told me then, his deep voice resonating like a radio announcer's. But Wedner was more bullish about the combination with Phillips.

Jim didn't have an office at Doubledown—he preferred to pop in twice a week, and either camp out with me or walk the halls—but he began coming in every day. Full battle mode invigorated him. A Phillips war cabinet was quickly drafted, with Jim as commander-in-chief. Greg Smith, a market-savvy buyout veteran and a new Doubledown investor, served as his deal chief of staff. Magnus would figure out how to make Phillips products more appealing for a wider audience of traders, and professional and amateur investors. I was charged with figuring how these two companies would work together. Specifically, how could Doubledown make Phillips three times as profitable in three years? It was the same benchmark, not coincidentally, that Jim pulled off at Petersen.

The bidding process for buying a company was similar to buying a house, except these houses were akin to the most exclusive neighborhood of the Jim Crow South. Step one was letting the right people—and only the right people—know that a company is in play. Generally, that involves hiring an investment banker with a specialty in the field to play the role of real estate agent, soliciting bidders and taking a cut of the sale price. In the Phillips case, they went with a media specialist, the Jordan, Edmiston Group.

Rather than place ads and put up proverbial yard signs, the bankers quietly passed around books to the hand-chosen. Secrecy was paramount. Employees, vendors, and clients justifiably freak out when hearing that management, dollar signs in their eyes, has put their livelihoods in play. If a pesky reporter catches wind, and asks whether a company is for sale, they'll get a blanket denial. Deal flow is king. If a dealmaker reads about a potential sale, he's likely already missed it. Jim Dunning got the book for Phillips; without him, the sale, and the company itself, would have remained invisible to me. In this clubby manner, entire industries were parceled out with the informality of a Tuesday night poker game.

Deal flow is more than knowing who's selling. Done right, it means knowing who's bidding, too. So unsurprisingly, Steve Schwarzman's Blackstone caught wind that we were working with CIVC; a partner named Jill Greenthal sent word to Jim and myself that they'd like to talk. Perhaps we would consider becoming the operator in partnership with them? After all, they had already raised $35 billion, and they had the ability to perpetually raise more.

The game for us was suddenly three-dimensional: we were in play, as an operator. We would then join whoever gave us the best terms to make a play for the acquisition. While comfortable with Wedner, we were obligated to seek the best deal for our shareholders. So I sent over our plan for the combined company, and scheduled a meeting for October 12. The day before, Greenthal canceled. Blackstone wasn't going to bid for Phillips, she said. But they had become a bit more knowledgeable about our company in the process.

Back firmly with CIVC, we went forward with the second step, an initial bid. As with houses, this isn't binding. But deal flow requires honor, lest those books not come your way next time. At this stage, there's a lot of winking: Wedner winked that we were interested. Scott Peters, Phillips's polished-looking banker, winked back that he'd like to get $200 million, but anything above $140 million would be considered. Wedner, rare in the private equity world for his determination not to overpay, blanched at even that lower number. But he wanted to go forward. So with our blessing, just in time for the October 16 deadline, the CIVC/Jim Dunning/Doubledown Media consortium submitted our bid: a range between $136 million and $146 million. No matter that Jim's commitment was coming in over time and we didn't have more than $200,000 in the bank. "It's just a game," explains Wedner. "The ultimate dance happens at some future date, and that negotiation depends on who has the leverage."

That brought us to step three, the parallel to a house inspection. This takes place in two parts. First, we were given the keys to their "data room." Although this is usually done electronically, in this case it was literally a room in their lawyers' office with every relevant document in Phillips's recent history. Anything could be viewed, nothing could be removed or copied. Wedner's nonbinding bid came with a cost: he was now paying tens of thousands of dollars for lawyers and bean counters to scour piles of paperwork measured by the yard. That research informed the second half of the inspection: the management meeting, scheduled at the investment banker's office in Manhattan for October 25, at 8:30 a.m. sharp.

On the appointed morning, Jordan, Edmiston had set up their boardroom like those old photos of the Paris peace talks that ended the Vietnam War. Long tables formed a U, with a projection screen filling the open side. The right prong was filled with the top executives from Phillips, up from Baltimore for the day. (Phillips himself, the great Oz of this whole process, chose not to attend.) The bottom was filled with the investment bankers, putatively honest brokers who, in reality, work for the sellers. Our team filled up the left prong: Jim, me, Greg Smith, Wedner, two of his colleagues from Chicago, and three people I didn't know.

"Who are they?" I whispered to Jim.

"Charlie, Bill, and Andrew."

"Who are Charlie, Bill, and Andrew?"

"That's our debt," he whispered back.

Our debt? My mind drifted to an Internet start-up at the time called Lending Tree, an online clearinghouse that allowed consumers to compare mortgages, running omnipresent commercials at the time with the slogan "When banks compete, you win." Apparently, in the buyout world, "you" meant money-losing microsized media companies. These guys, representing a giant Canadian bank, CIBC, and another private equity firm, Oaktree Capital, had won the ability to loan our little band of misfits, backed by the collateral of the combined companies, approximately $90 million. The Canadians would loan the first, safer $60 million (the "senior debt"), and Oaktree would loan an additional $30 million "mezzanine," which was riskier but paid a higher interest rate.

For the debt providers, the standards were even lower than for the investors. They too got a fee for all the money they lent. Generally, 2 percent. And most likely, they didn't even intend to hold on to these loans. Instead, they'd just sell it to a smaller bank, generating yet another fee. Banks didn't make loans in the Zeroes. They traded them. "It didn't mean shit if the bank thought it was a decent credit risk," recalls a private equity executive who spent the decade making several billion dollars' worth of acquisitions. "All that matters is that a guy on the syndication desk says he can sell it, then it got approved."

Like a baseball game, the meeting lasted about three hours, and featured a few bursts of intrigue, as well as long periods of people sitting around, bored, scratching themselves.

Each of the executives droned on about his or her division, and what he or she did. Besides encouraging high bids, they were pitching for their jobs—the new owner would decide who to get rid of, and who to keep, presumably with some ownership stakes as incentive. I spent much of the meeting pondering what an old-school guy like Carl Hess, who hated debt and never allowed mezzanine financing, would think about all this.

Meanwhile, Wedner, armed with the data room information, methodically led the questioning. Jim would occasionally chime in with an incredulous rejoinder, giving Team Phillips a proper taste of the Dunning Treatment. The debt teams asked perhaps one question each, like the Supreme Court justice who throws in a token inquiry from the end of the bench so the newspapers don't make fun of him. (Greg Smith and I stayed largely quiet, passing notes back and forth.)

The wow moment, for us, was when their database guru gave a fascinating introduction to the science of e-mail spamming, including which days and times work best, and how they played off the news. For example, down days on the market might result in a few million e-mails touting a newsletter with defensive strategies for your portfolio. Tellingly, while he could relate to you, in minute terms, the renewal rates on Tuesdays for Louis Navellier's fourth newsletter, no one mentioned how the recommendations performed in aggregate.

After the presentation, our group (minus the debt team, the lowest rung on this totem pole) repaired to Wedner's hotel for lunch. Questions were zooming around the room: What was the real reason they hadn't bothered to try to sell advertising themselves? (The managers had said they liked the idea, but Phillips himself had been against it.) Wasn't Phillips as vulnerable as a TV production company to the salary demands of its stars? (Long-term contracts were key, the team had said.) Who could Doubledown bring in to be the next Louis Navellier? (I had been discussing an energy newsletter with Eric Bolling.)

In the end, Wedner wasn't inclined to move off his low-ball bid. Winking time was over. Scott Peters informed him that while we might not chase it, others would. We were out.

I was mostly relieved. While heady to think about, Phillips was still tangential to our core mission of developing the world's largest database of rich people, profession by profession, using magazines as the entry point. It was a justifiable deal. It just wasn't a good one, especially after hearing the final sale price. In January, a buyout firm called Avista Capital Partners closed the deal for an undisclosed amount that was presumably somewhere near $200 million. The Zeroes buyout frenzy was clearly heading into 2007 unabated.

It wasn't a total loss for us. Marcus Wedner, who had been skeptical when we first met, was now a believer in me, and Doubledown. He wrote a personal check for $175,000 to jump on the investor bandwagon. That was a more significant endorsement in our future than the Phillips offer.

Jim, meanwhile, was dreaming even bigger. He wandered into my office the day the Avista purchase was announced, ready for more action. "Randall," he told me. "We're going to make this into a business of significance." He meant money, not influence.

PART 2

MANIA

(2006–2008)

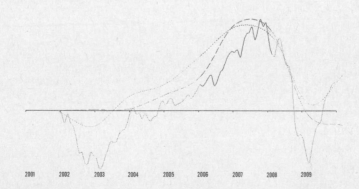

2001   2002   2003   2004   2005   2006   2007   2008   2009

——— S&P GLOBAL 100   ------ WORLDWIDE BONUSES   ——— GLOBAL CDO ISSUANCE

6

We Want Your Money

(Late 2006—Mid-2007)

Let's not beat around the bush.
You're rich.
You know it. We know it. The world knows it.
You also have style and taste.
We're not kissing your ass. It's simply a fact, based on what we
   know about you.
As such, we'd like to request the honour of your presence at a very
   private and exclusive, invitation-only fete.
W Las Vegas Hotel, Casino & Residences
Trader Monthly & CITYrem
Cordially invite you to:
BE THE HOUSE.

The gem above was akin to sending a note to your cousin Tilly saying "You're fat and obnoxious, but because we're family, why not have Thanksgiving dinner with us?" Propriety and tact, however, were in increasingly short supply as the rest of the human race finally awoke to the financial world's windfall. Technically, the invitation's text was correct. Our readers *were* rich. They knew it. We knew it. Increasingly, in part thanks to us, the world knew it. And the world *wasn't* interested in kissing their ass—it just wanted a piece of it.

By 2006, as the financial industry continued borrowing and gouging their way to hundreds of billions of dollars, it was becoming clear that Doubledown Media's best business proposition was helping luxury companies downstream on this cash river. We'd create a gold rush to exploit the gold rush. While our financial advertising had never fully recovered from the Refco implosion, there wasn't a purveyor of something frivolous that didn't find its way to our door, whether racehorse syndicates or special cards good for twenty-five hours of helicopter use. Space Adventures, a "space tourism" company, advertised heavily in search of precisely two customers willing to spend $20 million each to be shot around the dark side of the moon in a Russian spacecraft. They hung a real-life space suit at our parties, a tantalizing promise of the world's ultimate wall trophy.

Morally, I found it a pretty zero-sum role, letting stupid, obscene products fight for a share of stupid, obscene cash. Which is what brought Uri Litvak and Ghazzali Wadood into my life. They were an odd pair. Uri was tall and Ghazzali was short. Uri was pale and Ghazzali was dark. Uri was the serious lawyer and Ghazzali was the gregarious salesman. While it seemed like a good vaudeville act in the making, the Uri and Ghazzali Show was exclusively about luxury condominiums.

They ran a little company called CITYrem—the "rem" stood for "real estate marketing"—and since our launch they had been monitoring Doubledown. In the spring of 2006 they cryptically mentioned a "great project" to finally work together on, and when they trekked into our offices, they started the meeting with two powerful words: *Las Vegas*.

The same river of debt that had been juicing private equity and hedge funds, and prompting turf wars over lending $90 million to an unprofitable $4 million company, had also been transforming Sin City. As we heard out Uri and Ghazzali, $30 billion worth of buildings were going up in Vegas. Over the previous five years, people had been visiting more (up 13 percent), gambling bigger (up 53 percent), and filling every single hotel room on the Strip (room rates surged 74 percent, accordingly). John McCain wasn't a risk-seeking craps addict. He was the American mainstream.

Developers had even taken to throwing up condos with names like Turnberry and the Cosmopolitan, second homes for people who preferred a box looking over exploding volcanoes to a beach house. They all advertised in *Trader Monthly*, of course, buying pages that interspersed pictures of their generic-looking towers with a come-hither woman lying on the couch or carpet.

But those were Mickey Mouse projects compared with the proposition Ghazzali slid across my desk: the W Hotel, Casino and Residences, a three-thousand-room, $2.5 billion monstrosity located just off the Strip. Leveraging stylish minimalism and dark, trendy restaurants, the W had grown from a single hotel in New York in 1999 to twenty hotels from Mexico City to the Maldives by 2006. Vegas was next on their hit list, but rather than hewing to the quaint idea of building a hotel to, you know, rent rooms, the W would instead sell *condominiums*, available on a nightly basis when the owner wasn't using them. Why just be a hotel when you can be a real estate developer, using Other People's Money?

The only thing missing was a few hundred people ready to plunk down $650,000 for a one-room Vegas crash pad. Not unlike mortgage loans that were being repackaged and resold a dozen times by Wall Street, with every layer taking a fee, the W had hired a Las Vegas sales specialist, the Edge Group, to move the condo units, who in turn brought in Uri and Ghazzali, who in turn brought in us. Our deal: CITYrem would spring for lavish parties to introduce the W Las Vegas to *Trader Monthly* readers, buy a slew of advertising from us to promote it, and pay us an additional $5,000 finder's fee for everyone who coughed up. All we had to do was bring out the traders. In London.

Their venue choice struck me as moronic. We could deliver the audience—our London readers remained amazingly engaged with

the magazine. But distance-wise, it was like selling New York traders a pied-à-terre in Warsaw. And the W brand meant nothing in
Europe.

Their counterargument was the exchange rate. As hip-hop mogul
Damon Dash had posited as *Trader Monthly*'s first "Celebrity Trader"
two years earlier, the British pound "weighed more" than the once-
mighty dollar—almost twice as much by 2006. Currency speculators
had methodically pummeled the greenback as the Federal Reserve
pumped out cheap money to any financial institution trigger-
happy enough to reloan it, effectively rendering the United States
a continent-wide half-off sale for Brits. With the great American
real estate bubble hyperventilating into its fifth year, it was pounds
and euros and dinar—about one-third of all condos in Manhattan in
2006 and 2007 were sold to foreigners—extending the party.

Fissures in the partnership erupted immediately. First, there was
that cringe-inducing invitation language, submitted to us for approval. (Every invitation to our readers came through us, so that we
always retained a modicum of control over our audience, and the
message to it.) It broke the compact we had established with the financial community. Yes, our readers were filthy rich, or on their way
there. We could show it, or joke about it, or wink at it. But we never
just came out and said it. That was understood. I took my editor's
pen to their thirteen-line paean to gauche and replaced it with eleven
words: "Ever wonder what it would be like to 'be the house'?"

Unfortunately, I couldn't edit their expectations. "So what do you
think, ten percent, twenty percent?" Ghazzali would ask at almost
every meeting, delirious with gold fever, in terms of how many party
attendees would whip out their credit cards and buy a condo halfway
around the world. I kept trying to temper his expectations—sell two
condos, I consistently reminded him, and the program pays for itself.

The party was at London's trendy Penthouse Club, a reference to
the amazing view rather than any affiliation with the Candyman's
$10,000 proper night out. We rented out the sixth-floor "members'
lounge," which looked out over Leicester Square, seemingly across
the entirety of Britain's low-rise capital, as if it had all been built a
story shorter for our convenience. The room fit the W's sleek image:

white couches, columns, and booths, starkly offset by black tables and a stainless steel bar.

That bar was three deep with traders, two hundred in all, availing themselves of the W's free-flowing Champagne. Many had brought dates, as if they were going to a Vegas show, which is pretty close to what they actually got. There were burlesque performances, show-girls and several pretty brokers who could have been part of the team of seven from the W that had flown in from the States, trying to flirt their way to a sale.

I had arrived in London a few hours earlier. Stretched out across my flying Eos suite (my semiannual seven-hour taste of the trader lifestyle), I previewed the W's presentation. It ran thirty-five minutes. Five minutes on Vegas, Chamber of Commerce–style. Ten minutes on the W brand. And then twenty minutes to sell the condos.

I was aghast. We had been counting on, and advising, a soft sell. Show them a good time, make connections, and then tease them with an opportunity to buy into something exclusive and fun that generated income. Instead, what was planned was something right out of *Glengarry Glen Ross*: a canned, multislide hammer. Arriving at the Penthouse early, Magnus had already jumped up and down about this, but this was no longer our party. *Do you know how much this is costing us?* I was asked. *Sixty-three thousand dollars!* They were going to sell real estate, whether these rich traders wanted it or not.

With his understated eyeglasses and pleasant smile, Philip Fried-man, the lead salesman on the project, didn't look like a shark. Perhaps for that reason, armed with the kind of microphone headpiece you saw at the booths of large trade shows, he led the presentation. First, he introduced the W team, to a round of polite British applause— the payoff for an open bar and passed hors d'oeuvres. Magnus, the world's most famous trader, was introduced to a rousing cheer.

Then, without warning, came the PowerPoint, and suddenly the hosts' Champagne turned against them. As Friedman plowed through the Chamber of Commerce part—*Did you know that five thousand people a month are moving to Vegas?*—the formerly jovial crowd instinctively morphed into one organism, mob-rule-style. At first, the collective will was to ignore. People began turning away, resuming conversations with one another, or heading to the bar for more bubbly.

The presentation droned on—*the W brand is part of the Starwood family*—and the cold shoulder got more aggressive, the din of other conversations becoming as loud and unruly as third-grade recess. *Sit down!* barked one heckler.

So Friedman pulled out his trump card: *All of you who put down your completely refundable security deposit by tomorrow, and take advantage of the $100,000 price break we're already giving* Trader Monthly *readers,* he said, holding up a small black disk, *will get this $10,000 casino chip, which you can use upon closing.*

A coupon! The most market-savvy room in Europe that night was now enduring selling tactics straight out of a television infomercial (*call right now and we'll double your order!*).

At this point, the organism went into full tar-and-feather revolt. Even Friedman sensed this. You could see him almost give up, the censor button necessary for a salesman turning off. As his original invitation text had said, *Let's not beat around the bush.* And so he didn't. Friedman's first unscripted line came out so loudly and sincerely that it momentarily silenced the crowd.

"WE . . . WANT . . . YOUR . . . MONEY!"

We want your money?! Magnus and I were on opposite ends of the room, but our eyes instantly met, as if we both needed to verify what we'd just heard. So rude, so stereotypically ugly American . . . so blatantly true. Just as the financial industry was pillaging the world, marketers in the Zeroes viewed the financial industry as something to exploit. Friedman, looking wild-eyed, quickly stepped down from the stage.

"Buddy," Magnus said as he leaned toward me, after coming across the room, "I want to crawl into a ball and die." Of the 200 traders there, Magnus knew 50 and the other 150 knew him. His good name had now been commingled with a used-car pitch.

The traders, happily ensconced in the club with the World Cup playing overhead, were in no rush to leave until they had consumed every last drop of the offender's Champagne. Once it was gone, so were they, departing with gift bags full of Bliss Spa products—the

W planned to have a branch of it in Las Vegas—and reminders to make an appointment the next day to put down their six-figure deposits and claim their $10,000 chip. Uri and Ghazzali had secured a fleet of meeting rooms at the sculpture-filled Cumberland Hotel in Marble Arch, so the W's team of seven could divide and conquer the anticipated throngs of check-toting traders.

No one showed, from either this or a smaller London event that same week. Uri and Ghazzali wound up stiffing us for $17,849 worth of advertising. "Unfortunately," Ghazzali e-mailed months later, "we have been going through some financial turbulence." The W Las Vegas was never built.

$ $ $

When *Trader Monthly* first launched, the breathtaking wealth we unveiled was hard for most outside observers to fathom. They chalked up the huge figures to onetime aberrations, or confused it with net worth. But after a couple years, it dawned on people, luxury marketers like the W among them, that our audience was making these numbers *every year*, the hauls snowballing thanks to the perpetual fresh powder of the 2-and-20 compensation system.

The 2-and-20 snowball unleashed a powerful trickle-down effect among Wall Street's middle class. Specifically, it took the single most powerful word in the financial world and made it an obsession—the one word that generated more frivolous discussions and reckless decisions than any other. The almighty *bonus*.

As Wall Street's scorekeeper, tracking bonuses was a year-round exercise for us. Beginning early every summer we started getting initial dispatches from the field, much like the staff at the Department of Agriculture gets crop reports. *Goldman is accruing at 52 percent through the first half! Fixed income at Lehman making a killing! Prop desk at Credit Suisse got crushed!* We even had government agencies feeding us data: the richest city in the richest nation on earth had become so dependent on Wall Street bonuses—20 percent of its GDP—that the New York State comptroller's office, wary of tax shortfalls, issued periodic forecasts.

Like a presidential election, steady summer-long interest among our readers kicked into full-blown obsession beginning on Labor Day, continuing unabated through November. Each bank and fund followed a slightly different schedule, but by December, pretty much everyone had been told their Number. The checks then arrived in February or March, coinciding with our magazines' Bonus Issues, which chronicled who got what.

It all seemed so ingrained and regimented, despite the fact that Wall Street bonuses were a recent phenomenon. Until 1971, almost every single major bank was a private partnership. At the end of the year, the partners simply divided the profits between themselves; the vast majority of employees got regular paychecks like schoolteachers and firemen and other normal working people.

But then the big banks, save Goldman, went public, and the markets began ruling the market-makers, demanding consistent bottom-line performance. Power shifted to employees delivering alpha, and bonuses became standard, both as an incentive and as a retention device—most famously, Michael Milken's $550 million Drexel Burnham windfall in 1987, a number so out of whack that it took almost two decades, and Stevie Cohen, to top it. In 2000, a new overall bonus record was set—in New York State alone, $19.5 billion was divvied up. The ensuing recession, timed with 9/11, decimated financial compensation right up until 2004, when *Trader Monthly* unknowingly launched into the golden age of the bonus. Bonuses were up 15 percent in 2004, another 20 percent in 2005, and 17 percent in 2006. By 2007, Goldman Sachs alone was carving up more—$20 billion—than all of New York had at the beginning of the decade. The worldwide take was into the hundreds of billions.

Each year, I studied our figures before we published them, knowing they would be scrutinized like the Dead Sea Scrolls. Thanks to data from an industry headhunter, the Options Group, we precisely detailed the compensation for tens of thousands of financial professionals, down to job title and specialization. They were awe-inspiring, not for the nauseating heights achieved by the *Trader Monthly* 100, but rather for the breadth of the Wall Street money grab.

As an example, in January 2007 I stared at our chart denoting the average 2006 pay for bank traders specializing in mortgage-backed securities—the increasingly perilous practice of buying and selling the rights to people's home loans after they've been neatly packaged and bundled together. A typical vice president (four years' experience) earned himself a $100,000 salary, and a $450,000 bonus. (For comparison, the vice president of the United States, Dick Cheney, took home a $208,100 salary, no bonus.) A director (seven years' experience) took a salary of $125,000, and a bonus of $1.3 million. A managing director (just a veteran, despite the bosslike title) drew a $175,000 salary—and a $2.5 million bonus. And the desk's *real* boss, the "head," pushed close to $10 million in bonus payout.

It was dumbfounding: dime-a-dozen seven-figure earners, and twenty-six-year-olds pulling a half-million-dollar bonus? Worse, *indignant* twenty-six-year-olds. The financial industry doesn't produce anything physical—the product walks out the door each night at 5 p.m.—so while normal companies might spend 5 or 10 percent of revenue on compensation, the financial industry spends about 50 percent. That latter ratio mimics professional sports (they're both in the talent business, after all), except on Wall Street, everyone's pretty much a free agent *every* year.

Since no one left before the bonus check cleared, the herd migrated, en masse, every March. Thousands enjoyed Wall Street's spring ritual "garden leave," where the firm you just quit pays you to do nothing for ninety days, reducing your ability to steal away employees and clients at your new gig. Thousands more stayed put, renegotiating their roles, including those arrogant twenty-six-year-olds. Alpha was king. Revenue was surging. And bonuses spiraled ever upward.

But it was wrong to dwell on the totals. The real insanity in those 2006 numbers was *how* bonuses got paid—80 or 90 percent of total compensation in one giant year-end check. It was those checks that created the gold fever, dictating every portion of the recipients' lives, from where they lived ("A lot of my Wall Streeters have been pounding the pavement anticipating the bonuses," Louise Phillips Forbes of Halstead Property told the Associated Press in December 2006; "They're prepared to pay a tremendous amount of money") to whom they lived with (many strategically timed separations and divorces, depending on the size and arrival date of their bonus checks).

It was the uncertainty—a "bonus," by definition, is discretionary—that drove much of the paranoia. For those on the lower rungs, each bank and fund had compensation committees that divided the loot by group based on how the firm did overall, and how much each unit contributed to it, and then the head of each desk, like a Mafia boss, divided the spoils among his crew, based on individual performance and other intangibles. "I have some guys who work for me," says one manager, who oversees the bonuses of several dozen traders, "who I take $50,000 from just because I think they're a dick."

So much money. All in one check. All dependent on how much you make managing Other People's Money. It was a warped system that could corrupt even good people. "If I'm going to get paid zero," a money manager told me about his autumn mind-set during down years, "I might as well take some risk and try to make some money."

Wall Street was no longer aligned with those who put the money in its care. We'd see that dynamic play out at the end of the year, especially among the traders, as they frantically adjusted their portfolios. Those who were already up, particularly at hedge funds, began passing on good opportunities for their investors, content to run out the clock. If you were down, however, you'd leverage to the hilt. The only risk to your bonus was not taking risk.

In essence, long-term performance was irrelevant. Bonuses centered on the year at hand, and if that meant buying or selling junk that would explode later, that wasn't really an issue. "All you worried about was whether you could sell it," says one Wall Street sales executive. Wall Street's musical chairs meant you'd be at another firm, or somewhere else in your current firm, when the song stopped. Other People's Money met Someone Else's Problem. It was the world's largest game of Kick the Can.

In the fall of 2006, we began hearing about some particularly frantic maneuvering among two of the youngest members of the *Trader Monthly* 100. The first one we were told about, Brian Hunter, was as bonus paranoid as they got. The son of a concrete pourer in Canada's energy belt, Alberta, he studied physics and then moved just before 9/11 to New York to trade natural gas for Deutsche Bank in New York. He made the bank tens of millions in 2002, but his gains for 2003 eroded when his desk lost $51.2 million right before Christmas. Deutsche denied Hunter a bonus. He sued, lost, and left.

He wound up at a $9 billion hedge fund called Amaranth Advisors, which allowed him to set up his own operation in his hometown, Calgary. As with Deutsche Bank, his first full year was a blockbuster. He bet big that natural gas prices were going up, and as with Braveheart before him, the suffering of others—Hurricanes Katrina and Rita, which crippled Gulf of Mexico rigs—earned him a fortune. (Federal regulators later accused him of fixing prices; the firm paid a $7.5 million fine.) Amaranth made $1 billion; Hunter got nearly $100 million as a bonus, and a place on the *Trader Monthly* 100, the first time he had ever been written about.

Trying to replicate that performance entering the fall of 2006, he made the same enormous bet that natural gas prices would rise. But there were no hurricanes this Labor Day. Prices plummeted. If it were his own money, he would have presumably cut his losses. Instead, Hunter bet more.

On the other side of the trade was his doppelgänger, John Arnold, who ran a Houston-based hedge fund called Centaurus. He too was thirty-two, with blond hair, though Hunter's was curly and Arnold's straight. He too had had a bad experience with a former employer (he had been one of the trading whiz kids at Enron, before it melted down in the decade's first big financial scandal). He too had made $100 million the previous year, earning a precocious place on the *Trader Monthly* 100. He too was partial to natural gas trading, the infamously volatile "widowmaker."

There was only one immediate difference between them: Arnold thought prices would fall. As Hunter bet billions trying to force the market up, Arnold bet billions driving it down. In the end, Hunter blew his bonus and killed his firm. Amaranth lost $6.6 billion on Hunter's natural gas trades and had to shut its doors in one of the greatest wipeouts in financial history.

Much of that money went straight into Arnold's pocket, almost

$2 billion, to be specific. Not yet thirty-three, he supplanted Stevie Cohen atop the *Trader Monthly* 100. "You ask a big CEO what he makes, and it's a huge number, but it's all tied up in stock and options," gushed his lieutenant, Bill Perkins, when our chief trading sleuth, Rich Blake, called for details. "Traders get paid in cash. It's liquid. It's real. You can go, 'Here, look,' and slap someone across the face with it."

Hunter, meanwhile, faced no repercussions for the destruction he wrought. He quickly raised almost $1 billion to start again, this time as his own hedge fund, positioning himself in 2007 for yet more bonus riches using Other People's Money. The gold rush continued unabated.

$ $ $

Henry Hill, my addled buddy of *Goodfellas* fame, swore to the veracity of the scene wherein Robert De Niro, to the guitar solo of "Layla," kills his co-conspirators from their Lufthansa heist after they ostentatiously began buying cars and furs. Even faced with a police microscope and a boss's death threat, these wiseguys couldn't help themselves. Windfalls do that to people. I thought about that when a spy in Stevie Cohen's shop called in with a tip: the day after the bonus checks arrived, SAC Capital's Stamford, Connecticut, parking lot was filled with three Ferraris and no fewer than a dozen Bentleys.

Few trading outfits were more disciplined than Cohen's. He even had a rule that wasn't named for Brian Hunter, but should have been: if any position dropped precipitously, you automatically bailed, no matter how convinced you might be that it would come back. But it just wasn't human nature to ignore that once-a-year massive check.

We branded this phenomenon to the outside world as *Bonus Season!* in the same manner as other manufactured shopping holidays, like Back to School and Black Friday. Except that rather than new blue jeans and Sony PlayStations, our readers gobbled up cars, watches, and booze. As Bonus Season approached, the financial elite's knowledge of the latest and greatest in luxury mirrored a ten-year-old's post-Thanksgiving familiarity with the toy catalog. Christmas on

Wall Street came just a little bit later than it did for the rest of the world. And it was a lot more expensive.

We began polling traders on their Santa wish lists. In the same *Trader Monthly* issue chronicling the earning habits of mortgage traders, we learned about the thirst for $385 Macallan Sherry Oak, aged for twenty-five years in casks from Jerez until it smacked of dried fruit; $15,000-a-night vacations at the St. Regis in Bora Bora, a six-month-old resort with 13,000-square-foot suites built over a turquoise lagoon and room service from Jean-Georges Vongerichten; the new Ferrari 599 GTB Fiorano, a 611-horsepower beauty tricked out with a gearbox and traction control from Formula One race cars, which at $300,000, we deemed "almost something of a bargain."

Advertisers flocked to our Bonus Issues, but they almost universally exhibited the same tone-deafness as the W Las Vegas. One of New York's most luxurious new condo developments was going up directly across the street from my apartment. It was called, simply, The Prime, as if an apartment were a choice cut of steak. From the table in the area that triple-served as our dining room, a storage unit, and my home office, I watched it slowly rise, tall and thin, effectively giving me the finger. As I sat in my mouse-infested apartment, paying almost $4,000 a month for the privilege, my audience would get a beer out of the Sub-Zero and literally look down on me. For the Bonus Issue, The Prime amended its regular advertising with a message scrawled in thick black-marker letters designed to look like an informal trader-to-trader memo. *"J, just got my bonus. This place looks awesome. Let's check it out ASAP. See ya, D."* Awful.

Financial types discussed bonuses with each other incessantly, but for outsiders, I had learned, it was bad etiquette to bring it up, the same way only Jews can make Jewish jokes. So our bonus-centric parties celebrated the "Deals of the Year," or the "Trader Monthly Awards," using celebrating success as the proxy for avarice. Semantics aside, by Bonus Season 2007 we had finally perfected the riddle of efficiently connecting the money with the toys.

The answer had been inspired by something called a Maybach. Knowing how to pronounce it—*my*-bach, as in *my* money—signaled that you could afford it, and while many called it a private jet on wheels, that comparison would do a disservice to the Maybach. The 2006 edition of the Maybach 57S was three tons and came with a 612-horsepower V12 engine, seats made from the hides of twelve bulls, and heating, cooling, and massage treatment for all passengers. Tellingly, none of the new Bentleys or Ferraris at SAC Capital had belonged to Stevie Cohen himself. He had custom-ordered a new Maybach.

Similarly, we had custom-ordered the crowd that showed up at the Mercedes showroom on Park Avenue in Manhattan for the Trader Monthly Awards party in January, the fertile period when you knew your Number but hadn't yet received the hard check. We filtered our database geographically, inviting people in the New York area, and then sorted by title: managing directors or higher at a bank and portfolio manager or higher at a fund. That elegantly filled the room with people old enough to prefer comfort over speed, and rich enough to afford it.

Hundreds of men with salt-and-pepper hair put down the tuna sashimi floating around to run their hands over the nubuck leather, buffed until velvety, as they watched the honorees lift up their award, a Steuben glass sculpture called "Torch of Strength," that looked like a translucent swirl of custard. CNBC sent a camera crew, in part to recognize Eric Bolling, our Maybach "Man of the Year." We gave him the honor for three reasons. He'd had another monster year in the energy markets. He was developing into a superstar on CNBC. And we could count on him to show up.

Mercedes was happy, and we experienced an epiphany. Rather than big, random bashes, we began using our increasingly robust mailing list for targeted events. And the more exclusive we made them, the more desirable they became. A party for six hundred Wall Street women at Le Cirque drew a line a block long. Dusting off my sommelier degree, I started a Wall Street Wine Club, where traders and dealmakers paid $200 for exclusive tastings with winemakers. Then came a Wall Street Watch Club, for those who wanted to meet timepiece-makers. A party of Wall Street car buffs for the new BMW 7 Series resulted in four sales. My role changed accordingly. We were becoming a database with a magazine attached, rather than a magazine that happened to develop a database. Less of my time was spent concocting stories, and more time was spent concocting parties. "On Wall Street, a perk is a many splendored thing," wrote Jon Friedman, MarketWatch's well-read media columnist, in 2007. "When your employer springs for a Bloomberg terminal, you know you've arrived. And an invitation to one of *Trader Monthly*'s noisy, well-attended parties in Manhattan has become increasingly coveted, too."

Our two hottest tickets, by far, remained the ones focused on the young guns of Wall Street. In 2007, the *Dealmaker* 40 Under 40 attracted seven hundred people who packed into the Phillips de Pury auction house. Two $7,000 Carl F. Bucherer watches were sold right off the models showcasing them. But that still paled next to the *Trader* 30 Under 30, which had emerged as an annual celebration of youth and affluence. We decided to have three parties, with Magnus traveling to all of them like a global ambassador. In Chicago, three hundred traders crammed into Rockit, a bar in the trendy River North neighborhood; then London, at the Wardour Soho. And the flagship event in New York took place at Gold Street, a Wall Street bar with an outdoor patio allowing for a fleet of BMWs and a cigar tent.

Given the previous year's bacchanal, the New York invitation list closed early. Those left out lobbied furiously to get in. Confirmed RSVPs showed up for sale on Craigslist. None proved more frantic than our old friend Tim Sykes, who had leveraged his spot on the previous 30 Under 30 into a reality television gig as trading's designated jackass. Sykes had placed me on his e-mail list, and I watched his fund melt away month after month, charging investors 3-and-30 for the privilege, while he drunkenly dove into golf course lakes for the TV cameras and decided, at twenty-four, to write his autobiography, which he self-published. We had created this guy. It was embarrassing.

I was in Miami calling on advertisers in the days before our New York 30 Under 30 when our communications chief, Rachel Pine, began calling furiously. Sykes wanted to attend, a camera crew in tow, and attempt to rebuild some of his credibility at the expense of ours. Once she heard about the cameras, we decided to ban him. He in turn went into obsessive mode, bombarding her with e-mails and phone calls. And then me.

> Randall—
>   Just got off the phone with Rachel and
> she said I am no longer welcome at the '30
> under 30' party tomorrow night because 'I
> made a mockery' of the list last year. Even
> though I've definitely gone my own way, I
> definitely don't think that's the case as
> thanks to the popularity of my TV show, I've
> gotten thousands of emails from people who
> have been inspired by my story . . . I'd love
> to attend the party tomorrow night as I have
> already invited about a dozen trader friends
> and friends in the media to toast this year's
> newest members!

Ignore him, I figured, and he'll go away. Then came the voicemail bombardment. One, two, three, four, five messages. Looking for a backdoor entrance, he then began harassing the 30 Under 30's editor, Rich Blake, before returning to me via e-mail.

> Randall—
>   Rich emailed me saying you're holding firm
> that you don't want me there tomorrow night,
> but let me just try to change your mind
> because this last minute notification that I'm
> disinvited has put me in a jam. . . . I made
> plans to meet up with nearly a dozen friends.
> Some of these people I haven't seen in a very
> long time and we've been talking all weekend
> about what we'll do after the party. . . .
> I invited 2 female friends who went out and
> bought new dresses for this event. I don't
> know how to explain it to them that I can't

```
attend with them. . . . While you guys seem
to think 'I've made a mockery of the list'
with my eccentric behavior, other media
outlets now recognize me as a finance expert/
personality. . . . You guys took a pretty good
shot at me in this latest issue so even if you
really believe I somehow embarrassed you last
year, I consider us even.
```

The barrage continued unabated. E-mails, voicemails, phone calls; Rich Blake, Rachel Pine, me. Although I could only remember meeting him once, for five minutes, as he begged for inclusion in the 30 Under 30, it was clear that ignoring him begged more cross-company stalking. So I whipped out my BlackBerry and thumbed off a scolding, private response.

```
Tim,
    Acclaim comes with performance. While you've
been busily self-promoting, your track record
this past year for yourself and your investors
has been pitiful. Laughably horrid. If you
ever again become a real trader, rather than
ignore the hard work required and instead play
one on tv, you'll be welcome in our community.
Until then, including today, we will have
nothing to do with you, as we celebrate those
who actually perform versus those who pretend
to.
```

Sykes responded nineteen minutes later.

```
Thank you for your honesty, but I wish you
had read the book I sent you guys. you would
discover that ALL MY LOSSES have been caused
not by trading, but because I entered into an
illiquid stock that I have not been able to
```

```
sell. I am unable to raise any money, unable
to take any trading risk so all I can do is
take advantage of my publicity efforts and
turn that into my new career. I am a trader in
the truest sense in that I am willing to trade
professions to adapt to my environment.
```

Finally, that was that. I flew back to New York that morning, and the party came off without a hitch, eight hundred or so of the young and well-bonused drinking in Johnnie Walker Blue, some from bottles upon which their name was engraved.

But then the following day, I got an extended version of what follows:

```
Now that I've had a little time to calm
down and reflect, here is my response: You
should be ashamed of yourself for writing
such a spiteful email to me. As you sip
your overpriced champagne on your oversized
yacht (courtesy of your advertisers), I've
been working 20-hour days trying to claw my
way out of the hole I find myself in while
also nurturing a budding career in financial
journalism.

    Perhaps if you'd done a better job as
editor-in-chief of a magazine that purportedly
reports on the lives of traders, the public
wouldn't be so overwhelmingly lost, and I
could've gone on quietly managing my tiny
fund. But as it is, people are turning to me
because they see that I'm a person who tells
it like it is. So, no, I will not ignore
them. . . . I don't blame you personally—
you're merely a byproduct of your generation
and the Wall Street establishment, an
establishment I aim to change.
```

        Now, as you say, my fund's performance has
    been 'laughably horrid' and I am wiser for
    it. Instead of curling up in a shell as you
    apparently believe would be appropriate, I
    will use my self-promotional skills to the
    fullest . . . I've outgrown your juvenile
    ways. When you turn your back on a fellow
    trader, you turn your back on trading itself.
    And when you turn on trading, you no longer
    are worthy of running a magazine called
    'Trader Monthly.' Perhaps you should change
    the title to a more fitting description,
    'Traitor Monthly.'

"Wow—he might be certifiable," Rachel wrote to me when she saw this. "I had no idea he was actually such a sick person." Still, I was convinced we had *finally* severed ourselves from our most embarrassing by-product.

But then I got a call from a reporter from the highly influential Page Six section of the *New York Post*, wanting to know why I had banned Sykes from the party. The reporter quoted Sykes's letter, which I found odd since he had only sent it to me. Who leaked it? And who cared about Tim Sykes? Then it became fairly clear from the reporter who the source was—Sykes himself. His letter to me was just another press release.

The next day's gossip page announced that "a Wall Street war has erupted between influential *Trader Monthly* magazine and boisterous money manager Timothy Sykes." Meanwhile, Sykes had apparently spent the previous day priming financial blogs for the Page Six story. Hours wasted while his tiny fund continued to sputter.

Two weeks later, Sykes shut it down. He posted losses between January 2006 and July 2007 of more than 36 percent, while the overall market was up 25 percent.

Sykes announced the news, appropriately, in the form of a press release, citing not the hundreds of thousands of dollars he had lost for his investors, but rather, one of the very few regulations hedge funds faced—not being able to market to nonaccredited investors, little old ladies and the like. His hedge fund was crimping his media style. "No longer will I play by these misguided rules. I should be free to discuss my business, for I am an American entrepreneur. I call this freedom of finance." The bonus train would roll on without Tim Sykes, who would be stuck trying to extract his payment in the form of notoriety.

$ $ $

As the calendar turned from 2006 to 2007, those actually delivering alpha and pulling in obscene bonuses were attracting public attention. Not from the pitchfork-wielding mobs. That would come later. No, those pulling in seven to ten digits on Wall Street were acquiring another persona: pop culture hero.

The biggest movie in America the week before Christmas was *The Pursuit of Happyness*. The movie told the true story of Chris Gardner, played by the svelte Will Smith, but in reality an imposing bald man with a baritone voice who graced the cover of the concurrent issue of *Trader Monthly*. His rags-to-riches tale started with him as a homeless father and proceeded all the way to the classic Hollywood ending: he had become a trading tycoon. By the end of January, almost 20 million people had gone to see it.

At that same time, we were contacted by VH1, the cable network for those too old for MTV. One of their biggest hits at the time was a show called *The Fabulous Life*. It was an update on *Lifestyles of the Rich and Famous*, with typical episodes going inside the lives of Jennifer Lopez or Oprah. Their next goal: *The Fabulous Life Presents Wall Street's Billion Dollar Ballers*. Would we help them put it together?

Ever protective of our role as the nexus between the media and Wall Street, *of course we would*. They basically turned our magazines— the people, the numbers, the pictures—into a one-hour TV show. "Think stars are having all the fun?" intoned the narrator, in an intentionally corny British accent, at the show's beginning. "Ah, no . . . These days nobody is making more and spending more than

the buttoned-down bad-asses of Wall Street." Our editors and colum-
nists helped serve as the on-camera tour guides, while the channel's
viewers, accustomed to some of the network's usual fare, including
Behind the Music and *Flavor of Love*, a dating show involving over-the-
hill Public Enemy rapper Flavor Flav, gaped at Stevie Cohen's private
ice rink, Paul Tudor Jones's Greenwich mansion, and John Devaney,
his plane and helicopter behind him, smiling on our cover. Much of
the episode's focus: the "mind-boggling" bonuses.

One of *The Fabulous Life*'s breakout stars was Steve Schwarzman.
The directors cut to 740 Park Avenue, using special effects to make
the windows of Schwarzman's triplex glow as if magically blessed by
an Incan god. They failed to note that the building was known as the
"the world's richest apartment building" (Jackie O. grew up there)
or that Schwarzman's apartment had once been occupied by John D.
Rockefeller, Jr. But they got the gist: Schwarzman had paid $37 mil-
lion in 2000 for the thirty-five-room palace in the sky. "Steve likes
his square footage," the narrator gushed. Then came a dissection of
his $20 million Palm Beach winter home, "Four Winds," a landmark
owned by E. F. Hutton that Schwarzman had dismantled brick by
brick and then rebuilt—with a large expansion.

The thing was, it felt appropriate to help introduce Schwarzman
to the VH1 audience. As I had seen at the Four Seasons a few months
earlier, he was embracing the limelight. The signature social event of
the Zeroes, Wall Street or otherwise, took place the day before Valentine's Day, 2007: Schwarzman's sixtieth birthday. Limos lined up
for more than a block outside the Park Avenue Armory to discharge
their guests, as the paparazzi jostled under the snowy sky for position. Police had to push them back and install barricades as the likes
of Barbara Walters, Sir Howard Stringer, the heads of most investment banks and stock exchanges, the former governor of New York,
the current governor of New Jersey, and the most important man in
American Catholicism, Cardinal Edward Egan, queued up to kiss
Schwarzman's ring.

The armory's inside had been designed to mimic the Schwarzmans'
mega-sized apartment, down to replica paintings. The comedian
Martin Short roasted Schwarzman, Patti LaBelle sang a special song

with him, and then came a concert from Rod Stewart, as guests ate filet mignon and lobster. It was the kind of party we would aspire to throw, except that we would have tried to do it for free, leveraging sponsors, while Schwarzman just wrote checks for $3 million (including a cool $1 million for Stewart).

There was a huge backlash. Even in good times, filled with grand parties, throwing a bash like that *for yourself* seemed a new level of waste and narcissism. Rich, famous, and notorious, Schwarzman was the John Dillinger of his day.

From where I stood, the negative attention didn't faze Schwarzman a bit. Four months later, Jim wrangled invitations for Magnus and me to a party celebrating Qatar Airways' new service to New York. A pimple on the Persian Gulf, Qatar was trying to offset its lack of oil with banking and trading, and this new direct connection to the United States, less than six years after 9/11, was symbolic. So the airline spent the way Schwarzman did, renting out the soaring Jazz at Lincoln Center space at the Time Warner Center, and inviting about five hundred guests, who cleaved into two lines as they entered. The merely rich or connected were funneled straight into the receiving area, where bowls of caviar and bottles of Dom Pérignon awaited. The famous were shunted toward the left, where they walked over a red carpet set up for the benefit of the bank of photographers. In came Donald and Melania Trump. Chloë Sevigny and Andie MacDowell. Julianne Moore. Maggie Gyllenhaal and her husband, Peter Sarsgaard. Then the paparazzi scrambled again. Another celebrity was en route. Another couple. They were: *Steve and Christine Schwarzman!* The flashbulbs burst. Steve Schwarzman, king of private equity, poster child of decadence, was now certifiably paparazzi-worthy.

The famous guests were eventually discharged into the party's general population, milling in a cocktail area, and as Schwarzman made his way past us, Jim grabbed his wrist. We all talked shop for a few minutes. Since our quick introduction at the Four Seasons, *Dealmaker* had emerged as a force and I pressed. "We'd love to sit down with you," I said. Schwarzman, for his part, reacted diffidently. "I'll consider it." He looked bored, and soon excused himself to search for bigger social prey.

He found it as we all wandered into the performance hall, structured like a wedding cake, with five tiers of dinner seating rising up from the stage. Large circular tables filled each level. Jim sat at stage level. Magnus and I were on the fourth level, mostly with TV producers and other media friendlies. Directly below us, to my surprise, the Schwarzmans sat next to the Trumps for an ego-friendly double date.

Not unlike the W Hotel pitch, everyone from Schwarzman and Trump to Magnus and I had to pay for their attendance with their attention, as Qatar Airways CEO Akbar Al Baker, dressed in a blue pinstripe suit one size too big, droned on for twenty minutes in mediocre English about his airline and its unfathomable spending spree: he had just ordered eighty brand-new Airbus 350s (for $16 billion) and, one-upping Eos and other first-class airlines, built an entire first-and-business-class *terminal*, where massages and saunas greeted fliers from the moment they hit the curb.

We all remained respectful, especially because of the special guest he was promising.

A large band wandered onstage, and from behind a curtain, we began to hear the payoff. . . . *I'm . . . I'm coming . . . out . . .* and sprinting out, in a revealing leopard-patterned dress, came Diana Ross herself, to give a concert to five hundred lucky souls.

For ninety minutes, Ross belted out hits as the Dom Pérignon flowed and even the most jaded in attendance looked at each other giddily, heads bobbing, feet tapping. Magnus and I looked down to see one guy up from the table, dancing extra-effusively. There was Steve Schwarzman, awkwardly doing the white guy jig, a baby boomer less than forty feet from the siren of his youth, brashly dancing when no one else would.

As the night wound down, models dressed as Qatar Airways flight attendants lined up outside the hall, holding large silver trays stacked tall with gold and silver rectangular boxes, as if Fort Knox had just been raided. Party favors, in the form of 2007's ultimate must-have gadget: an iPod. The previous century's biggest female singer, now private entertainment, closed with "Ain't No Mountain High Enough," framed perfectly in the giant window behind her by Columbus Circle, the eye-level statue of Christopher Columbus, atop the obelisk at the circle's middle, looking away, as if embarrassed by the spectacle.

7

The Blank Check (2007)

To understand 2007, and the year the deal world—the entire world, actually—drove off a cliff, we first need to start with a quick story about John Travolta, John Travolta's hair, and me.

That unlikely convergence was set in motion during the second week of January, when Doubledown acquired our third magazine: *Private Air*. While there was some overlap with our other two audiences—John Devaney, for example, was reportedly the youngest person ever to buy a Gulfstream IV—this magazine, delivered to anyone who owned a plane or flew privately, gave us an entirely new swath of rich guys to plumb: business moguls, trust fund heirs, and Hollywood big shots, including Travolta, who had been taking flying lessons since before he began preening around as Vinnie Barbarino on *Welcome Back, Kotter*. "There's not a celebrity I know who doesn't do private flying," he told one of our editors, shortly after agreeing to appear on the cover of the first issue of *Private Air* published by Doubledown. "It's everybody's form of transportation."

Travolta lived in an Ocala, Florida, development called Jumbolair, which boasted America's longest driveway—a mile-and-a-half airstrip that allowed him to land and taxi his planes right up to his six-bedroom house. For Travolta, the commuter car was a plush thirteen-seat Gulfstream II, while the family car was a full-blown Boeing 707, originally used by Qantas and now reconfigured by Travolta into a flying apartment. The *Jetsons* fantasy of walking straight from your house into the sky had become Travolta's reality. "I'm just a citizen of the planet," he explained. "I think of the whole Earth as my home."

For thirty minutes—the time he allotted for our cover shoot—that home would be Newark Airport. He pulled up in his 707, repainted to mimic its 1964 Qantas glory days, with "Australia's Overseas Airline" on the fuselage and a giant *V* on the rear fin, denoting a once-revolutionary fan-powered engine, the V-Jet. Bounding out of the cockpit and down the stairs, Travolta quickly changed into a snazzy black leather jacket our stylist had waiting for him. Our chief photographer, Ian Spanier, then captured him in aviator glory, smiling triumphantly in front of the nose of his plane.

It was a huge moment for us. One of the most recognizable movie stars in the world fronting our newest, glitziest product. But it came with a catch: we had to grant him approval of the cover image we chose. A drastic change from our standard policy, but the price of admission if we now wanted to play with the image-frantic Hollywood A-list. Spanier and I picked out sixteen shots we liked, which would give us multiple options after Travolta's input, and down to Florida they went.

A few days later, we heard back from Travolta's assistant. Actually, he seemed to have about a dozen whom for storytelling purposes I'll amalgamate into one named Horshack.

"J.T. would like to see how the cover looks, professionally printed," Horshack told us.

So we took a couple of the images, and used the same expensive production process used for real covers. So which ones did he like best?

"None of them," said Horshack.

Spanier fumed. We had chosen the flawless shots, and he had spent hours digitally smoothing out the wrinkles and crow's-feet endemic even in well-preserved fifty-three-year-old actors.

So we instead sent him every photo from the shoot, good, bad, and ugly—more than one hundred in all. Even if he liked only a dozen, we'd have plenty of choices.

"J.T. is not happy," responded Horshack a few days later. "He doesn't like any of them."

"None of *one hundred* shots? What could possibly be the problem?"

Horshack paused. And sighed. "It's his hair."

Begrudgingly, Horshack let me in on an open Hollywood secret: the man who sported maybe the most iconic male head of hair in Hollywood history, from his disco helmet in *Saturday Night Fever* to the lubricated 'do in *Grease*, was bald. Or balding. It's hard to know when someone has the best fake mane money can buy.

"Would ya just watch the hair," Tony Manero had protested in *Saturday Night Fever*, after his father smacked his head. "Ya know, I work on my hair a long time." Life was now imitating art.

He was changing our deal. Cover approval didn't mean a blanket veto. There had been no fake-hair clause. Horshack, anticipating the impasse, offered a compromise: a reshoot in front of Travolta's planes in the run-drive-way of his house at Jumbolair. Peace reigned. Until another hairball cropped up: Travolta now insisted on bringing in his handpicked hairstylist. From Los Angeles. First-class.

This meant an $8,000 ticket, at our expense, plus a thousand or so for his day fee, plus other costs, including sending Spanier and his team down to Florida. All in all it came out to a $15,000 hairdo do-over, more than our entire editorial budget to produce the magazine. We offered to send up the best hair guy in Miami. No, said Horshack, it had to be the L.A. hair magician. We offered to fly him in coach. No, said Horshack, the hair magician only flies first-class. Or private.

There was *no way* I was authorizing that much money for a hairdresser's extra legroom. So Horshack came up with one last compromise. Travolta had just finished a plane-related advertising shoot for Breitling, a watch company that advertised with us and had a major aviator line. Would we be willing to use one of the outtakes?

It was an economical solution. But an awful one, on principle.

We always controlled our own photography. Otherwise, there was no way to know how it would be used going forward. It was core to our brand. "Not an issue," said Horshack. "We'll make sure that those images never get used anywhere else." What choice did we have? We had promised the entire media and aviation communities a big bang with the first issue, and Travolta was it. We had to make it work.

A few weeks later, as I was looking at a mock-up of a soon-to-print issue of *Private Air*, I saw an ad for Breitling. The photo caused me to double-take. It was "our" cover shoot. In our own magazine. Transformed into a watch ad.

A deal gone bad. It was an omen of things to come.

$ $ $

The most important skill in dealmaking is discipline. The discipline to develop investment criteria and stick with them, the discipline to kick the tires properly, and especially the discipline *not* to do a deal. While traders made their money in fixed hours, churning as much as feasible, success in the deal world was dictated by scouting infinite opportunities, and the infinite data points within those opportunities, like a diamond miner in an endless quarry.

This presumes, of course, a relative amount of sanity. By 2007, that was in short supply. More than $1.5 trillion worth of mergers and acquisitions would go down that year just in the United States, plus another $3 trillion in other countries. "It was a competitive situation," explains one private equity partner, who found himself outbid on a regular basis. "Multiple people would go after everything, and the crazy guy wins. So that became the new normal. If you didn't go into crazy mode, you weren't going to do many deals."

Crazy mode didn't cotton to discipline. Over the past few years, success had equated to simply *getting* the deal, no matter the terms or the cost. "You'd seen so many people pay these ridiculous prices, with so much leverage," says the private equity partner. "Then the private equity fund would dividend themselves back the money, or the hedge funds would trade away the risk. It just became part of what works. Next time, nobody would even question it." As with the housing market, where anyone who overborrowed and overpaid was now a real estate genius, the only losers were those conservative penny-pinching rubes on the sidelines.

Deals were getting done without requiring representations—a seller's pledge that everything they said was true. Loans were made without covenants, which required borrowers to pledge exactly what they would do with the money. The risks section of the deal memorandum, which lays out everything that could go wrong, was seen as just some legal boilerplate to be glanced over. Instead, the deal process, as explained by the private equity partner, worked like this: "You close your eyes, hold your nose, and figure that it will all somehow work out. When you want to be aggressive, you justify it by convincing yourself of anything."

Which is exactly how we would wind up running a glorified John Travolta watch ad on our cover. The world was shifting. Some were jumping on and surging forward, playing by the new rules of the day. Others were sticking to their principles, getting called old-fashioned, and being left behind. What my gut told me no longer seemed to be operative. So since we needed the new magazine to succeed, and thus needed Travolta, I ignored my principles, closed my eyes, held my nose, and convinced myself that it would somehow work out.

It was emblematic of everything I was about to do, on a far larger scale, with Doubledown. Other people, in fact, were putting *me* on the covers of their magazines precisely because of that attitude. At the same time Travolta began causing headaches, tens of thousands of copies of *Folio*, a magazine about the magazine industry, were flying off the printing presses. Their January 2007 cover story, entitled "All-In For Growth," featured two "bet-it-all entrepreneurs." In the background Jim Dunning stood in a dapper navy blue double-breasted suit, complete with pocket square. I stood centered in the foreground, in a beautiful Hickey-Freeman blue pinstripe suit, a sky blue shirt, and a purple necktie, my hands clasped together as if either plotting or praying.

No matter that I didn't own the suit, the shirt, or the tie. Our fashion director, Jennifer Lee, had borrowed them for the shoot at the insistence of Jim, who had tired of the frayed suits in my closet.

We were becoming a force in the luxury world, and our peers had taken notice of our aggressive growth. "Have you been to one of their parties?" a senior executive at a rival publishing company asked the writer of the cover story. "If you get invited to one, get an invite for me."

The more interesting quote came at the very end of the article. "We're fully backed and fully financed and have an open-ended commitment from me to continue," Jim told the reporter. "We want to see a business of significance, and by that we mean a business of $100 million."

He had privately been telling me about the commitment for months. We had a blank check from him, as long as I made a good case for where the money was going. He also talked loftily about the target value, except that when he talked to us versus a reporter, he would forecast far higher than $100 million. When Magnus and I had started Doubledown, we similarly talked a big game, but always privately, in the fun kind of way you talked to your brother after the lights went out about someday becoming astronauts. We were doing something we were good at, and we were enjoying it. The money would take care of itself.

But now, as Jim had made clear, money was the goal. The fun would take care of itself. "We're not going to have fancy offices," he said in the article. "We're going to have fancy houses at the end of this."

I fully bought in. While I had no interest in most of wealth's trappings, I very much wanted a house (although comfortable rather than fancy). I wanted security and funded college accounts for my daughters. And the further we evolved from Magnus and myself brainstorming in my apartment to legitimate international brand, the more ego kicked in. I wanted Doubledown to *succeed*. Money, I was reminded on a daily basis, was how you kept score in the Zeroes.

I was blessed and cursed with the knowledge of how my competitors were faring. Since every company in America was now either for sale, or buying, information-laden "books" floated around like bad résumés. I had seen the inner financials for almost every luxury or business magazine company, and I assumed they had all seen mine. Two really jumped out. Niche Media put out magazines (*Gotham*, *Hamptons*) for rich audiences, except they targeted city by city, rather than profession by profession. Between 2003 and 2006, they had gone from three magazines to seven, and jacked their revenues from $14 million to $36 million, generating cash flow of about $5 million. More impressively, Chicago-based Modern Luxury, following a similar strategy, had moved into a dozen cities, and quadrupled their revenue to $65.7 million, with cash flow of almost $20 million. In May, a private equity firm, Clarity Partners, bought them out for an estimated $250 million.

As bad as the magazine business was in general, and the independent magazine business particularly, there was clearly money creating luxury clusters "of significance," as Jim liked to say. Given our event and Internet capabilities, bringing our Rubik's Cube fully to life would prove his $100 million prediction low.

So we prepared for growth physically. Our sublease at the dumpy law firm digs had run out. Marc Feifer and I had found a new home for us in the Mary McFadden Building amid the dressmakers of Manhattan's Garment District. While named for a frilly designer rather than a Wall Street titan, it had space and windows and views and two outdoor decks, as well as the willingness to rent to a money-losing media company—provided I signed a personal guarantee. (On this issue, Jim demurred: "This is *your* company.") Although my dream of office barbecues ended when the fire department raided our first Friday beer-and-weenie roast, we now had room to grow, albeit at triple the rent.

So 2007 would be an expansion year. Jim would feed us as much cash as we needed—at the cost of an increasingly bigger ownership stake—as we tried to double our revenue yet again from our $4 million level. Jim continually tried to break me from "thinking small," my mind-set of incremental growth and tight belts.

Our new mantra: get big fast. I had convinced myself it would work. It certainly seemed to be working for everyone else.

$ $ $

This mind-set explains how we bought *Private Air* in the first place. Based in Birmingham, Alabama, the magazine had been owned by Edith Morrison, a fortysomething woman with a nest of auburn hair who went by the name Deedee. A fellow magazine entrepreneur had sent her to our new offices a few weeks before Christmas, where she told a story I was all too familiar with: an independent publisher covering payroll out of pocket, borrowing money from friends, her company spinning out of control.

My head swam in two directions. Part of my thoughts flashed back to the sleepless, hand-to-mouth days before Jim; another part thought forward, emboldened by our newly aggressive strategy.

Jim and Magnus instinctively brimmed with enthusiasm. Nothing induced more jealousy among the financial elite during the Zeroes than private jets. A trip to the airport in post-9/11 America meant arriving hours early, standing in lines appropriate for a Soviet bureaucracy, walking through security in your socks as agents picked through your underwear, and then waiting for your flight, delayed— nearly a third of all flights in 2007 were delayed—in part because of the thousands of other people undergoing the same tortured process. In this regard, the terrorists had won, unwittingly making hassle-free private flying the ultimate status symbol.

For supersized Magnus, even first class was constricting. When well-heeled friends flew privately, Magnus often tagged along (private jet hitchhiking was another Zeroes mainstay). Jim, meanwhile, only flew private. He vacillated all over the food chain, pricing out planes to buy and ripping through jet cards, twenty-five-hour blocks of charter time that you could pull out of your wallet and show off. At present, he was partial to playing charter companies off each other for the best rate. So on the day after Christmas, as I headed to Newark Airport and the flimsy seat of a Continental Express propeller plane in order to kick the tires of a magazine for people who never flew that way, his earlier pep talk rattled through my head: "This is a no-brainer. Don't get cute. Bring it home."

That implied that there was actually much to bring. Two of Deedee's seven employees didn't bother to show up to meet me. The office manager, a battlefield promotion, basically edited the entire magazine. Deedee's financial records were abysmal: files were missing, numbers didn't add up. And the company's most important person, the chief salesman, Doug Moore, doubled as Deedee's ex-husband.

Slightly paunchy with a baby face and a salesman's glib tongue, Doug, I discovered, had actually founded *Private Air*. When the pair got divorced, it seemed like he got the dog, and she got the cash-draining magazine. But Doug was still generating about half of *Private Air*'s $2 million in revenue. Over dinner at some dark local version of Houlihan's, he explained how he did it. Doug also had a gig consulting for Caribbean luxury real estate developments, helping them execute American advertising strategies. He directed a lot of that business to *Private Air*, for which Deedee paid him a 20 percent commission, on top of the 15 percent fee he was charging his Caribbean clients, which included his design services. In short, he was selling ads to himself.

Why would I want to get involved with people like this? I kept asking myself.

The answer, of course, was that I was seeing what I wanted to see—the third magazine in a $100 million empire—rather than a pig in a supersonic poke. It wasn't the first time I ignored my gut, and it wouldn't be the last. But in an environment where action equated to winning, my gut was no longer operative.

Within two weeks the deal was finalized. Our global sales force, which now numbered two dozen, from Miami to Mexico, San Francisco to Switzerland, was converging on New York on January 7 for their 2007 battle plan. Ad budgets for the year were nearly set, and it was our last chance to get a piece. We needed *Private Air* in their proposals.

While we were not immune from crazy mode, there was also protection for our haste. We would pay the princely sum of one dollar, along with an "earn-out." It was the same kind of deal I had worked under for *P.O.V.* If we did well, Deedee did well. If we didn't, she wouldn't. We'd pay Deedee a salary, but keep her in Alabama with nebulous responsibilities. We made no guarantees to Doug Moore, whom we viewed as a dicey short-term Band-Aid. We also tacked on a thirty-day out clause, in case we found anything else questionable as we completed due diligence. And we built a lie-detector test into the contract: if we ever discovered that she had misled us about what she was selling, we could immediately fire her.

Before we signed, however, I received a strange e-mail from someone who had set up an account under the name "Yellowbird":

```
Randall,
    I have had some albeit rudimentary
knowledge of the magazine Private Air and
its management. . . . Please look into the
situation closely for I do not want to see
anyone's company suffer any more from her lies.
```

We had a brief e-mail back-and-forth, where Yellowbird listed a series of unpaid bills, tens of thousands' worth, down to the dates incurred.

"A small question," I finally responded. "Who are you?"

Yellowbird replied with two words: "Your friend!"

When I confronted Deedee about this, she tearily chalked it up to jealous people out to get her. Given the contract's liar penalty, I felt protected, and given the blinders I was wearing, set by our need to get big fast, I saw only a glamorous new initiative as we sought to double our business.

I never heard from Yellowbird again. But she *was* my friend. I was just too caught up in the mania of the time to realize it. In short order, we discovered that Deedee, anticipating the sale to us, had cut back on the number of copies she printed of her last issue—a money-saver for her, but a ticking time bomb for us, as it would have caused the magazine to fail its circulation audit. She had been notified by the auditor about a different circulation protest a few days before our deal went through, but she neglected to tell us about it. She had represented advertising deals as "contracts" that soon disappeared. She sent the entire contents of her office to us by FedEx, incurring a $21,000 bill, and then falsely accused our sweet office manager of giving her written permission.

Some of these infractions were in the thirty-day probation period, which would have allowed us to walk, penalty-free. The rest triggered the lie-detector clause in our reps and warranties that would have allowed us to fire her. Instead, I sent her a scolding e-mail titled "Trust" ("Magnus and Jim know that Marc and I would sooner steal from our own parents than misappropriate one dollar or misstate one fact, and in fact we all feel that individually about each other. We must feel that from you. And frankly, we're not.").

And then we continued on with *Private Air*. We didn't have the discipline, or the desire, to say no.

$ $ $

For all the headaches and dubious partners, the plan was starting to work. Midway through the year, we were well on our way to doubling sales again—we wound up with almost exactly $10 million in revenue in 2007. But the bottom line remained unchanged—we would again lose almost $3 million, roughly the same amount we'd lost in 2006. And in 2005. We were on a treadmill. The faster we were running, the more we'd stay in place. That was the inherent problem with independent media, especially when our dominant business was expense-laden magazines. There's a certain amount of fixed cost required, and even with our 100-percent-a-year growth rate, we hadn't yet outrun it. Get big fast wasn't good enough. We needed to get big *faster*.

So during the last week of July, Jim began calling around, eventually dialing Bill Curtis, sometimes known as "Wild Bill" in the magazine industry. Like Jim, Bill was a high priest in the media dealmaker club, in which my auxiliary junior membership was pending. From his CurtCo headquarters, resembling a wooden spaceship just off the Pacific Coast Highway in glamorous Malibu, California, Bill had made a small fortune buying and selling magazines the way you might swap couches. He had even sold one to Jim when Jim was at Petersen.

I had met him eleven years earlier, on April Fools' Day, 1996, in Irvine, California. Minutes before we had met, my partner, Drew, and I signed our funding deal with Freedom Communications for *P.O.V.* magazine, and were squired into a large banquet room, where most of our parent company's top executives—every different flavor of old white guy—sat around a giant rectangular table, ready to haze us. Among them, seemingly the only person within fifteen years of us, was Wild Bill, another magazine entrepreneur funded by Freedom. A hefty man donning an Indiana Jones–style hat even though we were indoors, Bill pulled Drew and me aside, and handed us each an expensive cigar.

"Remember this night," he told us, like a cool older brother. "It doesn't get any better." After we plowed through $18 million of Freedom's money over the next three-and-a-half years, he was proven right.

Bill, on the other hand, did what he was best known for: getting Freedom to vastly overpay to buy him out. He, in turn, with private equity backing, plunked down about $30 million in 2001 to buy the ultimate luxury bible, the *Robb Report*. Founded in 1976 as the de facto newsletter for Rolls-Royce owners, it had since become an iconic symbol of the good life. No fewer than a half-dozen rappers had used it as a song lyric ("As you thumb through *The Source*," sang Jay-Z, "I read the *Robb Report*"), nearly as ubiquitous as Cristal Champagne. But like Doubledown Media, the *Robb Report* had yet to outrun its fixed costs, losing $3.5 million on $23 million in revenue, when Wild Bill rode in.

Bill had a toy-centric view of luxury. While Niche Media and Modern Luxury were slicing up rich people city by city, and we were carving them profession by profession (the "Working Wealthy," as we were now calling them), the *Robb Report* defined them by the stuff they bought. Besides the mother ship, there was *Robb Report Motorcycling* and *Robb Report Sports and Luxury Automobile*, and three or four others, as well as *Robb Report Collection*, covering anything expensive left over. Bill's timing and his knack for advertising sales couldn't have been better. By 2006, the *Robb Report* was doing $59 million in revenue, and produced $16.8 million in cash flow.

The only thing pricey that the *Robb Report* couldn't sell was itself. Wild Bill had hired Goldman Sachs to auction the magazine the year before; *The New York Times* reported that he expected to fetch up to $500 million for it. "He thought some Arab sheikh would buy it," recalls someone familiar with the proposal. "Talk about putting stars in your eyes." Not even those in crazy mode would touch it. Faced with bids not even half that figure, he embarrassingly pulled it off the market.

Now it was for sale again. This time, quietly. His banker, the media specialists DeSilva + Phillips, were handpicking prospects so it didn't get into the press. (*If this leaks*, said Bill, looking at me sternly when we eventually reconnected, *I'll fucking kill you.*) Bids were due August 15—his lawyers at Skadden, Arps had drafted a fifty-one-page, ready-to-go purchase agreement—in advance of a CurtCo board meeting.

So in a repeat of the Phillips newsletter pursuit a year earlier, the minnow again sought to swallow the whale. Back came our favorite private equity partner, Marcus Wedner at CIVC. Endless banks offered endless debt, with the Bank of Ireland and GE Capital, General Electric's giant financial arm, wining and dining us for the privilege of loaning us money. Once again, I spent sleepless nights figuring out how to put these companies together, developing budgets and presentations. And yet again, we made a "bid" that didn't mean anything more than agreeing to talk some more.

With great flourish, the Doubledown/CIVC team submitted its offer: $190 million.

As with Phillips, we were told that we were the low bidder, finishing third out of three. But this time, we were put through to the next round. In fact, within two weeks, Doubledown actually *controlled* the entire bidding process in a twist of fate directly attributable to one of the larger phenomena in media dealmaking: Bill's ego.

Wild Bill had the entrepreneur's version of bonus fever, translated into the currency of business sellers everywhere: the multiple. Historically, your typically mature private company sold at a price that equated to its cash flow multiplied by seven (or "7x"). The debt-fueled Zeroes had pushed that average multiple past 10x. And Wild Bill was transfixed by the price Modern Luxury had recently sold for, which equated to their cash flow multiplied by 12.5. As with Wall

Street's bonus culture, it really didn't matter what he thought he deserved, it mattered only what the other guy got. The other guy, in this case, got 12.5x. So Bill would get 12.5x, which equated to $211.5 million. "That's my price," he said, shrugging over $30 eggs at his New York hotel, the Ritz-Carlton. "That's what it will take."

We were the only ones, realistically, who could deliver it for him. The other bidders had money. That was fine to buy the *Robb Report*, but who would run it? And how were they going to justify 12.5x by making it vastly more efficient or valuable? Bill's ad sales engine already operated on full throttle, and he kept costs low. Doubledown had a management team in place, and a stable of magazines in need of the growth his sales machine could provide.

GE Capital fell in love with the combination. There's a joke about how the golden rule ("Do unto others as you would have them do unto you") works on Wall Street: he with the gold makes the rules. In the Zeroes, he with the debt made the rules. And GE Capital gave Doubledown a letter authorizing a loan of $120 million, no matter whom we partnered with.

Bill's banker, Roland DeSilva, understood this, too. Rather than just try to get CIVC to bid more, Roland introduced us to the other *Robb Report* bidders, in the hopes that one would see the logic of the combination and raise their offer to the magical $211.5 million threshold. Effectively, Roland was auctioning Doubledown in advance of auctioning the *Robb Report*; we would choose with whom we preferred to go forward.

The runner-up, a private equity firm named MidOcean Partners, had bid between $195 million and $200 million. Even after a long talk, they weren't inclined to go any further. So Roland phoned up the high bidder. In a decade of fanciful financial products, he had found the most ludicrous. He was about to introduce me to a SPAC.

$ $ $

In the four centuries since the Dutch East India Company first issued stock, unleashing the concepts of joint ownership and pooled capital, the road map to corporate riches had followed a pretty set formula:

you started a company, diligently built it up, and eventually took it public. From General Electric to Ford to Microsoft, virtually every company that mattered—and during the dot-com boom, many that didn't—followed this path.

In 2003, Wall Street came up with the special-purpose acquisition company, or SPAC. It's crazy-mode logic: if there's money to be made when a company goes public, let's skip the inconvenient company-building process, have the IPO first, and worry about plugging in an actual business later. A management team would essentially take *themselves* public, creating a war chest of hundreds of millions or even a billion dollars to go after targets in whatever industry they designated. For these reasons, SPACs were known by a more far descriptive term: a blank-check company.

From one in 2003, and a dozen in 2004, no fewer than sixty-six SPACs went public in 2007.

Big-time dealmakers like Nelson Peltz and Tom Hicks, who had access to as much money as they wanted through other channels, nonetheless stepped up to grab their blank check. Secondary players like grocery store magnate John Catsimatidis, of Gristedes, followed. He raised $450 million on the premise that his knowledge of vegetable oil might somehow help him buy a company that refined oil. Then came the floodgates, with virtually *anyone* with a useful name jumping on the gravy train: former vice president Dan Quayle, a national punch line during George H. W. Bush's term, was now smart enough to raise $433 million. Home run champion Hank Aaron helped raise a $200 million blank check targeting a professional sports business.

Somewhere below Nelson Peltz and above Hank Aaron fell David Marshall. The sharp, forty-three-year-old serial entrepreneur had made a quick fortune in vice, starting the first legal online gambling Web site, Youbet.com, which allowed people to wager on horse races from home. From there, he raised $50 million for what proved to be the biggest growth sport of the Zeroes: mixed martial arts, a euphemistic term for no-rules "ultimate fighting." Marshall's company ProElite staged regular fights on Showtime, pitting Brazilian jujitsu specialists against kung fu masters in octagonal steel cages.

His SPAC, Santa Monica Media, had $100 million, plus lots of debt, ready to deploy. With $205 million, they had been the high bidder in the Wild Bill sweepstakes.

Marshall had some time pressure. To prevent entrepreneurs from sitting on the money forever, these blank checks came with an expiration date, generally eighteen months. Six months had already ticked away. Thus, he was thrilled to start courtship, and moving with the haste I had demonstrated with *Private Air,* proposed to us within days. Santa Monica would buy Doubledown and *Robb Report,* fold them together into a company, trading on the New York Stock Exchange, that Jim and I would run, with one caveat: Jim would be the CEO.

It was a résumé issue. These blank checks required a countersignature. SPACs had been specifically invented four years earlier as a place to stash hedge fund cash. By the end of the first quarter of 2007 the 12,600 hedge funds now managed $2.3 *trillion* worth of capital, and they had run out of things to do with that money, much less trade. Hedge funds were behind everything from movies (*Poseidon,* a Kurt Russell flop, *We Are Marshall,* a Matthew McConaughey flop, etc.), to future sports stars (two British hedge funds invested in young soccer stars' contracts), to the sugaring of Broadway (*Legally Blonde: The Musical*)—absolutely anything to demonstrate enough action to keep that 2-and-20 rolling. So SPACs were a godsend. They were a chance to put billions to work by buying *nothing.* The funds earned a dividend on their money, retained the right to veto whatever deals were brought forward, and had a right to get back their money, held in trust, if no deal was cut within eighteen months. It was like a risk-free government bond.

Marshall's SPAC was even more aggressive—Citigroup would take it directly to the American investing public. That job would prove easier with a CEO who had already turned a publicly traded publishing company, Petersen, into one of the all-time media wins, rather than some journalist with an entrepreneurial streak.

At first, Jim demurred. But just as every coach secretly wants to play one more season, he convinced himself. It was exciting. Combined, we'd have over a dozen magazines in the United States and revenues quickly approaching $100 million. The company would be a publicly traded proxy for the luxury market. "You'll be the president and really run the company," Jim told me. "I'll do it for two years, and then you can officially take over."

Two days later, Jim unconvinced himself. Sarbanes-Oxley, the financial reform passed in the wake of Enron, now made running a public company about as fun as dental work—another factor in the private equity feeding frenzy—and even made the CEO personally liable for any irregularities. Jim had just turned sixty and was rich as Croesus. Who needed the trouble?

So Marshall endorsed me as the CEO. A year before I was emptying my bank account to cover payroll; now I would become, arguably, the most influential person in the luxury business. *What an insane world this was*, I thought. Especially since I'm about as luxurious as a used tire. My wife frequently described my personal style as "unmade bed." My wardrobe closet doubled as the floor. My shirts never stayed tucked in. With fatherhood curbing my high-adrenaline pursuits, fun now meant pounding beers while watching the Yankees from the nosebleeds. The only fancy thing I liked was eating and drinking well, and because of my hobby as a restaurant reviewer, even that was free. "You're going to have to have a total makeover," Magnus told me, laughing. Except he wasn't kidding.

We still needed to finalize the deal for Doubledown. We knew Wild Bill's number. I made it clear what ours was: $25 million, paid, in stock, to all the shareholders of Doubledown. An appropriate premium, I felt, over the $10 million Jim, Magnus, and the others already invested in the company. Marshall floated some drafts, but to make the offer formally, his team flew into New York for our first face-to-face meeting, where Citigroup would host us all at their downtown offices.

Banks like Citigroup were even hungrier for SPACs than the hedge funds. For the same reasons Jim didn't want to be CEO, Sarbanes-Oxley had dried up their huge IPO cash cow. Hence, we were treated like visiting dauphins, dispatched up by an internal elevator to the hallowed twenty-seventh floor, which looked less like a bank office than interconnected private restaurants. This was where Citi closed deals.

The SPAC guys were waiting for us. Marshall was only a few years older than I was but his graying temples gave him a distinguished look. The greetings were warm. An agreement was in the air. The two teams sat across from each other, with one banker on each side acting as the metaphorical peacemakers.

Over a sumptuous meal served on Citigroup's best china, they slid us their offer. For me, there was a five-year employment contract, with a $350,000 salary, an annual bonus of up to $350,000, and enough stock options to make those numbers small. After chronicling these kinds of compensation packages for three years, it felt strange to have my name attached to one. But it also felt vindicating, a manifestation of the endless hours and the stupid financial risk.

The offer was less impressive for our shareholders, which included Magnus, Jim, my staff, and many of my best friends. They were offering only $20 million in stock for Doubledown—a decent starting point until we saw what they proposed for themselves. In Wall Street shorthand, the SPAC management teams were called "promoters," without a shred of irony. Marshall and his partners owned a full 20 percent of the SPAC. Once everything was folded in, they would own more of the combined company than the entire Doubledown side, complete with the assets we were contributing, in recognition for the skill they exercised in "finding" us. That was a standard in the SPAC game; we realized that going in.

But Marshall and his team also baked in another one million stock options for themselves, $600,000 a year in consulting fees, and, if said consulting actually yielded some business, they wanted a cut of that, too.

Even in the gluttonous world of SPACs, it seemed gluttonous. I tried to convey that diplomatically for about twenty minutes, until Jim, now beet red, couldn't stand it any longer. He launched into a withering Dunning Treatment for the ages.

"This is the most ludicrous thing I've ever seen . . . we're the ones running this company . . . you guys don't understand this business at all . . . these negotiations

are going the wrong way . . . the market isn't going to buy it. . . . You guys HAVE NO CLUE."

He then mentioned that we had another suitor. Dealmaking in the Zeroes was a polyamorous affair; as with free love, more action was considered a good thing. We had never deactivated Wedner and our CIVC group, and Jim threw that in their faces.

The Santa Monica crew stared at him agape. "One of the most bizarre meetings I've ever had in my life," Marshall recalls. "Most of [the deal terms] had previously been laid out. There's no way in the middle of that meeting that you can throw out that you're going to do a deal with another partner." Wes Walraven, Citigroup's senior banker at the table, suggested that the groups take a break and pow-wow separately. They led the SPAC team out of the suite.

"I'm not doing a deal with these guys," Jim said, sternly. "If you want to, then it's your deal, and I won't stand in your way. But I don't like them."

"We always do everything unanimously, Jim, you know that."

"Well then," said Jim, "fuck these guys."

We already had our coats on when the SPAC team returned. Marshall appeared shocked; he had returned ready to negotiate. Instead, we marched out.

That didn't mean we were done with the *Robb Report*. By that afternoon the CIVC-Doubledown coupling had resubmitted its bid: $197 million, and a promise to close quickly.

$ $ $

The *Robb Report* wasn't just Wild Bill's business. It was his way of life, his image. He drove a *Robb Report* customized Rolls-Royce, and seemingly had a watch from every advertiser in the magazine. He was the king of luxury. "He grew into a lifestyle that no one else could get because of that magazine," says one of his former executives. "It's a hard thing to give up."

Accordingly, he wasn't inclined to sell without his precious 12.5x. Our $197 million offer, roughly 600 percent more than what he paid for it six years ago, was shot down.

Wedner dug deeper by reallocating money that otherwise would have been paid to Doubledown shareholders. The following week, we resubmitted: $202 million. A full 12x. There was no more wiggle room. Again, Bill shot us down. We weren't going to get to 12.5x without the SPAC; and since GE Capital was now insisting that any *Robb Report* bid include Doubledown, the SPAC couldn't do it without us.

So Citigroup brokered a rapprochement. "This is your deal now, Randall," Jim told me. "If you want to move forward with those guys, you have my blessing, but I don't want to have to deal with them." I did. The choice was life as a small independent company on a treadmill, or the largest luxury company in the history of media. Plus, I'd done the math. Jim would earn a fortune, plus glory. Magnus would have liquidity. The original staffers would have six-figure windfalls as a reward for taking a chance with me, plus extra stock options. And my stake would be worth almost $4 million. I would actually qualify for one of my own magazines.

To rekindle some good feeling, we kept Jim and the bankers at bay, focusing on just Marshall and me, as well as some new blood. Magnus flew in from Vancouver, while Marshall's right-hand man, Kurt Brendlinger, a television producer, flew in with Marshall from Los Angeles. We all met for lunch at a trendy New York hotel, the London, where foulmouthed TV chef Gordon Ramsay had opened his first American restaurant. The rapport was better. We were all within a few years of each other. Three of us had young kids. We slowly patched things up.

The end result was like a backroom congressional spending bill, with pork for everybody. Doubledown shareholders got our $25 million, sacrificing some of the stock options earmarked for senior managers, including me. The promoters got their deal by giving up some, but not all, of their extra goodies. Citigroup would get $9 million in fees. GE would get to loan us $120 million. And Bill would finally get his number. We formally bid $211.5 million—12.5x on the nose. It was a win-win-win-win-win. As with pork, the only loser was the public—in this case, the naïve market investor—who would be buying stock in a company bloated with overpriced assets and wasteful costs.

Bill, for his part, didn't act like someone who'd just been given a huge lottery ticket. It took four days, right before Halloween, for him to respond, sending an e-mail to me, Jim, and David Marshall that was as warm as an ice cube.

```
We request that you wait until November
15, 2007 to receive the revised 2007 business
diligence information. Starting at that time,
we are confident we can work within the time
frame you have suggested and provide you with
all the information necessary to consummate a
transaction.
```

Translation: Bill's number wasn't his number anymore. Yes, he got his multiple. But we now had every reason to fear a "revised" cash flow number, surely projected higher. Lucy was moving the football again. By this point, we weren't even surprised. We had already agreed to go up to $220 million—more than 13x!—if necessary, recognizing that the SPAC's cash, with all the regulatory steps required, wasn't as green as private equity's.

While we waited for Bill's revisions, I traveled to Napa Valley to marry my personal passion—food and wine—with our new toy, *Private Air*. I had talked the heads of the Napa County Airport into letting us take it over for a weekend in 2008. The vision: an aircraft clearance sale during the day, private wine dinners at night.

One of my recruiting stops was at something called the Napa Valley Reserve, the world's first "wine country club," where your membership fee of $150,000, plus hefty annual dues, gave you access to a few rows of grapes, complete with your name on them, which they bottled into up to seventy-five cases of wine for you to brand and label as you saw fit. The man who had everything could now have his own Napa microwinery. Pulling up late in my rented Hyundai, though, it felt more like a parking lot, albeit one from Magnus's dreams: Aston Martin V8 Vantage, Bentley Continental GT Speed, Ferrari 599, and the new Audi R8. A sign next to the gleaming white tent read "WELCOME TO THE ROBB REPORT CAR OF THE YEAR TESTING."

Maybe this is fate, I thought to myself as I rushed into the administrative building to meet with Philip Norfleet, the Napa Reserve's director. Waiting for him in a conference room, I ogled a stack of bottles, each labeled according to its owner's whims: family crests or cute kid pictures or just standard sketches of trees and vines. Then my eye caught a familiar face: Wild Bill's. He was apparently a member, and his bottles featured a cameo of himself, in full Roman statue mode, a toga draping his shoulders and a laurel around his bald pate like Julius Caesar. Or Nero. The emperor of luxury.

After the meeting, I detoured through the tent, and immediately encountered Bill. *Hail Caesar!* He in turn looked at me as if Brutus were upon him. He'd spent the past three weeks stalling us—unlikely to say yes, but unwilling to say no—yet here I was, three thousand miles from our last meeting, at his grand event, invading his club.

"Randall? What are you doing here?"

"Had a meeting with Philip to talk about an event we're putting together," I quickly spat out, attempting to demonstrate in one sentence that I was neither stalking him nor sitting around waiting for his call.

"Okay." Then he paused, thinking about what next to say to me. Choice one would have been, *Hey, since you might be running this business soon, you should hang out and see how our operation works.* Alternatively, he could have kept things murky with a *We're still working on our numbers—let's see where things stand next week, as planned.*

Instead, he went for curtain number three. "Well, nice seeing you." Translation: *get the fuck out.*

And that confirmed that. There would be no publicly traded mega-luxury company. No windfall for the staff, or bonuses for me, or liquidity for Magnus, or fees for Citigroup, or profits for Marshall. Wild Bill would keep his toys. "Entrepreneurs can be irrationally optimistic in their own ability to get things done," says

Marcus Wedner. "CurtCo became a company that lost touch with reality."

Jim got something out of it. He'd been taking notes the whole time. By the end of the year, he'd launched his very own SPAC, China Holdings, raising a $127 million blank check to pursue targets in the Far East. Meanwhile, Jennifer asked me how I felt having been one lost-touch-with-reality Bill Curtis decision away from millions of dollars in stock and a salary more befitting a football player. Even though I was disappointed, it didn't faze me. Doubledown now had swagger, and that swagger felt destined to translate into success. That was my detached reality.

$ $ $

By 2007, the emirate of Dubai, population 1.5 million, had broken ground on the tallest building in the world, the Burj Dubai, which would ultimately stand twice as tall as the Empire State Building, opened the world's first indoor ski mountain, and unveiled a $14 billion man-made archipelago of islands shaped like a world map, except that each of these "countries" cost as much as $200 million to build on. In another sign that Dubai had arrived, the local press would note, Doubledown Media's two flagship magazines, *Trader Monthly* and *Dealmaker*, finalized an agreement to launch in the capital of Arab capital.

Dubai represented everything we were about at the end of 2007: unfettered, self-generated growth, in all directions, from a tiny perch devoid of any inherent resources save pluck and ambition.

Our failed dance with the *Robb Report* had put us back on the treadmill. Given our recent track record, success would have to come through building rather than buying. As long as we had a cash source in Jim, that didn't seem particularly daunting. Trees still reached infinitely to the sky in 2007, and from what we gathered from our bonus forecasts, not even the increasing number of defaulting, junky subprime mortgages could put clouds on the horizon.

The international expansion was my hands-on passion. Our London operation would soon launch *Dealmaker* UK, and a licensing deal for Brazil followed fast on the heels of Dubai. I found interested parties in Russia, India, and China, and publishers in South Korea, Germany, France, and Japan all found me. Every developed or developing country was sprouting its own local Stevie Cohens and Steve Schwarzmans; we had the blueprint to tap them.

All these countries would be interlinked through our expanding Web sites and daily electronic newsletters; we experimented with mobile applications and digital magazine delivery; we launched a for-profit events division. And, of course, we launched more magazines. Since we already had the traders buying and selling corporate securities, and dealmakers buying and selling the companies themselves, the next natural targets were those who *ran* the companies. In November 2007, *Corporate Leader* was born. So we had yet another launch party. Same formula: five hundred suits swilling Patrón tequila and Hennessy cognac, ogling models of private jets. New venue: the Four Seasons.

We didn't stop there. Rather than cut our losses with Deedee Morrison and the floundering *Private Air*, we doubled down again, launching *Private AirMart*, a glossy pennysaver for used planes. Then came our first product-specific magazine: *The Cigar Report*, which tagged along with the other magazines, leveraging the fat-cat stereotype of our reader and that habit.

The latter effort came courtesy of Aaron Sigmond, who had originally sought to be our "chief luxury officer," aping an actual job title he had seen in the *Robb Report*. Ostensibly, he seemed even less fit for that position than me: think Groucho Marx's head atop the body of Barney the Purple Dinosaur. He signed his correspondence "Sig," but I was immediately told, upon asking around, that some friends referred to him as "Wilbur," as in the whiny corpulent pig from *Charlotte's Web*.

I surreptitiously checked out Sig the Pig the way Jim Dunning had done to me, only with opposite results. Of the three people I called, one gave me a two-word answer ("absolutely not"); one regaled me with stories about his expense accounts; another said, "I guarantee you'll fire him within eighteen months." But he also had complete mastery of one specific advertising category—cigars. And after ignoring him for three months, following those atrocious references, I found that the revenue temptation again proved too great. Character, focus, patience—all get sacrificed when you're starved for 100 percent annual growth. With the urgency of *yes* trumping the discipline of *no,* I rationalized by bringing him on part-time, commission-only, sans the silly Chief Luxury Officer title.

With Jim's encouragement, we hired more than twenty people during the second half of 2007 and beginning of 2008, most of whom were dedicated to revenue growth. The culture shift was palpable. The loyal crew who had originally come aboard believing in the cause clashed with the new crew and its heavy dose of luxury-world mercenaries. When I sat in on our weekly sales meeting, solutions that used to be admired, such as our use of an advertising trade to underwrite our swanky Four Seasons party, were now held up as symbols of what a "cheap" operation we ran.

That was half-true. Relative to the ambitious expansion we were undertaking we still ran remarkably lean. But our burn rate was soaring. The $75,000 biweekly payrolls that I had been forced to cover in emergencies had now swelled to $250,000. Jim's checkbook was wide open, but only on the assumption that our new sales army would quickly generate exponentially more revenue.

The one area we didn't spend on was administration, and that was to my detriment. My frantic days consisted of getting in by 9 a.m. for my morning call with Jim, nonstop meetings until 8 p.m., an hour of play with the kids until they went to bed, a rapid and text-filled dinner with an increasingly resentful Jennifer, and then editing the various magazines on my laptop until about 1 a.m.

I had convinced myself it would all be worth it.

8

Fight Night

In April 2007, we undertook one of the more comprehensive surveys of conspicuous consumption in the Zeroes: one thousand readers of *Trader Monthly* and *Dealmaker* answered some 150 questions about their spending habits, from how important "luxury" was to them to what drove their purchasing decisions. ("We're all like New Guinea tribesfolk—nice feathers in one's hair communicates status," one respondent explained. Another, referring to timepieces, was more specific: "Traders, in order to convey their success and attract more capital, *need* luxury watches.")

The results that startled me most involved real estate. Forty percent owned multiple residences; a quarter of those owned *four* or more. Roughly half were in the market for real estate over the next twelve months, and a similar number owned real estate for investment purposes. America was in the last throes of a real estate mania—the subprime mortgage meltdown was just a few months away. Our guys, purportedly the world's savviest financially, were still fueling it, pushing out NINJA loans (as in No Income, No Job, and No Assets required) and bundling them into Frankenstein-like trading contracts. Unbelievably, they were actually buying their own bullshit.

That was music to the ears of Raizy Haas, who had been scouring back issues of *Trader Monthly* trying to figure out how to move one of the largest inventories of luxury apartments in the world.

Her company, Extell Development, was another debt-fueled product of the Zeroes. Its arc almost precisely paralleled Doubledown's, only with different stakes. New York diamond merchant Gary Barnett, originally Gershon Swiatycki, shifted into real estate with the construction of the fifty-seven-story W Times Square in 2002. He then got the secretive Carlyle Group to back him on the $1.76 billion acquisition of a Donald Trump–owned tract of land on Manhattan's west side—the largest residential land purchase in American history. Extell was now hoisting up no fewer than six luxury condo buildings, most in the fifty-story range. They had thousands of apartments to sell, virtually none under $1 million.

From nowhere, they had become one of our five biggest advertisers. So when Extell's media buyer e-mailed us—"[Raizy] has a very creative idea on how she wants to partner with you. She wants to meet with the top brass"—we took it very seriously.

Raizy Haas was an interesting character. She never attended college, and was managing a building in Barnett's old stomping ground, New York's one-block Diamond District, when he plucked her from obscurity. Now the thirty-six-year-old mother of two was Extell's senior vice president for project management and development, displaying a demanding, erratic streak noteworthy enough even in a rogue-filled business to earn the nickname Crazy Raizy from those who'd worked with her before.

As we waited in her conference room, her deputies talked about Raizy with reverence (*you should be honored—she never meets with anyone!*) and fear (*don't shake her hand—she's very religious, and isn't supposed to touch other men*). When she finally appeared—her jowls morphed into her torso so that she looked like a thumb with a brown wig—she was doomed to disappoint. And she did so grandly.

"I have a weally big idea that I want to share," she announced, in a shrill Elmer Fudd lisp. She held up a recent issue of *Trader Monthly*, opened to our "Performance" column, which profiled traders through the oddball hobbies that honed their market skills, such as competitive sailing or musical theory. The specific story, "The Scrum and the Fury," detailed how arbitrage specialist Warren Rogers used rugby to stay sharp. ("The three best traits that a trader can have are aggressiveness, focus and determination," said Rogers. "And those are the exact same things that make you a good rugby player.")

"Are you weady?" She paused for dramatic effect.

"I found this story quite intwesting. So what we want to do is have a wugby match—the twaders versus Extell." In great detail, she then laid out her vision: A brisk Sunday morning. Wall Street's heretofore secret rugby community, having united for the coming battle, practice for weeks to tussle with their archrivals—a real estate firm none of them had ever heard of. After the grudge match, the whole group would repair for beer, and regale themselves with tales of just-missed tackles and the $2,000-a-square-foot apartments they would agree to buy in short order.

As she talked, I mentally glossed over what surely was the worst idea in the history of real estate marketing (or organized sports), and instead pondered what this all said about the current condition of private equity firms, which, like the hedge funds, were clearly having a hard time finding places to park their money: *Half the pension funds, endowments, and rich people in America are betting on the mighty Carlyle Group. . . . The Carlyle Group is betting on Gary Barnett. . . . And Gary Barnett is betting on Raizy Haas, real estate visionary/rugby evangelist.*

Of course, opportunity lies in insipidity. My eyes caught those of Pat Shannon, the first in our wave of newer hires, and the most important. The long-term prospects for the magazine industry were awful—luxury advertising was a lone, ephemeral bright spot. GE Capital, Santa Monica Media, and their ilk liked Doubledown because while print ads still generated three-quarters of revenue, our key assets were the various *communities* that the magazines spawned. Our master database now housed 400,000 of the most powerful people in the world, about 150,000 of whom proactively registered for our electronic newsletters, password-protected Web sites, and events. A Petersen veteran, Shannon had helped Jim Dunning launch the Gravity Games, an extreme sports Olympics that was eventually overtaken by ESPN's X Games. His Doubledown job was to help us escape the magazine ghetto by turning our event prowess into a profitable business, rather than an endless series of free parties.

Our favorite unhatched plan was a Wall Street black-tie boxing match. In Chicago, *Trader Monthly* helped publicize and find sponsors for Ringside for Mercy's Sake, a trader-versus-trader battle that for more than a decade had raised millions for a local orphanage. In London, we similarly supported Hedge Fund Fight Night, which raised $300,000 for Operation Smile, a charity that sends surgeons into poor countries to fix cleft palates and other easily repaired physical stigmas. We had developed our own plan for a blown-out version for New York, which was similarly swimming in money and testosterone. The only missing element: a title sponsor.

The first rule when dealing with your fastest-growing advertisers is that all their jokes are funny, all their ideas brilliant. Shannon indulged her for a while, before shifting the concept. "Raizy, that's a really powerful *out-of-the-box* idea," Shannon finally responded. Now *he* paused for dramatic effect, winking at me.

"But you know what might be as good as rugby . . ." He then pantomimed fisticuffs. "We've been noticing that Wall Streeters like to box. And maybe instead of fighting Extell brokers, they *might* be more into fighting each other."

So was born the Extell Wall Street Boxing Charity Championships. Within twenty-four hours, Shannon had repurposed our boxing proposal for Extell.

Five hundred traders. Black-tie dinner. Fights on behalf of a half-dozen good causes. And perhaps most critically for Extell, we'd get our audience into their overpriced boxes in the sky through a half-dozen hyped "weigh-ins," held on location at their apartment buildings around the city. The cost to them: $300,000, which included a large amount of advertising they would probably have bought anyway. With that money, we'd run the ads and then stage the event, Extell's name sitting right on top. Even if they didn't sell apartments, Extell was getting a robust marketing solution. We were taking some risk—we still needed ticket sales and other sponsors to make money—but kept the upside. The charities got a sure thing: Extell guaranteed them $40,000 in the contract with us. Raizy later added a lure, offering 3 percent from the sale of each apartment bought by our attendees. "She thought that would help us get into the chairmen and presidents of the big banks," remembers Shannon.

We confirmed the deal, and sent an e-mail to our New York database. Subject line: "Who wants to fight for charity?" No fewer than 120 volunteers immediately stepped forward. It was an amazing sign of the vitality of our community, their love for blood—oh, and helping those less fortunate.

It also was a good snapshot into the real estate business. Getting someone to commit (say, sell their old place), then take advantage of their vulnerability by changing the terms was a classic tactic of that cutthroat field. Once we sent that e-mail, we were committed. While the deal had been mutually agreed to, signed by us, and sent over for countersignature, Raizy still hadn't adorned it with her John Hancock.

Suddenly, Gary Barnett, who so far had been invisible to us in the process, wanted to speak with me personally. Now the deal wasn't good. Everything we'd negotiated was fine—except they wanted half of all profits. Our risk, their upside. Shouldn't we then get a share of the real estate we helped them sell? Over the phone, I heard a figurative shrug. "That's a lot of money we're offering. It's a good deal for you guys."

Sadly, given our desire to get into the big-ticket event business, he was right. In principle, I was furious. We had proceeded on the idea that handshakes and verbal approvals mean something; that we actually had a partnership. I had thought I was dealing with the Carlyle Group; culturally, Extell remained a Diamond District hustler.

$ $ $

Every year as we compiled the *Trader Monthly* 100 list, we faced a dilemma about where to place a London-based hedgie named Christopher Hohn, who ran something called the Children's Investment

Fund. Its mission was as unusual as its name. Hohn, the son of a cabbie who later became a Harvard MBA, made the money. His wife, Jamie Cooper-Hohn, who met him getting her public policy degree at the Kennedy School, spent it. Not on the usual stuff—Chris Hohn wore a $20 Swatch, rented his London apartment, and commuted to his St. James offices by tube—but rather on AIDS prevention, child poverty, and Third World development. Between the fund's founding in 2003 and the end of the decade, this unusual coupling—the market titan and the do-gooder—gave more than $1 billion of its hedge fund bonuses to charity.

But that wasn't what made Chris Hohn truly interesting. At the same time he was helping hungry kids, he was also making his name as one of the legendary assholes in the financial industry—and that's saying something. "He's not a nice guy," said one Wall Street executive familiar with his operation. "He doesn't care about money. He only cares about winning." Employees were chastised until tears flowed and target companies—Hohn was one of the new breed of "activist" investors who would buy into a company, and then bully its management to get the stock price up—were publicly tortured. For one of the great unsung philanthropists of the past fifty years, altruism was just an excuse to do what comes naturally: kick the teeth out of people. Charity as blood sport.

Chris Hohn neatly solves the riddle of why 120 traders volunteered to fight for us so quickly, or why the key word in our Extell event was "charity." For some, charity meant exactly what it said. But for a lot of these guys, charity was in fact yet another way—like making money itself—to publicly display who had the biggest dick on Wall Street. It was just another way to compete.

The standard forum is the annual dinner, held to laud a charity's accomplishments and invariably honor someone who happens to come from the financial world. It's how Wall Street socializes. During the spring and fall, there's a charity fete almost weekly in the major financial capitals. When I used to read about a given charity's "person of the year" award, I'd imagine some kind of Jimmy Stewart superman, working hard all day, then ladling soup to widows and orphans all night.

In reality, the charity finds someone in the financial industry who has shown interest in their cause. It tells him how much it wants to raise, and the honoree commits to getting it done. This "man of the year" then taps his network: friends buy tickets, or more likely, firms currying his favor buy entire tables, plus pages in a "program" that in reality is just a bunch of vanity ads from vendors and partners try-ing to kiss the honoree's ass. And so the symbiosis goes: the charity makes its budget, the financial titan basks in the goodwill created by muscle-flexing.

The senior prom of the Wall Street charity circuit each year was unquestionably the Robin Hood Foundation's annual gala. It was founded by hedge fund king Paul Tudor Jones in 1988—one year after his windfall during the stock market crash made him a house-hold name, and six years before he helped start the Greenwich man-sion arms race with his $11 million tear-down. Robin Hood, as the name implied, targeted the poor of New York. Its twenty-nine-member board of directors was a who's who of Wall Street, from Stevie Cohen to Goldman Sachs CEO Lloyd Blankfein, as well as a smattering of glitter, including Gwyneth Paltrow and Tom Brokaw.

Four thousand people attended the 2007 gala, paying an average of $3,000 a ticket to see Manhattan's Jacob Javits Convention Center transformed into an urban Sherwood Forest. Designer David Stark built a life-sized castle from 200,000 paper coffee cups, giant trees from wire frames with customized green lottery tickets as the leaves (the scratch-off yielded information about the foundation), and cov-ered the bars with medieval-style tents.

The highlight of the evening was a very public auction. The 410 dinner tables, adorned with 10,000 white hydrangeas, were carved into quadrants. In the center sat a small stage, like a theater in the round. From here, the high-low combination of Sotheby's auctioneer Jamie Niven and comedian Jon Stewart egged on the attendees, who bid via baton-sized light sticks, the neon green dancing like fireflies with each lot.

"We have ten thousand," shouted Niven, pointing frantically, as a private jet trip to meet Patriots quarterback Tom Brady at training camp came up. "Ten thousand, twenty, thirty, forty, fifty, sixty, seventy, eighty, ninety, one hundred . . . I have three hundred thousand in the back of the room." That took precisely four seconds.

Brady himself stood on the stage, and he and Stewart tried to rile up the crowd. "Three hundred eighty thousand—with an old friend," said Niven, acknowledging a wand in the air. "We have got to get to five," Brady shouted. As if the football star's voice could create money, $500,000 was bid. Then $560,000. *Sold!*

The numbers got bigger. Dinner for ten cooked by Mario Batali? *Sold!* $1.3 million. Trip to the following year's Beijing Olympics, where you get to meet *Today* show anchor Matt Lauer and a women's soccer player? *Sold!* $2.2 million.

"*Dayenu!*" Stewart, who is Jewish, shouted at one point, a joke about a Passover song. Loosely translated from Hebrew, *dayenu* means "had we gotten less, it would have been enough." Indeed, these absurd bids weren't economically rational. But neither were they purely an altruistic way to funnel money to the charity—that could be done quietly and anonymously. Instead, it was a way to do the right thing—while taking a bow with all of your friends and rivals watching.

The night's most interesting auction, in fact, came at the very end. Robin Hood was raising money for a specific fund to train public school teachers in New York, a point underscored by Graham Nash singing "Teach Your Children." Paul Tudor Jones himself started by asking who, in addition to himself, would donate $1 million to this cause? Twenty-three people stood up lifting glowsticks. How about $250,000? Twenty-two more. The staff frantically scribbled names and tables. What Jones was really auctioning off: acknowledgment. The more you gave, the longer, and more prominently, you stood out among your peers. It was Wall Street's hierarchy on display, for four thousand people to see.

The night's final total was an astonishing $71 million. Wall Street could feel pretty good about itself. With that, out came Aerosmith for a ninety-minute private concert, led by singer Steven Tyler, dressed in full rocker garb, down to the black tank top, yet completely comfortable with this crowd. (He would, in short order, appear on the cover of *Private Air*.)

Relative to this display, our magazines were positively penny ante. Since we were still bleeding cash, we weren't positioned to donate directly, but we used our media muscle to help as many of Wall Street's favored causes as we could. The magazines featured a column called "My Charity," where various honchos could plug the cause they support and why. Our top trading editor, Rich Blake, was quick to acknowledge the best annual dinners and similar events on our social pages. Often, we dug deeper, actively getting behind traders with pet causes. For three years, we helped Lava Trading's Dan Yu, who had been introduced to me through a mutual friend, host a reunion party for alumni of Instinet, an early electronic trading exchange, securing the venue, booze, and publicity, allowing him to raise enough money to build roughly a dozen libraries in Third World countries for a charity called Room to Read.

Another favorite was thirty-five-year-old Steve Drobny, a sandy-haired surf bum who ran Drobny Global out of Manhattan Beach, California. His business was improbability, which made sense, given that he and his unrelated partner, Dr. Andres Drobny, the former chief strategist for Credit Suisse, shared the 64,437th most common surname in America. They sifted through data for tradable anomalies, and hedge funds paid $50,000 a year and up for the privilege of hearing their macroeconomic trends. There was a waiting list.

Each year, Steve Drobny converted his magic Rolodex into a conference where the hedge fund elite laid down their weapons and swapped strategies. In 2007, he held it at the just-opened Wynn Las Vegas, a $2 billion statement that Sin City was now in the luxury business, with the idea of leveraging the location to help his cause, funding a model village in Haiti, through a full-blown Vegas poker tournament. The buy-in was $5,000 per seat. The prize: a new Mercedes convertible and a $10,000 entry to the World Series of Poker Main Event. And, most critically, bragging rights. Poker, as we've seen, has serious correlations with trading. But unlike trading, which is done secretly, with scores kept on spreadsheets, this was open-air combat, for all their peers to see.

In terms of his cause, Drobny walked the walk: a year prior, he and his wife had adopted a Haitian orphan. *Trader Monthly* eagerly got behind him, soliciting sponsors and promoting the tournament. In appreciation, Drobny invited me to Vegas to hobnob and play. My wife, who didn't appreciate my round-the-clock schedule, which involved work, time with the kids, and little else, sent me off with a message: *This had better be worth it.*

As I mingled among the sushi and shellfish at the opening cocktail reception, it didn't seem to be. Even though I was attending with the agreement that I would not report what was said at the conference—what happens in Vegas, stays in Vegas—most greeted me like I had 2007's designated plague, Ebola. Nothing ruins alpha talk like the presence of a journalist; I mostly cleaved to the other nontrader attending, financial historian Niall Ferguson, with whom I discussed the correlation between poker and the markets.

I had a monthly poker game in New York. But with relatively small stakes—forty bucks up or down was a huge night—we reveled more in creating exotic poker derivatives, christened with names like eBay Hi-Lo (players folding can auction cards to the survivors) and Rape of Ken (predatory betting, customarily involving heavy losses for Ken). The one hundred or so quants who gathered to play under the chandeliers of the grand ballroom at the Wynn the following night would not have been impressed.

But I had the best mentor of anyone in the room. Our poker/trading columnist, Johnny Chan, had passed on some advice for me before leaving for Vegas: *be hyperaggressive.* The tournament's compressed nature—three hours versus ten days for the World Series Main Event (which Chan had won twice)—made recklessness a virtue. Given what was going on at Doubledown—and in the world—that felt pretty natural to me. So when I had good hands, I bet big, though not until after milking my opponents for some easy money. When I had bad hands, I bet *bigger*, bluffing guys who ran $1 billion books by displaying something they had been trained to respect: overwhelming force. After ninety minutes, I had managed to collect the most chips in the room.

People stood three-deep around the final table of ten, as a professional announcer provided live play-by-play. Slowly, bizarrely, I continued to knock out the geniuses, including Andres Drobny,

Cambridge PhD. Eventually, the only one left was a young trader with a buzz cut and a poker background, Jason Self, from HFR Asset Management in Chicago. We'd battle head-to-head for the Mercedes, a chance to compete against Johnny Chan for $8 million—and the bragging rights that go with being the top cardplayer in the hedge fund kingdom.

After a twenty-minute seesaw, the fateful hand arrived. Me with an ace and nine of hearts; him with an ace and four, unsuited; an ace and two hearts flopped on the table. All of my chips, and most of his, in the pot. For those who don't speak poker, this meant I had a 90 percent chance of winning the hand, and then a 90 percent chance of finishing him off, given his meager remainders. His only hope: another four. My '97 Subaru, now approaching 100,000 miles, was about to be traded in for a brand-new Mercedes.

And then, nightmare: a four. Self caught the Hail Mary. With one card to go, disaster could yet be averted: any heart, or any nine, and the car would still be mine. The dealer, sneaking a peak before revealing, flashed us a big smile.

Another four. Defying odds similar to two unrelated Drobnys partnering, Self had pulverized my hand with two "bad beats" (lucky winning cards) on the same hand.

My runner-up prize was a cruise anywhere in the world. Not bad in a vacuum, but when I compared it with Self's haul—worth about $70,000—I was crestfallen. It mirrored the markets perfectly: second place gets punished.

Or does it? Drobny had arranged a post-tournament party at Myst, the Wynn's nightclub, which had cordoned off an entire section for the wealthiest group in the building with velvet ropes, right under a three-story man-made waterfall; pretty girls in skimpy outfits lined up on the perimeter, hoping to catch the eye of a math nerd and join our moneyed party.

But the hedgies, to the disappointment of the girls, seemed more eager to talk with me. *What was my strategy? What had I been holding on that hand I had knocked so-and-so out on? Where did I learn to play?* The group that had ostracized me the previous night now embraced me as a worthy colleague. My pockets filled with business cards, my calendar with invitations to reconnect. The kudos, fueled by vodka and Red Bull, lasted until dawn, at which point I headed straight for a 7 a.m. flight. No matter that I would be the only guy from the group flying home coach. I had publicly earned the currency that makes the Wall Street charity machine go: respect.

$ $ $

For the boxing event, we had a chance to direct some significant money for some good causes, and picked a passel of our Wall Street–backed favorites. Say Yes to Education, which motivates inner-city kids with guaranteed college scholarships; the Prostate Cancer Foundation; Hedge Funds Care, which fights child abuse; the NYMEX's philanthropic arm; the Valerie Fund, which helps children cancer victims; and Tuesday's Children.

This last one was run by Carmine Calzonetti, who had been inspired to change his life on 9/11 in ways exponentially more profound than mine. He was a former partner at the World Trade Center–based bond brokerage, Cantor Fitzgerald; 658 of his ex-colleagues (out of roughly 1,000 total) died that awful day. To honor their memory, his organization raises money for 9/11 orphans. I was thrilled that we could help his crusade.

Raizy, meanwhile, moved aggressively to wrap Extell in this mantle of goodwill. While our contract gave us responsibility for publicizing the event, Extell spent extra money to hire its own public relations firm to make sure nobody missed the connection. "WALL STREET IN A FIGHTING MOOD FOR CHARITY," blared the press release, which then declared: "Extell Development Company announces plans for 'The Extell Wall Street Boxing Charity Championship.'" Their camp then began coordinating with the charities, some of which put out their own press releases, creating an echo effect. "We would like to thank the Extell Development Company for selecting Say Yes to Education as one of the beneficiaries of this wonderful and exciting event," gushed Mary Anne Schmitt-Carey, the nonprofit's president, at the top of one. In the same release, Raizy could then take her bow: "Extell wanted to give back to the City as part of this dynamic and exciting event. We are delighted to be getting Extell and Wall Street together in the same corner to raise money for these fantastic New York charities."

Extell's self-congratulatory press push didn't surprise us. Having toured too many of these new "luxury" real estate developments flying up across the world, I found them singular in their uniformity. Same trendy kitchen appliances, same noise-proof, floor-to-ceiling windows, same once-edgy neighborhoods. The luxury condo glut made them a commodity, and few things work better to infuse a commodity with some positive branding than a little giving back.

That was the dirty secret of the luxury field, and true for most of its products. I used to think of "luxury" merely as something top-notch that I didn't really need. Over three years of producing magazines for the mega-rich, I eventually figured out the true meaning, even though I still couldn't dress the part. Luxury, as defined in the Zeroes, meant one of two things: either pretty stuff that, without marketing to infuse value, would either be virtually worthless (yellow diamonds, modern art, Steuben glass), or else something functional but no better than the same products available at a fraction of the price (just because you call it a "timepiece" and charge $10,000 for it doesn't mean you arrive at work any more promptly than with a watch selling for $10).

Take vodka. Back during my sommelier training, the class laughed like it had just heard an ethnic joke when someone asked what to tell a diner who wants a vodka recommendation. By legal definition, vodka has no taste, smell, color, or character. If you were forced to choose, the best, according to a 2007 comparison of 108 vodkas by the Beverage Testing Institute, was a no-frills Polish brand called Sobieski. Retail price: $11.

But after a brilliant octogenarian marketer named Sidney Frank turned Grey Goose into a luxury brand—Magnus ordered it up at $350 a bottle during our proper night out—and promptly sold it to Bacardi for $2.2 billion in 2004, just seven years after he launched it, half the world scrambled to churn out its own "ultra-premium" label. Donald Trump unveiled Trump Vodka. Fashion designer Roberto Cavalli poured his eponymous offering into a bottle enveloped in a glass serpent.

In all, over sixty new vodkas had been introduced to America the previous year, all of which pitched us on the superior qualities of their version of colorless, odorless, and tasteless. Some took special pride in filtering it through something expensive: Cavalli's $90 offering became tasteless via crushed Carrara marble, while $100 Diaka's lost its flavor over cut diamonds. Others laced it with some type of magical element: Pink infused caffeine, Lotus tried vitamins, while Gold Flake Supreme, skipping any subtlety, added twenty-four-karat gold shavings. It was Emperor Wears No Clothes–worthy stuff, custom-made for a business, luxury, whose ultimate product is how you feel about yourself.

Hence, the desire to associate their brands with charities as they wooed our Richie Rich audience. Imperia, of secret-formula-of-Czar-Alexander-III fame, offered not just five-liter bottles for each table at the boxing event, but ring-card girls worthy of a Moscow cat-walk. Watch companies proffered free timepieces for auction tables, if the do-gooders were demonstrably well heeled. The same attitude permeated our numerous in-store parties, where the "a portion of proceeds will go to charity" boilerplate became standard. Generally, I discovered, that translated into 1 or 2 percent.

That is, if we could get them to actually fork it over. Wall Street guys could be crass about it, but they actually gave. At one *Trader Monthly* event in May for Bulgari (which they brand "Bvlgari," since certain vowels late in the alphabet, apparently, have no class), christening their new Manhattan showroom on Fifth Avenue, we enlisted, at their request, a Robin Hood–endorsed charity, the Jericho Project, which aids homeless veterans.

It was a strange party. From our eyes, it looked like a huge success: three hundred of Wall Street's finest filling the triplex, respectfully studying, and sometimes buying, their overpriced accessories and baubles. Jim Dunning even went back the next morning to buy neckties to swell the charity's take. The Bulgarians, in turn, saw vulgarians ("Not to go down the list but we even had a fight break out because of a love triangle going on—our security guys felt like bouncers at some point," carped one of their marketers, in a follow-up e-mail to our sales rep. "I also forgot to mention some of the guys using the bathroom sink as a urinal in both the basement bathroom and the second floor bathroom"). And no sales. Zero.

We were skeptical of the rowdiness claims (it didn't jibe with what we saw), and knew their sales claim, because of Jim's purchase and bags we'd spied floating around, was wrong. But fighting with them for the measly cut—maybe a few hundred bucks—from the measly sales wasn't worth it. We needed their business, so we sucked it up. To compensate, Jennifer and I made a personal donation to Jericho.

This was typical. For all the perceived refinement, the frothiest of the luxury companies were the biggest bullies I'd ever worked with. The largest tussles occurred around editorial mentions. As with charity tie-ins, with the credibility they confer, positive mentions in the magazine were considered essential for these empty-vessel products, and we were pummeled on a weekly basis to grant them.

Such "church-state" battles exist everywhere. At *Forbes*, in my mid-twenties, I basically fed myself by attending "townhouse lunches," held in the private residence that Malcolm Forbes had purchased directly behind the Forbes building. Steve Forbes or his savvy brother Tim would host a fancy lunch for a visiting CEO, pouring the kinds of delicate wines I could never afford. The conversation was always lively, with my role defined: end any awkward silences with a smart question about the company. After the meal, when advertising deals would presumably be discussed, I excused myself. I was never asked or pressured to write or tone down an article. Quite the contrary, I found myself occasionally getting good ideas. The church-state wall held. And I'd held *P.O.V.* to the same standards.

These image-obsessed luxury marketers of the Zeroes didn't play by those rules. It was more like Henry Hill's Mafia *omertà*. If you took their money—we were now generating more than three-quarters of our $10 million revenue from luxury advertising—you agreed to their code, and it went far past the charity charade. Many of these brands were European, accustomed to the lax editorial/advertising divide there; others were simply taking advantage of the fact that dozens of luxury magazines had cropped up trying to join the gold rush. "Either you did what they said," remembers a top luxury publisher who competed against us across the Zeroes, "or you weren't going to get the business."

The first rule: don't criticize. The penalty was death, at least in terms of ever getting another advertising dollar. We paid that fine several times early in our existence after several of our cheekier barbs. Since this didn't affect our bread-and-butter—covering trading and the deal world—and since no one was picking up our magazines to find out which obscene watch *not* to buy, I gave Ty Wenger, our highly talented editor overseeing lifestyle coverage, complete freedom to recommend what he thought best for readers. But I also asked him to avoid criticizing those that fell short. I knew this was a long way away from my days at *Forbes*, but I also knew that the other option was bankruptcy. Look through *any* luxury magazine: dozens of adjectives like "beautiful," "rare," and "exquisite," but not a single diss. In luxury media, nothing ever sucks.

But that wasn't enough. As the Zeroes plodded on, the luxury *omertà* went further: the advertisers began requesting not just that we never slag them, but that we say nice things about them. Pay-to-play, as conveyed to our publisher, Wilkie Bushby, who would gingerly forward them to me, handcuffed by the standards of his competitors.

I tried my best to balance integrity and the need to stay in business. Often, we'd be covering them coincidentally—between all our magazines, we were now highlighting dozens of cars, scores of bottles, and hundreds of watches each year. Or else, we would happily use them as a prop in a fashion shoot, or steer them to a marketing event.

The story requests, however, became *demands*. Increasingly, marketers would wave deals with other luxury magazines in our face, claiming they had written guarantees for editorial mentions as part of their advertising contracts. Often, they would request to see me, wearing my editor-in-chief hat. One of Gary Barnett's competitors, Josh Guberman, president of Core Development, insisted to one of our salespeople that before he signed an advertising contract, he needed to meet me and show me his latest New York condo project, the Legacy. When I demurred, he sent a car and driver to fetch me.

Guberman met me at the ground floor, a young guy bearing the thin, intense face of someone who worked out a lot. Shoving a hard hat on my head, he took me through the work-in-progress: the Italian marble countertops, Jacuzzi bathtubs like small swimming pools, the floors, all six thousand square feet of them for the big units, warmed by radiant heat.

Then he got down to business. He showed me all of the other magazines that had done profiles of him. He wanted the same consideration from us. I suggested that maybe the Legacy would be a good site for a party or a photo shoot—ways I could mollify him while protecting our editorial sanctity.

But that wasn't what he had in mind. As our salesperson tried to close the deal, he kept harping back to an editorial guarantee. "What is agreement on editorial coverage (number of articles/# of pages/specific stories) and on site events?" he e-mailed urgently. Since I wasn't going to make any promises, the salesperson diligently tried to get him to sign off, leaving the editorial part vague. But that wasn't part of the code. "I will re-visit next week, and in turn, next deadline, the prospect of working with you and Randall," he eventually wrote. "To be quite frank, this was Randall's deal to close, not yours. His lack of participation spoke loudly with respect to our being a priority (or not)."

They never signed the contract—and never advertised with us again.

I eventually tried to stop putting myself in such awkward positions. I enlisted Sig, who reveled in these black arts. We named him "Luxury Markets Editor," which he crowed about in a press release he wrote himself, allowing me to focus on growing the business.

Still, not even that was enough. Apparently, the luxury *omertà* carries into your personal life, too. My pet Doubledown project was the Wall Street Wine Club, which brought Napa winemakers to New

York for dinners, hosted by restaurants trying to cater to the free-spending financial crowd.

There was no shortage of the latter. In fact, as with real estate or vodka, there was an arms race developing, with weapons measured by gluttony, absurdity, and cost. First came the burger wars. Daniel Boulud's $28 foie-gras-stuffed hamburger, introduced in 2001 to great fanfare across the street from the original Doubledown bunker, was eventually surpassed by a $41 burger from the Old Homestead steak house that used ground Kobe beef, made from cows fed a diet of beer and grass and given stomach massages to even out the fat.

Old Homestead then trumped itself with an $81 version that stuffed a small sirloin steak into the burger's center, the way others might infuse some cheese. Boulud fired back with a $150 burger topped with twenty grams of black truffles. Seeking the burger to end all burgers, a new entrant right near the New York Stock Exchange, the Wall Street Burger Shoppe, then unveiled a $175 burger with foie gras *and* Kobe beef *and* black truffles. In lieu of ketchup, this monstrosity came slathered in a healthy layer of edible gold leaf.

It got even more gross. Other New York restaurants joined the decadence, determining, independently, that $1,000 was now an appropriate amount of zeroes for a single menu item. For breakfast, one could eat a $1,000 bagel at the Westin (white truffles and gold leaf) or a $1,000 frittata at Norma's (six eggs, Maine lobster tail, Sevruga caviar). Lunch meant $1,000 pizza at Nino's Bellissima (more lobster, more caviar), dinner could start with a $1,000 martini at the Capital Grille (garnished with jewels) and end with dessert, a $1,000 sundae at Serendipity (more gold leaf). Most of these were designed as publicity stunts, of course, but then to the surprise of everyone except those who understood the Wall Street mentality, the Doubledown audiences began ordering them (the Wall Street Burger Shoppe averaged one $175 burger sale *every day*). They were the edible versions of burning a hundred-dollar bill to prove to everyone you could.

There was even a new restaurant entirely devoted to such absurdity: Kobe Club, which offered soup-to-nuts excess, from the $150 vodka punch bowl to the $160 shellfish plate to the $190 sampler of Wagyu beef, all served in a room more suitable to S&M fetishists, complete with the two thousand samurai swords hanging ominously from the ceiling. "Grossly calculated . . . absurdly crass," I had noted in my side gig as the top restaurant reviewer for *Time Out New York*. And for its times, brilliant.

Even the owner was excessive: Jeffrey Chodorow, fifty-seven, a real estate developer turned convicted felon (four months in prison for obstruction of justice after buying Braniff Airlines) turned mega-restaurateur, serving over $200 million worth of pricey meals annually, and achieving fame on reality television, depicted as an evil owner on *The Restaurant*.

Such were the kind of people who wanted to host Wall Street Wine Club dinners. So in July, two dozen oenophiles from the likes of Merrill Lynch, Morgan Stanley, and a slew of hedge funds found themselves sipping on St. Supéry, paired by the course by the winery's president, while brooding Jeffrey Chodorow, just in from the Hamptons and sporting a perpetual five o'clock shadow, held a silver tray of meat, with little country flags in each cut, lecturing about Wagyu beef with the kind of passion that causes men to spend $175 on a hamburger.

Several of the attendees, with more cash than sense, thanked us the next day, informing us that they'd already booked Kobe Club return visits. A partnership was born, with Chodorow's team offering one of their London restaurants, Suka, to host our upcoming 30 Under 30 party in the United Kingdom.

And then I unwittingly violated the *omertà*. The next week, *Time Out* assigned me to check out another new Chodorow restaurant (it was hard to avoid them: he had two dozen), a New York cuisine mishmash called Borough Food and Drink in the same doomed space where he had become a television villain in *The Restaurant*. Think of a meal of matzoh ball soup, followed by pork dumplings, followed by eggplant lasagna, with a few caloric atomic bombs (fried mac-and-cheese squares dipped in maple syrup; pickles fried in chicken fat) for good measure. The big-name consulting chef, Zak Pelaccio, was a personal favorite, but he clearly wasn't behind the dishes I alternately described as "puerile" and "disgusting." The final line: "Even given the reasonable prices, it's not worth eating here if Pelaccio's not cooking."

In retrospect, I should have recused myself. But reviewing restaurants was my personal hobby; it had nothing to do with Doubledown. And Chodorow hadn't protested my snarky Kobe Club barbs, which had appeared well before our respective marketing squads planned the event. He had better things to worry about.

Or not. The day after the review came out, I got an e-mail from Chodorow's top marketing executive. "How and why on earth would you choose to end it so negatively, in one single ending line? . . . How do you think Jeffrey feels after reading this last line of the review? He is hurt and doesn't understand why this had to happen. Needless to say, he is turned off by our relationship with the publication."

So I would be punished. "I am sorry I can't confirm this event at Suka," he then diplomatically wrote to our marketing department about the London party. "It's best you find another venue."

To a mutual friend, his e-mail was more direct: "It's about Randall . . . Jeffrey is not doing anything else with [Doubledown]. We were supposed to do a big event in London in September but Jeffrey was so turned off he had me decline."

The next time I reviewed a Chodorow restaurant, I did so with my byline removed. Witness protection for food critics. As with the Mafia, the luxury code was all-encompassing, for life. There was no getting out.

$ $ $

One of the better perks of the Wall Street–charity nexus is ringing the bell at an exchange. Unless you're taking a company public, some high-profile altruism is the surest path to the privilege of turning on or off the engine of capitalism. How else could a motley group of scrappy magazine types, nutty real estate developers, and four Wall Street boxers, clad in robes and gloves, find themselves atop the podium of the New York Mercantile Exchange on August 14, 2007? As those controlling the world's energy markets looked up, the exchange's giant tote board, usually filled with price quotes, welcomed the Extell Wall Street Charity Championships.

The boxers, including Josh "The Matrix" Weintraub of Bear Stearns and Dave "Minister of Pain" Smith of Lehman Brothers, actually did the honors, ending the daily chaos of the energy markets with the push of a button . . . *ring-ring-ring-ring-ring*. It sounded more like the beginning of a fight than the end of a trading day.

In many ways, it was. Like a marriage troubled even before the wedding, Extell's contract bait-and-switch had augured a rocky partnership. As the match got closer, Raizy began hiring consultants who answered directly to her rather than letting us, the appointed organizers, do the work. Her PR team shadowed our PR team, her production team shadowed our production team, her party expert clashed with our caterers. It was like the papal schism, with us in Rome, Extell in Avignon.

On the week of the match, all-day battles at the Hammerstein Ballroom ensued, as the two papal delegations devolved into screaming, very sacrilegious name-calling battles over timing, seating, lighting. Thankfully, I was far removed, dealing with other Doubledown headaches, but Pat Shannon finally called me in to referee an urgent dispute relating to, yes, flowers.

We had arranged for table centerpieces fit for Wall Street: autographed boxing gloves and giant bottles of vodka wrapped in a touch of frill. But Raizy was insisting on tens of thousands of dollars in flowers. "We are not using the [Doubledown] centerpieces," she summarily dictated to her party consultant in an e-mail forty-eight hours before the event, cc'ing Pat Shannon. "See if you can book centerpieces and let Pat know what it's going to cost him."

"I keep getting forwarded more emails about various small issues like floral arrangements . . . ," I e-mailed back. "Oversight lies specifically and solely with us in the contract . . . Pat has said for weeks that if you supply an alternative at your cost, we'll go your way. . . . No alternative was delivered . . . let's spend these last days focusing on the big picture."

Responded Raizy: "Sorry, Randall—I guess we are at an impasse," before trashing Doubledown's competence.

I tried again: "Obviously both sides are frustrated and we're all working very hard. Let's focus on the positive: we'll completely sell the event out—with an incredibly affluent and influential audience, we have amazing fighters and a healthy dose of boxing celebrities in the mix. And hopefully, we can help you sell more real estate."

Raizy's six-word response: "Terrific. Now what about the centerpieces?"

I overruled her (though I pulled them from the Extell staff tables), and things went downhill from there. The night before the biggest moment in our little company's existence, the Extell-hired production consultants informed us about a cache of secret videos. Extell's video team had filmed a series of lengthy real estate infomercials they were planning to play between fights.

Furious, Shannon and I called Raizy. With flashbacks to the "We want your money" debacle in London—except that here, the traders were paying up to $1,000 a ticket to attend—I first tried reason: "Raizy, there will be a riot if we play those before each fight."

"Wandall, if you don't run them, we're canceling the event."

"Raizy, you can't cancel the event. We booked the venue, we trained the boxers, we sold the tickets, and we have all the contracts with the vendors. We *are* having a fight tomorrow, whether you're there or not."

Raizy responded by becoming the Incredible Hulk of luxury real estate: "DON'T MAKE ME ANGWY!"

We'd been taking shit from the luxury bullies for three years. Success requires that you swallow your pride, I'd often remind myself. But here, at the very height of the market, Raizy knocked some sense back into me. There was *no amount of money* that justified working with people like this. It took about a half-second for the old reflexes to set in, and I responded in a voice even louder than hers. "OR . . . ELSE . . . WHAT?"

I felt liberated.

Raizy screamed. And hung up the phone.

By dint of some skill or luck or the pendulum of karma, everything the next night came off flawlessly. Almost one thousand people packed the joint, dressed to the nines. The beef tenderloin and Imperia vodka flowed. The boxer video introductions looked sharp (as a compromise, we also showed the real estate videos as an infinite loop during the cocktail hour, when no one was captive). And the boxers fought hard for charity—and glory. "They will channel the competitive nature of Wall Street into the ring," announced the evening's co-emcee (along with our favorite CNBC creation, Eric Bolling), boxing legend Bert Sugar. "Some of them will be bullish. Some of them will be bearish. But none of them will be sheepish." Each tribe chanted for their tribesman. (Sadly, while we had tribeswomen volunteer to fight, Extell nixed that on "religious" grounds.) Perhaps for the last time, history would show, Bear Stearns beat Goldman Sachs. The throngs went home happy.

Plus, we raised a good amount for charity. A silent auction of signed NFL football helmets, LeRoy Neiman paintings, and other things that twelve-year-old boys would buy if they made $1 million a year raised thousands of dollars. A live auction, Robin Hood–style, filled with race car weekends (*sold!*) and Super Bowl excursions (*sold!*), raised thousands more, as giddy audience members publicly jousted for charity, like the boxers but without gloves.

Even Extell was feeling the love. They announced that for all apartment sales, they'd *double* their previously pledged contribution; they'd now donate 6 percent of the sale price of each apartment to the charities.

Gary Barnett looked pleased. For her part, Raizy was beaming, posing for pictures as she swanned around the room. We'd made her look very smart for the boss.

As it became clear that we had a blockbuster on our hands—it would later be named the best magazine-related live event of 2007 by the folks at *Folio* magazine—I walked over to her to make peace. "Not bad," I said, giving her a thumbs-up. In response, Raizy turned her head dramatically and walked away.

Extell still owed $117,000—$77,000 for us, plus the $40,000 guarantee for the charities. Rather than their accountant, we heard from their lawyer, who began bleating about our need to reimburse Extell for the tens of thousands in redundant consultants Raizy had unilaterally frittered away.

As we also owed them a small rebate based on the strong ticket sales, we made an offer designed to wash our hands of Extell and avoid the lawyer fees that would surely run more than the upside: we'd forfeit all money owed to us if they just paid the charities the $40,000 they had committed. ("It's sports and charity," Raizy had told Bloomberg the day of the fight, after all. "How much more New York can this get?")

We got no answer. So Carmine Calzonetti, from Tuesday's Children, wrote to Gary Barnett on behalf of all the charities. "I'm sure you know the critical importance of the realization of funds for programs like this," his letter said, before describing how his nonprofit's share of Extell's promised donation would go to a special fund to help sick 9/11 rescue workers. Barnett's response? He forwarded the note to his attorney, who then told our attorney it had put them "in a difficult position."

I didn't fully understand until a random meeting on a playground. One Sunday morning, I took the kids to a local park in Union Square for some dad-and-daughters quality time. Sabrina was now three, Chloe was a precocious one. While pushing them on the swings, I ran into another new dad, Marc Sperling. A *Trader Monthly* booster, Sperling was the president of T3 Securities, a prop trading company similar to Magnus's old firm, MacFutures. He was training hundreds of young traders and taking a cut of their action. He and I occasionally brainstormed ways we could work together, including an online training site, T3 Live. We caught up a bit on trading, and parenthood.

"Yeah," he said. "We're getting more room soon. Just brought a new place."

"Cool. Where at?"

"A new Extell building that's still going up. The Rushmore. I first saw it at one of your weigh-ins. Got it right after that boxing match."

Five weeks after our event, on December 8, Sperling placed a down payment on a $4.5 million four-bedroom apartment (and he closed after the building was completed), thus generating a huge profit to Extell—and an additional $270,000 check due to the charities. "That donation definitely had sway," remembers Sperling. "Given what the prices were, knowing that a quarter-million was going to charity was very nice." Extell had never mentioned Sperling's sale to us. How many people whom I *didn't* happen to know and run into had also bought properties?

So I wrote a letter to Barnett. I included some flattery ("I'm writing this note, CEO-to-CEO, as someone who appreciates and respects what you've built"), a carrot ("My staff has already offered to forgive and forget the amount Doubledown is owed so long as the amount earmarked for charities is paid directly to them"), and a stick ("a lawsuit involving the six charities . . . would be both fruitless and a PR nightmare"). I also tried one last approach: a conscience. I appended a list of the charities, with a paragraph for each one describing their good works.

I sent it FedEx, so that he couldn't deny that it got there. He never responded.

We had written off the money owed to us by now, but we urged Carmine to sue and promised to help. Instead, he sent Barnett another letter. "Our financial foundation was crumbling," says Carmine, in recounting his decision not to pursue legal action. "We had bigger issues to worry about. I just chalked it up to a promise not kept."

Extell put that unpaid $310,000 donation (the $40,000 guarantee, plus the $270,000 for the Sperling sale) to other use, grandly announcing its own marketing event: the Extell Wall Street Rumble. They began recruiting boxers using a *Wall Street Journal* e-mail list and a familiar lure, without any irony: "Fight to raise money for the New York charity of your choice."

Even as the real estate market started to crest, Extell, less debt-ridden than many of their peers, had buildings flying up all over New York. I trembled with anger every time I passed their billboards at one of their construction sites. "I still can't figure out why they didn't [make the donation] ," says Shannon. As each month of the Zeroes progressed, and the money involved got incrementally bigger, I seemed to encounter increasingly capricious people. Looking back, only one rated worse in my mind than Raizy Haas and her crew. And I was about to meet him.

9

Nails

(Late 2007–Early 2008)

As siblings are wont to do, my younger brother and I grew up reflexively disagreeing on anything we were allowed to, most notably baseball. I became a fan of the New York Yankees, so Cary, taking advantage of his birthright in a region with two home teams, embraced the New York Mets. As I rooted for Ron Guidry and Reggie Jackson, he worshipped at the altars of Dwight Gooden and a center fielder named Leonard Kyle Dykstra, known even as a grown man as Lenny.

One of the smallest, scrawniest players in the major leagues, debuting in 1985 at five-foot-nine, 160 pounds, Dykstra played so fearlessly—a huge, nasty mound of chaw protruding from his mouth—that he earned the nickname "Nails." In Michael Lewis's book *Moneyball*, about a savvy baseball executive named Billy Beane who had proven too cerebral to excel as a player, Beane cited Mets teammate Dykstra as his polar reflection, a player "perfectly designed, emotionally" to play professional sports because he "had no concept of failure." He lived that attitude whether on the field (gleefully colliding his body into outfield walls) or off (drunkenly colliding his red Mercedes into thick-limbed trees, breaking three ribs, his collarbone, and his right cheekbone).

Slowly, the Nails physique had caught up with the persona. Mets manager Davey Johnson noted that Dykstra arrived in spring training in 1988 looking "like Popeye," and when he showed up another twenty-six pounds heavier to start the 1990 season, after he'd been traded to the Philadelphia Phillies, he explained to one of the beat reporters: "I did a lot of lifting and free weights. And I took some very good vitamins." More than a decade before steroids in baseball entered the public discussion, all anyone else noticed was that Dykstra made his first All-Star team. In 1993, now properly inflated to the size of a micro–Michelin Man, he produced one of the greatest seasons by a leadoff hitter in baseball history.

That was pretty much the last time I thought about him until July 27, 2007, when my phone rang, and a voice mumbled, "Hey, Randall Lane, this is, um, Lenny Dykstra. Do ya have a minute?" That minute turned into an hour, and that hour turned into a dinner invitation, which is how I wound up waiting at Coco Pazzo, a dated white tablecloth spot, to meet the man who claimed to have a plan that could revolutionize Doubledown Media.

I brought along Pat Shannon, our events guru, for some pro athlete credibility. Shannon's son, Ryan, had won the Stanley Cup as a fleet-skated forward for the Anaheim Ducks a few weeks earlier. While we waited, I relayed what I'd discovered about the last fifteen years of Lenny's life. Improbably, Nails had gone from pumped-up party animal placed on probation by the baseball commissioner for his excessive gambling to legitimate business tycoon. Back in his native Southern California, he parlayed his baseball fame into a huge car wash business (customers could treat their cars to a simple "double" or a deluxe "grand slam"). He was about to pay hockey legend Wayne Gretzky $17.5 million for a twelve-thousand-square-foot mansion on eight acres sitting high above L.A.'s ultra-premium Sherwood Country Club. He drove a Maybach. He had flown to New York for the week on a chartered private jet. He now spent most of his time trading, and writing a stock market column for Jim Cramer at TheStreet.com. I checked it out—thousands of people followed his picks, and hundreds slavishly made whatever bets he suggested.

Eventually, an entourage arrived, three middle-aged men plus a hunchback with a gait who bore precisely zero resemblance to the guy whose topless beefcake *NAILS* poster adorned the wall of every junior high school girl in Queens. *Yikes,* I whispered to Shannon, *what the hell happened to him?*

"Hey, bro," said Lenny, shaking my hand, his meaty paw trembling slightly, a tight grin fixed across his face.

As Shannon babysat the flunkies, only one of which, Lenny's accountant, Jeffrey Feinman, seemed to have any reason to be there, Lenny opened his laptop. Lenny, I would come to learn, traveled with three or four, just to be safe, each armed with a universal Wi-Fi card, still rare and costly in 2007. He sported another hot gizmo, an ear-mounted Jawbone cell phone, which he wore perpetually, as if he were on *Star Trek*. Like bats with perfectly shaved handles or a well-oiled mitt, this was now his equipment, and even if he displayed no innate knowledge of how this stuff worked—he typed with two fingers as if each were a chopstick—he treated it all with appropriate reverence.

Calling up a presentation, Lenny proudly flipped around his laptop to reveal the logo of his new project: The Players Club.

"What do you think of the name?" he asked, proudly.

"I think everyone will confuse it with that gambling card that Telly Savalas used to shill on TV."

"Nah, dude, it's perfect, it's about saving lives, saving families. Did you know that for pro athletes, eighty percent of marriages, eighty percent of families, break up in the first year after the player retires?" I looked at him skeptically.

"It's true, bro. And the reason is money. Everyone is accustomed to living at a certain level, but now after agents and taxes, there's no money coming in, you have no skills, and until you turn fifty-five, you have no pension. You're just a piece-of-shit broken-down ballplayer."

So Lenny Dykstra, who had offset his physical deterioration with a professional renaissance, would be their savior, escorting professional athletes—and the $5 billion or so they collectively made each year—to the omnivorous Wall Street fee machine. The main product of The Players Club, Lenny explained, flipping through his presentation, was a financial plan that would take players' money while they were still playing and turn it into an income stream to bridge their retirement and their pension. He called it "Guaranteed Cash Flow."

The reason Lenny was wooing me now came out of his leather satchel. Besides a financial service, The Players Club would be a magazine, leveraging Lenny's contacts to reach into every locker room in America. Athlete-to-athlete, they'd learn about their peers' successes off the field—and perhaps be enticed into some Guaranteed Cash Flow.

"Here's the sample," Lenny said, holding what appeared to be a magazine in his shaking hands. The cover was a white piece of paper, with the words THE PLAYERS CLUB above a bunch of sports league logos. It looked like it had emerged from a copy machine. He had then scotch-taped it atop an issue of the *Robb Report*.

It was a perplexing dichotomy, the high-rolling millionaire with his complicated stock trading column, and his sophisticated athlete retirement scheme, mixed with a guy whose magazine "prototype" could have been produced by my three-year-old, and who at various times during the meal slurred his speech, trailed off during sentences, and at one point nodded off at the table.

"Is he drunk?" I whispered to Feinman, the accountant, when Lenny excused himself for a cigarette, something he did to control his shakes.

"No, he never drinks anymore. He just gets like that sometimes. He's really smart."

He had absorbed enough, at least, to see how he fit with Doubledown and myself: we already put out glossy magazines for rich male-dominated audiences, we had connections to Wall Street, and I had personally spent five years at *Forbes* overseeing the coverage of athletes and wealth. Lenny began chasing me like a wayward fly ball.

"I know that I just met you, and I might sound like I am just *'feeding you the typical bullshit'* that we both receive when meeting new people," he wrote to me a few days later, availing himself of every emphasis icon known to e-mail, "so I am going to tell you anyways: You are the kind of person that I 'WANT' to partner up with; by the way, *we are partnering up . . . and I never lose money for my partners, as it is unacceptable!* Randall, you will be the single most important person to The Players Club as we prepare for The Players Club to 'BLAST-OFF!'

"Now, getting directly to the point: YOU ARE HIRED! It would be an honor to work with you, and your team at Doubledown Media. Also, it is very important for me that you know: 'You can count on being paid, that I can guarantee!' Money will not be an issue, I don't want you to worry about that part of the equation; as I must know that the 'PLAYERS CLUB will be the best magazine ever put out by Doubledown Media.'"

"Sincerely, Nails," the note ended, and in a show of good faith, he wired $50,000 to Doubledown the following week. Once we commenced our work on the magazine, I asked him for another $100,000.

"Here's $150,000," he said, reeling off a personal check. "No shortcuts. Major leagues all the way, bro."

$ $ $

Nails didn't chart time like the rest of us. While every other mammal on earth measures a day as one orbit around the sun, generally doing productive things when it's light and sleeping when it's dark, a day on Planet Lenny lasted a full week. During his increasingly frequent trips to New York, he basically went without sleep from Monday to Friday, and then hibernated over the weekend, a seven-day marathon turned into a single body cycle. Traditional working hours were spent taking endless meetings, and while the rest of us slept, he fumbled with one of his endless laptops, typing e-mails in slow motion or gazing at stock charts while banging out his cliché-ridden thrice-a-week column for TheStreet.com.

Accordingly, dealing with Lenny was a 24-5 exercise, exacerbated by the fact that, already a natural night owl, I covered the overnight feeding shift at home for our new baby, Chloe. Sometime between midnight and 2 a.m., my cell phone invariably would light up, displaying an 805 area code number from one of Lenny's three cell phones (his long-standing line, and then a pair of endlessly rotating "bat phones" for those currently in his inner sanctum). For as long as I would indulge him, he would talk about Wall Street or our business or whatever anal point of The Players Club he was presently stressing over; even after an hour, he saw through any veiled attempt to exit the conversation (Me: *Hmm, Lenny, I have a breakfast meeting tomorrow*. Him: *Come on, dude, why you trying to get off the phone with me?*) and continued droning into the night.

"I got nobody," he explained to me on several occasions. He claimed to have a restraining order against his brother, who he said sponged him for money, and didn't much trust anyone else. "Just the way I am. Growing up, I only had one friend, because I needed someone to play catch with." The only people he hung with were people he paid, including part-time hangers-on like Feinman, and his full-time Players Club staff, three sports nerds in their twenties he dubbed "the geniuses" who were busy assembling mailing lists and sorting through financial regulations. I was now Lenny's temporary best friend, the guy he needed so that he could play catch.

I usually indulged him. Besides his needy, cretin charm, Lenny offered me something else: a magic bullet for our short-term ills. The idea of sprinkling professional athletes into our "Working Wealthy" mix, from advertising packages to events, was formidable. More important, The Players Club would make Doubledown almost instantly profitable. In exchange for doing what we did better than anyone in the world—making glossy magazines for rich people in common professions—we would be paid a straight fee of almost $4 million a year, along with any advertising we could sell.

Best of all, the cash source was blue-chip. Nails was playing off The Hartford against JPMorgan Chase against AIG, copying me on his correspondence with their senior executives, who fawned over Lenny and his promised funnel of check-wielding pro athletes. His requirement: one firm would pay us, monthly, for our services, in exchange for the exclusive right to sell Players Club retirement plans. Lenny would then take a cut of their action.

So I made it my business to get his business funded. Wall Street had been a foreign world to me even five years earlier; now I was able to pick up the phone and blow open doors at the likes of Citigroup, Merrill Lynch, Alliance Bernstein, providing him more options.

Lenny's accountant hadn't lied. Early in a given week, when he was sharp, he displayed moments of intuitive brilliance. In a first meeting with a bank, he would lower expectations at the outset with a dumb jock shtick, mocking his lack of education, his fat, broken body, his bad Caesar haircut. If he held the upper hand—say, someone who wanted their company's services woven into The Players Club's offerings—he would often stop mid-sentence, wince, raise one of his butt cheeks and fart loudly, to make them uncomfortable, as he dictated terms. At every meeting, or any press interview, if he got a question he didn't like, he pretended that he didn't understand it.

As the week dragged on, however, his mind slowed and his speech slurred. That first dinner I had with him, on a Thursday, was typical. Sometimes, people would talk around him like he wasn't there: a mistake, as even on half-speed, he latently observed everything that went on the way only someone born to put a thin piece of wood on a 100-mile-per-hour fastball can, drily mentioning the following week what he'd picked up.

Our first July get-together had led to a weeklong August visit and then another in September. He now called or e-mailed every day, leaning on me like a consigliere, a role I was happy to play. Once he signed with any one of those financial giants, Doubledown was set. I began coaching him through the negotiations with the various financial firms. As the weeks went on, he acted increasingly dependent. During his mid-September meeting, when I informed him on Wednesday that I was leaving the next day to attend my brother-in-law's bachelor party—and thus wouldn't be around for him the rest of the week—he became visibly agitated.

"Bro, I need you here."

"Sorry, Lenny, only have one brother-in-law. Family first."

"Where's the bachelor party?"

"He lives in San Francisco, so they're having it on the west coast of Mexico, Puerto Vallarta."

"Shit, dude, that's right in my neighborhood. I'll drop you off Friday in the *bird*," he said, using Lennyspeak for his private jet. "We can do work the whole way across. Problem *solved*."

Puerto Vallarta is a three-hour flight from Van Nuys, California, the private airport Lenny used just north of Los Angeles—a significant detour. But to Lenny, it was just dropping off his best bud on the way home from work. So rather than fly coach all day Thursday on Continental, including a three-hour layover in Houston, Lenny and I would jet out Friday morning, he'd jump off, and then I'd continue south.

Of course, on Lenny time, the Friday morning departure dragged to Friday afternoon, a delay forgiven as we walked straight from a van through the FBO (the private terminal, grabbing a copy of *Private Air*) and onto the tarmac—no security, no delays—where Lenny's chartered $35 million G-IV sat washed and gassed, waiting for its two passengers. We'd owned *Private Air* for almost a year, yet this was the first time I actually got to fly on one of the jets we so fawningly covered.

"G-IV, dude," Lenny smiled, "the big dog of the tarmac."

The interior was as roomy as my apartment, complete with a full bathroom including a shower, a bed area, and a lounge with leather couches and a lacquered dining room table, where Lenny and I sat across from each other. The two pilots and three attendants followed, including Tim, who had called me that morning to find out what kind of food I liked, and now brought out a turkey-and-roast-beef hero with mustard, lettuce, and tomato, plus a diet Dr. Brown's black cherry soda, exactly as requested.

Even though he had slept little or not at all in the past five days, Lenny's bird made him feel euphoric. It was a billionaire's life— flying round-trip from Los Angeles, letting the plane idle unused all week at Teterboro, bunking the whole entourage at the St. Regis and feeding them in style. A $100,000 round-trip, even without the little detour to Puerto Vallarta. He began a private-jet-worthy bull session, explaining the imminent deal to sell his car wash business for $23 million and bragging about how he had "ripped off" the Gretzkys to buy his new $17.5 million mansion ("it's worth $25 million, easy"). Somewhere over Ohio, Ramon Manriquez, the president of the charter company, interrupted. "We have a problem."

The FBO terminal in Puerto Vallarta, they had learned, closes at 10 p.m. By the time we would arrive in Van Nuys, then head south, the computers said we'd miss the cutoff by an hour or so. A military pilot by training, Ramon had preemptively checked on plans B and C. The Puerto Vallarta control tower had refused to keep the FBO open late. Guadalajara would be open, but it was several hours away by car. The only option, Ramon had determined, was to take me to Los Angeles, bunk with Lenny (the Gretzky estate had three separate mansions), and then head down in the morning (I would then return to New York less than twenty-four hours later).

"No way, dude," Lenny barked. "Randall is my man. We have to do something for *my man*." So Lenny went back and caucused with the team.

Twenty minutes later, Ramon returned. "Okay, we have a solution. One of our other planes is taking off right now from Van Nuys and heading east toward us. And we've taken this plane to maximum speed. Somewhere in the middle—right now, it looks like El Paso—we'll both land, and hand off Randall for the trip down to PVR. Should land there with fifteen minutes to spare, based on what our computers tell us."

As promised, we put the G-IV down in the special private jet area of El Paso. As the pilots filled out the paperwork, Lenny smoked a cigarette just off the tarmac.

"Ain't this the life," he muttered. "The first time I flew private, I knew I could never fly commercial with all those sorry suckers again."

Our conversation was interrupted by another arriving plane, a Hawker. A mere flying limo versus the G-IV's flying apartment. Two new pilots rushed in to do their paperwork, leaving the engines idling. Then we all marched back into our respective planes. Lenny went up the stairs of the G-IV and gave me a half-salute. I jumped in the Hawker. The two planes taxied off together, as seamlessly as divorced parents handing off little Johnny at a 7-Eleven parking lot.

Like drinking or sex or going to the movies, flying private, it turns out, is one of those things that feels bankrupt alone. The self-important banter with Lenny was gone. As my two personal chauffeurs focused on getting their passenger to a low-budget bachelor party—a $10,000 flight to $70-a-night hotel so dilapidated that the entire group eventually moved—I was alone with my thoughts. And those thoughts latched on to guilt: the disgusting carbon footprint, the monetary waste, the inconvenience I had caused the two pilots, who surely would have preferred to have dinner with their families. Plus, the recognition that, until this Doubledown run, I had never been anything but one of the commercial "sorry suckers" that Lenny had referred to with disdain—and that, in my heart, I knew I still was.

If I could have gotten off, I would have. That wasn't an option. It wasn't unlike Doubledown. We had built something big, and innovative, and magnificent for what it did. But the underpinnings were shallow and getting worse. I was flying in the exact wrong direction from my post-9/11 self-image, the lofty idea of having a hand in this interesting financial revolution that would change the world. I recognized that. But I had also recruited more than fifty people, whose livelihoods I was responsible for; the company's investors, all of whom had been friends or become my friends, had collectively put in more than $10 million based on this vision; and my life savings was on the line. I had built this trip for myself. I needed to see the ride through.

Lost among his other accomplishments, Benjamin Franklin was also America's first financial guru. Through his *Poor Richard's Almanack* and then full-blown books like *The Way to Wealth*, Franklin developed a devoted following among the colonial population with aphorisms like "beware of little expenses; a small leak will sink a great ship" and "a penny saved is a penny earned." His financial gospel: thrift. And while, a quarter-millennium later, modern incarnations like Suze Orman were still scoring best-sellers with commonsense approaches, thrift had been replaced by another word: *alpha*. The Jealousy Machine that had prompted endless leapfrogging among

Wall Street managers, no longer content with $1 million, $10 million, even $100 million a year if they heard someone somewhere made more, had filtered its way down to the mom-and-pop investing public.

The high priest of the alpha gurus: Jim Cramer. Besides his influential perch as the cofounder of TheStreet.com, which six million people turned to for trading advice each month, almost 400,000 people nightly were now tuning in to *Mad Money*, making him the Oprah of options. "He moves the market," Gregg Goldstein, a Manhattan hedge fund analyst, told *BusinessWeek*. "He's really infiltrating all these areas—my friends, my co-workers, my clients. . . . Everyone knows who he is and what he's saying."

He had the proper bona fides for a guru. Pioneer hedge fund (Cramer and Co. launched in 1987), plenty of alpha (stellar 24 percent return annually after fees over the next fourteen years), and the personal trappings of success (net worth approaching $100 million). What he really loved to do, though, was scream into the camera. Every weeknight, he performed one of the great circus acts in financial history. He'd postulate on trades he'd like, and trends he saw, and then, like some nerd take on the king of the mountain, he'd challenge all comers during his Lightning Round. For eight minutes, viewers would name a stock—one of the five thousand listed on a major U.S. exchange—and Cramer would, Rain Man–like, not only recite what that company did, but give an informed opinion on whether to buy (a bull would rush across a screen) or sell (a bear would flash its paws). He had his own catchphrase—*Booyah!*—that he and his viewers would greet each with, the loud membership password for the community he called "Cramerica."

With Jim Cramer's stature as the nation's highest-profile market guru, it was hard, as counterintuitive as it seemed, to dismiss his star pupil, Lenny Dykstra. This odd couple—the human Bloomberg machine with two Harvard degrees and the idiot savant from the school of Nails—had a simple genesis. Lenny had seen his nest egg dwindle during the dot-com crash from $2 million to $400,000. So he started teaching himself the market, and then e-mailed Cramer out of the blue: "Let me show you my ideas."

Cramer claimed to be so blown away that he publicly stated he counted only four or five people in the whole world whom he would take a stock tip from—and one of them was Lenny.

"Not only is he sophisticated, he is one of the *great ones* in this business," Cramer told Bernard Goldberg, a correspondent for HBO's *Real Sports*, as we began to rev up publication of *Players Club*. "He is one of the great ones . . . a guy who applied the same skills to money that he applied to sports, it's brilliant."

More than just talk, Cramer gave him the legitimacy and platform of TheStreet.com, which tracked his performance. When I first met him, according to his Street column, he had picked *ninety-two winners in a row*. And like his mentor, Cramer, he moved markets. Lenny proudly forwarded one Street pick he had made in early October, a play on some options to buy shares of a mining company called Massey Energy, which had generated $20 million worth of purchases.

Lenny dubbed his gimmick "deep-in-the-money calls." When explained in Lennyspeak, it didn't make much sense. "I am going to feature Halliburton (HAL) this morning," he wrote in his very first e-mail to me. "The company reported a MONSTER NUMBER last week . . . because the operators on Wall St. want to get the public to sell . . . as they know the 'herd' will do whatever they tell them. It's hilarious how predictable these bozos work; they should just throw out a flare, it's so obvious." In person, it wasn't any better. Sitting in my office, Lenny once had me log on to his stock trading account at Wachovia to try to run me through his system, but he kept losing his thoughts mid-sentence. I was more impressed with his $1 million–plus in positions, providing extra comfort about his ability to pay his bills until he closed with one of the financial partners.

Fortunately, Magnus had met up with Lenny on a trip to Los Angeles and, besides returning with a dumbstruck description of the Gretzky house, down to the guest mansion that Lenny had transformed into a twenty-four-hour trading palace, he had a more cogent description of what Lenny did. A call, I already understood, was an option to buy stock at a certain price by a certain date. A deep-in-the-money call, Magnus explained, was an option when the stock price was already well above the option's trigger price. Because tons of leverage was built into the contract, a rise in the stock would disproportionately jack the price of the call, resulting in a big score. A price drop could be catastrophic. But Lenny, as chronicled by TheStreet .com, almost never missed.

Lenny loved his friendship with Cramer, and his Street column, which he displayed like a magic cloak of legitimacy, especially with me, the Wall Street media kingmaker. He would play me Cramer's voicemail messages, or forward their e-mail back-and-forths.

> "Jim, can you give The Players Club a little airtime" (Cramer: "Let me think about how to do this. I will mull.")
>
> "Nails is checking in . . . wanted to thank you again for the big-time support . . . FOUR MONSTERS RIGHT HERE . . . getting ready to POP! 1) SIGM, 2) PH, 3) UTZ, 4) DFG."

Watching Lenny operate, and TheStreet.com legitimize his results, I dusted off our proposal for Phillips newsletters. For over a year, I had been talking on and off to Eric Bolling and two other *Fast Money* stars we'd helped build up, Pete and Jon Najarian, about a Doubledown newsletter division. What better way to launch it than with a former Major League Baseball player whom Jim Cramer touts as a stock-picking genius? As I explained it to Lenny, if thousands of people were making money from his TheStreet.com picks, why not get into the guru game by charging for it? We'd do all the work and the marketing; he'd just need to make the picks, and we'd split the money that rolled into our partnership.

Lenny jumped right into it. "I am very excited for the opportunity to start an investment newsletter ASAP," he e-mailed me in mid-October. Frequent middle-of-the-night e-mails followed about strategy, from aesthetics ("There is something about opening a new envelope addressed directly to you and touching it, feeling it, this makes you focus on *that particular newsletter*") to the marketing ("I have approximately *FIVE THOUSAND (5,000) emails* waiting for you to retrieve on my 'thestreet.com' email system . . . THIS IS BIG! I CAN SAY WITH CONFIDENCE, *WE SHOULD GET AT LEAST 2,500 THAT SIGN UP!*") to the name (we all agreed on *The Dykstra Report*). We eventually hired a veteran newsletter editor named Christopher Frankie to run the division.

Others took notice of Nails's performance. A top literary agent named Dave Vigliano also reached out, and quickly secured Lenny a six-figure advance for a book on his Wall Street know-how. A top ghostwriter, Cal Fussman, who called himself the Maestro, was brought in to turn Lennyspeak into a best-seller. It was all teed up: from newsletters to bookstores to Web sites, in 2008, Lenny Dykstra was positioned to become America's next great Wall Street guru.

$ $ $

The security guard gave the driver's license a long, incredulous look, then ogled the unlikely person presenting it, before returning to the identification. The building he was paid to protect, the 950-foot limestone-covered global headquarters for the American International Group (AIG), located at 60 Wall Street, was a legitimate terrorist target, the tallest building in lower Manhattan since the Twin Towers fell. But that wasn't what had him flummoxed.

"Are you Lenny Dykstra . . . *the baseball player?*"

"Yeah, dude, Nails."

Only when he viewed the license of our colleague, Ron Darling, did he seem assuaged. Darling was a star pitcher for the Mets back in the eighties, and unlike Lenny, still looked the part, standing a trim six-foot-five. As articulate as Lenny was coarse, Darling, a French and Southeast Asian history double major at Yale, now broadcast games for the Mets. ("He's the smartest guy in the world," Lenny told me while preparing for the meeting. "Just ask him.") A starter for most of his career, Darling, like me, was there to close. It was the Tuesday after Thanksgiving, and we were going to help Lenny finalize his Players Club deal with AIG.

All the other financial firms had been relative tire kickers, as AIG tore through second, third, and fourth meetings. Deal terms flew back and forth, reaching all the way to the CEO of AIG Investments, Win Neuger. A full dozen executives stood ready to meet the three of us, ostensibly to show what they could provide the world's professional athletes. In reality, as we ascended in the elevator passing floor after floor filled with people creating endlessly complicated transactions, we were about to get a demonstration of why the global economy was about to implode.

The first culprit in the coming apocalypse was something called a collateralized debt obligation (CDO). Not just content to underwrite trillions of junky mortgages and other specious loans, Wall Street, led by big banks like Citigroup, Lehman Brothers, and Bear Stearns, began bundling them together and trading them like bonds. If you wanted relative safety, you could buy a bundle full of two-income couples in modest houses; if you wanted more money, you dabbled in migrant farmworkers living in McMansions. For the past few years, the banks had made billions this way, as everyone's American Dream, now a commodity, sold like a cattle future.

Then came AIG's demon offspring, the credit default swap (CDS). The general idea of interest rate swaps had been around since Dykstra and Darling were in their Mets heyday. It was little different from corporate insurance—companies could "swap" an income stream with a moving interest rate for a fixed one, with AIG setting the price.

But now the model was expanded. Rather than just corporate debt, why not start insuring pools of *consumer* risk? The CDS game— essentially guaranteeing the CDOs and other risky pools of assets in case they failed—went from a few hundred billion at the beginning of the Zeroes to roughly $50 trillion as we rode up that AIG elevator. Around 2003, Wall Street duped AIG and its ilk to insure subprime mortgages—loans to people, as the name implied, who could not usually be expected to afford them.

It was a fabulous racket. The only real risk: that all of them would default at the same time. Then AIG wouldn't have enough assets to cover all the guarantees they'd made. But as real estate prices soared to the sky, what were the chances that that could happen?

AIG had created a market out of thin air for student loans, car payments, and crappy mortgages and it was with great anticipation that the executives received Lenny, Darling, and myself. The retirement income of pro athletes was about to become a complicated financial product.

The figures AIG threw around were staggering. To prepare for the meeting, an AIG vice president, Steve Brenneman, had sent Lenny a preliminary partnership proposal, based on the premise that Lenny, armed with his charm, connections, and magazine, could bring one hundred professional athletes into the clutches of AIG in the first year, incrementally rising to six hundred new athletes by the tenth. By those assumptions, some $9.35 billion would flow into AIG from this pool of jocks over the decade, and then $724 million would flow back out to one jock in particular: Lenny Dykstra. "This does not include the additional multi-million dollar trail commissions that could be earned annually for the duration of the life insurance contracts," wrote Brenneman, meaning that as long as AIG milked these athletes, so would Lenny, "nor the millions from sales of additional AIG products."

It was a world gone mad. Lenny wouldn't keep all that money—his strategy, besides the magazine, involved throwing each player's financial adviser a huge commission for any business sent—but a farting, half-asleep former Met known as Nails stood to make *hundreds of millions* by delivering his brethren to AIG.

Our group of three was led into a conference room with a table built for fifty, the kind where important faceless people operating the machinery of capitalism made decisions that affected the world. To fill out our side, Darling sat at the far right end, and I spread out to the left, spaced far enough, with Lenny in the middle, for double play drills. Our roles were clearly defined: while the youngest on our team, I was The Players Club's "grown-up," trying to demonstrate to AIG that there was a real organization behind Lenny, and coherently explain how and why the magazine they were funding—no small commitment at almost $4 million a year—would penetrate locker rooms. Darling provided the testimonial, legitimizing the need for a product in the eyes of retired athletes and, since he still interacted with them because of his television gig, current ones. Lenny stayed largely silent.

When it was AIG's turn to present, they aped Lenny's terminology, unveiling their "Guaranteed Cash Flow" program, which they seemed determined to make as convoluted as a CDO or CDS. It started by touting AIG's monolithic position: 130 countries, 50 million customers, $1 trillion in assets, the tenth most profitable company in the *Fortune* 500, and purveyor of "leading edge retirement income products."

The latter was the key term. AIG would do to athlete retirement plans what it had done to everything else in the Zeroes, whether student loans, or car insurance, or mortgages: turn it into a "product" that required fifteen PowerPoint slides to explain.

This one was a doozy. Lenny's core idea, providing athletes an income between thirty-five (retirement) and fifty-five (pension), remained. The player would receive this in exchange for giving AIG $1 million a year for three years while still active. But AIG presented Lenny two choices. He could recommend that players buy true "Guaranteed Cash Flow"—a plain Jane annuity, the simplest, safest plan in investing, which would yield $170,000 in income each year. (*Not enough money*, Lenny grumbled.)

Or he could steer them toward curtain number two, a blend of an annuity and something that sounded vaguely robotic, an "AIG Elite Global IUL-LT" life insurance policy that invested money like a stock portfolio. What was retirement without a little risk? This option, we were told, projected to produce $300,000 each year, or the minimum Lenny had suggested any athlete worth his Maybach would need post-retirement.

The Players Club structure itself, as presented by AIG, was even more complex, with a flow chart that looked like a computer circuit board, encompassing three different AIG companies, Lenny's company (which now needed to register as a broker/dealer), the player, his agent, his money manager, the magazine, the purchase process, the commission schedules and bonus thresholds. All to help pro athletes retire stress-free.

A suite of extra services, for which Lenny would be paid separately based on sales, were laid out by a top executive from "the Private Client Group," whom I'll call Ken, since he looked like Barbie's boyfriend in middle age. His division offered special insurance for rich people. Art collection? *Covered!* Auto fleet? *Covered!* Kidnapping ransom? *Covered!*

Here's the best part, said Ken, handing us special baseball caps that read AIG WILDFIRE PROTECTION UNIT, flames emerging from the blue. *A lot of pro athletes have homes in California like you, Lenny.* Nails nodded. *Well, wildfires are a huge problem. We have six trucks armed with Phos-Chek, the best fire retardant in the world. Anytime there's a fire, we race in and cover your entire house.* He then went on to describe, in detail, a fire that wiped out an entire neighborhood, save the two homes under the protection of AIG's "private client" fire department, which came out nearly pristine.

I mentally imagined a scene, sipping a casual cup of coffee on the porch of your $8 million mansion as you survey the blackened landscape, watching all your neighbors pick forlornly through their charred possessions. I thought back to the biblical Exodus, and the Jewish slaves who, using a sacrificed lamb, painted their doors red to save themselves from the Tenth Plague, the death of the firstborn. Now it was the rich, not those under the yoke of bondage, who received mercy, the paschal blood replaced by AIG's Phos-Chek.

Of course, all this was an extended preamble for a deal, which Robert Conry, the number two executive at AIG Investments, now laid out. Tough and weathered, with a full head of white hair and a beard, he looked like a hearty New England boat captain. But while his parent company was creating more risk than any in the history of finance, AIG's game was promoting others to take chances, rather than putting their own capital in jeopardy. OPM (Other People's Money) redefined as OPR (Other People's Risk). So rather than direct $4 million to Doubledown for the magazine, they suggested a $300,000 "pilot" issue to see if it would work.

I cringed, as our financial salvation went out the window. Lenny was more direct. "I'm giving you $9 billion worth of accounts, and you expect an exclusive deal in exchange for a test?"

For the next three hours, the two sides knocked back and forth, before Conry put forward what I thought was a bluff. *Lenny, we'll front the $4 million, as an advance against your cut, if you personally guarantee it.*

To which Lenny, who as Billy Beane had noted, had no concept of failure, responded: *Sure,* as flippantly as I had personally guaranteed Doubledown's office lease. Conry grilled him on his financial assets, while Ken, fireman to the rich, probed the details of the Gretzky house. The five-hour marathon ended with a tentative deal in place: AIG would front the cash, Lenny would take the risk.

Back on the street, on the corner of Pine and William, Lenny, Darling, and I did a postmortem. "Goddamn pussies," Lenny grumbled, sucking a cigarette, before a voice—filled, refreshingly, with earnestness—interrupted the gripe session.

"Hey, Ron Darling!"

A man in his early thirties drove up in an electric wheelchair, adorned with Mets stickers. A few months with Lenny had provided a refresher course in how fame opens doors, whether to Jim Cramer or my willingness to have dinner on a few hours' notice. But it was also easy to forget the joy that it can produce if channeled correctly.

For fifteen minutes, Darling enthralled this guy with inside stories from the 1986 season, when he and Lenny led the Mets to their last world championship. This fan had no idea that yet another of his heroes was standing *directly next to him.* All he saw was Ron Darling, some random journalist-entrepreneur, and a fat, broken man. Yes, Lenny's name opened doors, especially in New York. But on the street, he was invisible.

I asked him if that bothered him. "I got the money," he said with a shrug. "At the end of the day, that's all that fucking matters."

$ $ $

Working with Lenny reached a new level of surreal, if that was even possible, in early December when Nails formally decided to fund the *Players Club* magazine out of his own pocket. For all the talk about the Gretzky house, AIG didn't actually loan money—they just enabled others who did—and thus Conry, in a follow-up note, declined to finance the magazine, even with Lenny's house as collateral. They remained interested in a pilot issue, to see if athletes took to the magazine—and AIG's retirement "product." Objectively, as disappointed as I was for Doubledown, it made sense. Why not test the idea first?

To Lenny, though, such thoughts were "minor league." We were going to launch fully, with him writing every check. I countered that, at the very least, we should launch bimonthly—we had done so with *Trader Monthly*; despite the name, we had never found an economically rational reason to change that frequency. No, insisted Lenny, it had to come out, from day one, every month, despite the frightful expenses that entailed. "Everything must be the best," he had scrawled on top of our services contract with him. "No short cuts."

So we began staffing up properly—just in time for a giant picture of Lenny to hit the top of the front page of *The New York Times*. On December 13, former Senate majority leader George Mitchell issued a highly anticipated report on the infiltration of steroids in baseball. The Mitchell Report was a cultural touchstone, an affirmation that "America's pastime" had lost its innocence. The 409-page report was exhaustive in its detail, and of the eighty-five players mentioned, few were featured more prominently than Lenny Dykstra, who, despite refusing to cooperate with the committee's investigators, was linked to taking Deca-Durabolin, Dianabol, and testosterone.

When I called him about it, he played dumb. "Oh, that? I haven't even seen it. I have a business to run." With reporters, he was far less vague, telling *The New York Times* that the allegations were "absolutely false." ("Instead of rewarding people for hard work, they threw people under the bus," he said of the report.) To the *New York Post*, he again "absolutely" denied taking steroids, and when a reporter for the sports blog Deadspin got him on the phone, his response was a more authentically Lenny, "What the fuck is this? I don't know anything about that, man."

Not surprisingly, the advertisers we'd been talking with about *Players Club*, ever image-conscious, freaked out. But that was largely our problem; that money was Doubledown's gravy. Lenny's money came from selling financial plans, and so he pushed forward, costs be damned.

Aside from the small inconvenience of Lenny's role in the biggest baseball scandal since the days of Shoeless Joe and the Black Sox, those early days of putting together *Players Club* proved kind of fun. Translating the Doubledown formula to cover professional athletes was easy, especially given Lenny's Rolodex. Darling sat in on one of our first brainstorming sessions, and Lenny put me in touch with everyone from former Heisman Trophy winner Tim Brown to tennis legend John McEnroe to flesh out ideas. We added another Mets legend, Keith Hernandez, as a restaurant reviewer ("Call him Mex," Lenny had instructed. "He has a new wife and she fucking hates that nickname"), PGA star Fred Couples wrote about golf, and the NBA's Kyle Korver covered video games. We developed "The Grid," where players from different sports filled in boxes explaining the gadgets they were buying, the cars they were driving, and the resorts they were visiting, balanced with lessons about fiscal prudence. We profiled high-profile spouses, successful retirees, and peer-chosen up-and-comers.

This general template turned into actual stories at editorial meetings, which I convened each Monday and asked Lenny to attend, usually by phone from California. I had thought it helpful to use Lenny as a sounding board, the way we did with Magnus before we launched *Trader*. But Lenny saw his role less as muse than as director, and so, his gravelly voice emerging from the speakerphone, Charlie to his Angels, he took us into the id of the locker room.

While we tried to give the magazine dual-gender appeal, including female golfers and tennis players in the mix, Lenny insisted that they must be "gasoline," his term for hot.

Anything that he didn't like was dismissed as "faggy." He measured length in decidedly unmetric units: Darryl Strawberry penises. At the end, Lenny signed off to our coed group with something that would become his weekly catchphrase: "Keep it stiff!"

It was during those "keep it stiff" weeks that the Lenny relationship changed. Maybe it was the pressure now that he was committing to write the checks himself, rather than gamble with OPM. Maybe it was the stress of actually enacting something he'd dreamed about for years. Or maybe it was just another side of Lenny emerging, one that either he had muffled or I'd willfully ignored. Regardless, the old

Lenny dichotomy—mumbling, bumbling Lenny versus jet-setting, stock-picking Lenny—was replaced by a new one: Charming Lenny versus Evil Lenny.

As I pulled the magazine together, Lenny began to complain about "not enough white meat," as in too many African-American players. Rather than winky jokes about "gasoline," women in the magazine became "bitches." Hispanics, Asians, gays—Lenny began slurring them all, and the more I asked him to stop, both as a courtesy to me, and for his own sake, the more he would say it, like some boundary-testing twelve-year-old boy.

Increasingly, this coarseness became personal. Lenny endlessly mocked the guy who financed the purchase of his Gretzky house for his stutter (*st-st-st-st-studder*, as Lenny would describe, jerking his head back and forth). And every time he hung up on his wife, Terri, who had stood with him since the time he was a poor, undersized minor leaguer, he would refer to her as his "fucking bitch wife," adding, "I'd divorce her tomorrow, but then she'd get half of what I own. No way I'm giving that bitch that." He said that so many times, with the exact same sentence construction, that I fully believed him.

A captive of his own riches at home, Lenny exorcised his Henry VIII demons professionally. The first to go was Eliot, the lawyer who led Lenny's young team of "geniuses." Lenny replaced him with a television producer named William Gregson, who had gotten to know Lenny when he appeared on Fox's *Bulls & Bears* to make stock picks. Then he fired the two remaining "geniuses" under William. And then William disappeared. Lenny hired the butler from his stays at the St. Regis Hotel, Israel, to become a concierge for Spanish-speaking Players Club clients. Then he fired him, too. Lenny's accountant, Jeffrey Feinman, whom I met that first night at Coco Pazzo, was next. So now he had no help developing the financial side of The Players Club, the part that was supposed to generate $9.35 billion worth of AIG contracts.

With no staff of his own, he turned to mine. Our deal gave me the authority to manage my own team, but Lenny was increasingly possessive of anyone dedicated to the project. He rented a large, expensive office suite in a Park Avenue tower that also housed the headquarters of Major League Baseball, and insisted that anyone working on The Players Club base from there. Then one by one, he insisted that I fire them, always accentuating these directives, in writing, with an exclamation point. First, my editorial lieutenant, John Capouya ("I must have told you 50 times: get rid of Capouya," he e-mailed. "Not my kind of guy, period!"). Then, the designer, Mitch Shostak ("I do not want this guy working on my magazine, period!"). Then Capouya's replacement, Jonathan Lesser. ("I'm sorry to say: Jon Lesser must go!") When I refused to fire Mitch or Jon, both of whom I had a prior relationship with, Evil Lenny stewed.

Lenny didn't just go through the motions of a professional executioner; he actually *enjoyed* it. Whenever I asked about another member of his staff that he'd removed, he'd laugh about what they said to him or how they begged him for their job. "Breathe deep," he would then say to me, pantomiming what it would be like to put a gas mask over someone's face and euthanize them, while making heavy-breathing sound effects.

No matter how much Lenny needed me right now, I knew that it was merely a matter of time before it would be my turn to "breathe deep." I just needed that moment to be after Doubledown got on more sure financial footing. On Wall Street, there's a term called "Fuck You Money." That's when you've finally socked away enough to tell your boss off if you don't like something. In my head, I knew what Fuck You Money—even a one-dollar profit—would mean to Doubledown: the freedom to stop dealing with Nails and the kind of people who bubble up when the world goes into a feeding frenzy, and you're viewed as holding the keys to the food silos.

$ $ $

"What kind of bullshit is this?" Lenny said to me, enraged.

The cause of this disturbance: a beautiful-looking plate of salt-and-pepper prawns, fried until the shell cracked. As he held one up, revolted, the manager of the new Columbus Circle branch of the well-regarded Blue Ribbon Sushi approached us on his rote table tour.

"How is everything?" he asked, innocuously.

"Terrible," snarled Lenny, "you sent us out this shrimp and forgot to peel it."

I should have known better. When Lenny came to town, I often took him out as my date to review restaurants for *Time Out New York*. Such was my life now that the only time I had for my sole remaining hobby was when I was working. Lenny, though, was an atrocious restaurant wingman, with the manners and palate of an eight-year-old. He gleefully slurped up watery pasta at a restaurant called Gemma that might have been my worst meal of the year ("this stuff is great"), while he mocked me for ordering sushi at Blue Ribbon ("you eat that raw shit?"). So when the cooked entrée I had ordered on his behalf didn't resemble a shrimp cocktail at Red Lobster, he blew up.

I endured it. Lenny was well overdue on his payments to us, so my mission this night, February 13, 2008, was not to leave him until he wired us a quarter-million dollars. It was a Wednesday, the midway point of Lenny's weeklong sleep deprivation, and always a crapshoot in Lennyland—sometimes he was still sharp, other times he was beginning his decline.

He was cranky, as evidenced by the blowup at the restaurant. The launch of *Players Club* was six weeks away. Lenny knew the cash request was coming this night, a topic as increasingly uncomfortable between us as a pubescent birds-and-bees sit-down, so he did his best to filibuster. We talked about what needed to be done for the magazine.

Derek Jeter had agreed to appear on the first cover, and we would need to shoot him in Florida during spring training. Lenny was insisting that we add a pictorial of his Gretzky house, which he now seemed keen to sell. And we discussed the possibility of a launch party, a magazine's best chance to introduce itself to the world. We had several venues interested in hosting the party for free, but as fate would have it, Blue Ribbon was located right across the street from the Time Warner Center and the Mandarin Oriental ballroom, where we had launched *Trader Monthly* and *Dealmaker*. On a whim, I took Lenny up to see it, and even Nails melted at the giant windows and their thirty-sixth-floor views of the Manhattan skyline. "This is where it's gotta be, dude," he said. "Everything has to be the best. This is the best."

A little after 9 p.m., I gave Lenny a ride in a cab to the St. Regis, which was on my way home, finally forcing the subject of money owed. "I hear ya, bro," Lenny responded. "Come up to my room, and let's talk about it."

"Room," it turned out, was modest. It was a breathtaking corner apartment overlooking both Fifty-third Street and Fifth Avenue, complete with shared butler, who rang the doorbell before entering to refresh the ice and fold the towels. The foyer opened into a grand living room, larger than the one I shared with my wife and two daughters, accented with antique moldings.

He had his laptops splayed around a little sitting area, creating his own multiscreen trading desk, and he instinctively migrated there. I sat in an overstuffed chair across from him. Grabbing the remote, he flipped on the giant plasma television sitting above the fireplace. It was tuned to CNN.

That day had been an epic one for television news. Roger Clemens, probably the best baseball pitcher of the past half-century, had been hauled in front of a congressional committee. Clemens was the biggest name outed by the Mitchell Report—he and Lenny had shared the spotlight atop the front page of *The New York Times*—and like Lenny he had steadfastly and publicly denied using steroids. Now, along with his former trainer, Brian McNamee, who had told Mitchell about injecting Clemens (and had the syringes to back it up), Clemens had been subpoenaed to testify, under oath, facing the possibility of jail if he lied.

The testimony was riveting. *"I fully support Senator Mitchell's conclusions that steroids have no place in baseball. However, I take great issue with the report's allegation that I used these substances. Let me be clear again: I did not."*

"Do I think steroids are good for helping someone's performance? No. In fact, I think they are detrimental."

"At the end of the day, I have been accused of doing something that I did not do. I have been asked to prove that I did not do it. How in the world can I prove a negative?"

When pushed further, Clemens eventually confessed—on behalf of his wife, citing her desire to look good for an upcoming photo shoot. *"She had been broken up over this a long time. . . . She said she feels like a pawn in his game."*

It was engrossing television. And for Lenny Dykstra and me, an even more awkward subject than the money talk. He had denied the Mitchell Report allegations to me on several occasions, as vociferously as he had to the press. I knew he was lying. He knew he was lying. But now CNN had Clemens's testimony on an infinite loop. Larry King played the highlights at 9 p.m., giving way to Anderson Cooper at 10 p.m., who repeated them for an hour again at 11 p.m., before ceding the network to a repeat of Larry King. It was like sitting in the Stuttgart living room of your grandfather, the rumored SS officer, as the History Channel played a *World at War* marathon. As we discussed everything and anything else, neither of us wanted to change the channel and acknowledge the steroid-pumped elephant in the room. So it just played and played.

"You know," Lenny finally said, breaking the ice, "I was like a pioneer for that stuff."

"Excuse me, Lenny?"

"The *juice*. I was like the very first to do that. Me and [José] Canseco."

He straightened up, as he prepared, somewhat proudly, to reveal his role in this dangerous, unseemly history.

Performance-enhancing drugs seemed to be everywhere at the time. Besides the almost-daily revelations that brought down one sports idol after another, *Trader Monthly* was increasingly getting tips about similar issues on Wall Street. These steroids were mental— amphetamine-based ADD drugs, particularly Adderall, as a way to sharpen focus and gain an edge. In late 2007, we conducted our largest—and last—survey of our readership, recording 2,500 responses to a variety of issues. We asked about Adderall, and 11 percent of our respondents admitted using it to get a boost against their peers.

Alpha, and the fantastic sums it created, did that to people. Our questions pushed further. If you received an illegal insider tip, a sure thing, and had a 50 percent chance of getting busted, would you use it? Only 7 percent would. What about only a 10 percent chance of getting caught? The number spiked to 28 percent. And what if you had zero percent chance of getting discovered? Suddenly, the number surged to 58 percent. To the majority of our readers, cheating wasn't an ethical issue. It was simply a matter of whether they'd get caught.

That seemed to have been Lenny's philosophy. "At first it wasn't even illegal. Then, after a few years, I had to go to a doctor, and get a prescription. You know how I got my stuff? Just walking into a pharmacy, bro. It was as simple as that.

"You gotta understand, there were only twenty-eight people who had my job in the whole world." He was referring to the fact that there were only twenty-eight Major League Baseball teams (there are now thirty-two), and that each only had one starting center fielder. "And thousands of people wanted those jobs, and every year, there were guys trying to take my job.

"So I needed to do anything I could to protect my job, take care of my family. Do you have any idea how much money was at stake? Do you?"

I gave him a generic shrug. I didn't express judgments, or ask any follow-up questions. I just listened, as a psychiatrist might.

"Twenty-five million dollars!" he said, answering his own question. "Twenty-five million!" He was referring to the final contract of his career. In 1993, bulked to dimensions approaching a fire hydrant, Dykstra had gone to the plate more times (773) than anyone in the century-long history of professional baseball. He led the National League in hits, walks, at bats, and runs scored, and set career highs in home runs, RBIs, doubles, stolen bases, on-base percentage, and slugging percentage. He finished second to Barry Bonds as the league's Most Valuable Player. And the Phillies rewarded him with a four-year, $24.9 million contract, giving him another baseball record: the highest-paid leadoff hitter ever. It was one of the worst deals in Phillies history: he quickly broke down physically, and never played another full season.

What Lenny Dykstra really did, by his own admission, was *cheat* his way to $25 million. He had duped the Phillies into that contract based on a completely manufactured performance. But he didn't view it that way. "Real money, bro, there's no way you can't do everything and anything you can to maximize that."

Of course, what he conveniently left out was the worthy candidate who played by the rules—and chose not to endanger his long-term health—and didn't get that job because Lenny cheated. Or the worthy pitcher on another team who lost his job because a 160-pound-weakling-turned-200-pound muscleman tagged an ill-timed, artificial home run off him.

Our meeting went long and late. Every time I brought up money, he smiled. "You're just trying to get out of here, dude." The quid pro quo was abundantly clear: he didn't want to be alone, and if I wanted to get paid, I'd keep him company.

At 12:42 a.m., he asked about wiring instructions. Even though I'd sent them before, I re-emailed them from my phone. Still, he didn't move to make the payment. Instead, he began talking about mortality. Lenny had turned forty-five three days earlier, and he bemoaned how broken down his body was, how he didn't expect to make it past fifty. As if to illustrate that, he removed his teeth, and put them on the table, flashing a gummy, toothless smile at me.

It was now 2 a.m.—Valentine's Day would begin with Lenny Dykstra—and the doorbell rang. The ghostwriter for Lenny's investing book, Cal "the Maestro" Fussman, bleary-eyed and dressed in sweatpants, was reporting for duty. He'd spent the early evening sleeping, knowing that he was covering the Lenny shift until dawn. I was dismissed.

"How much do I owe you?" Lenny asked quietly, even though he knew the answer.

"$250,000."

So he pecked out the wiring instruction to his broker with two fingers. As I left, the Maestro and I silently nodded to each other, coldly and knowingly, like night watchmen on a shift change, both all too aware of the ugly hours and nature of our work.

10

Maxed Out

(Early 2008)

A sure sign of imminent collapse is when the obscene becomes normal. It's the only explanation for why John Paulson, just
off the elevator, was heading in my direction.

Though I recognized him immediately, Paulson surely would have
had trouble getting anyone at a New York restaurant to give him a
decent table. Dark complexion, receding hairline, recessed eyes—a
slim, cerebral Paul Sorvino. He had come alone. No date, no entourage, no bodyguards, the latter perhaps the most unusual.

John Paulson, after all, had just made almost $4 *billion* in a single
year.

The previous spring, we had hosted a party to celebrate our *Trader
Monthly* 100 list. While Doubledown had become singularly good
at delivering whichever elite audience we promised our advertisers,
this event had largely been a charade. Hundreds of run-of-the-mill
$500,000 and $1 million and even $5-million-a-year traders came to
salute the best of the best, but none of the actual 100 appeared. Even
among our gauche crew, publicly celebrating your own nine-digit
haul was considered over-the-top.

By the spring of 2008, however, that had finally changed. This marked our fifth effort to keep score on who made what on Wall Street, and even by the grotesque standards we had been chronicling across the Zeroes, the final earnings figures for 2007 were so big that I was at a loss for what to call these people.

Billionaires? That didn't really cut it: we found five guys, including Paulson, who had just made at least $1 billion in *annual income*, not net worth. Comparing the magicians atop our list who pulled fortunes from the digital air to the old-fashioned titans of industry who spent their lives slowly building companies and employing people and producing things and funding libraries didn't seem to do the absurdity justice. In editing the list, I finally infused the term "billion-dollar earners," which more accurately reflected the concept: these guys were sitting on the most lucrative money machines ever invented, money machines capable of shooting out a billion dollars to them every single year.

Or in John Paulson's case, every three months.

"Thanks for joining us," I said, launching into babysitting duty for the orphaned guest.

"Glad to be here," Paulson replied cordially.

His demeanor matched his appearance; for all the sparkle of his wealth, he had the charisma of an accountant. We made the kind of awkward, idle chitchat that a struggling entrepreneur makes with a man who, over the past twelve months, had been pocketing money at the rate of $10 million a day, weekends and holidays included. Finally, we got down to business. I tapped my trophy guest on the elbow and ushered him over to a preview of what he, and the one hundred VIPs who would follow that night, had come to see. The sign, painted in vivid Day-Glo, that the apocalypse was near: the *Trader Monthly* 100, as interpreted by the Renoir of Hippies, sixties pop artist Peter Max.

$ $ $

When Peter Max's business manager left me a message a few weeks earlier asking me to contact him at my "earliest convenience," I knew

the name, but little more. I'd registered for art history the second se-
mester of my senior year in college, but dropped it when it became
clear that, amid one of the few periods in life when one counts on
taking it easy, it would require actual work. Before calling him back,
I checked out some art Web sites.

I recognized his *LOVE* poster, a woman's rainbow-colored hair
expanding from those four powerful letters, one of the iconic images of the sixties. His cosmic style inspired the Beatles' *Yellow Sub-
marine*. He'd been the official artist of the Super Bowl, the World
Series, the World Cup. He'd had ninety museum shows, and no less
a curatorial authority than Larry King dubbed him "America's artist
laureate."

And he loved money. At least that's what Paul Durante told me
when I called him back, and he asked me out of the blue if I wanted
to come to Peter's studio, located across the street from Lincoln Center. The next day, I found myself on a rickety elevator in a prewar
office building, ascending to a cryptically marked penthouse suite.

Whether or not the contrast with the entrance is intentional, stepping into Peter Max's studio feels like the miraculous scene from
Willy Wonka & the Chocolate Factory when Charlie Bucket emerges from
his dreary industrial London reality into a psychedelic fantasy of lol-
lipop flowers and chocolate rivers. There was Jimi Hendrix in a swirl
of red-white-and-blue, a Technicolor Bill Clinton tooting his saxo-
phone, and a piano bathed in rainbow swirls and autographed, with
panache, by Ringo Starr, who used a stylized pentagram to represent
his last name.

Durante emerged from the back to greet me. A Vancouver native
who stood a lean five-foot-ten, Durante didn't talk as much as he
announced, with every sentence coming across like a television commercial voice-over. He had ridden his pipes his entire adult life, from
a long stint in his teens and early twenties as a nightclub emcee to
the Catholic Channel on Sirius satellite radio. His new freelance gig
as head of business development for Peter Max, icon-turned-hustler,
had aspects of both.

The artist himself was running late, so I was parked in front of
a bank of eighteen televisions, six across, three deep, all of which

were running an infinite loop of Peter Max. Larry King fawning over him on his talk show, trippy videos from his sixties apex, a segment about a Continental 777 he painted, from nose to tail, to commemorate the millennium. As I saw later, this was mandatory operating protocol for first-time visitors, particularly for those who had needed the Internet to figure out who this guy was. It was a forty-minute infomercial drumming into my head, from eighteen directions, that you were now in the presence of America's *greatest living artist*, even if, as evidenced by the gaudy price tags on almost every work in his own studio, he seemed quite the sellout. By the end of the loop, not unlike anticipating the tasting room after a long brewery tour, you were foaming at the mouth to meet Peter Max.

My first encounter would have to wait some more. Forty-five minutes later, still no Peter. I was brought into a small conference room off to the side of the studio, where a pile of cashews and dark raisins sat idly on the tray, the stale centerpiece on a long table more befitting a dining room than a boardroom. While waiting, Durante discussed the power in Peter Max's right hand.

"Imagine," he said, "if you doodled some drawings and signed your name and it was the same as creating a one-thousand-dollar bill. That's what Peter does. He literally can print money out of nothing, as much as he wants. He's like King Midas." The difference, of course, is that gold has universal value, while only a very small percentage of people are willing to pay real money for some scribbles from Peter Max, which is apparently why I had been summoned. Durante had initially been intrigued by The Players Club, but as I talked about the incredible wealth of our traders and private equity hotshots, he adroitly went right to the hedge fund managers. "So these top guys all make one hundred million dollars a year?" he asked. I shook my head: "Some make a billion."

The mother lode has arrived! Almost conspiratorially, he told me about Peter's favorite way to make money from rich people: something known around the Peter Max studio as "One-Plus-Three." It worked like this: Peter would offer to paint portraits of as many people as were willing to donate $35,000 to a given charity. Unknown to them, Peter would then paint a polyptych—a four-panel painting,

Warhol-style, that he would intentionally render in such a way that each quarter's colors would seemingly bleed into the others, making the whole hard to break up. The altruist who went into Peter's studio expecting to pick up their $35,000 charity piece would, after seeing the video and then themselves in quadruple glory, invariably fork over another $105,000 directly to Peter for the other three panels. One-Plus-Three.

As I both cringed at the crassness and marveled at the ingenuity, Peter walked in, nearly two hours after our appointed time, huffing an apology in a weird continental version of a Brooklyn accent. Born in Germany, he and his parents had fled the Nazis, his mother and father toting him to China, Israel, and Paris before finally settling in Bensonhurst, Brooklyn, when he was a teen. He wasn't what I expected—most pictures of him are from his hippie heyday, when he looked a lot like George Harrison. Now he looked like Jerry Stiller, with his bushy mustache and stringy brown hair that seemed off-color. He was wearing a smock over a pullover V-neck sweater, and donning those wrist guards for people with carpal tunnel syndrome.

Paul gave him a quick synopsis of our conversation. "So you heard about One-Plus-Three," Peter said, flashing the toothy grin of an inventor discussing his latest patent. "The charity gives us the excuse to paint the first. Then people see all four, they have no choice. They fall in love. It works ninety-eight percent of the time." Peter cited a recent fund-raiser for Larry King, his high school schoolmate, where he sold twelve portraits for King's charity, and pocketed a cool million for himself.

"I'm not just an artist," he explained. "I'm a businessman. I love making money. I love doing deals." Later in our relationship, I would discover a 1969 issue of *Life* magazine, published two weeks after the Woodstock festival, with Peter on its cover, a photo of his face bubbling up from his candy-colored psychedelia, with the cover line: "Peter Max: Portrait of the artist as a very rich man." While his cultural peers were spinning naked around Max Yasgur's farm, Peter, the article detailed, had cut licensing deals with fifty different corporations, from General Electric clocks to Sears coffee mugs. I also came across a more disturbing clipping: Peter quietly pleading guilty in 1997 to federal conspiracy charges that he concealed more than $1.1 million in income from the IRS by swapping art as partial payment for houses in the Hamptons, the Virgin Islands, and, yes, Woodstock, New York. He wound up serving two months in a work release program. For Peter Max, Woodstock wasn't sex, drugs, and rock and roll—it was tax evasion.

As we discussed the upcoming *Trader Monthly* 100, and our billion-dollar earners, he began eagerly paging through the previous year's edition, tangible proof of numbers that, I'd come to learn, seemed impossible to Wall Street outsiders. The wheels turned in the artist's head: Peter Max loves making money. Peter Max paints rock stars. Rock stars were no longer making Peter Max enough money. Hedge fund managers were the new rock stars.

Within twenty-four hours, an agreement had emerged: Peter would do portraits to appear in the upcoming issue of the *Trader Monthly* 100. Similar to the charity fund-raisers, the magazine gave him the excuse to do the first painting. We would then host the *Trader Monthly* 100 parties at his studio, invite the honorees, and let Peter sell four-panel versions to them on the spot. It was a perfect arrangement for us: exclusive paintings from a world-famous artist in our magazine; an elite party venue; and yet another opportunity to get ourselves off the money-losing treadmill that was the traditional magazine advertising business, as we'd split Peter's take. "Plus, I always throw a little something from each sale to their charity," Peter added, giving us the chance to do some good, too.

The potential was huge: a dozen hedge fund managers, paying $140,000 for four portraits, would yield $1.68 million. After the hedge fund managers, we could repeat for the top players in *Dealmaker*, *Corporate Leader*, *Private Air*, and even *The Cigar Report*. We could then repeat this cycle annually. As the top of our readership gorged, here was a direct way for us to grab some of the crumbs. With Lenny Dykstra increasingly erratic, King Midas had the potential to rescue our struggling company with his right hand.

The only issue was timing. This was the very end of February, and the issue shipped in mid-March, which gave us all of two weeks to choose the subjects, get images for Peter to work from, have him paint the paintings, translate them into magazine-layout-friendly computer files, lay them into the larger story, correct the color, and get it to the printer.

Unbeknownst to me, however, I had just partnered with the Henry Ford of acrylics: if there's art in efficiency, as architect William Lethaby noted, then Peter Max proved that there's efficiency in art. Peter's bright penthouse was less a studio than a factory, similar to his old pal Andy Warhol's except that Wonka-style commerce had replaced speed-fueled orgies. The assembly line worked something like this: rather than paint from scratch, Peter's Oompa-Loompas, of which there seemed to be dozens, silk-screened a photograph of the subject directly onto the canvas, which they had prestretched and placed on an easel at a Peter-friendly height. Standing in his smock, Peter supposedly applied what in the business world would be termed the "value-added"—placing streaks and dashes and accents of groovy colors atop the picture, not unlike what Ted Turner had done when he colorized the MGM film library two decades prior.

His business, in other words, was selling rich people's photographs back to them, in quadruplicate. Now it was our business, too.

$ $ $

Our role as facilitator at this definitive crossroads of art-meets-commerce was winnowing the 100 to a dozen or so Peter-worthy subjects, and then obtaining photographs. Paging through the rough draft of the list, figuring out who merited the extra attention, was a strange experience. In the four months since the boxing match, the world had changed. The subprime meltdown, a problem for over-extended homeowners in 2007, was now infecting the country's financial institutions. The French banking giant Société Générale had turned up its own rogue trader, thirty-one-year-old Jérôme Kerviel, whose secret losses totaled an unheard-of $7 billion, the greatest fraud ever, or at least for a few months. Even bonuses were down.

Well, not *down*, as in less than the year before. In the mind-set of the time, that remained inconceivable. Just down, as in *up less*, percentage-wise, than the previous year's record haul. A record, but only barely.

Yet the top of the trading heap, as if from some parallel universe, had reaped astronomically. The total personal haul for these one hundred men (there were no women) was roughly $30 billion in 2007—a tidy $300 million each, on average. So much money had snowballed into hedge funds—more than $2 trillion—that a ludicrous pay system already stacked in their favor pretty much guaranteed the largest players a spot on the *Trader Monthly* 100 irrelevant of performance. The 2-and-20 compensation scheme had run amok.

How else to explain Bruce Kovner, the secretive sixty-three-year-old former cabdriver who managed $12 billion at Caxton Associates? When not gobbling up millions of dollars' worth of Beethoven manuscripts or serving as a veritable ATM for conservative causes, he turned in an essentially flat performance in a year when, even with subprime tremors, the overall stock market was up more than 5 percent.

Nonetheless, Caxton charged 3-and-30, meaning it took a 3 percent management fee off the top, charging investors $360 million for the privilege of this lousy performance. Even after overhead and salaries and, presumably, bonuses for his staff, we estimated that Kovner still had up to $200 million left for himself in 2007. "Turning on the lights," we noted archly in the magazine, "never paid so well."

Another hedge fund pioneer, Leon Cooperman of Omega Advisors, might have had a worse year. The former Goldman Sachs research guru's $5.6 billion flagship fund's return was barely above zero and his firm forked over $500,000 to settle federal allegations that one of its executives tried to bribe officials in Azerbaijan to sell the state-run oil company. His personal reward? An estimated $100 million to $150 million. JWM Partners' John Meriwether, famous in the 1980s for his $1 million *Liar's Poker* showdown and then in the 1990s for nearly collapsing the global financial system at Long-Term Capital Management, set some kind of record for profiting from underwhelming third acts. In 2007, he scratched his way to around $100 million for basically matching what my dad was getting in his index funds.

For those actually generating alpha, the 2-and-20 system yielded sums impossible to fathom. Quants fared particularly well. Chaotic energy prices, nervous equity markets, the subprime mess, all of it conspired to produce the effect most craved by quant traders— volatility. While markets had gradually become more price-efficient over the decade, erasing many of the opportunities for the scalpers at Magnus's old shop, the quants' "black box" computer robo-traders sucked up even the smallest opportunities like an Electrolux.

Jim Simons's machines proved particularly efficient. For the five years we had been estimating trader income, no one did better than Renaissance Technologies' former military code breaker: $6 billion combined, beating out Stevie Cohen by a cool billion or so. In 2007, his $7 billion Medallion fund nailed a 70 recent return. Given his insane 5-and-44 fee (staff who kept their money in the fund got an employee discount: 5-and-36), that put more than $1.5 billion in his personal pocket. Similarly, Ken Griffin's black boxes at Citadel collectively returned 32 percent for an asset pool that had swelled to $20 billion. The thirty-nine-year-old's estimated personal income for 2007: over $1 billion.

The truly great windfalls we had calculated for the prior year, however, surpassing even those of Griffin and Simons, belonged to those capitalizing on the subprime train wreck victimizing millions of subprime mortgage holders, unfortunate bank traders, and the entire economic system. As Braveheart proved on 9/11, as Steve Berkson did with Hurricane Katrina, in the zero-sum forum of trading, one person's losing position made another a winner. Disaster spelled opportunity for those who had foreseen the coming disaster and prepared an ambush.

Few were more poised than Harbinger's Phil Falcone. The forty-five-year-old hockey player who played at Harvard and professionally in Sweden, naming his firm's conference rooms after his favorite teams, had been bumping around the bottom of our list since we started counting. That was still plenty good enough to allow a recent $49 million bid, in cash, for the Manhattan town house belonging to now-bankrupt *Penthouse* founder Bob Guccione, complete with Roman-style indoor swimming pool, greenhouse, sauna, eleven bathrooms, and fire panels depicting a woman with five pairs of breasts. As I looked over his *Trader Monthly* 100 entry, I saw that he was converting the pleasure palace into a family compound for himself, his wife (another former model), twin three-year-old girls, and a pet potbellied pig named Pickles, which would get its own room.

In spite of his frothy personal real estate purchase, Harbinger's housing-related holdings gave Falcone a window into the trouble brewing. He responded by short-selling any and every subprime bond he could, betting 60 percent of his roughly $10 billion fund that they would go down. As the bonds plummeted, his fund more than doubled. Falcone personally took home almost $2 billion, the runner-up for 2007 (and all-time).

The new top dog, our early party guest, had emerged from nowhere. We first noticed John Paulson the previous year, when he debuted on the *Trader Monthly* 100 with an estimated $150 million income for 2006. For the decade prior, the onetime NYU valedictorian had run his eponymous fund, Paulson and Co., under the radar, earning him a great living—$5 million here, $10 million there—but in the pantheon of hedge fund managers, he was strictly middle-class, the high school gym teacher who lived in a neighborhood filled with doctors and lawyers.

Poring over the statistics and sure that the bubble would pop in 2007, Paulson, with one of his deputies, fifty-year-old Paolo Pellegrini, had developed two ways to take advantage. First, they would short the ABX, an index fund, like the vanilla's Vanguard 500, for subprime mortgages. Simple enough. Any trader in the world could have done that, though few ignored the euphoria to actually do so.

The evil genius came in the second approach. Using Goldman Sachs, Paulson hand-selected the junkiest of the junk CDOs, dubbed Abacus—Goldman eventually faced SEC charges for selling these specific bundles of garbage to investors—and then bought massive amounts of AIG's gift to the financial system, the swaps insuring them. As the CDOs began crashing, the swaps skyrocketed disproportionately as panicked traders began overpaying for some protection from their massive exposure. Paulson even did it one better. He specifically focused on a certain type of swap that required a *cash collateral* as the prices went up. So as his holdings exploded to the sky, those buying from him had to write him additional checks; one major bank angrily forked over $500 million.

Going into 2007, Paulson was managing $7 billion. Leaving 2007, that total had swelled to almost $30 billion. His investors made fortunes. His deputies made fortunes (Pellegrini's bonus, we estimated, approached $200 million). Paulson, meanwhile, made the kind of money that gets credited as the greatest trade of all time.

After a few days sorting through this new hedge fund hierarchy, and digging through our archives and wire services for photographs, Durante, Peter Max's business ringer, suggested that he reach out and try to get our choices to send in their own shots.

His effort turned into a Rorschach test for the gods of finance. *If Peter Max is immortalizing you for the world to see, how do you want to be depicted?*

To some, their wealth made them titans. Serious men doing serious work. John Paulson directed Durante to a photographer with a picture of him looking directly, solemnly, into the camera, a necktie tight at his cutaway collar, thick plastic frames atop his nose even though he appeared in most pictures—and at our party—without glasses. A short-seller named Jim Chanos who had rung up more than $300 million in 2007 desired to appear even more stoic in his picture. Chanos originally garnered attention in 2001 for publicly calling out the massive fraud that turned out to be Enron (his firm, Kynikos, is Greek for "cynic"). We had first gotten to know him in 2005 when his designer gave us photographs of his twelve-thousand-square-foot Hamptons beach house, inspired by King George IV's Royal Pavilion, for an occasional *Trader Monthly* column called "Spreads." Chanos blew a gasket, claiming he hadn't authorized them, and as a compromise, we ran them, in annotated detail, referring to the China-themed mansion as owned only by a "hedge fund mogul."

The following year, Chanos got divorced, and that house turned into some billionaire version of *Girls Gone Wild*, as Chanos hosted clambakes with dozens of sultry young women, most imported from Manhattan, including one named Ashley Dupré, the $5,000-an-hour call girl who helped bring down New York governor Eliot Spitzer during the very week Durante was soliciting Chanos's photograph. (Dupré reportedly referred to him as Uncle Jim. "She is one of many young ladies I have spent time with around town," Chanos shrugged to the *New York Post*.) Yet despite, or perhaps because of, this fun-loving alter ego, Uncle Jim gave Durante a dour picture, his lips pursed as if he were passing an oddly shaped kidney stone.

Paradoxically, others wanted to be seen in the same sunny way that Chanos apparently lived. Ken Griffin, master of the faceless black-box traders, approved one with a toothy grin. And while Peter had already painted one panel of Phil Falcone in an angry pose, appropriate for a short-seller whom *BusinessWeek* would soon dub "The Midas of Misery," Falcone submitted a photograph of himself smiling widely, with an open shirt, feathered hair parted down the middle, and little wired glasses. John Lennon reincarnated, save the love and peace stuff.

Then there were those who wanted to look on canvas the same way they did in their head. Marc Lasry (more than $200 million in 2007), a Democratic booster recently famous for hiring Chelsea Clinton as an analyst, sent in a tousled heartthrob shot more appropriate as the centerfold for *Tiger Beat*. Fifty-three-year-old Paul Tudor Jones ($650 million) did one better: he stepped into a time machine, and sent in his college yearbook shot, or one taken not too long after. ("I am wondering how large Peter's portrait of Paul would be as I think a decent size would make it more valuable to him," a Jones lieutenant wrote Durante. "Something to consider in Paul's case since he is a big fan.")

There were last-minute hitches. Traders who have worked for Stevie Cohen, another 2007 billion-dollar earner, describe his sixth sense in all things markets, the bomb-sniffing dog of price movements. He instinctively grasped the Peter Max/*Trader Monthly* 100 game. Not only would he not supply a picture, he relayed, he would not look if Peter ever tried to sell him one. Nevertheless, within a week of our first meeting, we had culled fourteen photographs from among the list's worthiest, and Peter Max's assembly line churned in advance of the looming deadline.

Then Durante called. "We have a problem," he boomed in his radio voice.

"What is it?"

"It's the Pope."

Pope Benedict XVI, some three years after his election to succeed John Paul II, was arriving imminently for his first American visit, including two masses at Yankee Stadium. Peter's pontiff painting would become 110,000 posters, to be given out at those masses. (Though Peter's signature would not go on them: "He's afraid of being targeted by al-Qaeda," I was told.)

So simultaneous with the fifty-six hedge fund paintings—the fourteen subjects in quadruplicate, which Peter now wanted to do all in advance—he now had one of the most important commissions of his career. Stress filled the studio, as the Oompa-Loompas went into overdrive.

With a day to spare, Durante beckoned me to return to the studio. It was awash in fresh canvases. Jim Simons had emerged from Peter Max's magic color machine with his white professorial beard streaked with yellow, his golf shirt turned electric pink. Paulson's suit was now eggplant, the sky Gatorade orange. Falcone's wavy hair looked like Raggedy Andy's. It was quite an effect: fifteen of the most powerful men on earth, lined up one after another; a collection of hedge fund moguls, who together made $10 billion the previous year—and the Pope, resplendent in white.

Only one of them looked humble.

$ $ $

Almost from the beginning, Peter Max wooed me in the same aggressive manner that Lenny Dykstra did. That should have been the first clue. Except rather than plane rides, Zeroes-style, Peter Max romanced with his tools of the sixties, art and love. During our very first meeting, where he had extolled his vision of One-Plus-Three, he asked for the names of my wife and daughters. He then went over to a large drafting table and took out a 240-page coffee table book, *The Art of Peter Max*. With a black Flair pen, on the first page he drew a heart containing all our initials, *R, J, S, C.* "Love, Max," he wrote at the bottom. Then, on the opposite page, he drew an elegant woman's face within another heart, a pen-and-ink riff on his famous *LOVE* poster. He signed another book to my father and stepmother, who were retiring from their respective academic posts.

A week or so later, Durante called me with an odd question. *If you could meet anyone in the world, who would it be?* Given that I had been expecting something more along the lines of what does Paul Tudor Jones really look like, this college interview chin-scratcher required a proper ponder.

"Probably the president, so I could give him my take on the world," I finally said. "But if it was just for jollies, I don't know. Maybe Muhammad Ali? Why?"

"Oh, nothing."

Two weeks later, a tube arrived at my office. Inside the tube was a rolled-up canvas, two-feet-by-three-feet: a Peter Max painting of Muhammad Ali, his face defiant, framed by orange and blue and purple. "To Randall. Love, Max, 2008," he scrawled on top, in thick marker, the *x* tilted more like a plus, a signature of his signature.

These gestures were far less touching after I later received two invoices, confirming that, while I had paid nothing, the book and the painting were worth $1,000 and a few thousand, respectively. I felt like Peter had given himself a tax write-off, rather than me a gift. Perhaps that's the real way that tax felons express "love."

The real love I was looking for was a signed contract. At our first meeting, I'd laid out Doubledown's position: an elegant fifty-fifty revenue split. Art galleries generally take 50 percent of the sale, and by bringing the *Trader Monthly* 100 to him, we were essentially serving that function. Any other arrangement was a messy haggle. Peter responded amenably, and given the immediate turnaround required, we pushed forward.

However, the Extell bait-and-switch had taught me that the handshake Magnus and I had founded Doubledown with, in the spirit of trust, didn't work outside the family. Until the magazine actually printed, we had the leverage. All I wanted out of it was a binding contract, without any headaches.

Yet Peter didn't seem interested in formalizing anything. So about a week before the final deadline, as I made hollow threats about pulling the images from the issue, Paul Durante asked me to meet him and Peter at a Le Pain Quotidien across from his studio at 7 p.m. to break some bread and cut a deal. Now familiar with Peter Max time, I showed up a half-hour late, and I was still the first to arrive. Peter finally showed, at 8, just in time for the bakery to close.

Peter insisted that we go to dinner, a more complicated process than it sounds. Peter Max is a vegan; only a handful of restaurants in New York pass muster for him. His wife, Mary, was already at one of them, a utopian-sounding place called Blossom. So we would make it a table for four: me, and Peter, Paul and Mary.

Unfortunately, this Peter, Paul and Mary show was canceled as soon as we arrived at the restaurant. Mary was already dining with a friend, and she treated Peter with all the warmth of a bill collector. When I reached out to shake Mary's hand, I was met with a nod and a recoil. As we walked to our table in the back, Durante grabbed my wrist. "Don't be offended," he whispered. "It has nothing to do with you. Mary doesn't like to touch people. It's a germ thing."

For the next few hours, Peter, seizing on my restaurant critic hobby, was keen to convert me to the wonders of vegan cooking. "It's just like chicken!" he explained, trying to push seitan, a wheat gluten, on me. He also shilled for the "bacon cheeseburger," made from soy-bacon, soy-cheese, and soy-burger. (I don't happen to like foods that mean "I am" in Spanish.)

After I eschewed the fake meat for real vegetables—great butternut squash soup, so-so fettuccine primavera—Peter told stories. How he learned about colors in China. How he and Andy Warhol used to go to flea markets and stage cookie-jar-buying competitions. And he talked a lot about money. How much he got paid for this and that, that and this. Everything except finalizing our deal. I made eye contact with Durante, who finally forced the issue.

"I've never done fifty-fifty," Peter responded. "We'd generally do something more like seventy-thirty."

"Peter, it's really about principle," I said, then trying to throw some New Age hokum at the hippiecapitalist. "Good karma. A symbiotic deal. Anything other than fifty-fifty seems odd. Plus, you already agreed to that."

"Okay, I get that, Randall Lane." For whatever reason, he called me, and almost everyone else, by both names. "So how about sixty-forty?"

When Peter began bellyaching about out-of-pocket costs, I volunteered that those could come out first before the revenue split. Plus, we'd cover the full costs of the parties.

"Okay, this is the first time I've ever done this," he said. "Why not?" Hailing a cab outside Blossom, I turned around to shake hands with my new partner. Peter ignored my hand, and gave me a kiss, wetly, on my cheek.

"I love you," the hippie painter told me.

With Peter Max, though, love is complicated. While he granted me fifty-fifty, once we put it in writing, he insisted that his "costs" were $2,500 per painting, or $10,000 per quartet. He then revised the number to $3,500. And then, on third thought, $4,000. King Midas was creating money for himself again, this time at our expense through the cost line in a contract.

"Peter, canvas and paint costs more like forty dollars than four thousand," I told him, with the confidence that comes when your brother is an art professor. "You *know* that."

"I don't know anything," he said shrugging, conveniently retreating from the "I love doing deals" mantra of our first meeting. "I'm just an artist, not a businessman. I just pass on what my accountants tell me."

$ $ $

Since the Peter Max studio didn't comfortably fit more than one hundred or so, we staged the parties over three consecutive nights, April 22, 23, and 24, each proving as big a headache as the contract, from the caterer (vegan-only, of course) to the photography (Peter was manic about approving every frame released). But as various members of the list, beginning with John Paulson, walked in, it all felt justified.

Each night had the same rhythm. The guests would come in and mingle. The video would play in a constant loop, a valentine to the world of Peter Max. I would make the welcome remarks, thanking our guests and sponsors and giving a brief biography of Peter Max. Properly teed up, Peter would give a little speech, and then a tour of the studio by dint of his finger. The Ringo Starr piano here. Ronald Reagan's dark brushstroke atop his Statue of Liberty painting there. The Andy Warhol cookie jars filling the rafters above.

The audience ate up this nexus of twentieth-century pop culture. Each night, supposedly two hours, ran closer to four. Few wanted to leave—least of all, the honorees. Jim Chanos, accompanied by a classy, appropriately aged blonde rather than some bimbo harem, smiled the entire time, far more jovial (and handsome) than the stark picture he authorized. The legendary Mario Gabelli made an appearance despite the fact that his son Marc had been charged with securities fraud that very morning.

John Paulson, meanwhile, soaked it all up. My babysitting duties ended a minute after he walked in. He was swarmed from beginning to end, as the various dukes and archdukes jockeyed for some words with the king. Jim Dunning took responsibility for filling in any holes, as the pair sat down at one point for a half-hour to talk about things men who fly privately discuss with one another.

What was more interesting was Paulson's reaction. To the outside world, he was either anonymous or a greedy billionaire. Here, among a curated cross-section of his people, he was secure. He posed eagerly and often for pictures, which we intended to post on our Web site the next morning.

But of course, nothing was ever so easy with Peter Max. He insisted that our freelance photographer leave her photo disk so that he could review each one. When she balked at letting him keep it, he became exceedingly agitated. I pulled Durante aside.

"What's going on?"

"Peter is very particular about photography, what shows up in public."

"I don't get it. All these paintings are in the magazines. We have him with John Paulson. What's bad?"

"Okay, I'll level with you," he said, pausing. "Peter has issues with how his hair appears."

As I had a Travolta flashback, Durante promised that we would get the film disk back. But not before Peter's hair—toupee or sensitive dye job, I still don't know—got a frame-by-frame vetting.

$ $ $

Back in the eighties, the now-defunct *Spy* magazine pulled off an insightful prank. It set up a fake company and issued obscure, incrementally smaller refund checks to fifty-eight of the rich and famous to see who would cash them. For $1.11, twenty-six made the effort. When it got down to thirteen cents, only two did. One of them was Donald Trump.

The lesson, a creative way of recycling Benjamin Franklin, was that great fortunes are built by minding pennies. But Zeroes traders, and increasingly dealmakers, didn't build or actually earn fortunes. They *made* them. Watches and houses and cars didn't come incrementally by pinching pennies: they came instantly from alpha. So as Peter and Paul set out to sell portraits to the *Trader Monthly* 100, the ultimate ego buy for the ultimate egoists, I sat back with the popcorn, expecting quick action.

Paulson was the first to engage, and rather than have some deputy handle the details, he did it himself, swapping cell phone numbers with Durante, who figured it would take five minutes to simply collect a credit card number. Wrong. Paulson wanted to know what his discount for all four was. "Thirty-five thousand times four equals $140,000," Durante said. "This is Peter Max, the Picasso of his generation. Picasso wouldn't discount."

"$110,000," replied Paulson. "That's my best bid."

The trading gene—the one that defines success by buying at the lowest possible price, down to the fourth decimal point (the "pip")—doesn't turn off after hours, it seems.

Some perspective: $140,000 to John Paulson, coming off an almost $4 billion year, was the equivalent of about two bucks to someone making $60,000 a year. The discount he was asking for translated to about 50 cents. No matter. Paulson wanted—he *needed*—to know he bought low.

Durante failed to grasp that for weeks as he tried to outstare

Paulson. The newly crowned greatest trader in the world, correctly gauging the tiny market for Peter Max portraits of obscure hedge fund billionaires, didn't budge. Overmatched, Durante eventually blinked, and with that, off to the office went the $4 billion man, in discounted rainbow quadruplicate.

It's ingrained. Not a single subject who bought his own portrait paid full price. Each followed his own trading style. Paul Tudor Jones, the hedge fund pioneer, preferred the scalping approach: he knocked the price down to $120,000 and cut the deal immediately. Mario Gabelli, rivaling Warren Buffett in terms of global fame as a value investor, applied his philosophy consistently: the billionaire bought just one, for $35,000, with Peter Max responsible for the $200 shipping. Chanos, the fun-loving short-seller, went for a heavy-duty block trade. He bought all four giant panels at full price, then commissioned an extra two, getting the second one free. The order, a volume discount, totaled $175,000.

From there, things slowed drastically. The decade's most audacious trader, Texas-oilman-turned-dealmaker-turned-hedge-fund-manager T. Boone Pickens, a billion-dollar earner in 2006, made the most audacious offer: *$250 per painting, four for $1,000, nonnegotiable*. And Pickens never blinked. The paintings went unsold. Boyish Marc Lasry was the only hedgie to mention charity. Like Gabelli, Lasry wanted just one. When Durante talked him into two, he agreed only if half the money went to charity. They offered One-Plus-Three, but Lasry wouldn't budge. He eventually reduced his offer, posturing that he wanted just one, except that *all* of it must go to charity. Their negotiations dragged on for months. In the end, they didn't cut a deal. Chicago's Ken Griffin, who had recently spent $80 million for a Jasper Johns, didn't even make an offer.

The final challenger to engage Durante was the runner-up on our *Trader Monthly* 100 list, Phil Falcone. Durante held out hope that a full-price sale was possible, as Falcone came by the studio to ogle them privately.

Falcone's offer: $90,000. As with Paulson, he seemed to enjoy the cat-and-mouse, holding a firm line.

"I'm going to be honest with you," responded Durante. "John

Paulson already paid $110,000. I can't give it to you at $90,000, or even $100,000."

Of course, this just gave Falcone a price to beat. Employing his wife as the emissary, the haggle dragged on for almost six months. In the end, he paid $110,000, the same amount as John Paulson. Except rather than just the four Happy Falcones, he negotiated the extra Angry Falcone that Peter had originally painted as a throw-in for his mother in Minnesota, to be shipped out immediately, with Mrs. Falcone insistent that Peter Max pay for the shipping.

After Falcone sent the check, Durante called him, his wife, and his office roughly a dozen times over the ensuing year asking for a delivery address for the Happy Falcones. But the hedgie already had what he wanted: besting the most elite of his peers to buy at the lowest price. He had won the game. The paintings themselves were superfluous. As of this book's printing, they were still sitting unclaimed in Peter Max's warehouse.

$ $ $

As I scanned the news on Friday, May 30, 2008, trouble signs abounded. The Commerce Department said first-quarter growth had been a paltry 0.9 percent. A new report showed that housing prices had fallen 14 percent over the past year, the largest drop since records had been kept. And our daily electronic newsletter, the Morning Call, now sent to almost 100,000 traders, carried a prediction from former Federal Reserve chairman Alan Greenspan—now a paid adviser to John Paulson—that the U.S. economy had a "50 percent chance" of going into recession during the latter half of 2008.

Greenspan bore a large degree of responsibility for that ominous prediction. For the first half of the decade, he had kept the prime rate—the rate the government loans to banks—at historically low levels. That meant financial institutions could borrow endless money cheaply, and then reloan endless money expensively to anyone who could sign their name onto a subprime loan document. In the end, $1.4 trillion of these crappy loans were made, and housing prices soared. Even better, banks, working with AIG and other insurance giants, took junk like this, bundled it together, and turned it into tradable contracts, passed around endlessly like a Christmas fruitcake. These contracts had so much perceived value and so much leverage that $14 trillion worth of these ticking time bombs, now labeled "toxic," were presently circulating, the long fuse lit years earlier by Alan Greenspan, minder of Uncle Sam's infinite printing presses.

Of course, that's all easy to see in retrospect, with Greenspan's "fifty-fifty" estimate looking naïvely optimistic. But as I was scanning the e-mails in my in-box that day, it was easy to see the glass full if you wanted to, at least in Doubledown Media's world. The head of our Internet unit sent a report crowing about his first-ever six-figure revenue month. Offers of wine and planes, cars and cigars flooded in for my pet project, the Flights of Napa event, now scheduled for late September. A new sponsor for our annual boxing event, the government of the Turks and Caicos, had stepped forward with a richer deal than Extell had paid. And kudos continued to come in for a recent profile of Doubledown Media on the front page of the *New York Times* business section, entitled "Where Wall Street's Caviar Set Still Thrives," with a photograph of Magnus and me holding giant blowups of all of our magazines. "However the economy is doing," I told the writer, "we always know we'll be reaching those who are doing the best." More comforting, the magazine expert quoted in the article heartily agreed, lauding our "laser shot at the market."

One of my e-mails, a forward, filled me with an extra boost of confidence. "I have the check," Paul Durante wrote to the accounting department that afternoon. "If Randall has time, Peter would love to see him today." Given that I had planned to take Jennifer on a restaurant review not too far from the studio, bringing her up to meet Willy Wonka sounded like a fine way to end the night.

We didn't arrive until 10 p.m., which on Peter Max time means things were finally percolating. Paul Durante greeted us coming off the elevator, immediately handing me an envelope. Doubledown's take from the sales to Paulson, Jones, Chanos, and Gabelli (the Falcone face-off was still pending) came to $107,900, even after the usurious $4,000 per painting charge for "costs." Not the company-changing money that I needed, but a start.

Durante walked us in to see Peter, who already had other guests. A few minutes earlier, Peter had bumped into Gordon Bethune, former CEO of Continental Airlines, who had recently purchased an apartment around the corner (and a decade prior commissioned Peter to paint the Boeing 777), dragging him and two friends to our nascent party. The whole studio seemed in a grand mood. Durante, the smartest and hardest-working of Max's crew, had also gotten a commission check, his first. Peter had cleared $300,000 on the hedgies so far. While he didn't drink and seemed far removed from his acid-era heyday, money got him high, and he was feeling it tonight.

"Let's do something special," he announced.

Leading the group, Willy Wonka took us through a door into the drip-splattered back chamber where he did his painting (the "inner sanctum," as Durante put it). From there, we ducked through yet another door, into the beginning of a catacombs, filled floor to ceiling with binders, books, canvases. We were now in his archives. Peter Max, it turns out, is a hoarder. He has never thrown anything out. Not an etching, a scribble, a doodle. Every time he sells something, it is photographed before going out the door and then filed away.

Peter grabbed a binder at random. It was crammed with kaleidoscope-looking patterns, repeated endlessly in different color schemes, like particularly groovy wallpaper swatches. "Do you know how valuable this stuff is?" he asked rhetorically. Back went that book, reconsigned to eternal obscurity, like the Holy Ark at the end of the first Indiana Jones movie. There were thousands of these binders. Half the Oompa-Loompas, it now appeared, were employed to sort and catalogue the endless volumes.

Back in the studio, Jen and I had fun with Bethune. A pilot, he was fascinated by *Private Air*, and with Jennifer, a writer for *Fortune*, he caught up on corporate scuttlebutt. Eventually, though, it was time to relieve the babysitter.

Peter wasn't anywhere to be found. Looking to thank the party's host, I eventually found him in a corner, at the same large drafting table where he had inscribed the book to my family on the first day I met him. He focused on a stack of mass-printed posters as thick as a phonebook, autographing his way through them as fast as he could.

"You know, each of these signed is worth one thousand dollars," he said, offhandedly. He paused. "Everything you saw tonight, total it all up and I'm a billionaire. Really."

It was an odd comment, and it made me think back to the Muhammad Ali painting he had sent me. A classic artist's series might run ten, or even one hundred. (A Red Grooms lithograph I had bought at a charity event to support New York firefighters sat in my living room, numbered 5/10.) The Ali painting bore a stamp on the back: *266414*.

Whether it's Alan Greenspan's dollars or Peter Max's art or my magazines, printing more of something doesn't mean you're rich. Flood enough of anything into the market, and everything collapses. But Greenspan hadn't seen that and Peter didn't want to hear that. Nor did I. Nobody in America did. We had collective blinders on, which some were shedding faster than others. Though we would deal with each other frequently in the ensuing months, that was the last time I ever saw Peter Max in his studio: alone, signing and signing, creating wealth that would ultimately prove ephemeral.

PART 3

RECKONING

(2008–2009)

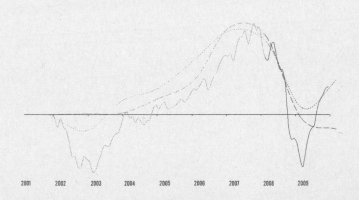

2001   2002   2003   2004   2005   2006   2007   2008   2009

—— S&P GLOBAL 100   ------ WORLDWIDE BONUSES   --- GLOBAL CDO ISSUANCE

11

Leverage

(Mid-2008)

In 2008, Doubledown received its first credit line, a $1.5 million facility from Keltic Financial, a small firm based in a generic Tarrytown, New York, office park. Such modesty belied Keltic's mission: the giant Hong Kong bank HSBC had helped empower it to find little lending deals like ours, injecting leverage into every possible nook and cranny of American business.

Assets were rising endlessly, and cash, in the form of loans, was automatic if you wanted it. With that cash you could then accumulate more assets. In the Zeroes, that was how you became rich. Doubledown, poised to double revenues again from $10 million to $20 million, finally stood ready to play the game. Hedge funds buying $1 million contracts for $50,000. Private equity funds turning healthy companies into debt-ridden ones with the goal of "extracting value." U.S. homeowners turning the American Dream into an ATM, borrowing $1 trillion against their castles in 2007 alone to go and buy other things, including, too often, yet more castles.

The trend could be seen on television, as new programs espousing maximum real estate exposure for regular folks proliferated as quickly as the judge shows earlier in the decade: There was *Flip This House* on A&E, and *Flip That House* on TLC. *The Real Estate Pros* and *The Property Ladder*. *House Hunters* and *Flipping Out*. The big banks, insurance companies, and the Fed had all enabled this cycle, creating an unprecedented asset bubble, particularly in housing, which they perpetuated by pumping yet more money into the system, justified by the same trees-grow-to-the-sky illogic of their borrowers.

By March, Keltic had raised our limit to $2 million, which we made still more potent by taking out an insurance policy covering any advertisers that stiffed us. From a dollars-and-cents standpoint, it was a loser—the insurer set a price designed to exceed the claims they'd have to pay. But from a *leverage* standpoint, it allowed Keltic to lend us even more money, since we had essentially traded away the risk from the collateral. The media version of an AIG "swap."

Meanwhile, Jim Dunning, the advocate for manic growth in the model of his legendary Petersen windfall, put his money where his mouth was. In late 2007, as the *Robb Report* deal imploded, he had invested another $1.5 million on the same terms as we'd earlier agreed upon, and in early 2008 added $1.1 million more. In many ways, Jim was more eager to give us money than Magnus and I were to take it. Each of these infusions raised Jim's ownership stake: by June 2008, he owned 46 percent. (Magnus stood at 20 percent; I now owned 14 percent.)

These were important numbers. While we sniggered about Lenny Dykstra's self-imagined valuation for his Wayne Gretzky house, $25 million plus, we strutted around, cocksure confident about the valuation of our collective asset, Doubledown Media: $25 million plus. Emphasis on *plus*. The SPAC offer had given our company a market value, no matter how silly or inflated, of $25 million. The "plus" came from a new wrinkle.

The hottest area in media in 2008, by far, was a new genre called social networking—closed communities interacting online. There were now hundreds of these sites, with three—Facebook, LinkedIn, and a fading pioneer, MySpace—each worth about $1 billion (in Facebook's case, far more). Every social network plan we saw dreamed about monetizing their communities someday through parties, newsletters, conferences—the kind of things Doubledown Media *already did*.

Players Club, Peter Max, even the boxing event—these were all Band-Aids, quick fixes designed to stem our losses and ween us off our dependency on paid print advertising. Turning our vibrant communities and database into online *professional* social networks—Facebook for traders and the like—was a transformative idea that could get us out of the magazine ghetto once and for all.

Magnus and I began a venture capital tour in the spring, traveling from Route 128 in Boston, to Sand Hill Road in Silicon Valley, to Silicon Alley in Manhattan, meeting two dozen leading firms, from Draper Fisher Jurvetson to Battery Ventures to NEA. Most of them, rewardingly, already read *Dealmaker*. Even more rewardingly, these discussions veered into the kind of long-term thinking—*Where is this business going? How will it get there?*—that I had always focused on when writing about companies in the nineties, yet seemed completely foreign to everyone I came across running a company in the Zeroes, including, too often, me.

By the summer, one New Jersey firm, Edison Venture Fund, stepped forward. The lead partner, Joe Allegra, however, didn't buy $25 million plus, and after much back-and-forth, we finalized a term sheet at a $17 million valuation. At that price they'd invest $7 million in Doubledown.

It was a revolutionary deal for us. Rather than perpetual handout requests, we'd have a predefined war chest big enough not just to ride Doubledown into profitability, but to transform it into a digital media company—social network, robust Web sites—that also owns magazines, rather than the opposite, which I continued to consider a dying proposition. The final hurdle was an August 12 meeting with the full investment committee in Edison, New Jersey—a rubber stamp, I was assured by the CEO of another Edison-backed company whom I called for advice.

In the interim, we needed money—the summer was always cash-intensive, with advertising revenue clustered in the spring and, especially, the fall. Jim proposed the world's most aggressive loan: as many quarter-million-dollar checks as needed, each carrying a 15 percent annual interest rate. Fair enough. For ninety days, we could either pay them off or, if we finished the Edison deal, convert them to stock under the previous terms. Also fair enough. Here was the catch: for every loan not paid off, he'd get 10 percent of the company. Nothing was ever free with Jim, and Tough Love Dad had presented us a dare. Pay off his loans. Or get a deal done. Or else.

Such stakes didn't faze us. We had an asset that a signed piece of paper said was now worth $17 million. What could go wrong?

$ $ $

Lenny Dykstra frequently used a one-word code when he didn't like something: *Joke!* As in, what a joke! For example, three weeks before the launch of *Players Club*, Lenny's new squad of independent party planners recommended that he hire a Grammy Award–winning Israeli "hip-hop violinist" named Miri Ben-Ari. Lenny's predictable forward to me: *Joke!*

He couldn't have been more prescient. The last launch party that Doubledown Media ever hosted—located at the site of our first one, the Mandarin Oriental ballroom-in-the-sky—took place on April Fools' Day, 2008, and proved a farce of epic scale.

Concerned about the thrifty Doubledown Way, Lenny had removed us from direct oversight of the launch party, forking over $58,000 in management fees to his "big league" party planning team. When I approached the hotel an hour before the event, I got a preview of what the eight hundred giddy attendees, drawn by $30,000 worth of invitations, embossed gold on handmade paper worthy of a royal wedding, would soon experience. Maybachs lined the red carpet outside, courtesy of $3,300 in permits. Inside the ballroom, Lenny obscured the best (and free) feature, the thirty-sixth-floor views of Manhattan, approving $40,000 for flowers, $40,000 for special lighting, and a $45,000 magazine highlight video loop, the kind Doubledown generally produced for a grand.

Then there was the $190,000 spread: sliced prime rib, endless Champagne, and, most visibly, a giant raw bar, with shrimp and clams and king crab, piled by the trawler-load onto an ice sculpture embossed with the Players Club logo. Still, that wasn't enough fine food for the palate-challenged Lenny. He independently hired one of the best Italian chefs in New York, Marco Canora, to set up a separate $15,000 pasta station.

For the gift bags, Lenny wanted every attendee to leave with Jawbone ear-mounted cell phones like he wore. When I urged him to reconsider, noting that such goodies are generally supplied, gratis, from actual sponsors, and this had zero connection to The Players Club, he scoffed and grabbed up one thousand of them, at retail. Cost: $77,000. He did ask us to buy one thousand baseballs, which he would sign. Our staff executed scrappily, as trained, finding balls on the Internet at two bucks a pop. "Do I look like a Little Leaguer?" Lenny exploded, dressing down one of our marketing executives, holding the offending sphere. He insisted that he would sign only balls manufactured by Rawlings, which supplied the majors, and ran $15 each.

The grand total for the party, based on the last budget I was privy to: $600,000, almost *twenty times* what we'd spent entertaining the same number of people at the same place when we launched *Trader Monthly*.

Here's where it gets *really* funny: by the night of the party, April 1, 2008, Lenny Dykstra, Pied Piper for professional athlete fiscal responsibility, was out of cash.

Six weeks earlier, the Monday after the night Lenny held me financial hostage at the St. Regis during his endless steroids confession, he had started another of his seven-day body cycles with an e-mail to Magnus and me. He attached the contract that he had crowed about to me on our G-IV flight, the $23 million sale of his car wash business, along with a message: *Please help me move this*.

How—and why—was Nails selling his car wash a second time? Despite his boasting, it turns out that Lenny didn't get a big $23 million check, like some grinning sweepstakes winner. Instead, he had traded the car wash for a $23 million *promissory note*—a promise to pay him $22 million on the deal's tenth anniversary, with a $1 million appetizer scheduled on the fifth anniversary. Until then, he would get $125,000 a month in interest payments.

In fairness, an income of $125,000 a month, or $1.5 million a year, with the knowledge that the full $23 million balloon will be yours in late 2017, is a pretty remarkable retirement package—*that's* Guaranteed Cash Flow, with a jackpot, rather than a pension, waiting on the other side.

But Lenny needed the cash *now*. His lifestyle was everything *Players Club* preached against: reckless borrowing and wanton spending. In the launch issue that Doubledown had produced, now en route to twenty thousand lockers across North America, Lenny, leaning on his ghostwriter, had penned a four-page manifesto entitled "Making It Big and Keeping It."

"Greats of the game have seen tens of millions of dollars slip through their hands," Lenny warned. "It was easy to always pick up the dinner check no matter how many people were at the table. Great business opportunities that couldn't miss caved in." This was written directly before Lenny picked up what turned out to be a $600,000 dinner check for eight hundred people, and directly after he spent $17.5 million on the Gretzky estate, which he justified as a business opportunity that couldn't miss, despite ubiquitous headlines about an imminent real estate cave-in.

Flipping the Gretzky home was such a sure thing that Lenny financed it with *$20.5 million* worth of loans—a $12 million first mortgage and an $8.5 million second mortgage, respectively—according to financial records he sent us to help sell the car wash note. With that extra $3 million in cash from the mortgages, he bought himself a "starter jet," a $3.7 million G-II. Then he borrowed millions more against *that*, using me as a professional reference.

Magnus and I had gone with Lenny to Teterboro, the private jet airport outside Manhattan, to kick the tires of his gleaming new toy, tail number N5DL, in mid-October, the apex of our Nails honeymoon phase. As we all lounged on the plane's sofas, I mentioned a marketing idea we had for *Private Air*, a partnership with a designer to style a plane in, say, all-Hermès trappings. Lenny decided that he'd outfit his interior like a Maybach—he wound up spending some $75,000 just on interior sketches—and rent it to *Players Club* readers. He looped us in, too: in exchange for running ads for the plane in *Private Air* and our Wall Street magazines, Doubledown could use the plane whenever it wanted. "It'll have the the Players Club logo on one side," Lenny promised, "the Doubledown Media logo on the other, and the Maybach logo on the nose."

Meanwhile, after swiftly moving into the Gretzky house, Lenny kept his original mansion, a five-bedroom 8,100-square-foot palazzo just down the hill, complete with spa, pool, and four-car garage, despite the $4 million mortgage he still owed on it. Then he took out an additional $750,000 line of credit against that house from Wachovia. When I asked him why he wanted to carry the exposure of two homes, he reverted to his guru alter ego. "They call it real estate for a reason," he explained. "Because it's *real*."

Here's what was real: Lenny now had four loans against two mansions exceeding $25 million, and requiring payments of $126,990 a month—single-handedly absorbing the $125,000 monthly income he received from his nest egg, the car wash note. The aggressive jet financing payments totaled another $70,000 a month. Then, there was the cost of living life like Lenny: hotel suites, jet fuel, and whatever his family expenses were. Plus, The Players Club, which, since he always e-mailed his broker about wiring money, presumably came by draining that $1 million stock trading account he had shown me.

Those big, early checks, the nonchalant jet rides, the Jim Cramer endorsement. It had thoroughly convinced me, and Magnus and Jim as well, that Lenny was "money good." But as I sized up his balance sheet, it became clear that not only were we working for an asshole, we were working for a broke asshole. He was no better positioned than the unemployed dropouts whose no-money-down subprime loans entitled them to five-bedroom McMansions.

He had bet everything on the theory that asset prices would never fall. He put the Gretzky house back on the market for $27.5 million—$10 million more than he had paid for it six months earlier, and $7 million more than the mortgages he owed on it. As for the jet, Lenny took the money borrowed against the first one, and reached a deal to buy a *second* G-II, for $4.9 million. His plan, according to the personal financials he sent me, was to buy sixty Gulfstreams, each financing the next, turning them all into "Flying Maybachs," including newer models that "will be auctioned off, with an expected starting bid of $100 million."

While the ability to borrow cash hadn't been crimped—yet—signs now emerged weekly that asset prices weren't infinite. In mid-March, as Lenny finalized the budget for the *Players Club* party, the first Wall Street tremor hit. Bear Stearns went into free fall after it revealed that two of its internal hedge funds had previously blown up betting on subprime mortgages. From $172 a share a year earlier and $93 a month earlier, JPMorgan Chase agreed to swallow Bear for scraps, $2 a share (later adjusted to $10). A firm founded in 1923 had been erased from history in a matter of days.

Mind-sets don't respond as quickly as the merciless markets. While mortgage defaults soared throughout 2007, real estate prices had continued to inch up, flattening only at year-end. In the spring of 2008, most people held on, rather than sell assets for anything less than the inflated number in their head. Housing sales ground to a halt, including the Gretzky mansion, which Nails continued to maintain was worth millions more than what he paid. Lenny went into similar denial over the value of his car wash note: he was offered $16 million for it but held out for $19 million.

Meanwhile, I begged him to stop spending. He sneered that I wasn't "big league." Anticipating the same spend-versus-thrift fight I had experienced with Extell and its boxing table center-pieces, we had changed our deal. Rather than oversee the *Players Club* budget, Doubledown would simply manage the project, taking a $50,000-a-month fee, plus half of the advertising profits. Lenny would be directly responsible for every budget decision, and clear his tab by the eleventh of every month.

With Lenny holding the purse strings, spending went unchecked. New design consultants were hired for $100,000, even though Doubledown was already paying Mitch Shostak to design the magazine. Seventy grand for the Derek Jeter cover shoot, plus the cost of flying the whole photo entourage by private jet. Twice as many articles, printed on twice-as-thick paper. (A typical magazine costs maybe 40 cents to print and mail, including the paper. At Doubledown, our thick, glossy magazines for the rich came in closer to $1. *Players*

Club? $6.) Then he demanded that the entire magazine be translated into Spanish, separately designed and separately printed, tens of thousands of dollars more each month so shortstops from the Dominican Republic wouldn't feel left out.

As for that $600,000 party, Lenny bought himself a legitimate spectacle. Paparazzi jostled as everyone from John McEnroe to Donald Trump, Jr., to Jim Cramer to half the New York Rangers came to pay respect, standing with Lenny, in a dark blue suit and a blue-and-white striped tie, in front of a screen that alternated the Players Club and Doubledown logos, like the shared jet that never would be.

My whole world was there. Our hardworking staff, biggest advertisers, best friends. Eric Bolling, lugging along a camera crew from Fox Business, where Roger Ailes had personally recruited him to become the in-house trading god. The team from AIG (Lenny had allowed them to sponsor the first issue, after all—and inexplicably neglected to charge them for it). Peter Max. ("Peter wants to send Lenny a signed book," his deputy wrote after the party, presumably beginning the Peter Max gift write-off ritual anew. "What is the correct spelling of his wife and kids and what address should we ship it to please.")

The only person I didn't talk to was Lenny Dykstra, as we pointedly ignored each other the entire night. For the past week, we'd warred, by phone and e-mail, mostly about cash, or his lack of it. For his March 13 payment to us, supposedly $300,000, he came up with only $200,000. And then he tried to get Doubledown to front the absurd party costs I had begged him not to incur, which I resolutely refused to do.

"This is ridiculous, how can you let this get to this point?" Lenny e-mailed me, four days before the party, when various unpaid vendors tried to shut down the event (we wound up stepping in with $44,000, enough to avert disaster). "TO JUST TURN YOUR BACK ON ME IS AS LOW AS YOU GO. . . . You cannot control the situation any better than this?"

"How can I 'control the situation' if I am not in charge of the situation?" I wrote back. "You're blaming the wrong guy, bud."

In theory, Lenny was stuck with us. We had a one-year contract.

But now that we'd readied *Players Club* for launch, Nails was doing whatever he could, besides running up extraordinary bills, to make us miserable, berating staffers high and low. The locker room epithets he knew I disdained ratcheted up. All women were "bitches." Blacks had become "spearchuckers." My assistant, a gay man who loyally served as Lenny's de facto concierge when he was in town, became "your fag." I had previously looked the other way because I liked the project and we needed his money; by now, it was clear that I had wrongheadedly introduced a toxic substance into our company. Even if he sold the car wash note, the $1 million annual profit we'd make, and desperately needed, from The Players Club could no longer justify the cost of dealing with him every day.

So at the party, it was left to others to go to the podium to toast Nails, most notably Jim Cramer. When it came Lenny's turn, he thanked half the room—but didn't mention me, or anyone from Doubledown. "You can't play professional sports forever," he told the audience. "You either have to grow up or die, so I grew up." And with that, the grown-up financial guru revealed a special "surprise" for the guests.

Clad in a kimono, out walked Miri Ben-Ari, the hip-hop violinist, hired to play a few songs for $10,000 that Lenny Dykstra didn't have. As she fiddled away, one word popped into my head: *Joke!*

$ $ $

A few days after the party, I sent Lenny a breakup note. Not the usual sentimental kind, but rather crafted between Magnus and me and discussed with our general counsel, Andy Mirsky. It encompassed a reminder that we had a signed, one-year contract in force, some self-indulgent predictions that he would never find a partner as good as us—and then the split-up, written in legalese ("We can amend our agreement to allow for an amicable parting that transitions you away from Doubledown") that boiled down to a single condition: *please pay us what you owe us.* With that, I enclosed the latest itemized, line-by-line costs, totaling $351,000.

"All good dude," Lenny said, calling me the next day. "We're still friends. We can still work on other projects together." A sane breakup with your crazy boyfriend. Relief.

We agreed to meet the following Monday, April 14, at 4 p.m. at his hotel. Lenny had changed hotel allegiance from the St. Regis to the Carlyle, best known as the meeting place for the financiers that formed the Carlyle Group and John F. Kennedy's preferred spot for assignations (including Marilyn Monroe on the night of her "Happy Birthday, Mr. President" torch song). This powwow, putatively in the spirit of the former, felt uncomfortably like the latter when Lenny greeted me, fresh from the shower, naked except for a towel, beads of water hanging on him like a walrus newly lunged from the sea.

His suite was even bigger than his St. Regis digs, a Versailles-in-the-sky, with giant mirrors reaching up to high ceilings and walls painted with dark, rich colors, framing windows that looked across the Upper East Side. A 2003 Opus One, a killer $175 bottle of wine, sat in a basket, compliments of the hotel. "Take it, dude," said Lenny, now dressed, studying me studying it. "You know I don't drink that shit anymore."

The tension between us was gone. We went over every expense, line by line. When he complained, I defended. If he insisted, I relented. We wound up agreeing to knock $23,000 off the bill. This divorce would be amicable.

The final total, including the $44,000 we loaned him for the launch party and the full production costs of the second issue, which was printing the following Monday, came to $328,000. As our team was already knee-deep assigning and editing the third issue of *Players Club*, we also agreed that Doubledown would produce the words, photos, and design for an additional $200,000 flat fee, and then turn it over to his new partner—he said he was leaning toward American Express's publishing arm. We were out of the Players Club business. Bad for our bottom line; good for our sanity.

The only unresolved issue was the *Dykstra Report* newsletter. We had built a Web site, with Lenny's approval, and begun marketing it, testing different price points. Lenny boosters, it turned out, gladly forked over $995 up front a year for wisdom from their toothless guru. We had quickly collected $87,000; a $1 million newsletter in the first year seemed realistic. For the past few weeks, Doubledown's newsletter editor, Chris Frankie, had been ghostwriting Lenny's free columns for TheStreet, as a dry run for the paid version. Perhaps we would continue to distribute it? Or else take a cut of the first year in exchange for the development effort and costs? "We'll figure that one out, dude," Lenny said. "All good."

The next day, I was introducing Lenny at a long-planned speech to a financial marketing association. Because Lenny was late, I wound up making his entire presentation. When Lenny stumbled in with ten minutes remaining, he started taking questions from the audience before making his way to the front. "You were a better me than me," he said as the crowd laughed, a fresh audience for the Nails play-it-dumb rap.

"I'm working on getting that money transfer done," he whispered to me, nodding, as we swapped places on the podium.

The wire didn't come Tuesday, or Wednesday. On Thursday, I called. For three more days, no response. We were heading for a showdown. In the magazine world, a print date has huge significance. Besides making a bunch of computer files a major asset—a living, breathing magazine—it creates significant liabilities. Debt to the printer for its time and resources; to the paper company, whose dead trees you've now covered with ink; to all the writers and photographers who get paid for their hard work upon publication. There was no way, of course, that we were willing to incur any of that on behalf of cash-strapped Lenny Dykstra. So I sent Lenny a note on Sunday letting him know, firmly, that we needed the wire or we couldn't print the next day.

Lenny's response displayed a new side of him: *nuclear*.

$ $ $

Nuclear Lenny differed from Evil Lenny, who could be mean and brutish but whose hate was at least tempered by self-interest. "He thinks I'm going to buckle," Nails said about me to the *New York Post*, one of several news outlets that began covering this suddenly high-profile face-off. "I don't buckle—I go to war." ("If he wants to pay us the money he owes," I responded to the reporter, "we'll let him go on his merry way.")

First, Nuclear Lenny threatened us, using his nuclear litigator, David Schack, whose collection of quality clients also included Joe Francis, a convicted child pornographer who had become a Zeroes tycoon by filming young women removing their tops at spring break for the *Girls Gone Wild* video series. "I do not know why you believe you are free to take any wrongful action that you wish," Schack faxed, mailed, and e-mailed, "but it will not be done with impugnity [*sic*] as you will soon see if you don't change your course of action immediately."

Then, by that Friday, he did in fact sue—Doubledown *and* me personally ("unbelievably nasty," our lawyer said, shaking his head, about including me individually in a business dispute)—alleging that my failure to print the magazine he refused to pay for was damaging his business.

Then he tried to *steal* the magazine, flying his Gulfstream to the rural Pennsylvania plant where the printing plates stood ready. Doubledown had produced and supplied the files. It was clearly our property until he paid for it. "They had security waiting for him," remembers Richard O'Connor, a California entrepreneur who replaced me as Lenny's business consigliere and flew overnight to help him get the magazine printed. "They said, 'Leave now or we'll have you arrested.' "

And then he actually stole it.

Mitch Shostak, the designer whom I had shielded from Lenny's direct order to fire him during Nails's Henry VIII period, decided he wanted to keep working on *Players Club*. So he had signed a contract directly with him, and now handed over the articles that Doubledown had created. (*He was in a tough spot,* Shostak's lawyer later told ours.) Lenny was armed and dangerous.

For the next two weeks, Nails and I played transcontinental chess. One nice dividend of a decade of launching magazines was that I knew half the printers in the country. I tracked the course of Lenny's Gulfstream based on the area code of the printing executive calling me, asking why some semicoherent former All-Star had a bunch of files that clearly had "Doubledown Media" marked on the masthead. I'd explain the situation, and then Lenny would jet on, to try again elsewhere.

Nuclear Lenny was spending countless more on lawyers, jet fuel, new vendors—not to mention time and goodwill—than if he'd just paid us what he had already agreed. But his "war" brain wasn't processing that way anymore, and despite my putting the entire American printing community on alert for flying Lenny and his stolen magazine files, Nails finally found one, California's Trend Offset, apparently willing to avert its eyes as the figurative Rolexes emerged from the back of the trunk. *Players Club* issue two, with basketball star Chris Paul on the cover, eventually landed on my desk.

Nuclear Lenny's exact pattern repeated regarding the *Dykstra Report* newsletter. First, the threats (*give us the money and the Web site or else*). Then the illogical lawsuit (*Lenny never permitted Doubledown to launch the newsletter!, ignoring the pesky details that we agreed on the name, designed the site together, and solicited subscribers using the list Lenny gave us*), which he folded into the Players Club litigation. Then the theft.

In this case, besides the core idea I had provided, and the development we had put in, he stole away our newsletter editor-in-chief, Chris Frankie. Then he stole our nascent division, inviting Eric Bolling to join him. And then he dug in for the $87,000 we held from the initial sales of *The Dykstra Report*. We maintained that he should simply send those subscribers the newsletter until a judge sorted out the money. After briefly complying, Lenny sent an e-mail to the subscribers on the list informing them about a "very serious matter." It began with a lie—"*The Dykstra Report,* which you signed up for and paid for, was started without Mr. Lenny Dykstra's permission by a company named Doubledown Media"—and moved on to a crisis: he was cutting them all off, unless they paid him directly. He then gave each person my e-mail address and *personal* cell phone number to demand a refund from Doubledown, effectively filling my in-box and voicemail with expletives and hate. "It is very disturbing that once again an effort to defraud the public has been brought to the attention of the many who are just trying to get ahead," read one typical note. I felt violated.

This was all enabled by, of all people, Jim Cramer. *Nails on the Numbers,* Lenny's new $995 service, mimicking the test marketing we had conducted, magically appeared under TheStreet.com's "premium newsletter" umbrella.

I flashed back to *Players Club*'s launch party a few weeks earlier and my odd conversation with Cramer. We'd had two or three encounters over the years. Most substantively, in 1995, Cramer's original TheStreet .com partner, Marty Peretz, recruited me to become the new venture's editor-in-chief, an opportunity I declined. That job eventually went to a more talented financial editor, Dave Kansas, whose TheStreet.com stock at the height of the dot-com craze hit almost $10 million. I went up to Cramer at the launch party and reintroduced myself; Cramer, in turn, did everything he could to get as far away from me as possible, as fast as possible. I found his diffidence, particularly given my connection to *Trader Monthly*, peculiar. Maybe he already had a deal to bring Nails into his newsletter fold. Maybe he just sensed that Lenny's future was with him, and there was little to be gained by chatting with the awkward past. Either way, it suddenly made more sense.

$ $ $

"Lenny would kill me if he knew I was calling you."

That's how Richard O'Connor, the man who had assumed the ever-rotating role of Lenny's best friend and business adviser, introduced himself. O'Connor said that he had been trying to get Lenny to pay what he owed us, so that he could move forward with his company, but Nails refused to end our "war." "It's irrational," O'Connor said as he tested theories on me, a knowledgeable refugee from Lennyland. *Had I ever seen Lenny take Oxycontin? Did he suffer from syphilis?*

Lenny was also becoming increasingly reckless, O'Connor confided, with his newsletter and relationship with TheStreet.com. I was simultaneously uncovering similar concerns.

While preparing our court documents, our IT team fished through all the e-mails in our system regarding *The Dykstra Report*. Once there, they stumbled upon the secret to Lenny's stock-picking success.

Almost every morning, Lenny would receive a list of "deep-in-the-money calls" picks from an actual market analyst, Richard Suttmeier. Lenny then chose "his" picks, which Chris Frankie would write up. That explained how a ballplayer who didn't even know how to use a computer until 2003 was transformed into a guru of financial derivatives that he couldn't cogently explain. I had blindly accepted his three-year stint writing his column for TheStreet, and his endorsement by Jim Cramer as "one of the greats," but even his 99-and-1 track record chronicled on TheStreet.com was now suspect. "Lenny doesn't count a position as a loser until it is closed out," explained a market blogger, Michael Comeau, who subsequently pored through his accounting. In other words, Lenny counted the winners, but let the losers twist indefinitely—good for his "stat sheet," disastrous for those who actually put money behind his picks.

O'Connor's information was even more damning. On June 6, D-Day, some six weeks after our professional divorce, Lenny e-mailed out a copy of *Nails on the Numbers,* but instead of one of the thrice-a-week "deep-in-the-money calls" that his subscribers paid $995 a year for, this was an unsolicited "bonus" recommendation: a plain old stock. "I will occasionally alert readers to other great investment ideas I have," wrote Lenny, explaining the aberration. "I have one today." Specifically, a pimple of a company called Automated Vending Technologies, or AVT, which did less than $3 million in revenue in 2008, or Doubledown's take in three months. AVT existed mostly as an excuse to buy and sell—a classic "penny stock," it traded for about $1, and a measly ten grand worth of shares might move on a given day, versus billions for Google or General Electric, the kind of easily manipulated security embraced by "pump-and-dump" boiler rooms for decades.

Even by Lenny's keep-it-stiff communications standards, this day's special "great investment idea" came across about as stunted as a prisoner of war extolling the cause of his captors for the cameras. All that was missing was the hidden message blinked in Morse code.

> While exiting an airplane at McCarran Airport in Las Vegas recently, I noticed a large 011 Mobile Kiosk while I was on my way to the baggage claim area. It was selling prepaid cell phones. . . . This blew me away! I was so impressed by the capabilities of this Kiosk that I did some poking around and found a press release talking about it on Yahoo.com. As it turns out, the company that manufac-

tures this Kiosk is called Automated Vending Technologies and is located in Corona, Calif.

So, I hit my Google search to try and find contact information for the company. I got it and gave them a buzz. The receptionist put me in contact with W. Chris Moore, the publisher of their magazine; AVT Magazine. . . . Mr. Moore told me that their engineer, James Winsor, has developed two new kiosks called the 24 Hr Tech Mart and 24 Hr I-Vend that are spin-offs of the 011 Mobile Kiosk and have even greater potential. . . . I know what you are thinking—vending machines? But these are different and in my opinion have really great potential. . . . The company's shares are under a buck and give investors a lot of potential upside. In the interest of full disclosure, I am long in shares of AVT and am now a consultant to the company's CEO Shannon Illingworth. I like this company so much that I have some skin in the game. You can't ask for much more of an endorsement than that.

According to O'Connor, he introduced Lenny to the CEO, Illingworth. He later sent me a copy of their consulting agreement, signed on March 15, just as Lenny started going south on us. The contract cited his "management expertise in basic industry related businesses." What possible "expertise in basic industry" could Lenny have? "Relationships with the TheStreet.com, Cramer," Illingworth now admits to me. Lenny was selling direct access to Jim Cramer. Illingworth said that because Nails didn't deliver any meetings, he wasn't paid anything—unless you count the $15,000 the CEO says he put in an account for Nails to trade on his behalf, which disappeared.

The "skin in the game" was even more puzzling. "As noted above, I am long in shares of AVT," Lenny wrote at the bottom of his newsletter post, for double emphasis. Plugging a stock you already owned became increasingly common in the Zeroes as professional traders, with an assist from us, morphed into television gurus. In theory, as long as there was disclosure, they were simply putting their mouth where their money was.

But O'Connor said that Lenny never *bought* the stock. He had been *given* it, in exchange for promoting it using TheStreet.com's platform. Even Lenny had understood the ramifications.

"This is illegal," O'Connor said Nails told him.

O'Connor's plan—the reason he made the original introduction—was to put Lenny on the company's board, which would entitle him to legitimate stock options.

Lenny, according to O'Connor, had another idea: "We can just put the stock in Keith's name," referring to his brother-in-law, Keith Peel. And on March 25, AVT quietly issued Keith 250,000 shares of AVT, a quarter million dollars' worth of stock. So quietly, O'Connor now says, that he's sure "Keith didn't know anything about it." The stock certificates—numbered 11205, 11206, 11207, and 11208, each for 62,500 restricted shares—were held at the Gretzky mansion, and O'Connor made copies of them, which he subsequently showed me, "in case I ever needed to go to war with Lenny." (Despite the certificates, Illingworth denies Keith Peel was ever issued any stock, or that Lenny ever received free shares.)

Illingworth says the decision for Lenny to send out a newsletter column touting his stock was "mutual," "It wouldn't hurt the company to have someone say something good about it," the CEO explains. (True in a vaccum; illegal if the plug was paid for.) O'Connor further claims that Illingworth and Lenny had a handshake agreement to allow Lenny to sell 50,000 shares each time the stock rose 25 cents.

For the week following Lenny's endorsement, AVT's stock volume jumped 50 percent, but the price stayed fixed near $1. Illingworth was furious that the "bonus recommendation" went out only to the few hundred subscribers of Lenny's TheStreet-affiliated newsletter, O'Connor says, rather than his enormous audience on the actual Web site. Four days after the initial plug, Illingworth sent out a press release, paying to disseminate it far and wide. "I remember Shannon calling me going, 'He hasn't done a fucking thing,' " O'Connor recalls. " 'You got to get my stock back from that guy.' "

O'Connor, meanwhile, was sure that Lenny had other such deals going. He saw $25,000 offers for Lenny from small-company CEOs, following the HBO segment, just for a meeting. The reason? "Cramer said he only listens to three or four guys," O'Connor explained, "and Lenny's one of them."

As I heard all this, one feeling washed over me: *relief*.

Lenny's litigiousness had saved us. His newsletter pick cribbing, the deal for access to Cramer, the shares issued to his brother-in-law, all that took shape while we were still working with him—it took the lawsuits to reveal it to me. I shuddered thinking about what might have happened on our watch had we gone forward with him. He was Jim Cramer's problem now.

Yet even after we pointed out in our lawsuit that Lenny didn't make his own picks, and after O'Connor repeatedly called Cramer's office, trying to get Mr. Mad Money to intervene, Lenny remained on the reputable, otherwise excellent TheStreet.com, charging a thousand dollars a year for extra wisdom. His followers paid up front— Nails boasted it was $3 million a year, though Chris Frankie later put the figure closer to $1 million. Like everything in Lenny's life, and in the greater economy, cash was flying in, under questionable circumstances, resulting in liabilities down the road.

$ $ $

It wasn't just Lenny. As well as we could tell, we didn't have a partner, small or big, old or new, that wasn't leveraged to the hilt or engulfed in legal issues. As 2008 pushed on, that caused no shortage of problems.

The first headache, less destructive than Nails but equally incorrigible, was *Private Air*'s Deedee Morrison. In 2007, she made, by far, more than anyone else at Doubledown Media—a $100,000 signing bonus plus a $125,000 salary—for doing less than anyone at Doubledown Media. She remained in Alabama, with no specific day-to-day responsibilities. A featherweight job had been our price of admission to the world of private jets, and what had seemed a slam-dunk deal.

But then her provided list of "prebooked" advertising proved fleeting, and her ex-husband took his cozy Caribbean advertising system to greener pastures. The contract's simple premise—win together, lose together—kicked in. As Doubledown lost roughly $800,000 on *Private Air* in 2007, revenue didn't even remotely approach the threshold to qualify Morrison for her first $125,000 "earn-out" payment.

But by early 2008, Deedee had picked up on the ways of Wall Street: she wanted her 2007 bonus anyway. She, too, had leverage issues: a mortgage she'd taken against her house, a $125,000 loan from a family friend. If she couldn't earn her way out of debt, she would sue her way out. She hired a litigator who told me that our contract "guaranteed" these annual payments, conveniently neglecting the next sentence that made them "contingent" on hitting the revenue threshold. Foiled there, the litigator then accused us of covertly sneaking in that second sentence without Deedee's knowledge, before we produced the electronic paper trail that showed that *Deedee's lawyer* had added that language—and Deedee had e-mailed me the version with the addition.

Meanwhile, we had just been notified that *Private Air* had failed its circulation audit—when Deedee owned the magazine, the auditors discovered, names were swapped in and out every issue, rather than maintained as a stable, legitimate list. We expected an apology and a pledge to do better. Instead, we got a lawsuit, throwing out two new conspiracy theories (that we bought *Private Air* as part of a scheme to secretly smother it and/or we had intentionally forgone revenues, and incurred that $800,000 loss, in a mathematically brilliant plan to deny her $125,000 bonus) and one from the Lenny Dykstra school of magazine management: we didn't hit the revenue because we didn't *spend enough*. We, in turn, fired her, in accordance with our contract, for hiding the newly revealed circulation problems.

The binding arbitration hearing, which played out over the summer of 2008, was a complete waste of time and money. Deedee rang up yet more debt for herself—some $250,000 in legal fees—and inflicted similar bills on us. In the end, our methodical lawyer, Katharine Parker, defeated all of Deedee's original counts. Yes, the earn-out was valid, which meant she fell well short of her bonus. In fact, the arbitrator *raised* the earn-out threshold going forward, based on an agreement Deedee and I had made the previous summer as we poured extra resources into *Private Air*. The only setback: the arbitrator ruled we shouldn't have fired her, saying that while the circulation data she supplied us was inaccurate, he wasn't convinced that she understood it was inaccurate, or at least that we hadn't made our purchase decision based on it. Ignorance, apparently, *is* a defense under the law, or at least enough of one in the Zeroes to continue to draw a salary for doing nothing.

$ $ $

For the most important meeting of his career at Doubledown Media, Henry Watkins, our travel advertising director, was perfectly prepared to take a cab from his budget accommodations in Berlin, where he was staying for the giant ITB Travel Show in March. *No*, his hosts insisted, *we will send our stretch Mercedes limo*. That's how it works when the leader of a country summons you to his hotel room to talk deal.

Well, technically not a country: Turks and Caicos, twenty-eight swampy islands near the Bahamas with less collective landmass than New York City and fewer citizens (twelve thousand) than Dickinson, North Dakota, was mostly a pirates' hideout until it was annexed by Great Britain in 1799. And not technically a hotel room: within the Ritz-Carlton, the three-thousand-square-foot, $8,000-per-night space that Henry stepped into was internally known as "the apartment," complete with working fireplace, exercise room, and views over Potsdamer Platz.

But forty-two-year-old Michael Misick, with the good looks of Cuba Gooding, Jr., really was the islands' leader. In 2006, he had implemented a new constitution, giving the Turks a large degree of self-rule after more than two centuries of direct colonial yoke, installing himself as the archipelago's first-ever "premier."

Economically, the Turks were pretty much irrelevant, with a GDP of $750 million, or what John Paulson personally made in two months. But the charismatic Misick had a vision: "The Riviera of the Caribbean," filled exclusively with new five-star and "six-star" resorts (similar to the famous Spinal Tap amplifier which was surely louder because, rather than having a dial marked one to ten, "it goes to eleven"). To pull this off, he needed lots and lots of Wall Street money to finance the buildup, and lots and lots of Wall Street money spent enjoying it. Thus, he was keen to hear about a partnership with Doubledown Media—specifically about becoming the new title sponsor of the Wall Street Boxing Charity Championships.

Watkins brought a video loop of the previous year's event to the meeting. As the group, including what seemed like half his cabinet, splayed themselves across the apartment's living room, the premier projected the DVD onto the forty-two-inch flat screen. *Millionaires slugging millionaires . . . Men in suits dancing in the aisles amid jumbo-sized vodka bottles . . . Goldman Sucks, Goldman SUCKS!* He gazed at the strange spectacle once, then a second time, and then a third, before directing everyone into the dining room for a catered lunch.

Champagne was poured, and lobster cocktails emerged, followed by foie gras and then a meat dish smothered in freshly shaved truffles. (With a little caviar and gold leaf, he could have covered all the official food groups of the Zeroes' decadence.) "So how much did you pay to be the sponsor of this boxing event?" the premier asked in his crisp British accent, a product of his UK schooling, weakly attempting to haggle on price.

"Three hundred and fifty thousand dollars," Watkins replied, and as he was about to launch into a defense of that number, the Honorable Wayne Garland, tourism minister, cut him off.

"Don't worry, Mike," he said, addressing the premier, "we already set the price."

"The message was clear," Watkins remembers. "We pay top price—we don't care."

That message was heard worldwide. Debt-fueled spending was far from a private sector phenomenon, as the entire world took a cue from the U.S. government and the more than $6 trillion in debt it ran up during the Zeroes. The tiny Turks and their flashy leader, married to a beautiful American actress named LisaRaye McCoy, had an especially Dykstraesque way of borrowing and squandering.

Tapping the Turks treasury, Misick leased two Gulfstreams to jet around in, as well as a Rolls-Royce for on-island transportation. And while he had entered public office in 2003 with a stated net worth of $50,000, he was now building a personal $8 million mansion, complete with $1 million in interior design work. When a bank in the tiny European duchy of Lichtenstein issued him a personal $21 million loan, Misick later boasted that he had more than enough assets to cover it.

Meanwhile, favored real estate developers chomped up the Turks' prime waterfront real estate, using billions in borrowed money. As I flew into the main airport, on the island of Providenciales, to check out some of these developments, a detour from visiting my mom in Miami, cranes filled the horizon out my window like little flamingos.

Misick was particularly proud of Nikki Beach, a nightclub chain often described as Playboy Mansions on sand popping up in sunny hot spots from Miami Beach to Cannes. For the Turks, the concept had been turned into the first-ever Nikki Beach Resort, five-star of course, complete with private butlers, slick pool cabanas, and menus giving all guests their pillow options. The premier had personally flown to St. Barts to woo Nikki Beach executives. Since it was scheduled to open on April 5, Misick told Watkins, why didn't the Doubledown team join him for the festivities, and sign the boxing contract in style?

Our sales and marketing heads, Wilkie Bushby and Pat Shannon, eagerly joined Watkins for the trip. With the colorful Mediterranean architecture contrasting with the bleached white that almost everyone wore, it did indeed feel like the "Riviera on the Caribbean," and everyone from boxer Lennox Lewis to Hollywood glamour couple Michael Douglas and Catherine Zeta-Jones took in the fire dancers and fireworks. "Welcome to paradise," Misick said in formally opening the resort. "What Nikki Beach stands for is consistent with what we're trying to do here in the Turks and Caicos . . . we can now claim to be the sexiest destination in the world." With that, two women lugged out what was touted as the "world's largest bottle of Champagne," at thirty liters. Misick unsheathed a sword, and with great flair, sheared off the top, the bubbly flowing for all.

Midway through the party, Misick came up to the Doubledown group and gave everyone a hug. "This is the event," he beamed, already looking toward October, "that is going to make us the top destination with Wall Street." No haggles, no hassles, Nikki Beach parties—it was quite an upgrade from Extell. Plus, this was a government contract, the one type of deal that always gets paid, with the first installment check, for $83,333, quickly due.

Fast-forward six weeks: the Turks still hadn't paid. *The check is in the mail,* Watkins was told repeatedly, from low-level flunkies up to Misick's office. Our finance department had used that line for vendors when cash was tight; dozens of advertisers had used it on us. But never a head of state. And never so brazenly, for so long. Finally in mid-June, we were told it had been sent FedEx. When it didn't arrive, we asked for a tracking number. That conveniently could not be found. On June 24, Watkins was dispatched to a travel trade show to drag a check in by hand. No luck.

On July 3, the Honorable Wayne Garland, tourism minister, chimed in: "It is with regret that I write this email. I only today learned that the funds were not wired as previously indicated. Honestly, I am rather embarrassed. . . . I will give you my personal assurance that you will have the first deposit payment by Friday 11th and the subsequent second payment by the end of July."

Minister Garland's personal assurance wasn't worth very much. The eleventh came and went, as did the twelfth, thirteenth, fourteenth, fifteenth, and sixteeth. Finally, on July 17, roughly ten weeks late, an $83,333 wire showed up in our account. But by the end of the month, there was no second check, as had been promised.

Instead, the only other thing to appear in July in regard to the Turks was an investigation. The British government began looking into widespread corruption and questionable deals involving Misick, his ministers, and various developers. Meanwhile, their initial survey had indicated what our finance department already sensed: the Turks and Caicos, waterlogged by debt, was now broke.

$ $ $

At least we still had Peter Max. Unlike our legally inept *Private Air* employee or our apparently corrupt Caribbean partners, America's "artist laureaute" was a self-styled King Midas, able to produce cash at will. While he refused to sign our deal ("Peter has a problem with signed contracts," his business development contractor, Paul Durante, finally admitted), he actually forked over our cut of art sales, with Durante diligently providing updates.

The great hedge fund colorization project had proven a mixed success: less than half the hedgies bought their portraits. But those who supplied their own picture, or showed up in person to view the finished product, almost universally succumbed. As long as our subjects engaged with Peter from the beginning, we envisioned an autumn filled with Peter Max acrylics, toasting the "rainmakers" of the deal world, the world's top CEOs, the most charitable jet owners.

To test this new model, we had a quick opportunity. Every summer, the entire cigar world descends on some city or another with loose antismoking laws for four days of puffing and networking. A painted portfolio of a dozen cigar tycoons for *The Cigar Report* "Hall of Fame"—unveiled at the convention, this year in Las Vegas—would be a triple win: a great editorial package for the magazine, a chance to impress the decision-makers who could lift *The Cigar Report*'s advertising from financial mediocrity to solid profit, and a financial score from the art. When Peter sent them all autographed books, imploring them to send in photos, they almost universally complied.

Then came a call from Paul Durante. "We have a problem." Last time I heard that from him, it was the Pope. But Durante sounded dire this time.

"Peter changed his mind. He doesn't want to paint the cigar guys anymore."

"Why not?"

"He's decided that it goes against his whole 'natural' thing."

Cigars *are* natural—they're just rolled leaves, versus the tar-and-additive delivery system known as cigarettes. And Peter Max's entire fame and fortune derived from people staring at his paintings under the influence of bad-for-you substances. Cigars were just how Wall Street took an acid trip. But I didn't have a problem with Peter's principle—cigars surely cause mouth cancer, providing moral qualms in conflict with my libertarian instincts. I just objected to his timing.

"Paul, do you think he could have thought of this *before* he promised to paint the owner of every cigar company in North America?" Teasing cigar royalty is a pretty effective way to snuff a cigar magazine.

I eventually took it up with Peter himself, who relented after an hour on the phone, setting one condition: none of the subjects could have a cigar in their painting.

Of course, that's like promising to paint jockeys without horses, or fashion designers buck naked. Every single one approved a picture of himself smoking, holding, chewing, or caressing his "stick," which Peter's Oompa-Loompas digitally erased before applying them to the canvas.

A few days before the cigar-less cigar barons were set to ship to Vegas, Durante ominously called again.

"We have a problem . . . Peter is insisting he be paid in advance for his expenses for these paintings."

His "expenses," the bogus $4,000 per painting, were just a backdoor way for Peter to tip the scales on his fifty-fifty deal with us. We all knew that. But now he was twisting that concept to make us *front* him money.

"Paul, that's extortion."

"I know it is," replied Durante, always a straight shooter. He sighed. "Can I level with you?"

"Please."

"Peter's desperate for cash."

Peter had a full-time staff of about fifty: assistants, lawyers, archivists, canvas-stretchers. He doubled his commercial real estate holdings, to cover the spillover from the hoarding. He had thirty-six vintage Corvettes gathering dust in a Brooklyn parking garage. But at the same time, sales were tailing off. That was precisely why Durante reached out to me months before. For all the bluster about having archives worth a billion dollars, Peter Max was in the same straits as Lenny Dykstra, another victim of overleveraging.

The larger moral, however, was less important to me than the fact that *The Cigar Report* was dead unless I paid Peter Max his extortion money. Phil Falcone's $110,000 for his soon-to-be-unclaimed portraits was due any day, so Durante and I worked out a compromise. We'd write postdated $24,000 checks for July 15 and July 31, respectively.

If Falcone or some of the cigar money showed up first, we'd be off the hook. My only stipulation: Peter had to sign a written contract. It's one thing to trust a tax felon when he's forking over the money to you; how do you justify giving him a loan on a handshake?

You don't. On July 15, the same day as the Vegas cigar party and the date on the first check, our general counsel, Andy Mirsky, sent the Max team a letter informing them that until they formalized the contract, which "has been in your possession for several months awaiting your signature," don't bother cashing the check.

The party itself had some excitement—the paintings didn't arrive until fifteen minutes before the cigar gods, eleven out of the twelve of whom showed up—but the real fireworks happened when I got to New York. Cash-starved Peter Max still refused to sign the contract. Instead, he tried to cash the check anyway—and then received a surprise when he learned that we had issued a stop order on it.

"You . . . FUCKING . . . ASSHOLE!!!!" he screamed at me through the phone. It wasn't those harsh words spouting from the *LOVE* poster creator that struck me; after the de facto extortion, I was primed for anything. It was the high, wheezing octave, somewhere between a seven-year-old-girl and a Bee Gees falsetto. Peter Max had an honest-to-goodness adult hissy fit that ended with his slamming the phone down on me.

It quickly became a moot issue. While cigar tycoons sans cigars proved a tough sell overall, even when discounted to as low as $5,000 per portrait, Sig sold the father-son Bahamian duo who owned Graycliff Cigars, Enrico and Paolo Garzaroli, a pair of portraits for $50,000. And Falcone's $110,000 check finally arrived, as did other *Trader Monthly* dribs and drabs. Peter's costs were taken care of—and he now owed us more than $50,000.

Yet he refused to pay. "You're being punished," Durante explained, apologetically. "He's still mad at you for stopping that check."

Now I was having the hissy fit: "He wouldn't sign the contract. We told him not to cash it. And now he's more than covered. This is *stealing*."

"I'm just as angry as you are," Durante replied. "But he needs cash. I guess this is his way of getting it."

$ $ $

"We're not going to make payroll."

Those were six words I hadn't heard in two years, and they had come from our financial controller in response to the most innocuous question someone running a company can ask: how's everything going?

It was the middle of July. We had a $2 million credit line, an unlimited, albeit onerous, backup credit line from Jim, and a $17 million valuation for the company in the offing. So how the heck were we not making payroll? The answer pretty much summed up the summer of 2008 for us, and too many others: money coming in at a glacial crawl, money flying out like the economic party would last forever, and a management team too blind to see the obvious.

Marc Feifer, our pay-as-you-go CFO, had managed our books with such precision that our financial auditors genuflected. But that immaculate record-keeping came at a cost: perpetual one-hundred-hour weeks that he felt incapable of shirking, no matter how much I implored him to hire help or delegate. The previous summer, he burned out, and stepped down. "I need to for my health," Feifer told me. "It's gotten to the point where I can't stay at Doubledown and keep any balance."

I replaced him with Paul Fish, an *expansion* CFO. Fish had previously been CFO of Dennis Publishing, the folks behind *Maxim* magazine, helping to take it from start-up to a $200 million sale. A perfect fit. It was Fish who had gotten us the Keltic credit line, yet more leverage from our printer, and worked nights and weekends to churn out financial models anytime a VC wanted to explore a new theory about how to grow our business.

But for all his nimble financial wizardry, Fish fumbled with the operating basics—collecting money in, paying it out, and communicating to those involved. He had left for a family visit in England a few days earlier, assuring me all was fine, and now the controller was telling me that we were $200,000 short of payroll. At the same time, our auditors reached out to us, alarmed over the state of the financial records. People who were owed money increasingly reached out to me as well. It wasn't that they were getting paid slowly—we had always paid slowly, but also surely—but that they weren't being given reliable information from the finance department.

"Growth for the sake of growth," Edward Abbey once wrote, "is the ideology of the cancer cell." He was referring to the environment, but we surely had a cancer building up within Doubledown. As I spent all my time scrambling manically to Get Big Fast, from the venture capital meetings to rancorous quick-fix partnerships to gobbling up a second suite of offices in our building, and then a third, and then a fourth, more liabilities incurred with little more than my personal guarantee, I neglected the day-to-day operations, delegating them to Fish, to my deep regret.

Now I had to take my medicine. Even after Jim became chairman, I never flat-out asked him for money. I was always too proud, too able to triage the situation; Jim invariably sensed a need, and *offered* cash. That kept our relationship healthy. Tracking him down in Hong Kong, on vacation with his family while kicking tires for his China SPAC, I groveled for a $400,000 loan, the prodigal son finally reduced to sticking out his hand and asking Dad to bail him out.

Realizing that I had dropped the ball on the CFO, I then tried to send a quick message to the staff and the world, with a new head of finance. I called the country's top media head-hunting firm, Howard-Sloan-Koller, and within a week, they delivered the perfect candidate: Pete Cipriano, a stable, veteran CFO for similarly sized media companies. He'd start immediately—part-time, as he transitioned out of his old job at LTB Media, then full-time after Labor Day.

"Those who work with Doubledown," I wrote to the company in announcing Cipriano, "will be able to count on two things:

- If we have a business relationship with someone, and they contact us, we will contact them back promptly.
- If we promise something to someone, we will deliver it."

Problem solved. Until Cipriano, still working at his old company during the transition, took a counteroffer from LTB, resigning, meekly, via a voice message. That bothered me: he had seen under the hood enough to get spooked. When I hired another established media CFO, John Orr, he insisted on keeping Fish, now integral as the sole person who could decipher our suddenly complex finances and abysmal record-keeping. The same dynamic would play out across Wall Street over the next few months. The safest job in finance: creating a mess. It was those who kept everything neat as a pin who faced the layoffs.

This was all just housekeeping until the Edison venture capital deal closed.

But then it didn't.

The meeting in front of the full investment committee seemed cursed from the outset. We brought a Mac laptop; their projector worked only with PCs. The one-two patter Magnus and I had perfected over a few dozen VC meetings broke down, as our larger group of managers, a five-headed hydra, stumbled over one another. Most of all, though, the larger Edison group discerned that, rather than an unconventional technology company, we remained a vulnerable magazine publisher. "We were becoming more risk averse on companies that were so heavily dependent on advertising," Edison's Joe Allegra now recalls, "as we had started to see it slow down."

Engorged with debt, we were again left to grow ourselves out of our problem, with the calendar serving as our key ally. The biggest advertising season, by far, is autumn. Each year for the past four, we'd beg and borrow our way through the first six months, when 40 percent of our revenues arrived, and then wash away all our sins each fall, when the remaining 60 percent flooded in, almost entirely after Labor Day.

A few weeks before September, with $6 million logged for the first half of 2008, history indicated that we'd bring in $9 million in the second. Far short of our $20 million goal—unsurprising, given the Dykstra implosion and the softening economy—but still enough to turn a small profit, paying all our bills and knocking out all our debt.

The latest lender: me. Jim's 2008 hefty contributions had come with a stipulation: Magnus and I needed to raise another $250,000 from our friends. If his ass was getting deeper into this, Jim insisted, so would ours. One of my college buddies threw in another $50,000, solely on my word that it was a good investment, and Magnus had a friend put in $35,000. But as the markets hiccuped, that was it. So, mindful of my word to Jim, I did something really stupid. Borrowing to the maximum against the stocks in my retirement account, which had appreciated, as all assets had, over the past two years, I scraped together $50,000 personally. Completely drained, I then turned to the only other source that would blindly deliver for me, on my personal guarantee: my mom. A widow on a fixed income, she had a credit line, which she tapped for the last $115,000.

My first $233,000, back in 2005, had been extraordinarily risky—there was no safety net in those days—but also smart. It allowed Doubledown to grow up and become worth $25 million, or $17 million, or whatever it was worth now.

This new money felt dumb and safe. Dumb because I wasn't getting anything—I didn't ask for any interest or any extra equity stake—other than a leadership statement. Safe, in the sense that, since it was avowedly a short-term loan, it would get paid back with the autumn's torrent of cash, or any company sale. As long as the asset was worth even the few million needed to wipe out our debt, much less $17 million, it was risk-free. Right?

For all my time inside the heart of Wall Street, I still hadn't embraced the game: OPM, or Other People's Money. I had again put up MOM—My Own Money (and far worse, MOM, via my mom). And while risky and smart was a time-tested formula for entrepreneurial success, dumb and safe were two words that historically clashed, rather than complemented.

As we approached September 2008, the most fateful month in global finance since October 1929, dumb was about to trump safe.

12

The Party's Over

A decade-long mania ended with a brutal forty-eight-hour spasm. On Monday, September 15, 2008, two Wall Street pillars—158-year-old Lehman Brothers and 94-year-old Merrill Lynch—essentially disappeared, drowned by massive subprime losses. Bank of America swallowed Merrill in a fire sale; Lehman, unable to find a financial suitor or a government savior, filed for bankruptcy. On Tuesday, September 16, the global markets panicked; banks stopped lending money to individuals, companies, or each other. AIG, which had insured all those junky subprime losses through their swaps, but now didn't have enough cash to cover the payoffs, was deemed "too big to fail" by the federal government, which took it over, injecting $85 billion in emergency taxpayer-funded capital.

So how did Doubledown Media, chronicler and celebrator of the financial industry, react to the two days that introduced "financial meltdown" into the global vernacular?

We had a party.

Not just any party, but a proper doozy, our annual *Dealmaker* "40 Under 40," held that fateful Tuesday, September 16, at the Stone

Rose, a Manhattan lounge owned by nightlife impresario Rande Gerber, model Cindy Crawford's husband.

Canceling was never considered. Quite the opposite: as the carnage accumulated through Monday and Tuesday, our reservation line exploded. RSVPs flooded in, by the dozen, by the hundred, surging toward one thousand in all. The shell-shocked *Dealmaker* community wanted to lick wounds, compare notes, and, of course, drink— Facebook for the deal world in live action.

All the trappings were still properly pre-meltdown. The de rigueur Maybach parked in the lobby, the skimpily dressed models displaying $10,000 Carl F. Bucherer watches. Trying to horn in on the Turks and Caicos, the Bermuda Department of Tourism dragged in a putting green, while the folks behind Seaside Marina tried to entice bankers and private equity partners to buy lots in their new luxury development in . . . *Nicaragua*. Daniel Ortega, leader of the Sandinista Communists whom America covertly battled throughout the eighties, prompting the Iran-Contra scandal that crippled Ronald Reagan, had returned to power the previous year and promptly embraced the real-estate-for-millionaires boom. Seaside Marina, according to the presentation, boasted an equestrian club, "massage center," and Jack Nicklaus championship golf course, carved right against the Pacific.

As to be expected from ex-Communists in a hypercapitalist decade, the Nicaraguans were too late to the party. While crowds elbowed to the bar featuring four different levels of Johnnie Walker—red, black, green, and gold—the Maybach looked lonely and no one bought watches off the models. The room was searching for its new September 2008 equilibrium. Had we just experienced a paradigm shift, or merely a momentous hiccup?

The highlight of the evening came when I shushed the crowd. After thanking the sponsors and welcoming the 40 Under 40 honorees in attendance, I passed the microphone to the man with the best job in the world, Steve Wilson, Johnnie Walker's goateed "Whisky Master." Dozens of waitresses fanned across the room, with tumblers filled with the Holy Grail of brown liquor, Johnnie Walker Blue.

"What unites the honorees is their drive and determination," crowed Wilson, announcing that the entire 40 Under 40 list would receive personally engraved bottles, from the Carlyle Group's Brett Wyard, who stared out confidently from the magazine's cover, to Lehman's Frank Cicero and Punit Mehta, who presumably no longer had jobs. "If everyone could please raise their glasses in a Blue Label toast."

He raised his left arm and I raised my right. And down the $200-a-bottle nectar went into everyone's gullets. Scottish whisky at an Irish wake.

$ $ $

"We have come a long way, partner."

Magnus sent that e-mail on Thursday, September 25, attaching a jpeg of the cover of the first-ever *Dealmaker Middle East*, a screaming "Hello Dubai" cover line sitting above Essa Kazim, chairman, and Soud Ba'alawy, vice chairman, of the regional stock exchange, resplendent in white Arabian robes and kaffiyeh. Even more monumental than the striking global image was Magnus's location when he sent it—Dubai itself. Doubledown's representative at the launch party, he was swarmed by a dozen Gulf television networks, radio stations, and newspapers, and treated as if he were a visiting member of the British Parliament. "Magnus," reported the president of our Middle East licensee, Avi Bhojani, "has become a celebrity in Dubai."

I received his note precisely halfway around the world, in Napa Valley. I was preparing for three winery welcome dinners, two days of private-jet-tire-kicking, and one Saturday night charity auction at the Flights of Napa, our most ambitious event yet. For all the crazy times and the crazy people around us, that e-mail exchange physically underscored the precise apex of our influence. We now sent magazines to 500,000 different people worldwide, and reached over 100,000 people a day with our electronic newsletters. Tens of thousands of people attended our events. *Trader Monthly Brazil* and *Dealmaker* UK were preparing to launch. Our Web sites now brought in $1 million in annual revenue. We had indeed come a long way, actualizing the vision—if not the profit—of the expansive Working Wealthy business plan.

But by September 25 much of our audience, like the world as a whole, was no longer working and no longer wealthy. As Magnus and I corresponded between Dubai and Napa, Washington Mutual, holding $300 billion in assets, collapsed, the biggest bank failure in U.S. history. Meanwhile, President Bush, his cabinet, congressional leaders, and both presidential candidates, Barack Obama and my old craps buddy John McCain, were holed up at the White House, desperately trying to hammer out a Wall Street bailout package. Treasury Secretary Henry Paulson literally got down on one knee to beg for Speaker of the House Nancy Pelosi's support. And while Federal Reserve chairman Ben Bernanke had reportedly told members of Congress that "we might not have an economy Monday" without a bailout, Bush was, typically, more direct when addressing the room: "If money isn't loosened up, this sucker could go down."

With such a backdrop, Flights of Napa was, predictably, a letdown. Sure, over eight hundred people came to the Napa Airport for the daytime festivities to gawk at the planes and taste wine samples from thirty vintners who poured in front of the aircraft. But eight hundred people on an airport tarmac, over two days, feels like a tea party in a barn. And no one wanted planes. Or cars, to the concern of those at the Mercedes display. Or the financing to buy either, from the looks of the forlorn AIG booth, a sponsorship sold during the good times whose $50,000 fee now came guaranteed by U.S. taxpayers.

As for the evening events, one of the remaining signs of the apocalypse was revealed to us in the form of Al Gore attending our Napa gala. The most indulgent pollution machines on the planet would be saluted in the presence of the most famous environmentalist on the planet, a year after his Nobel Prize. The world was officially upside down.

The seventy-five guests with $500 VIP packages, cleaved into small groups for the three different welcome dinners across the valley floor on Friday night, were scheduled to come together for a big dinner auction on Saturday night, hosted by Garen and Shari Staglin of Staglin Family Vineyards. Their house was Hollywood worthy (Lindsay Lohan filmed *The Parent Trap* there), a Tuscan villa carved into the hills, with a loggia high enough above the valley floor to emulate a balloon ride.

The Staglins represented everything the Working Wealthy *should* be. Garen made a fortune in venture capital, and they lived a beautiful life in a beautiful home. But they also gave back in equal measure: after their son Brandon developed schizophrenia, they started the Music Festival for Mental Health, held at their house with acts ranging from Pat Benatar to Gladys Knight. Since 1995, they had raised $83 million for the cause. The entire proceeds from the Saturday auction would go to their fight; I was thrilled to help.

Besides mental health advocates, the Staglins were also influential Democrats, and ten days before our event, Garen called with the kind of sentence I was now hearing on a daily basis: "We have a problem." Specifically, the Staglins had offered to host a big Napa fund-raiser for the Democratic National Committee's "Victory Fund"—$2 million big, as in fifty people at $40,000 a pop. Al Gore had signed on as the headliner—as long as they could do it on the same Saturday evening as our auction.

Garen wasn't going to disappoint Gore or Obama. But he wasn't going to let me down, either. Per his venture capital background, we brainstormed. Hold the auction Friday? Too complicated with the other wineries. Move the event site? A bummer for those coming to see the Staglin estate. Finally, a *Dealmaker*-appropriate solution: a merger. The Staglins would host the fund-raiser on the early side, segregating Gore and the Democratic donors on the front loggia while our GOP-leaning guests arrived for cocktails, shunted into the garden through the back door. The carbon-haters could then join the carbon-spewers for the poolside dinner, common ground (even Gore sometimes used Gulfstreams during the Zeroes) forged by private jet.

The Staglins graciously sat me at Gore's table. Dressed in a blue blazer atop a blue button-down, he focused on politics rather than jets, launching into a droning series of mini-lectures that passed for conversation until Garen tapped me on the arm. Rather than engage a bloated, drowsy audience—bellies full of Dungeness crab pasta, summer-vegetable-and-citrus salad, morel-and-foie-gras ravioli, spring lamb osso bucco, and buttermilk vanilla panna cotta, with Napa wines to match all five courses—we had decided to start the auction before the food came out. Standing at the head of the pool, surrounded by sculptures and a terraced garden, Garen discussed the charity, and I talked about the importance of giving back. "Please bid high and bid often," I implored, mimicking the language of the auction program, anticipating the rapid action we had seen at the previous fall's boxing event, a mini–Robin Hood frenzy.

The first of the seven lots was a "front-row" tour of New York, complete with VIP tickets to the David Letterman show, a suite at the Affinia Manhattan, and three gourmet dinners, including one as my guest on a *Time Out New York* restaurant review.

We're going to start with the minimum bid, $3,500, announced the auctioneer, Napa favorite Ursula Hermacinski. *Who has thirty-five hundred?*

The answer, on the last Saturday of September 2008, was, nobody. Silence. A pit welled in my stomach.

Okay, let's drop down to $2,000. Who has two thousand?

A long pause. Very long. Then a jet broker with a bushy mustache, dressed Napa casual, a beige sports coat over a black T-shirt, lifted his paddle. *We have two thousand!*

Across the pool, another paddle went up. *Twenty-five hundred!* Then the bushy mustache responded. *Three thousand! Sold!* Relief.

Lot two came up. A bicycle and spa trip through Napa. Market value: $6,000. Ursula started the bidding lower. Nothing. A weekend for four at the Staglin estate, valued at $15,000? Nothing. A South American wine tour, opening bid twenty-five grand? Nothing. Even the chance to be painted by Peter Max, donated before he wigged out on us, went bidless, depriving me of the delicious chance to warn the winner about Peter's One-Plus-Three tactic. As Gore looked on, a random sliver of America's rich had surveyed the new economic landscape and effectively voted with their fallow auction paddles about the direction of the economy.

Ursula prepared to relaunch the auction at lower numbers, but

Garen, who solicited most of the lots, intervened. He'd try to re-auction them at a more fruitful time.

"I feel like I let you down," I told him as we returned to Gore's long dinner table.

"The world is crazy right now," Garen replied, supportively. "We'll try again next year."

The next evening, after we packed up the Napa Airport, I flew to New York on the red-eye, arriving just in time Monday morning for Congress to reject the bailout. The weekend that started with the largest-ever bank collapse ended with the largest-ever drop in the Dow Jones Industrial Average, 778 points. The traders sensed the same undercurrents as our auction bidders: this sucker could go down.

$ $ $

There's a difference, as any gazillionaire will tell you, between wealth and *liquidity*. Jim Dunning, the wealthiest man that I had a personal relationship with, had the kind of investments that make, as F. Scott Fitzgerald noted, the rich different from you and me. Hedge funds, private equity funds, limited partnerships, three houses, his China SPAC, not to mention the $6 million or so he'd now plugged into Doubledown Media. Unlike Lenny Dykstra or the tens of millions of other overleveraged Americans and Europeans who paralleled him, Jim carried almost no debt. Most of those investments, however, were completely illiquid, and the source of his mad money, a fund affiliated with Lehman Brothers, had been frozen since that firm's rapid demise, placing Jim in the same adrift, cashless boat as the rest of the world.

The cavalry that we had originally counted on to rescue us— the surge of fall advertising that had rolled in as predictably as San Francisco fog since our company's founding—never showed. Wilkie Bushby, our dogged group publisher and Doubledown employee number one, whose autumns had always encompassed whipping our far-flung sales reps to *pile on* the ads, instead scrambled to prevent already committed advertising from *pulling out*. "It was like a freight train coming down the tracks," Bushby remembers. "There was no getting out of the way." The entire media industry was going backward—magazine advertising dropped 15 percent in the fourth quarter—and with our twin foci on Wall Street and luxury, few were more vulnerable.

Meanwhile, our costs remained stuck in growth mode. We'd built a platform designed for a big company, and every trim—from the chief revenue officer, who hadn't been generating revenue even before the market explosion, to slimmer magazines, to suspending *Corporate Leader,* which failed to gain traction—met offsetting increases. Most notably, we were still dancing to the tune of the venture capitalists. Several, including Verizon's investment arm, pledged a check as soon as we could prove that our audiences would engage in one of these mini-Facebooks, so we scrambled to build a test version for *Dealmaker*.

We needed money from Jim. And with the entire world in panic, he dictated the terms. He would convert all those short-term loans into stock, and put another $750,000 into the company. In exchange he would own 70 percent of Doubledown (if the company did well, he offered to rebate 20 percent to the employees). From the $17 million term sheet I had held in my hand just weeks before, Jim's investment now valued the company at roughly $5 million. Dreams of a big score for any of us were largely gone. This was survival mode, and we needed to do what it took to weather the storm.

Even if that meant compromising with Lenny Dykstra. Litigation with Nails had proven as event-filled as working with Nails. On the morning of his deposition—a chance for our lawyers to grill him under oath—he called me out of the blue (*Yo Randall, man, it's Lenny!*) suggesting that we settle "before we go spending all this money." I let him buy me breakfast at the W Hotel, near Union Square, and shook his shaky hand on a package where he'd pay us about $350,000.

But once inside the lawyers' office, when he discovered that he'd have to agree with the attorneys and court stenographer present, he waffled. Sure, Lenny would pay $350,000, but "only after I go over all the charges to make sure they're legitimate."

He and I had already agreed on the charges at the Carlyle. And we had already sent him a copy of every receipt, itemized. This was just more games.

"Lenny, either honor the $350,000 we agreed to," I said, pointing at him, "or you can go do your testimony." Lenny asked to meet with his lawyer. Then he snuck out the door.

It didn't get any less surreal when both sides showed up for our first court date, more late-September absurdity in the form of a "settlement conference." Magistrate Andrew Peck ordered us into the cafeteria of the federal courthouse to try to work out a deal. I remained attached to the $350,000 we'd already committed to. Lenny's new line: he would do me a favor and just dismiss both cases without money changing hands. When I laughed, he looked at me, with a darkness I had never seen in his eyes, not even when firing staffers with the epitaph "Breathe deep." "You know what I've paid my lawyers?" he said, pointing at the poor sap representing him. "Four fucking million dollars. I do this for a living! I will *ruin* you."

When we came back without a deal, Magistrate Peck tried to mediate using shuttle diplomacy. First, I'd march into Peck's chambers to get beat down. Then Lenny would march in to get beat up. This went on for three rounds. We never had to look at each other.

Eventually, Peck came to a compromise number: $200,000—about enough to pay the outside vendors for the magazine that Lenny had stolen, sticking us with the bills, including $75,000 that would go to the printer for the expensive glossy paper Lenny ordered but never used.

On Lenny's last trip into the chambers, he threw in a wrinkle: he needed 90 days to pay some of it and 180 days to cover the balance. Nails apparently still hadn't cashed in his car wash note.

I dug in. I wanted Lenny out of my life, and I needed those bills paid now. But the magistrate looked me in the eye. "I'm going to slap on a healthy interest rate—do you think you're gonna do better in the markets right now?" We'd avoid more legal bills. And now, he added, he'd serve as our collection agent. In the middle of a credit crunch, a federally enforced payment down the road was about as close to upfront cash as we could find.

$ $ $

"When we come back, we will be talking about a real Wall Street party," intoned television anchor Rick Sanchez, CNN's resident populist, before looking at the reporter sitting next to him, Abbie Boudreau. "You actually take us into one of those. Right?"

"A rare glimpse!" She nodded.

Sanchez then broke for a commercial: "I guess we could call this 'fat cats in their element' when we come back."

Since its inception, Doubledown's events had been eagerly attended by the press, who could ogle and poke and prod the traders/hedgies/bankers/private equity partners—these exotic creatures seemingly making us all rich, even if they were keeping the outsized share of the loot themselves. Since 2004, we had used the on-air comments from another CNN anchor ("I went to the *Trader Monthly* launch party. Live band, great food, open bar, fancy cigars. I really enjoyed the vicarious experience") in our sales presentations. For four years, that had been the near-universal response to that "rare glimpse" we offered almost weekly to anyone who asked.

Thus, Doubledown's public relations team reflexively welcomed Boudreau and her camera crew to the first-ever Wall Street Smoke, *The Cigar Report*'s attempt to leverage the *Trader Monthly* and *Dealmaker* databases into a competitor for *Cigar Aficionado*'s highly profitable Big Smoke. October 7 had already proven a lousy day globally—the Dow dropped another 508 points, putting it below 8,000, nearly halved from just a year earlier, and Iceland, the country, imploded financially. Doubledown's day followed suit, after our PR squad failed to note the FBI-worthy title of the CNN producer person asking for entry: "Producer, Special Investigations Unit."

The following Saturday and Sunday, CNN devoted an entire hour at 8 p.m., the heart of prime time, to a special, "Fall of the Fat Cats." The very first thing CNN viewers saw: Sig. "All the good things in life," he cackled. "Caviar! We have a lot of caviar!"

"They lived the high life," said Sanchez, introducing the special, over a visual of Sig's sweaty forehead. "Now it's come crashing down."

Most of the hour was taken up by an interview with a crooked trader from the nineties and a newly laid-off banker, as well as an exposé on Dick Fuld, the former CEO of Lehman Brothers. But the centerpiece was the *Cigar Report* party.

CNN viewers saw a typical Doubledown Media event: more than eight hundred traders and bankers at the Hudson Terrace, a Manhattan party space with an outdoor roof overlooking the river, each handed $150 worth of cigars from manufacturers paying us handsomely for the privilege. The one hundred VIP tickets, at $75 each, sold out immediately: those folks had access to still-better smokes, manicures and shoeshines, and a caviar bar stocked from Petrossian, the world's top purveyor of pricey fish eggs since the Roaring Twenties. But what, even two months ago, would have been chronicled with wide-eyed amazement, was now viewed from the other side of the mirror.

"I have to ask you, because I think some people at home are wondering about this party," Sanchez said to Boudreau. "How did you get in?"

"We just asked," replied Boudreau, ". . . and they said 'come on in.'"

"*Come on in,*" marveled Sanchez, getting on his soapbox. "It's interesting. Is it really about a lack of fear? When there is not enough fear, and the greed exceeds that fear, don't we know we will get into trouble? Weren't we taught this by our grandparents?"

I couldn't speak for my grandparents, but the past month had me scared shitless, which is why I wasn't at the cigar event, but across the country, at the American Magazine Conference in San Francisco, trying to gin up interest in a sale or investment with various media company heads. Fortuitously for CNN, in the tone-deaf Sig, they found their willing poster boy for that greed.

"All right, guys, follow me," said Sig, preening for the camera. "This is Big James. We're going into the VIP lounge. Can I have some caviar, please? Thank you so much. That is delicious. Thank you so much."

The camera pans around. "A true story," Sig boasted. "That beer was flown in straight from the Dominican Republic for me for this event."

To really drill it in, the producers brought in a live three-person panel—a laid-off plant manager, a Realtor, and a former intern for

Lehman Brothers—to heap on derision. And after a commercial, the American public was invited to follow suit, via Twitter and Facebook. "We welcome you back. I'm Rick Sanchez. People all over the country are watching with amazement, as are we, by the way. Some of them are commenting to us. . . . Let's go to the one that says 'Rick Young' on it. It says 'The arrogance of those people is amazing. They spend as much in a week as many of us earn in a year. It doesn't bother them a bit.' "

"I don't think that they feel bad," added Boudreau as she signed off at the end of the show. "I think that they feel like things will get better. They look at it as if they are living in the moment right now, they worry about tomorrow, tomorrow. And they are optimistic. It might have slowed down the party a little bit, but the party on Wall Street, according to people that I talked to, is not over."

Technically, she was right. We had parties locked in throughout the fall, commitments to advertisers and attendees we needed to follow through on: a Wall Street Smoke in Miami; an October 14 party in Chicago, hosted by Bears star linebacker Lance Briggs, who had just appeared in a *Trader Monthly* fashion spread; the official *Dealmaker* UK launch party in London; an October 30 party on a one-hundred-foot megayacht at the Fort Lauderdale Boat Show, sponsored by a Costa Rican real estate development; and our trifecta of "30 Under 30" bashes, drawing turnouts larger than ever, in New York, Chicago, and London.

Spiritually, though, they now felt dirty. For four years, people had told me what a great job I had, lording over these events. As in having people at your house, though, the host never had fun. Every event was stress-filled, as I troubleshot problems, mollifying high-maintenance sponsors and babysitting entitled attendees. The real thrill came from being at the center of seemingly the most important phenomenon of the decade, and building something amazing and unprecedented within it. The glowing media coverage stemmed from the fact that everyone thought of Wall Street as the engine of prosperity, putting an SUV in every driveway, an organic hen in every pot.

Now that the game had been revealed as a corrosive fraud—

painfully obvious in retrospect, yet ignored by the regulators, the general public, and the supposedly vigilant media like us—these same events effectively honored those blamed for millions of bankruptcies and layoffs. The torrent of public hate wasn't entirely fair: I knew hundreds of hardworking financial types who had nothing to do with the meltdown, and were in fact victims themselves, losing their jobs as their nest eggs, in bank stock, melted away. But like most stereotypes, there was also an inescapable, underlying truth to it.

So why was I still doing this? I asked that myself every day. The bankrupt societal value had revealed itself. After the new Jim Dunning deal, there was no longer any financial upside for me. And it was no longer fun. I worked around the clock, never saw my family or friends, and spent my waking hours managing crises. But what option did I have? I needed to recoup the money I'd recklessly sunk in, make good on the commitment I had given Magnus and then Jim, do right by every person I had recruited into the company and every vendor we did business with, all of whom we invariably owed money to. It's precisely why smart investors back only entrepreneurs with skin in the game. In situations like this, there's no escape.

As we scrambled for a solution, we all put on a good face. On October 23, we repeated the Wall Street Boxing Championships. If anything, it was more spectacular than the first: we crammed one hundred more people, over one thousand in all, into the Hammerstein Ballroom. Del Frisco's Double Eagle Steak House, the second-highest-grossing restaurant in America, offered all-you-can-eat stations of butterflied lamb chops and Angus beef filets—and that was just hors d'oeuvres. The giant bottles of Imperia vodka gave way to giant bottles of Bocaj vodka, "distilled in individual batches by the finest-choice grapes." Gerry Cooney returned, along with a passel of B-list celebrities. The Hard Rock Casino in Las Vegas ran blackjack tables in the back. Nikki Beach supplied ring-card girls. Jeremy Schaap brought an ESPN camera crew, and a European documentary team dragged along real film cameras, boom mikes, the works.

The title sponsor, meanwhile, offered still more drama, though none of it, fortunately, had to do with us. As the British colonial overlords launched their investigation, the Turks continued to dodge their payments. Then, on September seventh, the week before the Lehman bankruptcy/Merrill fire sale/AIG bailout, the Turks went underwater—literally. Hurricane Ike leveled the island chain; while it didn't kill anyone, miraculously, it inflicted $500 million worth of damage—the rough GDP equivalent of a $10 trillion storm in the United States. When the Brits went looking for money to rebuild, they found less than $100,000 in the emergency fund.

The Misick administration, however, somehow eventually found another $125,000 for us, and sent up a delegation of *seventy-eight* people to the event; the VIPs via Gulfstream, the rest, I surmised, merely first-class. The entourage filled up the trendy Hotel Gansevoort, a Meatpacking District spot more common for the Hollywood/rock star set, and included everyone who mattered from the Turks and Caicos, save one person: Premier Michael Misick.

Misick had planned a grand welcome, the premier of a pseudo country addressing an audience controlling hundreds of billions. But sometime between the contract signing and the event, Misick was accused of raping a woman in Puerto Rico. The FBI was seeking him for questioning, making travel to the United States a no-go. "He was afraid that the moment he stepped off the plane, he'd be arrested or at least investigated," remembers our travel advertising director, Henry Watkins.

Instead, we got stuck with Deputy Premier Floyd Hall, the Dick Cheney of the Turks. The live auction was feeble—Jim Dunning, trying to seed some action, got stuck with two of the lots. We raised just $100,000 for the charities, though this year, we made sure they got paid. The crowd, while larger, was less euphoric. The fights seemed less dramatic.

In professional boxing, the winners get a belt. The Wall Street champion, in October 2008, got a watch. The gaudiest, flashiest, tackiest watch in the history of male accessories—one from Jacob Arabo, aka "Jacob the Jeweler," whose diamond-encrusted monstrosities infiltrated more than fifty hip-hop song lyrics across the Zeroes, from Jay-Z to R. Kelly to 50 Cent. Having moved from rappers to basketball players, Arabo excitedly targeted the next rung on the funny money ladder, Wall Street, spending $100,000 to sponsor everything from the Peter Max package in the *Trader Monthly* 100 to the boxing event.

Like Misick, Arabo planned on making a dramatic personal appearance. And like Misick, the feds had provided him a detour. Four months before the match, Arabo was sentenced to thirty months in prison for making false statements about his connection to Detroit's notorious Black Mafia Family drug cartel, after accusations that he laundered $270 million worth of narco-profits through his company. His marketing chief, Denise Scala, was left to present the Fighter of the Night timepiece to Andre "The Greek Sheik" Ameer, of Copper River Management.

A charitable event, produced by a cash-strapped company, held for a despised audience, sponsored by a corrupt regime, and crowned with a felonious watch.

The party was over.

$ $ $

What does it feel like to lose $60 million in a single day?

Imagine you're sitting on a beach and you see this tsunami far on the horizon, explained this unfortunate trader, one of the world's biggest, from the couch of his psychologist's office. *And there is no way, even if you run, that you can get away from it.*

The markets drew control freaks in the first place, those who preferred individual sports over team sports, snipers over infantrymen. Thus, as the mistakes of the few punished the many on Wall Street and the billions on earth, despondency engulfed the financial industry.

"There was a deer-in-the-headlights fatalism," remembers Dr. Douglas Hirschhorn, the in-house psychology PhD at Deutsche Bank and a half-dozen top hedge funds. "I'm going door-to-door with clients and they were *all* feeling this way."

Just as Oprah Winfrey transformed Phil McGraw into "Dr. Phil," America's shrink, *Trader Monthly* had turned a similar trick with "Dr. Doug," who wrote the popular "Head Coach" column and quickly proved another beneficiary of our star machine. Hirschhorn was the real deal, counseling hundreds of top traders on mental toughness, including the tsunami-dreamer. Besides helplessness, his clients felt another newfound stress: embarrassment. The rock stars of the Zeroes had instantly become social pariahs; their kids were taunted at school. "If you didn't have coping mechanisms," Hirschhorn says, "there was no way to pull yourself away from the ledge."

This despondency manifested itself in many ways (some of which, ironically, had also symbolized success): Drugs and alcohol. Strip clubs and prostitutes. Divorce and nervous breakdowns, as the Wall Street elite bawled to Hirschhorn like newborns.

Then came the suicides. A Bear Stearns executive named Barry Fox jumped off the twenty-ninth-story roof of his New Jersey office building after that firm melted down. Kirk Stephenson, the dark-haired COO of a City private equity fund with a $5 million flat in Chelsea, a country house, a caring wife, and an eight-year-old son, jumped in front of a London express train traveling one hundred miles per hour. German billionaire Adolf Merckle ended his life that same way after his industrial conglomerate reportedly defaulted on a loan. The head of insurance in the United Kingdom for HSBC, a father of four, was found hanging, naked, in the closet of his $800-a-night London hotel room, after a cocaine-and-women bender. An aristocratic French money manager locked himself in his office on New York's Madison Avenue, gobbled sleeping pills, and slit his wrists with a box cutter. Reports piled into our office from around the world.

Our company, sadly, wasn't immune. Four days after a locomotive took Adolf Merckle, the former publisher of now-defunct *Justice* magazine, Alan Stiles, parked his car along the Massachusetts Turnpike and stepped in front of a train barreling west from Boston's South Station. He was fifty-four. The former publisher of *Esquire*, he had, since *Justice* folded, bumped around various other struggling media entities. "We had adjoining offices," I wrote to his eighteen-year-old daughter, Christina. "I had just had my first daughter, and was learning how to be a dad, and I was struck by how he talked to you, how much he loved you, how he used to call you 'Squirt.'" Now, without an outward sign of trouble, he was gone. For days, I was numb. With the global economy, Wall Street, and Doubledown swirling together in a tight, concentric, rapidly downward circle, sickness surrounded me.

On a day-to-day basis, I had to deal with Rachel Pine, off-kilter even before our world stopped rotating. One of our original employees, hired as head of communications, Pine, who had worked for me at my previous venture, was alternately talented and insidious. She diligently cranked the PR machine and helped install the frugal ethos of our expensive-looking events. But virtually no one who worked under her lasted very long before she fired them or they quit, usually in tears. She refused to report to anyone but me. And she introduced so much office poison that a half-dozen staffers formed a committee to demand that I fire her. "We never had the guts to come to you," remembers a member of the group. "We knew you were too loyal to her."

Every few months, she would pretend to quit, and I would pretend to talk her out of it. On June 22, faced with yet another resignation letter, I accepted. "Unfortunately, there is no way around this," I wrote to Jim and Magnus. "The seventh floor [sales and marketing] is literally at war, and she is the catalyst every time." She responded to my acceptance apoplectically, even after I agreed to severance and an over-the-top written recommendation.

For safety, I brought Magnus into my office to discuss the transition. Over two hours, she emoted and threatened and cried, her anger intensifying as Magnus and I refused to raise our voices, no matter what she said. She finished by smashing my door into the wall four times, amid a primal scream, until the handle created a cantaloupe-sized crater in the Sheetrock.

At home, without a full-time job, Rachel's primary focus apparently remained Doubledown. She had penned a bitter roman à clef about her last long-term employer—creepily, in retrospect, dedicating it to my "exquisite" newborn daughter. Now, almost every day, current employees, ex-employees, even investors would tell me how Rachel called them to rail on endlessly, and negatively, about Doubledown, and me. "Literally, she would talk for forty-five minutes," remembers someone who talked with her regularly, "and every other sentence was 'What does Randall think of me? Does Randall mention my name?'"

Then came the media inquiries—the downside of your PR chief losing her shit. First, the leaks targeting specific rivals at Doubledown that Pine didn't like. Then came leaks dealing with Doubledown's increasingly worrisome financial situation. Then a leaked investor update (the copy specifically sent to Pine). Any tidbit that one reporter left out would be releaked to a different reporter, and so on, extending the meme.

It made no rational sense. Pine had *quit*. She had signed a nondisparagement clause as part her severance, and now risked thousands of dollars by her daily disparagements. And when Doubledown looked like a sure thing after Jim Dunning made the water safe for others, she had asked to invest $10,000, her husband another $75,000—plenty of incentive to let us succeed. "If she wasn't there," says one of the staffers she regularly called, "she'd rather have it fail."

On the unhinged barometer, though, Pine scored relatively low compared with Teri Buhl, one of our editorial interns. Before Doubledown, Buhl hadn't really worked in five years; she lived with a rich Connecticut trader, who covered her costs. In her mid-thirties, Buhl decided she wanted to try journalism, working for us for free as an apprentice as she learned the ropes. But her personal conflicts caused problems.

"Need some advice," our top Wall Street editor, Rich Blake, e-mailed me in early 2008. "I would like to send an email to Teri explaining why she can't write her 'scoops' for the website. She bothers me all the time with web scoops that either smack of an agenda, or are shaky or could get us in trouble . . . she is too inexperienced and I can't trust her reporting."

In response, Buhl quit. "Being a good investigative reporter means knowing and understanding the basics," I wrote to her as she left. "I worry you're too trigger-happy, especially given your level of experience."

Her parting gifts from us were a $350 freelance (noninvestigative) writing assignment and $2,600 to help finish reporting the *Trader Monthly* 100. When our fact-checkers corrected the asset number she submitted for Phil Falcone, the winner of the Peter Max negotiation contest, making it less favorable, Buhl exploded. "This unfortunately has gotten to a level that I can't ignore now," she e-mailed me. "This doesn't need to get ugly and I hope we can work it out professionally. But don't mistreat me."

I kicked it to Blake, who decided to stick with the fact-checkers' account. Buhl's last words to him, memorialized in an e-mail: "I'm going to get them," referring to Jim Dunning and me. "They're going to pay."

That payback began as she started reporting for the *New York Post* on our battle with Lenny Dykstra, taking the nonsensical position that Dykstra was in the right. Then came extortion threats to continue to tar us unless we accelerated the $350 payment for her final freelance article (after already paying the $2,600 for her *Trader Monthly* 100 research).

An e-mail from my assistant: "Teri Buhl just called me pissed off and threatened to continue writing negative things about Doubledown until she gets paid."

An e-mail from Buhl to group publisher Wilkie Bushby: "I will follow up publicly tomorrow if I do not receive a confirmed answer today as to the date my check was mailed."

An e-mail from Buhl to Magnus: "Please make sure some one gets back to me tomorrow . . . and then we can all move on in piece [*sic*]. I am giving your company a chance to avoid more bad press here."

Alarmed, Magnus called her. For our collective protection, he recorded the conversation.

"Some of the things I'm hearing about you wanting to do big stories about Doubledown and what a terrible group of people we are," Magnus began. "I just want to kind of keep it all in perspective."

"You know, it should've never gotten this bad, and you know I go, 'If you don't start communicating with me this is going to get ugly,'" Buhl eventually responded. "And they didn't communicate."

"Let's just try to figure this out, 'cause I think this is just going to a silly place that it doesn't need to go to," said Magnus. "I just don't like feeling that people are making threats against me or my company or my business partner for no reason. You have to admit, Teri, this is a little extreme. Come on."

Buhl's two-word response: "I know." Then she laughed.

"That might be your signature style," sighed Magnus, "but I don't think it's actually warranted."

Buhl laughed again: "It's been a great start for the last three days," referring to her currying favor at the *Post*, "thanks to Doubledown!"

And throughout the fall, Buhl, who added that she was "harboring a lot of anger because of the way things ended," kept at it: she began calling our vendors, saying she was a reporter for the *New York Post*, and suggesting that they sue us. She lied to our printer, pretending that she worked for our database provider, trying to get information. She began to e-mail, text, and Facebook message our employees, making absurd statements (we had influenced *The New York Times* for favorable coverage; we had stolen *Private Air* magazine; I had purchased secret shares of Doubledown stock), then asking for comment. It was siege by "journalism," wigging out the staff, who weren't privy to the whole backstory. Her final point to Magnus before hanging up lingered chillingly: "You guys created me."

And the freak show played on with another of our creations. More than a year after I had the temerity to disinvite Tim Sykes from the 30 Under 30 party as his fund imploded, he found two new focuses in life. First, freed from the promotional restrictions that come from managing Other People's Money, he hawked a how-to-trade DVD series and a stock-tip service to the unsuspecting general public, burnishing his credibility by invoking the British behemoth Barclays (rather than Iowa's small Barclay Group, which had actually measured his fund). This lie helped him generate more than $1 million a year, a testament to how fame and fibbing can trump failure. And second, he indulged in a bizarre fixation on me.

As best I can remember, my entire interaction with him of any kind comprised one five-minute conversation at a party, and one curt e-mail, which I sent privately to him, an attempt to sever his publicity-seeking self from our cornerstone franchise. To him, though, I was now important enough in his life that 10 percent of his biography on his Web site was devoted to *me*. Glomming on to me, apparently, provided him an identity.

"Hey, Randall Lane, you sick twisted son of a bitch, remember me?" was how he reintroduced himself in his Internet posts. He filed dozens of dispatches, on his Web site, across Twitter, and using comments on other Web sites, obsessively coming back to the subject of the party he was disinvited to.

He aped the paranoid language of conspiracy theorists: I was "powerful," I had "powerful friends," I made my "enemies look bad." When *Forbes* did a story quantitatively proving that most of Lenny Dykstra's newsletter picks were just repeats of what Richard Suttmeier picked in his newsletter, Sykes stood up for his fellow market savant and penny stock aficionado. "Forbes The Latest Victim In Randall Lane's Web Of Deceit," blared a headline on Sykes's Web site, using the crisp logic that *Forbes* wrote the article only because I asked my wife, who wrote for their archrival *Fortune*, to influence them. "Yes, Joshua Lipton of *Forbes* [the article's author], I'm talking to you, because you've allowed yourself to be influenced by scum."

He placed a picture of me on his site, and it was easy to imagine him staring intently at it, mumbling to himself in a room full of candles. His posts didn't bother me—his Web site received less traffic than cityofelmira.net. But they encapsulated the moment. "I learned long ago that there's no such thing as bad press," he wrote in his self-published autobiography. The right sentiment for a time when anger for the sake of being angry, sickness for the sake of being sick, turned nary a head.

$ $ $

Sleep again became a stranger. The year we were supposed to grow into profitability had turned into a four-season pressure cooker—internal soap opera in spring, financial tremors in summer, meltdown in autumn, frigid winter looming—and each night my subconscious took a predictable voyage. First, I thought about my kids, and the frightful risk—$283,000, plus $115,000 I owed my mom—that now undermined their future. Then I started thinking about *other people's* kids—Will Dawson and T. J. Wenger, the infant sons of two of Doubledown's original, most dedicated employees. Then came the fifty-plus employees, with rents, mortgages, or student loans. From there, I thought of my personal friends, who had dropped roughly $1 million into Doubledown, not to mention the $10 million from Magnus and Jim, all betting, in varying degrees, on me, and the belief that the wealth and power of our audiences could trump the rapidly evaporating prospects for print media. By that time, the sun would be rising, and I would grab a giant cup of coffee and trudge back into the office.

I generally didn't leave until midnight. I had given up my restaurant reviewing gig, and every other hobby. Marooned eighteen hours a day at the office, I bought a giant tub of peanut butter at Costco to eat at my desk, but never much had the stomach for it. From 200 pounds on my six-foot frame, I began melting, at first garnering compliments, then looks of concern as my weight plummeted into the mid-170s.

Exhausted and emaciated, I developed the personality to match. I would snap when I heard an answer I didn't like. I would cut people off mid-sentence. Rather than develop media products and conjure business strategies—my strengths—I now spent my entire day curtly managing the revenue mercenaries I had knowingly brought on.

Sig epitomized it. When he derisively called Doubledown's oldest female employee "mom" via e-mail, I responded in the bark that had become my correspondence style: "WTF?! . . . In my office in 15 minutes."

"From my point of view there is nothing to chat about," Sig responded, using the argument that he needed nothing from this woman and thus had no reason to talk it through. So I barked at him by e-mail again: "When will you be honoring us with your presence?"

But rather than show up, he sat at home and penned a breathless letter, which he sent within the hour to Jim, Magnus—and me. "Given these tumultuous times, decisive and strategic actions are required to not only survive, but thrive," he wrote. "Randall Lane is not a leader who can bring any of these qualities to the table. He is not one to guide us through treacherous waters." The core reason: *lack of empathy.*

Magnus and Jim laughed it off, but there was a delicious irony. I couldn't even express empathy—sticking up for an employee against a loutish barb at her age and gender—with empathy.

I had become a loud, unpleasant, cranky mess, not unlike the seven-figure Wall Street studs lining up for Dr. Doug's couch. Babson College once published a study showing that entrepreneurs cease to function well when their companies move above $10 million in sales—from there, the role shifts to managing managers. "If we have five hours to come up with fifty grand, there's no one in the world better than you," says Magnus, before his voice trails off. Left unsaid: how I had become a case study once Doubledown hit $10 million.

As this meltdown played out, I celebrated my forty-first birthday. Every year since Doubledown's founding, the staff had thrown me a surprise party. It was something I actively discouraged—I felt uncomfortable, as the boss, getting special treatment—but also counted it as a healthy benchmark that I was doing a decent job as a manager. For my thirty-eighth birthday, there was a bake-fest, and for my thirty-ninth, the team lovingly produced and framed a joke *Trader Monthly* cover with my head Photoshopped on top. ("10 Launches in Six Months? Piece of Cake, Baby!" the headline blared.) The bash for my fortieth featured Champagne toasts.

For my forty-first, my assistant and our can-do circulation director, Nora Pastenkos, bought a cupcake, a party of three among the seething dozens. No one else wanted to be with me. No offense taken: I didn't much want to be with me, either.

$ $ $

Cash at Doubledown no longer meant dollars and cents, profit or loss. Cash represented *time*.

Two venture capitalists promised big money if we could successfully test one of the social network channels. Other media companies approached us about selling. There was safety somewhere, whether VC cash or within a larger entity. Either would solve the increasingly untenable reality of an independent magazine company—we just needed to buy time to get there.

Unfortunately, the credit crunch that our magazines and Web sites, particularly *Dealmaker,* now slavishly chronicled, wasn't academic. Our advertisers owed us $2.4 million, but with bank lending frozen, every business in the world hoarded cash. Those who owed us went from paying in 60 to 90 days to between 120 and 150 days; we were now paying at the same glacial pace.

It would be left to Jim Dunning to buy us the time. Even the man who had publicly promised to fund us forever was, in this environment, a tough sell. He had seen his net worth cut in half, his private equity deals reeling, his Chinese SPAC deal undermined, his cash account frozen at Lehman Brothers. But he now had $7 million invested in Doubledown, which would evaporate without one more hit. Eventually, he came up with his number: $300,000—the last check ever, and it would have to last us until February.

Between September and November 2008, the U.S. economy shed more than one million jobs. We staved off such bloodbaths, but now saving the body meant losing a leg. Or both legs. From our staff of fifty, I laid off twenty. The survivors won ninety-day pay cuts. Everyone earning above $100,000 would have their salaries slashed in half, starting with me (from my salary now of $157,000, I went to $78,500). Everyone between $50,000 and $100,000 would get a 25 percent reduction. The difference would be made up in stock. Those who could least afford the haircut, making $50,000 or less, remained untouched. Our bloated payroll, $250,000 per every two weeks in the summer, was back down to $75,000.

Whether they were laid off or reduced, I tried to meet each employee personally; it seemed cowardly to do it any other way. But what had been intended as a short, painful morning played out slowly, as every person wanted—and deserved—to vent, discuss, plan, or question. For two full days, I was the grim reaper; I felt people cower when I approached.

Yet no one quit, even among those getting halved. The economy was in meltdown; there was simply no place to go.

Cash was now life. It was treated like a water bottle in the desert, used solely for essentials: payroll, expenses, or whittling down the oldest invoices. Magazines were mailed at the latest dates allowable under our circulation audit rules. Big debts were put on a payment schedule.

Then there was the rent. I had personally guaranteed the lease, but why pay $40,000 each month to a faceless, ball-busting landlord when it could be better spent on writers, Web developers, and sales commissions? What was another $40,000 in risk for me each month? Just like the Wall Street millionaires we covered, my relationship with money had now become hopelessly skewed. On a day-to-day level, I was strapped, eating my Costco peanut butter, driving across state lines to New Jersey to buy gas cheaper, trying to save $3 here and there. Those kinds of savings felt reflexive and tangible—a physical $10 bill still felt like ten real bucks. But when dealing with Doubledown, like throwing around casino chips instead of real cash, all those zeroes felt like funny money as the decade approached its close.

Many businesses resorted to a barter economy, and we now ran Doubledown with the economic sophistication of Paleolithic cavemen. We swapped the extra office space I had foolishly leased to software developers in exchange for coding necessary for our social network. We traded advertising to an air charter company for hours on their jets, which we then sold to Jim. The salon that had provided manicures at the infamous Wall Street Smoke paid for the sponsorship with free haircut memberships for staff and clients.

As we approached Thanksgiving, I began eyeing two giant boxes of watches sitting in our office closet as a heroin addict might eye a poppy plant. Even during the boom times, a Swiss watch company named Gevril advertised only if they could pay, at least in part, in timepieces. If I ever wanted to know which luxury magazines were hurting financially, I just paged through looking for the Gevril ads.

Curious about the cash value of $3,000 watches in an economic collapse, I dispatched my assistant, Tony, to Forty-seventh Street, New York's Diamond District, the block that gave us Extell's Gary Barnett and Raizy Haas, to see what we could get for the box. From store to store, most had no need for thirty to forty watches from a second-tier manufacturer. A few bottom-fishers dangled 5 cents on the dollar, or $5,000, for a crate that sold for $100,000 at retail.

One guy, let's call him Stu, offered Tony $10,000, a number I still found insulting. For weeks, those watches sat there. As those who owed us still failed to pay, and we still failed to pay those we owed, they beckoned. It had become that pathetic: Doubledown Media, a company with almost $15 million invested in it, which even in the slowdown would do $12 million in revenue for 2008, needed a $10,000 cash fix.

Tony checked back with Stu to make sure he still wanted them. And then he and I lugged the two enormous boxes—each watch came in a case the size of a small bread loaf—to the store. Well, technically, a *stall*, on the balcony of a garish bi-level bazaar that better resembled a flea market than a luxury retailer. As Tony and I unloaded the boxes, Stu removed each Gevril from its case with the suspicious manner of a drug dealer tasting the coke to make sure we didn't sell him a bunch of baking soda.

Satisfied that we hadn't snuck in some $20 Timexes, he left the stall to get the money, but returned instead with his boss, über-Stu, who took his turn poring skeptically over the Gevrils. And then he shook his head. "It would take me years to move all these watches."

"Why didn't you tell us that," I nearly exploded, "before we dragged these down here?"

But über-Stu merely shrugged, and regular Stu looked away embarrassed. Now Tony and I had to drag these huge watch boxes back to the office, at rush hour, when available cabs are nonexistent. And then, as if in a movie, the skies opened up with a cold, drenching, miserable rain. After getting waterlogged, we split up: I sought cover with the watches, while Tony scrambled, unencumbered, to find us a ride home.

It was so beautifully pathetic that I called Magnus. "Hey," I said to my partner in one of the Zeroes' great luxury media companies, "I'm standing here, soaked to the bone, trying and failing to sell barter watches at ten cents on the dollar." And then we laughed and laughed until we cried. Or perhaps cried until we laughed.

$ $ $

In a long-term sense, the market implosion doomed Doubledown Media. As we looked toward 2009, advertisers weren't merely holding back, but actively shunning us. "We know your ads work," our BMW contact told group publisher Wilkie Bushby. "We just don't even want to be *seen* marketing to these guys." Wall Streeters were the bad guys, and the luxury toys—particularly cigars and jets— were metaphors for the destructive depravity. To compound this, our primary media, print magazines, quickly went into a death spiral. Big companies began shuttering titles, and independents like us fared far worse. For all my manic scrambling looking for a cure— *social media! merger! electronic distribution!*—we had contracted a fatal form of corporate cancer.

It merely came down to cause of death. Just as AIDS patients often die of pneumonia, we technically fell to the financial toxin that the entire world had been swallowing—leverage—introduced by a somewhat innocuous letter in late November from our credit line, Keltic Financial, informing us that we were now in default.

Default is how lenders begin calling in their loans. At this given moment in history, that meant that half the world was seemingly in default. Keltic cited two primary reasons. First, the slow rate at which our advertisers were paying (fair). Second, we had borrowed money against "foreign" advertisers, like BMW and Mercedes (unfair—when Keltic wanted to loan us money, they happily over-looked that clause).

We had borrowed $1.2 million from Keltic, and advertisers owed us $2.4 million. In theory, there was plenty to go around. To us, the default seemed more like a way to pile on extra fees. By declaring default, they were able to jack up our interest rate another 3.5 per-cent, plus an extra $1,500 fee per month. So we scrambled to get out of default. "We have to give them a couple of things (more accurate reporting) but at the end of the day we should be fine," John Orr, the new financial chief, wrote me.

But Keltic's contract gave them sole discretion as to what con-stituted legitimate collateral. They said we remained in default. So we remained in default. In early December, they upped the ante, sending a letter to all our advertisers instructing them to pay Keltic directly, properly spooking them.

Then they asked Jim Dunning and me to head up to Tarrytown

to meet their president, Jack Reilly. Shuttered into a windowless room for what we had been told would be a friendly meet-and-greet, we were instead introduced to Reilly's tough-talking associate Tony Bucci, who had been hired as the Doubledown "workout guy." His job was to legally do what my old *Goodfellas* pal Henry Hill did furtively: make sure Keltic got paid back.

The more Tony got to know our company, the more he liked it. He scoured our books and deemed it an honest operation. But that didn't help matters much. All incoming payments now came to him. Any money going out required his blessing. It was a thousand times worse than asking Jim for money. Jim was a tough love dad, but still our dad. Tony was our lovable loan shark. He wished us well, but readily admitted that he would trade our survival for making Keltic whole.

Tony understood that we needed time. He and I just disagreed on what constituted necessary capital. For the next six weeks, Tony doled out the bare minimum to keep our company alive—payroll, mailing out issues, and keeping the phones on. Occasionally, if there was an emergency—say, cutting a $6,800 check to keep the Web sites up—he'd make a dispensation. When rent came due, he let me chose between it and payroll. I chose payroll, incurring yet more personal liability.

Meanwhile, we prepared for a fire sale. I gave up trying to save the investors money. Or my own money. The goal now was simply money to pay our creditors, and save everyone's jobs. The new price of Doubledown Media: the difference between what we owed and what was now owed to us, between $1 million and $2 million.

I told anyone on staff who asked that we would get something done. The game face was critical. The only sure way to kill Doubledown Media, at this point, was to start a panic; telling people their jobs were in jeopardy was a self-fulfilling prophecy. But I remained convinced that we would find a way. We had two of the world's best media investment bankers, Mark Edmiston and Jonathan Knee, helping, and a dozen companies kicking the tires. We had been in dire situations before, and always escaped, into a place better than where we started. If I worked hard enough, thought outside the box enough, and *willed* it enough, history had shown, it would happen.

But the waves I was accustomed to conquering were run-of-the-mill swells. This was a tidal wave, way out of paddling depth. Companies that would have snapped us up for $10 million even six months ago would not touch a Wall Street–based magazine company if we paid *them*. "You were in the exact wrong categories," remembers our banker, Polly Perkins Johnson. "Life changed in the blink of an eye."

The last stand came at the end of January. I begged Keltic for $100,000; they stuck firmly at $75,000. Enough for payroll. Or a final mailing of *Trader Monthly* issues, which was mandatory to bill advertisers in accordance with our audit rules. But not both. So the fate that had caused me endless stress in 2005 and 2006 finally came to fruition: we missed payroll.

Actually, we missed only half of payroll. All the lower-salaried workers were paid. One by one, I asked the higher-earning salaries to take one for the team. If they did, it would buy us another two weeks to find a solution.

But over the weekend, the panic that I'd feared set in. As with Bear Stearns and Lehman Brothers, both of which seemingly collapsed overnight, once confidence goes, you can't function. Keltic took note; we'd seen our last cash infusion. Keeping the company open just meant having people work another pay cycle for free. We were done.

So Monday night, Groundhog Day, 2009, at 10:35 p.m., I sent out an e-mail to our now thirty employees. Hitting the Send button felt like hara-kiri, a forlorn move that you regret the second you follow through. It read in part:

```
Regretfully, we have some very bad news
to share. The bank that's been supplying our
credit line for the past year, an affiliate
of HSBC, has ceased to provide working capital
for Doubledown Media. Thus, this forces us to
suspend operations effective immediately.
    I cannot begin to convey how heartbroken
we are. These are unprecedented times: the
```

> combination of the media depression, the Wall
> Street implosion and the credit slowdown were
> collectively too much for our company—probably
> any company in our shoes—to overcome.
>
> We have approximately a dozen organizations
> who have actively expressed interest in some
> or all of Doubledown's assets—we hope to both
> generate money for those who are owed, and
> also help us save as many jobs as we can.

The first condolence note came at 10:58 p.m. It was from Sig: "I'm sorry man, I really, really am."

The team-oriented reflex pleasantly surprised me, until I was later forwarded another e-mail he had sent. Five minutes *before* he sent his sorry note to me, he forwarded the announcement to our embittered ex–PR chief, Rachel Pine. *That* had been Sig's first reaction. And before I had even arrived at the office the next morning, my memo, leaked to the Web site for *Folio*, on whose magazine cover I had triumphantly appeared two years earlier, was streaking around the planet.

What I had hoped would be a quiet, dignified public funeral became an instant circus. Reuters was calling—please talk to us for five minutes. The *New York Post. Mediaweek. Advertising Age. Bloomberg. The New York Times* was so eager to get into the fray that they rushed out a story on their DealBook blog, ahead of their story in the physical newspaper the next day, which itself dwarfed an adjacent article about the removal of the head of CNBC, the same guy I had met with to brainstorm *Fast Money* during happier days. It included my headshot, an outtake that made me look like a deer in the headlights, staring out into the schadenfreude.

No less than the definitive arbiter of capitalism, *The Wall Street Journal*, termed our demise "one of those moments when a chance arrow of history scores a perfect bull's-eye on a deserving target." But the overall tone of the press frenzy was best summed up by the New York gossip Web site Gawker, which went out with the headline "Magazine Company for Wall Street Pricks Is Dead," and eulogized us thus: "no other media company embodies the boom and bust quite so well." I couldn't disagree.

$ $ $

The legacy of my own personal real estate mania, Doubledown Media's twenty thousand square feet of tattered office space, stood eerily intact—idling computers and goodie bag vodka mini-bottles and bartered *Private Air* neckties, all frozen in time, as if a neutron bomb had efficiently removed the humanity, but left all the stuff. On the afternoon of February 26, 2009, while the Dow closed under 7,300 for the first time in more than a decade, a routine 80-point loss on the heels of the worst January in market history, I sat alone on the seventh floor, like the sole survivor in a science fiction movie, kept company only by the grinding hum of the electric lights, which I feared might be shut off at any moment. Only the ring of my cell phone, courtesy of our attorney, mercifully offered another human voice.

"The trustee is coming over in two hours," he said with an unexpected urgency, referring to the court-appointed officer newly charged with disposing of our corporate remains. "And he's bringing the locksmith."

I had filed the paperwork putting Doubledown Media into bankruptcy a few hours before. Not the friendly, Chapter 11 kind that involves maintaining control, beating up your creditors, and reorganizing to fight another day. This was the strong stuff: Chapter 7, liquidation. Everything would be sold off, like a corporate garage sale, the proceeds going to everyone to whom we owed money.

For the previous three weeks, we had been a zombie company, neither dead nor alive. Media brands are like milk: the longer they're out, the more they spoil, at least in the eyes of advertisers. So I had scrambled, an unpaid dealmaker trying to hock the assets before the expiration date, hoping to save jobs and pay off those we owed. Two dozen bottom-fishers stepped forward. Some dangled a few hundred thousand for what had been worth, on paper, $17 million six months earlier. Others offered a hundred grand for one brand or another.

Others wanted to pay nothing up front, with millions down the road if the brands turned around. But no one seemed in a hurry to write a check: throughout February, the news kept getting worse and worse—more bailouts, more layoffs—with our audiences smack in the middle. Only the headaches came quickly. The phones were shut off. The landlord sued me for the back rent, plus all the rent due until the end of the lease the next August. *Private Air*'s Deedee Morrison filed yet another claim, arguing that she was somehow owed $1.25 million, despite the arbitrator's ruling, and further claiming that ceasing operations was part of our master plan to deprive her of it. In all, the zombie process had all the horrible effects of death and none of the closure.

Bankruptcy, at least, was clean: we could let the court set a deadline with teeth, and parcel out the proceeds. Jim and Magnus concurred. The only party that didn't: Keltic, which favored the status quo, collecting the money owed without interference. They urged me to hand them control of the company—a legal concept known as "peaceful possession"—and as incentive, offered me a consulting contract for $60,000, payable as soon as the incoming money wiped their slate clean.

With one signature, it would be the easiest money I'd ever made. And the most necessary, partially offsetting the gigantic real estate liability—up to $450,000—that I had incurred by choosing payrolls over rent. But it would also have been the most unfair. How could I take out sixty grand when so many people were owed money? Bankruptcy also protected our employees' previous health insurance claims; the zombie status left everyone vulnerable. It wasn't a choice. We filed Chapter 7.

Which brings us back to the empty office and my urgently ringing cell phone. As our new bankruptcy lawyer explained it to me, the randomly assigned bankruptcy trustee, Robert Geltzer, was an infamous ball-buster. Dressed in a sharp gray suit and walking with the puffed gait I imagined MacArthur had when he returned to Manila, Getzler arrived ten minutes early, an accountant, a liquidator, and the locksmith in tow.

I moped out to meet him. "Please have a seat," I said, pointing to our conference room. "We'll tell you anything you want to know about our company." Geltzer waved his hand. "I want to walk around." The trustee, it was made clear, was to speak, not be spoken to. *What's in that box? Open it! Is there a computer missing here? Is the copy machine owned or leased?* To Getzler, it appeared, Doubledown was worth no more than the sum of its physical parts. His squad was concurrently dealing with a restaurant in New Rochelle, which now made the agenda grills, pans, ovens—and the most finely tuned media machine for rich people ever created.

When our IT team stumbled onto our little entourage, and asked Geltzer who he was, his answer was succinct.

"I own this place."

A small part of me felt relief. For the past eight or so months, owning this place was a daily, perpetual burden, which those four words plainly removed. Mostly, though, I felt loss, and failure. I had let down most of the people I knew, and myself.

The locksmiths finished their work. Satisfied that he had a fix on his new assets, Geltzer then respectfully escorted me out of the company I had built, and the office space I had personally guaranteed with my own money.

13

See It, Spend It, End It

(2009)

The very first mock cover of *Trader Monthly*, worked up in 2003 and good enough to bluff Refco into a $360,000 advertising contract, had declared: "Blood on the Streets!" Ejected from my warped bubble, I now saw what that actually looked like. The entire world was melting down, simultaneously, and average folks were getting crushed. In the week before we filed bankruptcy, a record 667,000 people, including myself, petitioned for unemployment. (A bureaucrat held up my claim because I was still "working" on selling the assets, even though I wasn't getting paid.) The fancy types we had chronicled and catered to across the Zeroes were simultaneously getting their comeuppance.

The hedge fund industry spent February tallying its 2008 losses. The typical fund was down 20 percent, trading through a market that humbled even the immortals. Ken Griffin, the crown prince of the quants, found himself with a lot of subprime mortgage exposure, and his funds plummeted 55 percent the past year. While his Peter Max paintings idled in the warehouse, Phil Falcone's fund dropped 28 percent. Befitting his reputation as the world's greatest trader, Stevie Cohen beat the average: his fund dropped a mere 19 percent. (The Greenwich real estate market dropped in lockstep.) Only John Paulson seemed to defy the odds, yet again. Still bearish on junky mortgages, he threw another $2 billion profit onto his personal pile.

The flashiest of the big hedge fund managers, our former cover boy John Devaney, took one of the biggest public spankings. His funds, specializing in subprime and other junk that he had helped create, encompassing over a half-billion dollars, were completely wiped out. Devaney, who estimated his personal hit at $100 million, sold his 142-foot yacht, *Positive Carry*, the Gulfstream he insisted on posing in front of for our cover, and many of his houses on Key Biscayne. "We put a lot of properties on the market—my father-in-law's, my mother-in-law's, my sister-in-law's, my mother's," Devaney told *The Miami Herald*. The Scarface mansion, however, remained his. Pain in the hedge fund world has its limits.

In all, 1,471 hedge funds closed their doors in 2008, with dozens more failing each week in 2009. As with Doubledown, many lost access to their credit sources, with death following quickly. Still more had a redemption crisis: investors withdrew their money, leaving many without enough funding to continue. Those who wanted to keep playing with Other People's Money had to come down in price. The 2-and-20 pay standard, as sacrosanct as the 15 percent restaurant tip minimum, was now up for negotiation.

Private equity fared better: while suffering from the same problems, most of those funds had long-term commitments from investors. Still, belts tightened. Steve Schwarzman, who set the tone for the industry at Blackstone, took a $350,000 salary—and no bonus. And celebrated his birthday privately, a new personal preference. "Obviously, I wouldn't have wanted to do that and become, you know, some kind of symbol of sorts of that period of time," he told a conference in New York, referring to his now infamous 2007 bash. "Who would ever wish that on themselves? No one."

In a matter of months, private jets had gone from symbols of cool to the embodiment of Zeroes evil. When the CEOs of the Big Three Detroit automakers had the gall to fly privately to ask Congress for a government bailout, they were nearly decapitated by the rightly furious lawmakers. They all returned commercial.

Governments buckled globally. On the same day that I had told the staff about Doubledown's suspension of operations, Avi Bhojani, the well-connected owner of our Dubai offshoot, coincidentally wrote a note informing us that he was suspending operations in the Middle East. "Our advertising sales have dried up almost entirely . . . all rather unfortunate." It was like those stories you read about twins separated at birth dying on the same day. Within months, this barren speck of a city-state, built into a glittering Oz on the foundation of free trade, needed to be rescued by its neighbor, Abu Dhabi, which sat on all the oil.

Dubai fared well compared with the Turks and Caicos. During our last communication shortly before we folded shop, the Misick regime asked us for a plan to repeat the Wall Street boxing event in 2009, with a twist: we would physically host the event down there, a U.S. versus UK financial brawl held at an outdoor ring erected above the beach. A month later, the British governor, Richard Tauwhare, suspended self-government on the islands. A week after that, Misick resigned. "This is tantamount to being re-colonized," he grumbled. By August, the entire government had been stripped of its power and the legislature was suspended for two years. Misick fled to the Dominican Republic, where as of this book's printing he remains in exile.

Our previous boxing title sponsor, Extell, fared better. While most New York real estate companies suffered, Gary Barnett and Raizy Haas expanded (although they canceled their rival Wall Street Rumble). They finished all the buildings we had helped them promote and broke ground on several more. They never made their charitable donations, which remains a tragedy. Tuesday's Children, the boxing event's lead beneficiary and a chief supporter of 9/11 orphans, ran into trouble, as charitable giving sank with the respective fortunes of their regular donors. Carmine Calzonetti, who left Wall Street to become the charity's president, had to lay off eight employees and then vacate his own post. "It affected us," he now says. "We counted that money in our budget." Calzonetti's salary would have been largely offset if Extell had donated what it committed.

As for Doubledown, we contributed five of the more than four hundred American magazines that would fold in 2009, including stalwarts like *Gourmet* and cultural icons like *Vibe* and fellow up-starts like *Condé Nast Portfolio*, another glitzy new business title that had gone through more than $100 million, or seven times what we had spent, producing a single magazine and Web site. The luxury magazine company juggernauts we had emulated in our Get Big Fast mode, Modern Luxury and Niche Media, staggered under their new ownerships. And the granddaddy of luxury media, the *Robb Report*, saw its pages plummet across 2008, and then drop another 24 percent in 2009. If Bill Curtis had taken either of our $200-million-plus offers, whether via private equity or the SPAC, he would have been rightly hailed as the greatest media dealmaker since Jim Dunning. "He'd be lucky to get a quarter of that today," says someone familiar with the company and the market.

Regarding the SPACs themselves, Jim Dunning's China gambit proved successful, acquiring a ceramics company. (Ironically, Jim also became chairman of Freedom Communications, which funded my last company and now found itself in bankruptcy.) Meanwhile, right before Doubledown filed for Chapter 7, I received a call from a deal broker who thought he had the answer for our problems.

"Are you familiar with SPACs?" he asked.

"Sure," I replied, guffawing.

"Have one that's perfect. They have a hundred million dollars to put into a media company, and they're basically out of time. If they don't get something done immediately, they're going to have to give the money back to their investors."

"Is the company called Santa Monica Media?" I responded, refer-ring to our partners in the *Robb Report* bid.

"Yes," he answered, startled. "How did you know?"

$ $ $

I began accompanying my eldest daughter, Sabrina, to preschool, the kind of thing I hadn't been able to enjoy enough over the past few years. Every class at the school was named for a bird; her group, the Blue Jays, was having a special event that they had prepared for weeks. The classroom had been transformed into a "town" for the day. There was a restaurant, and a doctor's office and a beauty salon.

Sabrina, now almost five, was the Blue Jays' postmaster, running a post office comprising a little table, a giant box of envelopes, and ink-pad stamps. As I sat next to her, she wrote a letter to me. Grabbing an envelope, she scrawled "D-A-D-D-Y," in the uneven, all-capital manner common to all preschoolers and Charles Manson, before stamping it and "delivering" it to me. As I gazed at it proudly, I noticed the return address: Refco. Some other parent who had presumably lost a job in the Zeroes had salvaged a big box of envelopes, putting the fruits of Phil Bennett's firm, perhaps for the first time ever, to good use.

Random things like that happened on a daily basis, as much as I tried to run out the decade with the mortals whose lives didn't revolve around their bonuses and expensive toys.

Partly, I could now clearly see the influences of Wall Street and luxury, previously invisible before Doubledown instructed me in the various codes and brands. Partly, these things were now a greater part of our culture. Partly, it was unavoidable. Although I was technically unemployed, I had to deal with the landlord lawsuit and answer questions from the bankruptcy trustee's team as they tried to sell the assets.

I picked up some of the things I liked to do before I had become warped, a spring thaw for a winter that had lasted since 9/11. While I had met incredible people and done incredible things across the decade, it had come at a huge price: myself. For my high school yearbook, every senior provided a quote next to his picture. I chose something from William Penn: "I expect to pass through life but once. If therefore, there be any kindness I can show, or any good thing I can do to any fellow being, let me do it now, and not defer or neglect it, as I shall not pass this way again." Other than still expecting to pass through life but once, there wasn't a single clause in that text that I adhered to in the Zeroes. Sometimes it takes a cataclysmic event to reinforce what's important in life. And it takes a lack of money to appreciate its irrelevance.

Besides spending time with my kids, I began writing about food again. My wife and I went to movies. And I went to Opening Day at the new Yankee Stadium. The old ballpark had been one of my favorite places in the world—an original stadium blueprint from 1922 remains perhaps my most prized possession—full of grace and elegance and ghosts. The new stadium was a monstrosity, a $1 billion shopping mall with baseball, and as I took in the Hard Rock Cafe and little Yankees department store, I stopped in my tracks. Snug on the ground floor between first base and the right-field foul pole: a Peter Max outlet. A big crowd clustered around Peter himself, who was gabbing and shaking hands and no doubt looking for new marks. I thought for a moment about going in, but I didn't know what to say. I just kept walking.

But Peter would not leave me alone. In August, Jennifer and I took the kids on the first vacation in years where my phone wasn't ringing. It was a weeklong cruise to Alaska, courtesy of my runner-up finish in the hedge fund charity poker tournament two years prior—one of the few tangible things that remained from five years in the business. One night, we returned to the cabin after another large meal; along with the ship's schedule for the next day, something else awaited us on our pillow: a $1,000 coupon for a Peter Max painting.

Cruise ships and painters alike generate a huge revenue stream from art sales, and the *Serenade of the Seas* was crammed with lithographs from the famous (Dalí) and original works from the cheesy (Thomas Kinkade), as well as a dozen-plus Peter Maxes, from flowers to Statues of Liberty, chunked out from the Oompa-Loompa factory. "Welcome to the world of Peter Max," declared the auctioneer, a smooth talker with a shaved head in a beige three-piece suit, "in my opinion, one of the most important artists alive today." Out came one of the hearts Peter loved to paint. Its value, the auctioneer declared, was $12,300, but—just for us—he would start the bidding at $9,000.

The results followed the arc of the Napa event. There were no bidders. "A thunderous applause for Peter Max," the auctioneer shouted in face-saving mode, as staffers wheeled it back to the shitpile.

The following month, a number showed up on my phone that I hadn't seen in a year, but whose name remained programmed into my cell: Peter Max, whose distinct digits ended in double-zero. I had the same reaction as I did at Yankee Stadium, and let it go to voicemail.

"Hey, Randall, it's your buddy Peter Max. I'm calling to say hello. I know you're not doing the company anymore, blah, blah, blah. Call me back. I have a lot of nice ideas. Maybe we'll make some money. Nothing you've got to put up, it's all going to come from me. I just want to make sure that you're doing well. Don't be shy. Call me. Really, I really mean it. Don't be shy. It could only turn to good. Or else it's just a phone call, but I have some nice ideas, where we can make some money together. Stuff I'm doing right now. You're gonna love it. Give me a call, okay? Please."

Preferring my current blah, blah, blah state, I never called him back. And I didn't think about him again until October, when I returned to Yankee Stadium for game two of the World Series. As I cruised the lower concourse, trying to find a better perch than my nosebleed seats, I noticed, between first base and right field, that the Peter Max store was gone.

Over the summer, he'd been evicted. The reason, I was later told: he had refused to sign a written contract.

$ $ $

"Hey Randall, it's Lenny," said the familiar slurring voice that popped into my voicemail on a mid-April night, pausing pensively before adding "Dykstra," in the impossible case that I'd forgotten him. "It's, I don't know, about eleven. I want to talk about a couple things that might be interesting to you. So give me a buzz." He left two numbers, his longtime cell and the latest of his "bat phone" rotating numbers. "Call me anytime."

That was April, and I didn't call back. I needed to cleanse, and move forward. A few weeks later, he left another message: *I have an idea for a way to work together,* he teased, in a Peter Max kind of way.

Lenny had just skipped his court-ordered $200,000 payment to

Doubledown, which could have paid off a lot of people owed money. Before that, he had illogically sued us, compulsively lied about us, and menacingly threatened us—and now he was chummily calling to work together again. Screwing people as a way of life, it seems, means assuming that people willingly accept you for that. At least if you're somewhat famous.

Lenny remained top of mind throughout the spring as another professional screwer dominated the headlines. Every year as we put together the *Trader Monthly* 100, the name Bernie Madoff popped up. To our trading editor Rich Blake's credit, he always nixed him. Famous for generating between 10 and 12 percent annual returns— never more, never less, no matter the market conditions—Madoff didn't smell right. The decade of ever-larger financial scoundrels ended with a new king—Madoff copped to stealing $18 billion— and while the other crooks used electronic trading to hide their mischief, Madoff never even bothered to make trades, instead leveraging his fictional track record to collect ever more money, which he'd spend or pay earlier investors who asked for their money back. The classic Ponzi scheme.

Like Madoff, when it came to trading, Lenny never lost, selling newsletters on the premise that his recommendations made money no matter the market. In April, a full year after our lawsuit raised questions about his stock-picking prowess, ten months after he was apparently paid to tout a stock, and six months after *Forbes* methodically chronicled how most of his recommendations came from someone else, TheStreet.com finally stopped running Lenny's column or selling his newsletter, *Nails on the Numbers*. Undaunted, Lenny quickly set up "Nails Investments" to market the newsletter to me and anyone else on his e-mail list. "My record is now 106 (wins) and 0 (losses)," he declared.

Like Madoff, Lenny always found a new sucker to give him money, in ever smaller amounts. He managed to sell his car wash note for about $13 million, which immediately disappeared to pay off the second mortgage on the Gretzky house and other debts. Then he got an $850,000 loan from a private equity fund, using the house, which still had a crippling $12 million first mortgage on it, as collateral.

His book agent loaned him $250,000 on the promise that he'd get $300,000 back in six months.

Then came loans to feed his jet habit. One of his pilots put $7,000 on his credit card for fuel, under, he claimed, the threat of termination. His flight attendant fronted $10,600, and said she was fired when she wouldn't lend him another $30,000. The photo editor for *Players Club*, which Lenny was now publishing independently and intermittently, similarly put $18,000 on his credit card for fuel, on the failed promise that Lenny would reimburse him an extra five grand. Nails even called his estranged mother, waking her up at six in the morning. "He is on the phone, crying to my mom, saying he has got to get home and he is in Cleveland, Ohio," his brother Kevin recalled to ESPN's Mike Fish. "He asked my mom to put up her credit card for twenty-three grand. That is just sick, dude." And she complied. Lenny flew back private, as he was now accustomed.

Finally, like Madoff, the money ran out. A Ponzi scheme is the most suicidal of frauds. Nick Leeson and Jérôme Kerviel and the rest of the rogue traders at least maintained the *hope* of trading themselves out of the hole, but a Ponzi scheme always gets exposed when the finite supply of the rich and gullible runs out. Lenny's checks began bouncing. Between November 2008 and April 2009, eighteen people sued him, claiming he owed them money. In February, his Gulfsteam was impounded. The Maybach and a Rolls-Royce Phantom were repossessed. In April, concurrent with his calls to me, his wife, Terri, filed for divorce after twenty-three years of marriage. Lenny's litigation attitude, in regard to her, seemed remarkably similar to his attitude when he sued me. "From now on everything is going to be bad," he allegedly told her via voicemail message, "the war is ready to begin and I play . . . dirty!" A court then awarded Terri the rights to Lenny's baseball pension, the last-resort paycheck The Players Club's financial plan was supposed to shield.

Meanwhile, Nails's final assets, his two houses, were thrown into foreclosure. In July, the day before the Gretzky estate was set to be auctioned on the steps of the Ventura County Courthouse, Dykstra filed for bankruptcy, listing $31 million in liabilities, and $50,000 in assets.

Lenny had filed for the "good" kind of bankruptcy, Chapter 11, but the court quickly forced him into Doubledown's kind, Chapter 7 liquidation, and Nails spun into a new level of dysfunction. He claimed he had been the victim of "bank fraud," forced to take loans he didn't want, and ripped flooring and fixtures from the Gretzky house in an attempt to prove it had water damage. When the company appointed by the court to manage the estate entered, they found it "littered throughout with empty beer bottles, trash, dog feces and urine and other unmentionables." Raw sewage filled the backyard.

Dykstra was banned from both homes. An insurance policy provided a temporary rental home—which was claimed by Terri and their thirteen-year-old son. Nails was broke—and homeless. A boutique hotel booted him after he ran up a $2,500 tab he couldn't pay. He slept in an office in the hangar he had rented for his impounded Gulfstream, until he was evicted for nonpayment of rent. That left him with one final housing option—his car, an existence he would, out of necessity, supplement with hotel lobbies. "I don't mean to be crude," he explained to CNBC. "But where do they expect me to shit?"

"So here's reality," Lenny had presciently written a year earlier in his four-page mission statement, highlighting our glamorous launch issue of *Players Club*. "Players who've won championship rings have ended up living under bridges." Nails, whose ring commemorated the 1986 New York Mets' win over the Boston Red Sox, a legendary World Series known for the ball that dribbled through Bill Buckner's legs, now lived under bridges, depending on where his car was parked.

Nails used to wax on endlessly about that ring, the thrill of sliding it onto the fingers of his children. He kept it tucked away in a safe, retrieving it on days when he felt bad, like a toddler's fuzzy security blanket. On one of his trips to New York, he toted it along to show me. It looked like a single brass knuckle, with WORLD SERIES CHAMPIONS in gold capital letters encircling the perimeter and a round diamond, placed on a gold setting shaped like a baseball diamond, set on a field of blue. On the side was his name: DYKSTRA, above the Mets logo.

Because the ring, in Lenny's mind, represented success and security, he had us photograph it to illustrate his essay, a paean to AIG's complicated retirement products. We ran a full-page picture of it in its mahogany case next to the opening page, and then the empty case and the ring on his finger, respectively, to represent the two financial doors a player could choose to walk through. Under the empty case, Lenny declared, in thick, bold letters: "You can see why I get sad when I hear about athletes—champions!—who're forced to pawn their rings or put them up for auction because they weren't financially prepared for life after they retired."

Late in the year, I stumbled across an odd video parked on the nether reaches of the Internet, a segment from a Toyko news program about America's "once-in-a-century recession." The correspondent, a Japanese man of about forty in blue jeans and a white shirt, walks up and down Rodeo Drive in Beverly Hills, pointing out all the "FOR LEASE" signs, before entering a pawnshop with a neon "WE BUY AND LOAN" sign in the window.

"I deal with a lot of people who'd surprise you—a lot of actors and stars," Yossi Dina, an Israeli commando turned "pawnbroker to the rich and famous," tells the reporter. He takes the camera crew into his vault, where he brings out a garish timepiece from Jacob and Co., our former boxing sponsor whose owner now sat in a federal prison. "Look at this watch," he says. "It's worth $225,000, I gave a loan of $25,000."

Back at the front counter, as the Japanese camera crew keeps filming, a lumpy man in an off-white golf shirt walks into the store.

It's Nails.

"There's only one of these in the world," says Lenny, handing Dina the mahogany ring case we shot for *Players Club*, before turning, a bit confused, to the reporter and shaking his hand. "I'm Lenny Dykstra. I played baseball."

Dina, who sports a muscular, shaved head like Mr. Clean, removes the box's contents. The gold lettering, the blue backdrop, the diamond within the diamond: it's Lenny's prized World Series ring.

"When is this from?" asks Dina, barely audible over the Japanese dubbing.

"1986 World Series."

"Was that Boston?"

"That's right," says Lenny, before nervously addressing the camera. "I only come here because these are my life's treasures. I come here because I trust him."

"Banks don't lend to these people anymore," says Dina, shrugging, as he glances down at Lenny's ring. "They know that."

After the pawnbroker entombs Lenny's ring in his vault, the female anchor in Tokyo ends the segment with a quote from Dina about his confidence that the owners "will come back and buy back their possessions once the economy improves."

But the economy did not improve by the end of the Zeroes. And Lenny never came back. So Dina consigned the ring to a liquidation company in Dallas. In October, it was auctioned off for $56,752.

$ $ $

Lenny's ring could have fared worse: the market for baseball memorabilia, a proxy for American nostalgia, transcends fad or era. The media assets most associated with Wall Street's "see it, make it, spend it" decade? Suddenly and painfully worthless. Our company's print magazine genesis didn't help: even juggernauts like *Reader's Digest* (filed for bankruptcy) and *BusinessWeek* (essentially given away) no longer had value. As the months dragged on and the media economy worsened, Doubledown's bankruptcy trustee, seeking to force the issue, held an auction in August, setting six-figure minimums for each of the core properties. No one showed up. Eventually, a small newsletter company gobbled up the brands and the lists and the content and everything else we built over five long years. Price: $55,000. By the end of the Zeroes, Doubledown Media, which churned out $12 million in revenues in 2008, was worth a grand or two less than Lenny's World Series ring.

Studying the list of people we owed money to in the end—the people due to be paid back in the event of a successful asset sale—was a wrenching experience. I reached out to a lot of them, to listen, or explain, or apologize. Many were comforting and gracious when they didn't have to be. ("We definitely appreciate you [apologizing] even though you don't have to," wrote Bart Codd, who comanages a talent agency, The Hired Guns, that was owed more than $20,000. "At the end of the day friendship and trust are what matters.") The investors almost uniformly responded with compassion rather than blame. ("Sorry it turned out this way," wrote Chip Block, who had celebrated our partnership with Martha Stewart. "The perfect storm.") A dozen ex-employees, mostly from before our late-2008 train wreck, called to console me, or thank me for the opportunity I had given them.

But many others were angry, especially the dozen-plus employees who had been left short on that last paycheck and summarily sent into a bleak job market. "Everyone felt abandoned. It was emotion driven, fright driven," remembers Brian Dawson, our group managing editor. "Everyone wanted to blame someone and you were closest at hand." For weeks, rumors proliferated. "You were the guy in the corner office," says Ty Wenger, another of the founding editors, "so people were like, 'You don't think Randall was taking money out on the side?'"

Alas, that's one Wall Street lesson I didn't take to heart. My final tally, financially: the $233,000 that had gone for four early payrolls, the $50,000 I had loaned during the summer of 2008, the $115,000 I'd borrowed from my mom, and then, like a nightmare that won't let you wake up, the rent money that I had instead directed to payroll. I eventually paid $110,000 to settle the lawsuit with the landlord, after burning through $20,000 in legal fees. All told, the personal hit came to almost $530,000. A sickening amount of zeroes. Only Magnus and Jim lost more in absolute numbers, and in terms of loss relative to wealth, no one did.

And that's the way things *should* work. Back in the financial industry's functional days—when it was a well-paying career providing the lifeblood of capitalism, rather than an absurd casino promoting perilous, systemic risk—partnerships ruled Wall Street. The principals risked their own capital—even those managing Other People's Money coinvested—and made risk-rewards decisions based on the firm's common good. Yes, I lost more than a half-million dollars, but by sticking my neck out as far as it could stretch, I purchased frightfully expensive peace of mind. Maybe, in that example, there was a lesson for Wall Street.

But then came something unexpected, at least to me. After trillions of dollars of government bailouts and guarantees for Wall Street amid a continuing recession worldwide, I glanced at the bonus forecasts for the end of 2009. Better than 2008, admittedly a horrible year. But also better than 2007. Better, in fact, than any year ever—a new record. Again playing with Other People's Money—this time, the taxpayers'—Wall Street reflexively returned to its new normal.

Except in one aspect. In August, as Goldman Sachs came off its most profitable second quarter ever—$2.3 billion—firm CEO Lloyd Blankfein sent a message across the company: *no conspicuous spending*. No jet cards or Maybachs or Johnnie Walker Blue or Panerai watches. The looting would continue, but this time with the hope, reflective of a world without *Trader Monthly* and *Dealmaker,* that no one would notice.

I couldn't help but think of Nick Carraway, the everyman narrator of the last Gilded Age's definitive work, *The Great Gatsby*. Nick had come to New York to work in the bond market, and the novel ends with him fleeing town, after the wanton destruction that he witnessed had changed precisely nothing, reflecting on the species who "smashed up things and creatures and then retreated back into their money or their vast carelessness, or whatever it was that kept them together, and let other people clean up the mess they had made."

Nick to his credit, walked away. I had been ejected. Either way, while others dealt with the epic mess, the game played on, timeless and unabated.

ACKNOWLEDGMENTS

This book could not have been written, at least not with this level of detail, before the Zeroes. For all the decade's unseemly legacies, historians may yet view them as blips compared with the wonders spawned by the ones and zeroes of the digital revolution. Thanks to Google, I flexibly searched the bodies of 43,528 e-mails that I received between 2004 and 2009, as well as the 19,296 that I sent, allowing me to reconstruct every day with a dizzying degree of minute-to-minute precision. The 1,000-plus related contracts, memos, presentations, and other documents that would have filled enough filing cabinets to create a government agency instead rest comfortably on my four-year-old MacBook. Events otherwise left to reside only in memory were relived via YouTube.

This digital trail was buttressed by interviews with more than fifty people who were there with me, imbuing the book with still more solid details and perspective. A solid half of them are credited in the book—and I offer my sincere thanks to you all, particularly Magnus Greaves and Jim Dunning, with whom I forged a true partnership that I will never forget. Also, a warm thank-you to the two dozen or so who talked with me on the condition of anonymity—mostly Wall Street heavies interested in both sharing the truth and continuing to earn oversized paychecks in the financial industry. You know who you are.

I want to tip my cap to three classics: Fred Schwed's *Where Are the Customers' Yachts?*, George "Adam Smith" Goodman's *The Money Game,* and Michael Lewis's *Liar's Poker,* each of which provided inspiration. They reinforced three facts: that a book like this is needed for the record, that money can be funny, and that absurd periods in our history come and go like the tides.

As every work of nonfiction is colored by the person telling the story—this one especially so, given that it's based on my own experiences—I tried to offset that by hiring Avi Zenilman, who put his *New Yorker* experience to great use, independently and skillfully fact-checking the book line by line. In contract with my first job as a *Forbes* fact-checker nearly twenty years ago, here any errors remain solely my responsibility. Clark Merrefield did a fine job of providing research. (The book's endnotes can be found at www.RandallLane.com.)

Since the daily experiences I had at Doubledown Media, whether events attended or thousands of stories edited, are the heart of this book, so too are the one hundred–plus people who worked at Doubledown. *The Zeroes* stands on your talented, dedicated shoulders. I know how hard you worked, and I am so sorry for the tumultuous ending.

This book took full shape in Sag Harbor, New York. Katharine and Bret Parker graciously let their house there become mine for weekends, even weeks at a time. I will always appreciate that. The words also flowed with hosting assists from Laura Gellert and Pranav Ghai, Barry Diller and his beautiful IAC building, the Jefferson Market branch of the New York Public Library, a half-dozen Starbucks, and a few other special nooks.

Huge kudos to the team at Portfolio: Adrian Zackheim, who saw the need for a book like this in a sea of seemingly similar tales; Courtney Young, who championed the cause; Eric Rayman; Will Weisser; Maureen Cole; Bruce Giffords; Michael Burke; Emily Angell; and Jeffrey Krames, among many others.

My deepest appreciation to Tina Brown and Edward Felsenthal at *The Daily Beast* for their support and flexibility. Michael Finkel was my main outside reader; he made *The Zeroes* better. Various others watched my back, from helpful introductions to key bits of knowledge to timely words of encouragement: Rafe Sagalyn, Charles Fishman, Ned Rust, Bill Rowan, Jon Wilner, Nora Magid, Nina Munk, Bob Frost, Richard Creighton, Neil Weinberg, Sonoko Setaishi Weinberg, Bob Appleton, Fred Lane, Madeleine Adler, Cary Lane, Bill Lewis, Tanya Rodriguez, Joshua Lane, Stuart Bussey, Carol Levy, Mark and Susan Reingold, and Jackie and Rodney Schapiro.

As I sat around, shell-shocked, in early 2009, my mom, Lea Lane, was the first to suggest that there was a book in all of the disparate and bizarre experiences I'd had. A formidable wordsmith herself, she then read the whole thing in serial form and encouraged me the whole way, in the unique manner that mothers do. My proceeds from *The Zeroes* will pay her back the money I owe her, as well as cover my office lease obligations, the last debts from my Doubledown financial folly.

Besides supporting this project, my wife, Jennifer Reingold, carried the familial lode as I went into a de facto bunker for six or so months to finish this. Yet despite her full-time job and full-time parenting responsibilities, she still found time to read every word of the manuscript and make exceptional suggestions. Passionate individual, devoted mother, amazing editor.

Finally, I want to thank two book lovers, Sabrina Lane and Chloe Lane, who patiently made do without their daddy for too many days. When you're old enough to read this properly, know that everything I did, and do, was and is for you. Over the past year, as I taught myself how to write again, Sabrina learned for the first time. She even extracted a promise from me, completely on her own initiative, that she could pen the last line of *The Zeroes* on my behalf: Now I can play with my daughters, Chloe and Sabrina, who are three and six.

INDEX